# ARM System Architecture

Test Development Group

4/19/2000

Copy #2

# ARM System Architecture

*Steve Furber*

University of Manchester

## ADDISON-WESLEY

Harlow, England • Reading, Massachusetts • Menlo Park, California
New York • Don Mills, Ontario • Amsterdam • Bonn • Sydney • Singapore
Tokyo • Madrid • San Juan • Milan • Mexico City • Seoul • Taipei

© Addison Wesley Longman 1996

Pearson Education Limited
Edinburgh Gate
Harlow
Essex CM20 2JE
England

and Associated Companies throughout the World.

Published in the United States of America by Addison Wesley Longman Inc., New York.

Cover designed by odB Design & Communication
Cover photograph of a StrongARM die above a StrongARM wafer kindly supplied by Digital Equipment Corporation (© DEC)
Typeset by the author
Printed in the United States of America

The publisher wishes to thank Acorn Computers Ltd, Apple Computer UK Ltd, Advanced RISC Machines Ltd, GEC Plessey Semiconductors, Digital Equipment Corporation, VLSI Technology Inc. and the University of Manchester for their kind permission to reproduce material in this book.

First printed 1996. Reprinted 1997 and 1999

ISBN 0-201-40352-8

**British Library Cataloguing-in-Publication Data**
A catalogue record for this book is available from the British Library.

**Library of Congress Cataloging-in-Publication Data** is available.

# Preface

**Aims**

This book introduces the concepts and methodologies employed in designing micro-processors and in designing systems around microprocessors. The principles of micro-processor design are made concrete by extensive illustrations based upon the ARM.

The aim of the book is to assist the reader in understanding how microprocessors are designed and used, and why a modern processor is designed the way that it is. The reader who wishes to know only the general principles should find that the ARM illustrations add substance to issues which can otherwise appear somewhat ethereal; the reader who specifically wishes to understand design of the ARM should find that the general principles illuminate the rationale for the ARM being as it is.

Other commercial microprocessor architectures are not described in this book. The reader who wishes to make a comparative study of such architectures will find the required information on the ARM here but must look elsewhere for information on other designs.

**Audience**

The book is intended to be of use to two distinct groups of readers:

- Professional hardware and software engineers who are tasked with designing a product which incorporates an ARM processor, or who are evaluating the ARM for a product, should find the book helpful in their duties. Although there is considerable overlap with ARM technical publications, this book provides a broader context with more background. It is not a substitute for the manufacturer's data, since some detail has had to be omitted, but it should be useful as an introductory overview and adjunct to that data.

- Students of computer science, computer engineering and electrical engineering should find the material of value at several stages in their courses. Some chapters are closely based on course material previously used in undergraduate teaching; some other material is drawn from a postgraduate course.

**Prerequisite knowledge**

This book is not intended to be an introductory text on computer architecture or computer logic design. Readers are assumed to have a level of familiarity with these subjects equivalent to that of a second year undergraduate student in computer science or computer engineering. Some first year material is presented, but this is more by way of a refresher than as a first introduction to this material.

No prior familiarity with the ARM processor is assumed.

**The ARM**

1995 was a good year for the ARM.

Ten years earlier, on 26 April 1985, the first ARM prototypes arrived at Acorn Computers Limited in Cambridge, England, having been fabricated by VLSI Technology, Inc., in San Jose, California. A few hours later they were running code, and a bottle of *Moët & Chandon* was opened in celebration. For the remainder of the 1980s the ARM was quietly developed to underpin Acorn's desktop products which form the basis of educational computing in the UK; during the 1990s, in the care of Advanced RISC Machines (ARM) Limited, the ARM has sprung onto the world stage and has established a market-leading position in high-performance low-power and low-cost embedded applications.

This prominent market position has increased ARM's resources and accelerated the rate at which new ARM-based developments appear.

The highlights of 1995 were:

- The introduction of the novel compressed instruction format called 'Thumb' which reduces cost and power dissipation in small systems.
- A significant step upwards in performance with the 'StrongARM'.
- A state-of-the-art software development environment in 'Tools 2.0'.
- A range of new embedded applications based around ARM processor cores.

These developments make this a good time to be writing about the ARM. Most of the principles of modern processor design are illustrated somewhere in the ARM family, and some concepts (such as dynamically decompressing the instruction stream) are unique to ARM. The inherent simplicity of the standard ARM core makes it a good pedagogical introductory example to real processor design, whereas the debugging of a system based around an ARM core deeply embedded into a complex system chip represents the cutting-edge of technological development today.

**Book structure**

Chapter 1 starts with a refresher on first year undergraduate logic and processor design material. It illustrates the principle of abstraction in hardware design by reviewing the roles of logic and gate-level representations. It then introduces the important concept of the *Reduced Instruction Set Computer* (RISC) as background for what follows, and closes with some comments on design for low power.

Chapter 2 describes the ARM processor architecture in terms of the concepts introduced in the previous chapter, and Chapter 3 is a gentle introduction to user-level assembly language programming and could be used in first year undergraduate teaching for this purpose.

Chapter 4 describes the organization and implementation of the ARM6 processor core at a level suitable for second year undergraduate teaching.

Chapters 5 and 6 go into the ARM instruction set architecture in increasing depth. Chapter 5 goes back over the instruction set in more detail than was presented in Chapter 3, including the binary representation of each instruction, and it penetrates more deeply into the corners of the instruction set. It is probably best read once and then used for reference. Chapter 6 backs off a bit to consider what a high-level language (in this case, C) really needs and how those needs are met by the ARM instruction set. This chapter is based on second year undergraduate material.

Chapter 7 introduces the 'Thumb' instruction set which is an ARM innovation to address the code density and power requirements of small embedded systems. It is of peripheral interest to a generic study of computer science, but adds an interesting lateral perspective to a postgraduate course.

Chapter 8 raises the issues involved in debugging systems which use embedded processor cores and in the production testing of board-level systems. These issues are background to Chapter 9 which introduces a number of different ARM integer cores, broadening the theme introduced in Chapter 4 to include cores with 'Thumb', debug hardware, a more sophisticated pipeline and even fully asynchronous operation.

Chapter 10 introduces the concept of memory hierarchy, discussing the principles of memory management and caches. Chapter 11 reviews the requirements of a modern operating system at a second year undergraduate level. Chapter 12 introduces the integrated ARM CPUs (including StrongARM) which incorporate full support for memory management. Chapter 13 describes a number of systems which incorporate these CPUs.

Chapter 14 covers the issues of building system chips with embedded processor cores. Here, the ARM is at the leading-edge of technology. Several examples are presented of production embedded system chips to show the solutions which have been developed to the many problems inherent in committing a complex application-specific system to silicon.

A short appendix presents the fundamentals of computer logic design and the terminology which is used in Chapter 1.

A glossary of the terms used in the book and a bibliography for further reading are appended at the end of the book, followed by a detailed index.

**Course relevance**

The chapters are at an appropriate level for use on undergraduate courses as follows:

Year 1: Chapter 1 (basic processor design); Chapter 3 (assembly language programming); Chapter 5 (instruction binaries and reference for assembly language programming).

Year 2: Chapter 4 (simple pipeline processor design); Chapter 6 (architectural support for high-level languages); Chapters 10 and 11 (architectural support for operating systems); Chapter 13 (system design).

Year 3: Chapter 8 (embedded system debug and test); Chapter 9 (advanced pipelined processor design); Chapter 12 (advanced CPUs); Chapter 14 (example embedded systems).

A postgraduate course could follow a theme across several chapters, such as processor design (Chapters 1, 2, 4, 9, 10 and 12), instruction set design (Chapters 2, 3, 5, 6, 7 and 11) or embedded systems (chapters 2, 4, 5, 8, 9 and 14).

**Support material**

Many of the figures and tables will be made freely available over the Internet for non-commercial use. The only constraint on such use is that this book should be a recommended text for any course which makes use of such material. Information about this and other support material may be found on the World Wide Web at:

http://www.cs.man.ac.uk/amulet/publications/books/ARMsysArch

Any enquiries relating to commercial use must be referred to the publishers. The assertion of the copyright for this book outlined on page iv remains unaffected.

**Feedback**

The author welcomes feedback on the style and content of this book, and details of any errors that are found. Please email any such information to:

sfurber@cs.man.ac.uk

## Acknowledgements

Many people have contributed to the success of the ARM over the last decade. As a policy decision I have not named in the text the individuals with principal responsibilities for the developments described therein since the lists would be long and attempts to abridge them invidious. History has a habit of focusing credit on one or two high-profile individuals, often at the expense of those who keep their heads down to get the job done on time. However it is not possible to write a book on the ARM without mentioning Sophie Wilson whose original instruction set architecture survives, extended but otherwise largely unscathed, to this day.

I would also like to acknowledge the support received from Advanced RISC Machines Limited in giving access to their staff and design documentation, and I am grateful for the help I have received from ARM's semiconductor partners, particularly VLSI Technology, Inc., Digital Equipment Corporation and GEC Plessey Semiconductors.

The book has been considerably enhanced by helpful comments from reviewers of draft versions. Mainly these were engaged anonymously by the publishers, but my colleague, Viv Woods, deserves special mention for volunteering to review several draft revisions and for acting as a sounding board for proposed modifications. I am grateful for the sympathetic reception the drafts received and the direct suggestions for improvement that were returned. The publishers, Addison Wesley Longman Limited, have been very helpful in guiding my responses to these suggestions and in other aspects of authorship.

Lastly I would like to thank my wife, Valerie, and my daughters, Alison and Catherine, who allowed me time off from family duties to write this book.

Steve Furber
August 1996

# Contents

# 6   *Architectural Support for High-Level Languages*   *159*

# 7   *The Thumb Instruction Set*   *199*

## Trademark notice

Acorn™, Risc PC™, Econet™, Acorn Archimedes™ and Online Media™ are trademarks of Acorn Computer Ltd.

ARM™, EmbeddedICE™, StrongARM™ and Thumb™ are trademarks of Advanced RISC Machines Ltd.

Apple™, Newton™, NewtonScript™, LocalTalk™ and MessagePad™ are trademarks of Apple Computer, Inc.

Verlilog® is a registered trademark of Cadence Design Systems, Inc.

Digital™, Digital Semiconductor™, PDP-8™ and Alpha™ are trademarks of Digital Equipment Corporation.

TimeMill™ is a trademark of EPIC Design Technology, Inc.

BµILD™ and Butterfly™ are trademarks of GEC Plessey Semiconductors.

Hagenuk® is a registered trademark of Hagenuk Telecom GmbH.

IBM® is a registered trademark of International Business Machines Corporation.

Inmos® is a registered trademark and transputer™ is a trademark of Inmos Group of Companies.

Intel® is a registered trademark of Intel Corporation.

MS-DOS®, Microsoft® and Windows® are registered trademarks of Microsoft Corporation.

MC68000™ is a trademark of Motorola Corporation.

UNIX® is a registered trademark of Novell, Inc.

Oracle™ is a trademark of Oracle Corporation UK Ltd.

Partner-ET™ is a trademark of Partner-ET.

$I^2C$ Bus® is a registered trademark of Philips Electronics N.V.

SPARC® is a registered trademark of SPARC International, Inc.

SUN™ is a trademark of Sun Microsystems, Inc.

3DO™ is a trademark of The 3DO Company.

JumpStart™ and Ruby II™ are trademarks of VLSI Technology, Inc.

Xilinx® is a registered trademark of Xilinx, Inc.


Within this publication, the term BBC is used as an abbreviation for British Broadcasting Corporation.

# 1 An Introduction to Processor Design

**Summary of chapter contents**

The design of a general-purpose processor, in common with most engineering endeavours, requires the careful consideration of many trade-offs and compromises. In this chapter we will look at the basic principles of processor instruction set and logic design and the techniques available to the designer to help achieve the design objectives.

Abstraction is fundamental to understanding complex computers. This chapter introduces the abstractions which are employed by computer hardware designers, of which the most important is the logic gate. The design of a simple processor is presented, from the instruction set, through a register transfer level description, down to logic gates.

The ideas behind the *Reduced Instruction Set Computer* (RISC) originated in processor research programmes at Stanford and Berkeley universities around 1980, though some of the central ideas can be traced back to earlier machines. In this chapter we look at the thinking that led to the RISC movement and consequently influenced the design of the ARM processor which is the subject of the following chapters.

With the rapid development of markets for portable computer-based products, the power consumption of digital circuits is of increasing importance. At the end of the chapter we will look at the principles of low-power high-performance design.

## 1.1   Processor architecture and organization

All modern general-purpose computers employ the principles of the *stored-program digital computer*. The stored-program concept originated from the Princeton Institute of Advanced Studies in the 1940s and was first implemented in the 'Baby' machine which first ran in June 1948 at the University of Manchester in England.

Fifty years of development have resulted in a spectacular increase in the performance of processors and an equally spectacular reduction in their cost. Over this period of relentless progress in the cost-effectiveness of computers, the principles of operation have changed remarkably little. Most of the improvements have resulted from advances in the technology of electronics, moving from valves (vacuum tubes) to individual transistors, to integrated circuits (**ICs**) incorporating several bipolar transistors and then through generations of IC technology leading to today's very large scale integrated (**VLSI**) circuits delivering millions of field-effect transistors on a single chip. As transistors get smaller they get cheaper, faster, and consume less power. This win-win scenario has carried the computer industry forward for the last three decades, and will continue to do so at least for the next few years.

However, not all of the progress over the past 50 years has come from advances in electronics technology. There have also been occasions when a new insight into the way that technology is employed has made a significant contribution. These insights are described under the headings of computer architecture and computer organization, where we will work with the following interpretations of these terms:

**Computer architecture**
- Computer architecture describes the user's view of the computer. The instruction set, visible registers, memory management table structures and exception handling model are all part of the architecture.

**Computer organization**
- Computer organization describes the user-invisible implementation of the architecture. The pipeline structure, transparent cache, table-walking hardware and translation look-aside buffer are all aspects of the organization.

Amongst the advances in these aspects of the design of computers, the introduction of virtual memory in the early 1960s, of transparent cache memories, of pipelining and so on, have all been milestones in the evolution of computers. The RISC idea ranks amongst these advances, offering a significant shift in the balance of forces which determines the cost-effectiveness of computer technology.

**What is a processor?**
A general-purpose processor is a finite-state automaton that executes instructions held in a memory. The state of the system is defined by the values held in the memory locations together with the values held in certain registers within the processor itself (see

Figure 1.1; the hexadecimal notation for the memory addresses is explained in Section 6.2 on page 162). Each instruction defines a particular way the total state should change and it also defines which instruction should be executed next.

**The stored-program computer**

The **stored-program** digital computer keeps its instructions and data in the same memory system, allowing the instructions to be treated as data when necessary. This enables the processor itself to generate instructions which it can subsequently execute. Although programs which do this at a fine granularity (**self-modifying** code) are generally considered bad form these days since they are very difficult to debug, use at a coarser granularity is fundamental to the way most computers operate. Whenever a computer loads in a new program from disk and then executes it the computer is employing this ability to change its own program.

**Computer applications**

Because of its programmability a stored-program digital computer is **universal**, which means that it can undertake any task which can be described by a suitable algorithm. Sometimes this is reflected by its configuration as a desktop machine where the user runs different programs at different times, but sometimes it is reflected by the same processor being used in a range of different applications, each with a fixed program. Such applications are characteristically embedded into products such as mobile telephones, automotive engine-management systems, and so on.

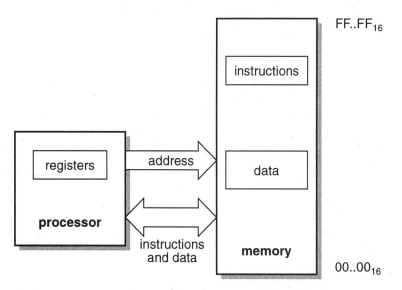

**Figure 1.1**  The state in a stored-program digital computer.

## 1.2   Abstraction in hardware design

Computers are very complex pieces of equipment that operate at very high speeds. A modern microprocessor may be built from several million transistors each of which can switch a hundred million times a second. Watch a document scroll up the screen on a desktop PC or workstation and try to imagine how a hundred million million transistor switching actions are used in each second of that movement. Now consider that every one of those switching actions is, in some sense, the consequence of a deliberate design decision. None of them is random or uncontrolled; indeed, a single error amongst those transitions is likely to cause the machine to collapse into a useless state. How can such complex systems be designed to operate so reliably?

**Transistors**    A clue to the answer may be found in the question itself. We have described the operation of the computer in terms of transistors, but what is a transistor? It is a curious structure composed from carefully chosen chemical substances with complex electrical properties that can only be understood by reference to the theory of quantum mechanics, where strange subatomic particles sometimes behave like waves and can only be described in terms of probabilities. Yet the gross behaviour of a transistor can be described, without reference to quantum mechanics, as a set of equations that relate the voltages on its terminals to the current that flows though it. These equations **abstract** the essential behaviour of the device from its underlying physics.

**Logic gates**    The equations that describe the behaviour of a transistor are still fairly complex. When a group of transistors is wired together in a particular structure, such as the CMOS (Complementary Metal Oxide Semiconductor) NAND gate shown in Figure 1.2 on page 5, the behaviour of the group has a particularly simple description.

If each of the input wires (*A* and *B*) is held at a voltage which is either near to *Vdd* or near to *Vss*, the output will will also be near to *Vdd* or *Vss* according to the following rules:

- If *A* and *B* are both near to *Vdd*, the output will be near to *Vss*.
- If either *A* or *B* (or both) is near to *Vss*, the output will be near to *Vdd*.

With a bit of care we can define what is meant by 'near to' in these rules, and then associate the meaning **true** with a value near to *Vdd* and **false** with a value near to *Vss*. The circuit is then an implementation of the NAND Boolean logic function:

$$output = \neg (A \wedge B)$$                                    Equation 1

Although there is a lot of engineering design involved in turning four transistors into a reliable implementation of this equation, it can be done with sufficient reliability

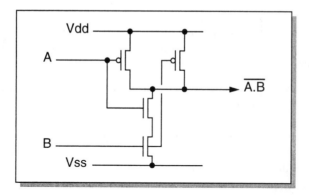

**Figure 1.2**   The transistor circuit of a static 2-input CMOS NAND gate.

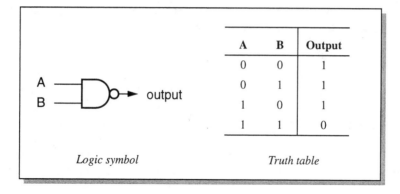

| A | B | Output |
|---|---|--------|
| 0 | 0 | 1 |
| 0 | 1 | 1 |
| 1 | 0 | 1 |
| 1 | 1 | 0 |

*Logic symbol*                    *Truth table*

**Figure 1.3**   The logic symbol and truth table for a NAND gate.

that the logic designer can think almost exclusively in terms of logic gates. The concepts that the logic designer works with are illustrated in Figure 1.3, and consist of the following 'views' of the logic gate:

**Logic
symbol**

- A logic symbol.

  This is a symbol that represents a NAND gate function in a circuit schematic; there are similar symbols for other logic gates (for instance, removing the bubble from the output leaves an AND gate which generates the opposite output function; further examples are given in 'Appendix: Computer Logic' on page 389).

**Truth table**      • A truth table.

This describes the logic function of the gate, and encompasses everything that the logic designer needs to know about the gate for most purposes. The significance here is that it is a lot simpler than four sets of transistor equations.

(In this truth table we have represented 'true' by '1' and 'false' by '0', as is common practice when dealing with Boolean variables.)

**The gate abstraction**

The point about the gate abstraction is that not only does it greatly simplify the process of designing circuits with great numbers of transistors, but it actually removes the need to know that the gate is built from transistors. A logic circuit should have the same logical behaviour whether the gates are implemented using field-effect transistors (the transistors that are available on a CMOS process), bipolar transistors, electrical relays, fluid logic or any other form of logic. The implementation technology will affect the *performance* of the circuit, but it should have no effect on its *function*. It is the duty of the transistor-level circuit designer to support the gate abstraction as near perfectly as is possible in order to isolate the logic circuit designer from the need to understand the transistor equations.

**Levels of abstraction**

It may appear that this point is being somewhat laboured, particularly to those readers who have worked with logic gates for many years. However, the principle that is illustrated in the gate level abstraction is repeated many times at different levels in computer science and is absolutely fundamental to the process which we began considering at the start of this section, which is the management of complexity.

The process of gathering together a few components at one level to extract their essential joint behaviour and hide all the unnecessary detail at the next level enables us to scale orders of complexity in a few steps. For instance, if each level encompasses four components of the next lower level as our gate model does, we can get from a transistor to a microprocessor comprising a million transistors in just ten steps. In many cases we work with more than four components, so the number of steps is greatly reduced.

A typical hierarchy of abstraction at the hardware level might be:

1. Transistors.
2. Logic gates, memory cells, special circuits.
3. Single-bit adders, multiplexers, decoders, flip-flops.
4. Word-wide adders, multiplexers, decoders, registers, buses.
5. ALUs (Arithithmetic-Logic Units), barrel shifters, register banks, memory blocks.
6. Processor, cache and memory management organizations.

7. Processors, peripheral cells, cache memories, memory management units.

8. Integrated system chips.

9. Printed circuit boards.

10. Mobile telephones, PCs, engine controllers.

The process of understanding a design in terms of levels of abstraction is reasonably concrete when the design is expressed in hardware. But the process doesn't stop with the hardware; if anything, it is even more fundamental to the understanding of software and we will return to look at abstraction in software design in due course.

**Gate-level design**

The next step up from the logic gate is to assemble a library of useful functions each composed of several gates. Typical functions are, as listed above, adders, multiplexers, decoders and flip-flops, each 1-bit wide. This book is not intended to be a general introduction to logic design since its principal subject material relates to the design and use of processor cores and any reader who is considering applying this information should already be familiar with conventional logic design.

For those who are not so familiar with logic design or who need their knowledge refreshing, 'Appendix: Computer Logic' on page 389 describes the essentials which will be assumed in the next section. It includes brief details on:

- Boolean algebra and notation.
- Binary numbers.
- Binary addition.
- Multiplexers.
- Clocks.
- Sequential circuits.
- Latches and flip-flops.
- Registers.

If any of these terms is unfamiliar, a brief look at the appendix may yield sufficient information for what follows.

Note that although the appendix describes these circuit functions in terms of simple logic gates, there are often more efficient CMOS implementations based on alternative transistor circuits. There are many ways to satisfy the basic requirements of logic design using the complementary transistors available on a CMOS chip, and new transistor circuits are published regularly.

For further information consult a text on logic design; a suitable reference is suggested in the 'Bibliography' on page 405.

## 1.3   MU0 – a simple processor

A simple form of processor can be built from a few basic components:

- A **program counter** (PC) register that is used to hold the address of the current instruction;
- A single register called an **accumulator** (ACC) that holds a data value while it is worked upon;
- An **arithmetic-logic unit** (ALU) that can perform a number of operations on binary operands, such as add, subtract, increment, and so on;
- An **instruction register** (IR) that holds the current instruction while it is executed;
- Instruction decode and control logic that employs the above components to achieve the desired results from each instruction.

This limited set of components allows a restricted set of instructions to be implemented. Such a design has been employed at the University of Manchester for many years to illustrate the principles of processor design. Manchester-designed machines are often referred to by the names MU$n$ for $1 \leq n \leq 6$, so this simple machine is known as MU0. It is a design developed only for teaching and was not one of the large-scale machines built at the university as research vehicles, though it is similar to the very first Manchester machine and has been implemented in various forms by undergraduate students.

**The MU0 instruction set**

MU0 is a 16-bit machine with a 12-bit address space, so it can address up to 8 Kbytes of memory arranged as 4,096 individually addressable 16-bit locations. Instructions are 16 bits long, with a 4-bit operation code (or **opcode**) and a 12-bit address field (S) as shown in Figure 1.4. The simplest instruction set uses only eight of the 16 available opcodes and is summarized in Table 1.1 on page 9.

An instruction such as 'ACC := ACC + mem$_{16}$[S]' means 'add the contents of the (16-bit wide) memory location whose address is S to the accumulator'. Instructions are fetched from consecutive memory addresses, starting from address zero, until an instruction which modifies the PC is executed, whereupon fetching starts from the new address given in the 'jump' instruction.

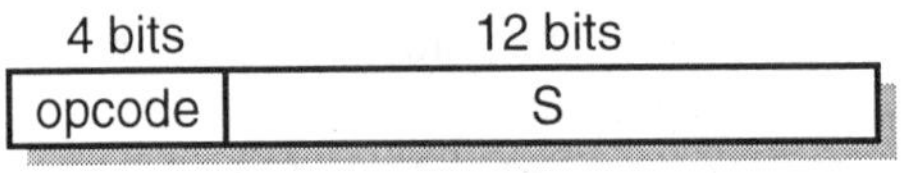

```
 4 bits           12 bits
┌────────┬──────────────────────┐
│ opcode │          S           │
└────────┴──────────────────────┘
```

**Figure 1.4**   The MU0 instruction format.

**Table 1.1**   The MU0 instruction set.

| Instruction | Opcode | Effect |
|-------------|--------|--------|
| LDA S | 0000 | $ACC := mem_{16}[S]$ |
| STO S | 0001 | $mem_{16}[S] := ACC$ |
| ADD S | 0010 | $ACC := ACC + mem_{16}[S]$ |
| SUB S | 0011 | $ACC := ACC - mem_{16}[S]$ |
| JMP S | 0100 | $PC := S$ |
| JGE S | 0101 | if $ACC \geq 0$  $PC := S$ |
| JNE S | 0110 | if $ACC \neq 0$  $PC := S$ |
| STP | 0111 | stop |

**MU0 logic design**

To understand how this instruction set might be implemented we will go through the design process in a logical order. The approach taken here will be to separate the design into two components:

- The datapath.

  All the components carrying, storing or processing many bits in parallel will be considered part of the datapath, including the accumulator, program counter, ALU and instruction register. For these components we will use a register transfer level (**RTL**) design style based on registers, multiplexers, and so on.

- The control logic.

  Everything that does not fit comfortably into the datapath will be considered part of the control logic and will be designed using a finite state machine (**FSM**) approach.

**Datapath design**

There are many ways to connect the basic components needed to implement the MU0 instruction set. Where there are choices to be made we need a guiding principle to help us make the right choices. Here we will follow the principle that the memory will be the limiting factor in our design, and a memory access will always take a clock cycle. Hence we will aim for an implementation where:

- Each instruction takes exactly the number of clock cycles defined by the number of memory accesses it must make.

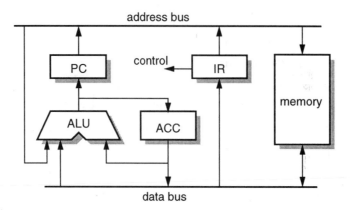

**Figure 1.5**   MU0 datapath example.

Referring back to Table 1.1 we can see that the first four instructions each require two memory accesses (one to fetch the instruction itself and one to fetch or store the operand) whereas the last four instructions can execute in one cycle since they do not require an operand. (In practice we would probably not worry about the efficiency of the STP instruction since it halts the processor for ever.) Therefore we need a datapath design which has sufficient resource to allow these instructions to complete in two or one clock cycles. A suitable datapath is shown in Figure 1.5.

(Readers who might expect to see a dedicated PC incrementer in this datapath should note that all instructions that do not change the PC take two cycles, so the main ALU is available during one of these cycles to increment the PC.)

**Datapath operation**

The design we will develop assumes that each instruction starts when it has arrived in the instruction register. After all, until it is in the instruction register we cannot know which instruction we are dealing with. Therefore an instruction executes in two stages, possibly omitting the first of these:

1. Access the memory operand and perform the desired operation.

   The address in the instruction register is issued and either an operand is read from memory, combined with the accumulator in the ALU and written back into the accumulator, or the accumulator is stored out to memory.

2. Fetch the next instruction to be executed.

   Either the PC or the address in the instruction register is issued to fetch the next instruction, and in either case the address is incremented in the ALU and the incremented value saved into the PC.

**Initialization**

The processor must start in a known state. Usually this requires a *reset* input to cause it to start executing instructions from a known address. We will design MU0 to start executing from address $000_{16}$. There are several ways to achieve this, one of which is to use the reset signal to zero the ALU output and then clock this into the PC register.

**Register transfer level design**

The next step is to determine exactly the control signals that are required to cause the datapath to carry out the full set of operations. We assume that all the registers change state on the falling edge of the input clock, and where necessary have control signals that may be used to prevent them from changing on a particular clock edge. The PC, for example, will change at the end of a clock cycle where *PCce* was '1' but will not change when *PCce* was '0'.

A suitable register organization is shown in Figure 1.6 on page 12. This shows enables on all of the registers, function select lines to the ALU (the precise number and interpretation to be determined later), the select control lines for two multiplexers, the control for a tri-state driver to send the ACC value to memory and memory request (*MEMrq*) and read/write (*RnW*) control lines. The other signals shown are outputs from the datapath to the control logic, including the opcode bits and signals indicating whether ACC is zero or negative which control the respective conditional jump instructions.

**Control logic**

The control logic simply has to decode the current instruction and generate the appropriate levels on the datapath control signals, using the control inputs from the datapath where necessary. Although the control logic is a finite state machine, and therefore in principle the design should start from a state transition diagram, in this case the FSM is trivial and the diagram not worth drawing. The implementation requires only two states, 'fetch' and 'execute', and one bit of state is therefore sufficient.

The control logic can be presented in tabular form as shown in Table 1.2 on page 13. In this table an 'x' indicates a *don't care* condition. Once the ALU function select codes have been assigned the table may be implemented directly as a **PLA** (programmable logic array) or translated into combinatorial logic and implemented using standard gates.

A quick scrutiny of Table 1.2 reveals a few easy simplifications. The program counter and instruction register clock enables (*PCce* and *IRce*) are always the same. This makes sense, since whenever a new instruction is being fetched the ALU is computing the next program counter value, and this should be latched too. Therefore these control signals may be merged into one. Similarly, whenever the accumulator is driving the data bus (*ACCoe* is high) the memory should perform a write operation (*RnW* is low), so one of these signals can be generated from the other using an inverter.

After these simplifications the control logic design is almost complete. It only remains to determine the encodings of the ALU functions.

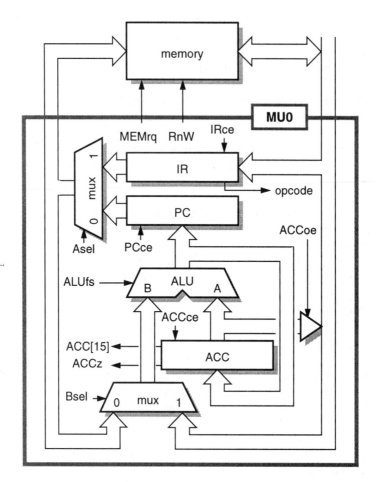

**Figure 1.6**   MU0 register transfer level organization.

**ALU design**   Most of the register transfer level functions in Figure 1.6 have straightforward logic implementations (readers who are in doubt should refer to 'Appendix: Computer Logic' on page 389). The MU0 ALU is a little more complex than the simple adder described in the appendix, however.

   The ALU functions that are required are listed in Table 1.2 on page 13. There are five of them ($A + B$, $A - B$, $B$, $B + 1$, 0), the last of which is only used while reset is active. Therefore the reset signal can control this function directly and the control logic need only generate a 2-bit function select code to choose between the other four.

**Table 1.2**   MU0 control logic.

| | Inputs | | | | | Outputs | | | | | | | | | |
|---|---|---|---|---|---|---|---|---|---|---|---|---|---|---|---|
| | Opcode | | Ex/ft | | ACC15 | | Bsel | | PCce | | ACCoe | | MEMrq | | Ex/ft |
| Instruction | | Reset | | ACCz | | Asel | | ACCce | | IRce | | ALUfs | | RnW | |
| Reset | xxxx | 1 | x | x | x | 0 | 0 | 1 | 1 | 1 | 0 | = 0 | 1 | 1 | 0 |
| LDA S | 0000 | 0 | 0 | x | x | 1 | 1 | 1 | 0 | 0 | 0 | = B | 1 | 1 | 1 |
|  | 0000 | 0 | 1 | x | x | 0 | 0 | 0 | 1 | 1 | 0 | B+1 | 1 | 1 | 0 |
| STO S | 0001 | 0 | 0 | x | x | 1 | x | 0 | 0 | 0 | 1 | x | 1 | 0 | 1 |
|  | 0001 | 0 | 1 | x | x | 0 | 0 | 0 | 1 | 1 | 0 | B+1 | 1 | 1 | 0 |
| ADD S | 0010 | 0 | 0 | x | x | 1 | 1 | 1 | 0 | 0 | 0 | A+B | 1 | 1 | 1 |
|  | 0010 | 0 | 1 | x | x | 0 | 0 | 0 | 1 | 1 | 0 | B+1 | 1 | 1 | 0 |
| SUB S | 0011 | 0 | 0 | x | x | 1 | 1 | 1 | 0 | 0 | 0 | A-B | 1 | 1 | 1 |
|  | 0011 | 0 | 1 | x | x | 0 | 0 | 0 | 1 | 1 | 0 | B+1 | 1 | 1 | 0 |
| JMP S | 0100 | 0 | x | x | x | 1 | 0 | 0 | 1 | 1 | 0 | B+1 | 1 | 1 | 0 |
| JGE S | 0101 | 0 | x | x | 0 | 1 | 0 | 0 | 1 | 1 | 0 | B+1 | 1 | 1 | 0 |
|  | 0101 | 0 | x | x | 1 | 0 | 0 | 0 | 1 | 1 | 0 | B+1 | 1 | 1 | 0 |
| JNE S | 0110 | 0 | x | 0 | x | 1 | 0 | 0 | 1 | 1 | 0 | B+1 | 1 | 1 | 0 |
|  | 0110 | 0 | x | 1 | x | 0 | 0 | 0 | 1 | 1 | 0 | B+1 | 1 | 1 | 0 |
| STOP | 0111 | 0 | x | x | x | 1 | x | 0 | 0 | 0 | 0 | x | 0 | 1 | 0 |

If the principal ALU inputs are the $A$ and $B$ operands, all the functions may be produced by augmenting a conventional binary adder:

- $A + B$ is the normal adder output (assuming that the carry-in is zero).
- $A - B$ may be implemented as $A + \overline{B} + 1$, requiring the $B$ inputs to be inverted and the carry-in to be forced to a one.
- $B$ is implemented by forcing the $A$ inputs and the carry-in to zero.
- $B + 1$ is implemented by forcing $A$ to zero and the carry-in to one.

The gate-level logic for the ALU shown in Figure 1.7 on page 14. *Aen* enables the $A$ operand or forces it to zero; *Binv* controls whether or not the $B$ operand is inverted. The carry-out (*Cout*) from one bit is connected to the carry-in (*Cin*) of the next; the carry-in to the first bit is controlled by the ALU function selects (as are *Aen* and *Binv*), and the carry-out from the last bit is unused. Together with the

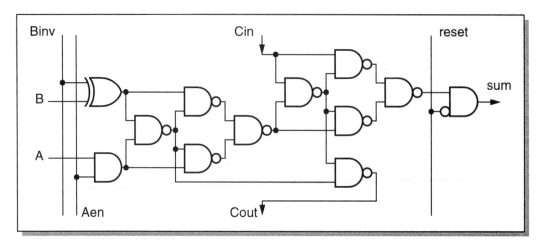

**Figure 1.7**   MU0 ALU logic for one bit.

multiplexers, registers, control logic and a bus buffer (which is used to put the accumulator value onto the data bus), the processor is complete. Add a standard memory and you have a workable computer.

**MU0 extensions**

Although MU0 is a very simple processor and would not make a good target for a high-level language compiler, it serves to illustrate the basic principles of processor design. The design process used to develop the first ARM processors differed mainly in complexity and not in principle. MU0 designs based on microcoded control logic have also been developed, as have extensions to incorporate indexed addressing. Like any good processor, MU0 has spaces left in the instruction space which allow future expansion of the instruction set.

To turn MU0 into a useful processor takes quite a lot of work. The following extensions seem most important:

- Extending the address space.
- Adding more addressing modes.
- Allowing the PC to be saved in order to support a subroutine mechanism.
- Adding more registers, supporting interrupts, and so on...

Overall, this doesn't seem to be the place to start from if the objective is to design a high-performance processor which is a good compiler target.

## 1.4   Instruction set design

If the MU0 instruction set is not a good choice for a high-performance processor, what other choices are there?

Starting from first principles, let us look at a basic machine operation such as an instruction to add two numbers to produce a result.

**4-address instructions**

In its most general form, this instruction requires some bits to differentiate it from other instructions, some bits to specify the operand addresses, some bits to specify where the result should be placed (the **destination**), and some bits to specify the address of the next instruction to be executed. An assembly language format for such an instruction might be:

```
ADD     d, s1, s2, next_i ; d := s1 + s2
```

Such an instruction might be represented in memory by a binary format such as that shown in Figure 1.8. This format requires $4n + f$ bits per instruction where each operand requires $n$ bits and the opcode that specifies 'ADD' requires $f$ bits.

| f bits | n bits | n bits | n bits | n bits |
|--------|--------|--------|--------|--------|
| function | op 1 addr. | op 2 addr. | dest. addr. | next_i addr. |

**Figure 1.8**   A 4-address instruction format.

**3-address instructions**

The first way to reduce the number of bits required for each instruction is to make the address of the next instruction implicit (except for branch instructions, whose role is to modify the instruction sequence explicitly). If we assume that the default next instruction can be found by adding the size of the instruction to the PC, we get a 3-address instruction with an assembly language format like this:

```
ADD     d, s1, s2           ; d := s1 + s2
```

A binary representation of such an instruction is shown in Figure 1.9.

| f bits | n bits | n bits | n bits |
|--------|--------|--------|--------|
| function | op 1 addr. | op 2 addr. | dest. addr. |

**Figure 1.9**   A 3-address instruction format.

**2-address instructions**

A further saving in the number of bits required to store an instruction can be achieved by making the destination register the same as one of the source registers. The assembly language format could be:

```
ADD      d, s1    ; d := d + s1
```

The binary representation now reduces to that shown in Figure 1.10.

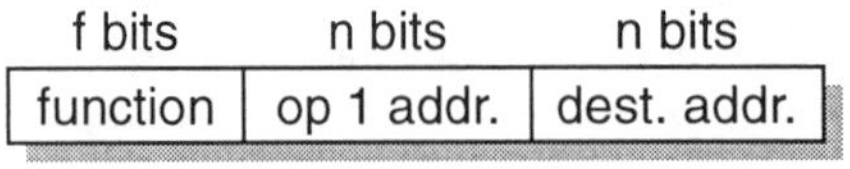

```
 f bits      n bits        n bits
 function | op 1 addr. | dest. addr.
```

**Figure 1.10**   A 2-address instruction format.

**1-address instructions**

If the destination register is made implicit it is often called the **accumulator** (see, for example, MU0 in the previous section); an instruction need only specify one operand:

```
ADD      s1       ; accumulator := accumulator + s1
```

The binary representation simplifies further to that shown in Figure 1.11.

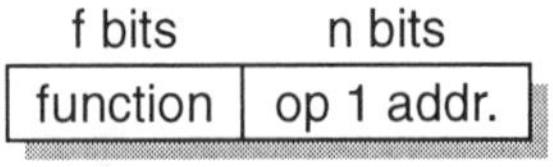

```
 f bits      n bits
 function | op 1 addr.
```

**Figure 1.11**   A 1-address (accumulator) instruction format.

**0-address instructions**

Finally, an architecture may make all operand references implicit by using an evaluation stack. The assembly language format is:

```
ADD      ; top_of_stack := top_of_stack + next_on_stack
```

The binary representation is as shown in Figure 1.12.

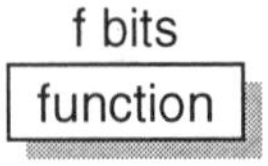

```
 f bits
 function
```

**Figure 1.12**   A 0-address instruction format.

**Examples of n-address use**

All these forms of instruction have been used in processor instruction sets apart from the 4-address form which, although it is used internally in some microcode designs, is unnecessarily expensive for a machine-level instruction set. For example:

- The Inmos transputer uses a 0-address evaluation stack architecture.
- The MU0 example in the previous section illustrates a simple 1-address architecture.
- The Thumb instruction set used for high code density on some ARM processors uses an architecture which is predominantly of the 2-address form (see Chapter 7).
- The standard ARM instruction set uses a 3-address architecture.

**Addresses**

An address in the MU0 architecture is the straightforward 'absolute' address of the memory location which contains the desired operand. However, the three addresses in the ARM 3-address instruction format are register specifiers, not memory addresses. In general, the term '3-address architecture' refers to an instruction set where the two source operands and the destination can be specified independently of each other, but often only within a restricted set of possible values.

**Instruction types**

We have just looked at a number of ways of specifying an 'ADD' instruction. A complete instruction set needs to do more than perform arithmetic operations on operands in memory. A general-purpose instruction set can be expected to include instructions in the following categories:

- Data processing instructions such as add, subtract and multiply.
- Data movement instructions that copy data from one place in memory to another, or from memory to the processor's registers, and so on.
- Control flow instructions that switch execution from one part of the program to another, possibly depending on data values.
- Special instructions to control the processor's execution state, for instance to switch into a privileged mode to carry out an operating system function.

Sometimes an instruction will fit into more than one of these categories. For example, a 'decrement and branch if non-zero' instruction, which is useful for controlling program loops, does some data processing on the loop variable and also performs a control flow function. Similarly, a data processing instruction which fetches an operand from an address in memory and places its result in a register can be viewed as performing a data movement function.

**Orthogonal instructions**

An instruction set is said to be **orthogonal** if each choice in the building of an instruction is independent of the other choices. Since add and subtract are similar operations, one would expect to be able to use them in similar contexts. If add uses a 3-address format with register addresses, so should subtract, and in neither case should there be any peculiar restrictions on the registers which may be used.

An orthogonal instruction set is easier for the assembly language programmer to learn and easier for the compiler writer to target. The hardware implementation will usually be more efficient too.

**Addressing modes**

When accessing an operand for a data processing or movement instruction, there are several standard techniques used to specify the desired location. Most processors support several of these **addressing modes** (though few support all of them):

1. Immediate addressing: the desired value is presented as a binary value in the instruction.

2. Absolute addressing: the instruction contains the full binary address of the desired value in memory.

3. Indirect addressing: the instruction contains the binary address of a memory location that contains the binary address of the desired value.

4. Register addressing: the desired value is in a register, and the instruction contains the register number.

5. Register indirect addressing: the instruction contains the number of a register which contains the address of the value in memory.

6. Base plus offset addressing: the instruction specifies a register (the **base**) and a binary offset to be added to the base to form the memory address.

7. Base plus index addressing: the instruction specifies a base register and another register (the **index**) which is added to the base to form the memory address.

8. Base plus scaled index addressing: as above, but the index is multiplied by a constant (usually the size of the data item, and usually a power of two) before being added to the base.

9. Stack addressing: an implicit or specified register (the **stack pointer**) points to an area of memory (the **stack**) where data items are written (**pushed**) or read (**popped**) on a last-in-first-out basis.

Note that the naming conventions used for these modes by different processor manufacturers are not necessarily as above. The list can be extended almost indefinitely by adding more levels of indirection, adding base plus index plus offset, and so on. However, most of the common addressing modes are covered in the list above.

**Control flow instructions**

Where the program must deviate from the default (normally sequential) instruction sequence, a control flow instruction is used to modify the program counter (PC) explicitly. The simplest such instructions are usually called 'branches' or 'jumps'. Since most branches require a relatively short range, a common form is the 'PC-relative' branch. A typical assembly language format is:

```
        B           LABEL
                ..
LABEL       ..
```

Here the assembler works out the displacement which must be added to the value the PC has when the branch is executed in order to force the PC to point to LABEL. The maximum range of the branch is determined by the number of bits allocated to the displacement in the binary format; the assembler should report an error if the required branch is out of range.

**Conditional branches**

A Digital Signal Processing (DSP) program may execute a fixed instruction sequence for ever, but a general-purpose processor is usually required to vary its program in response to data values. Some processors (including MU0) allow the values in the general registers to control whether or not a branch is taken through instructions such as:

- Branch if a particular register is zero (or not zero, or negative, and so on).
- Branch if two specified registers are equal (or not equal).

**Condition code register**

However, the most frequently used mechanism is based on a condition code register, which is a special-purpose register within the processor. Whenever a data processing instruction is executed (or possibly only for special instructions, or instructions that specifically enable the condition code register), the condition code register records whether the result was zero, negative, overflowed, produced a carry output, and so on. The conditional branch instructions are then controlled by the state of the condition code register when they execute.

**Subroutine calls**

Sometimes a branch is executed to call a subprogram where the instruction sequence should **return** to the calling sequence when the subprogram terminates. Since the subprogram may be called from many different places, a record of the calling address must be kept. There are many different ways to achieve this:

- The calling routine could compute a suitable return address and put it in a standard memory location for use by the subprogram as a return address before executing the branch.

- The return address could be pushed onto a stack.
- The return address could be placed in a register.

Subprogram calls are sufficiently common that most architectures include specific instructions to make them efficient. They typically require to jump further across memory than simple branches, so it makes sense to treat them separately. Often they are not conditional; a conditional subprogram call is programmed, when required, by inserting an unconditional call and branching around it with the opposite condition.

**Subprogram return**

The return instruction moves the return address from wherever it was stored (in memory, possibly on a stack, or in a register) back into the PC.

**System calls**

Another category of control flow instruction is the system call. This is a branch to an operating system routine, often associated with a change in the **privilege** level of the executing program. Some functions in the processor, possibly including all the input and output peripherals, are protected from access by user code. Therefore a user program that needs to access these functions must make a system call.

System calls pass through protection barriers in a controlled way. A well-designed processor will ensure that it is possible to write a multi-user operating system where one user's program is protected from assaults from other, possibly malicious, users. This requires that a malicious user cannot change the system code and, when access to protected functions is required, the system code must make thorough checks that the requested function is authorized.

This is a complex area of hardware and software design. Most embedded systems (and many desktop systems) do not use the full protection capabilities of the hardware, but a processor which does not support a protected system mode will be excluded from consideration for those applications that demand this facility, so most microprocessors now include such support. Whilst it is not necessary to understand the full implications of supporting a secure operating system to appreciate the basic design of an instruction set, even the less well-informed reader should have an awareness of the issues since some features of commercial processor architectures make little sense unless this objective of potentially secure protection is borne in mind.

**Exceptions**

The final category of control flow instruction comprises cases where the change in the flow of control is not the primary intent of the programmer but is a consequence of some unexpected (and possibly unwanted) side-effect of the program. An attempt to access a memory location may fail, for instance, because a fault is detected in the memory subsystem. The program must therefore deviate from its planned course in order to attempt to recover from the problem.

These unplanned changes in the flow of control are termed **exceptions**.

## 1.5   Processor design trade-offs

The art of processor design is to define an instruction set that supports the functions that are useful to the programmer whilst allowing an implementation that is as efficient as possible. Preferably, the same instruction set should also allow future, more sophisticated implementations to be equally efficient.

The programmer generally wants to express his program in as abstract a way as possible, using a high-level language which supports ways of handling concepts that are appropriate to the problem. Modern trends towards functional and object-oriented languages move the level of abstraction higher than older imperative languages such as C, and even the older languages were quite a long way removed from typical machine instructions.

The **semantic gap** between a high-level language construct and a machine instruction is bridged by a **compiler**, which is a (usually complex) computer program that translates a high-level language program into a sequence of machine instructions. Therefore the processor designer should define his instruction set to be a good compiler target rather than something that the programmer will use directly to solve the problem by hand. So, what sort of instruction set makes a good compiler target?

**Complex Instruction Set Computers**

Prior to 1980, the principal trend in instruction set design was towards increasing complexity in an attempt to reduce the semantic gap that the compiler had to bridge. Single instruction procedure entries and exits were incorporated into the instruction set, each performing a complex sequence of operations over many clock cycles. Processors were sold on the sophistication and number of their addressing modes, data types, and so on.

The origins of this trend were in the minicomputers developed during the 1970s. These computers had relatively slow main memories coupled to processors built using many simple integrated circuits. The processors were controlled by microcode ROMs (Read Only Memories) that were faster than main memory, so it made sense to implement frequently used operations as microcode sequences rather than them requiring several instructions to be fetched from main memory.

Throughout the 1970s microprocessors were advancing in their capabilities. These single chip processors were dependent on state-of-the-art semiconductor technology to achieve the highest possible number of transistors on a single chip, so their development took place within the semiconductor industry rather than within the computer industry. As a result, microprocessor designs displayed a lack of original thought at the architectural level, particularly with respect to the demands of the technology that was used in their implementation. Their designers, at best, took ideas from the minicomputer industry where the implementation technology was very different. In particular, the microcode ROM which was needed for all the complex routines absorbed an unreasonable proportion of the area of a single chip, leaving little room for other performance-enhancing features.

This approach led to the single-chip Complex Instruction Set Computers (**CISCs**) of the late 1970s, which were microprocessors with minicomputer instruction sets which were severely compromised by the limited available silicon resource.

**The RISC revolution**

Into this world of increasingly complex instruction sets the Reduced Instruction Set Computer (**RISC**) was born. The RISC concept was a major influence on the design of the ARM processor; indeed, RISC is the ARM's middle name. But before we look at either RISC or the ARM in more detail we need a bit more background on what processors do and how they can be designed to do it quickly.

If reducing the semantic gap between the processor instruction set and the high-level language is not the right way to make an efficient computer, what other options are open to the designer?

**What processors do**

If we want to make a processor go fast, we must first understand what it spends its time doing. It is a common misconception that computers spend their time computing, that is, carrying out arithmetic operations on user data. In practice they spend very little time 'computing' in this sense. Although they do a fair amount of arithmetic, most of this is with addresses in order to locate the relevant data items and program routines. Then, having found the user's data, most of the work is in moving it around rather than processing it in any transformational sense.

At the instruction set level, it is possible to measure the frequency of use of the various different instructions. It is very important to obtain **dynamic** measurements, that is, to measure the frequency of instructions that are executed, rather than the **static** frequency, which is just a count of the various instruction types in the binary image. A typical set of statistics is shown in Table 1.3 on page 23; these statistics were gathered running a print preview program on an ARM instruction emulator, but are broadly typical of what may be expected from other programs and instruction sets.

These sample statistics suggest that the most important instructions to optimize are those concerned with data movement, either between the processor registers and memory or from register to register. These account for almost half of all instructions executed. Second most frequent are the control flow instructions such as branches and procedure calls, which account for another quarter. Arithmetic operations are down at 10%, as are comparisons.

Now we have a feel for what processors spend their time doing, we can look at ways of making them go faster. The most important of these is pipelining. Another important technique is the use of a cache memory, which will be covered in Section 10.2 on page 273. A third technique, super-scalar instruction execution, is very complex, has not been used on ARM processors and is not covered in this book.

**Table 1.3** Typical dynamic instruction usage.

| Instruction type | Dynamic usage |
|---|---|
| Data movement | 43% |
| Control flow | 23% |
| Arithmetic operations | 15% |
| Comparisons | 13% |
| Logical operations | 5% |
| Other | 1% |

**Pipelines**

A processor executes an individual instruction in a sequence of steps. A typical sequence might be:

1. Fetch the instruction from memory (fetch).
2. Decode it to see what sort of instruction it is (dec).
3. Access any operands that may be required from the register bank (reg).
4. Combine the operands to form the result or a memory address (ALU).
5. Access memory for a data operand, if necessary (mem).
6. Write the result back to the register bank (res).

Not all instructions will require every step, but most instructions will require most of them. These steps tend to use different hardware functions, for instance the ALU is probably only used in step 4. Therefore, if an instruction does not start before its predecessor has finished, only a small proportion of the processor hardware will be in use in any step.

An obvious way to improve the utilization of the hardware resources, and also the processor throughput, would be to start the next instruction before the current one has finished. This technique is called **pipelining**, and is a very effective way of exploiting concurrency in a general-purpose processor.

Taking the above sequence of operations, the processor is organized so that as soon as one instruction has completed step 1 and moved on to step 2, the next instruction begins step 1. This is illustrated in Figure 1.13 on page 24. In principle such a pipeline should deliver a six times speed-up compared with non-overlapped instruction execution; in practice things do not work out quite so well for reasons we will see below.

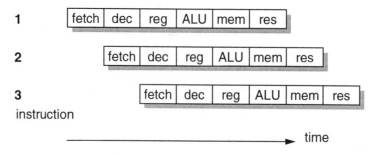

Figure 1.13  Pipelined instruction execution.

**Pipeline hazards**

It is relatively frequent in typical computer programs that the result from one instruc-tion is used as an operand by the next instruction. When this occurs the pipeline oper-ation shown in Figure 1.13 breaks down, since the result of instruction 1 is not available at the time that instruction 2 collects its operands. Instruction 2 must there-fore stall until the result is available, giving the behaviour shown in Figure 1.14. This is a **read-after-write** pipeline hazard.

Branch instructions result in even worse pipeline behaviour since the fetch step of the following instruction is affected by the branch target computation and must therefore be deferred. Unfortunately, subsequent fetches will be taking place while the branch is being decoded and before it has been recognized as a branch, so the fetched instructions may have to be discarded. If, for example, the branch target calculation is performed in the ALU stage of the pipeline in Figure 1.13, three instructions will have been fetched from the old stream before the branch target is available (see Figure 1.15 on page 25). It is better to compute the branch target earlier in the pipeline if possible,

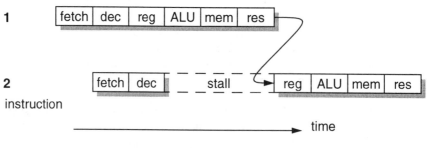

Figure 1.14  Read-after-write pipeline hazard.

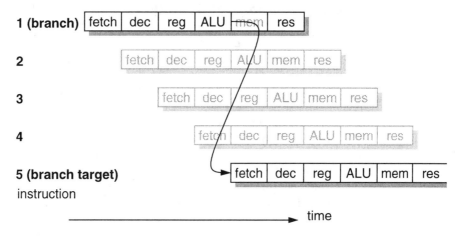

**Figure 1.15**   Pipelined branch behaviour.

even though this will probably require dedicated hardware. If branch instructions have a fixed format, the target may be computed **speculatively** (that is, before it has been determined that the instruction *is* a branch) during the 'dec' stage, thereby reducing the branch latency to a single cycle, though note that in this pipeline there may still be hazards on a conditional branch due to dependencies on the condition code result of the instruction preceding the branch. Some RISC architectures (though not the ARM) define that the instruction following the branch is executed whether or not the branch is taken. This technique is known as the **delayed branch**.

**Pipeline efficiency**

Though there are techniques which reduce the impact of these pipeline problems, they cannot remove the difficulties altogether. The deeper the pipeline (that is, the more pipeline stages there are), the worse the problems get. For reasonably simple processors, there are significant benefits in introducing pipelines from three to five stages long, but beyond this the law of diminishing returns begins to apply and the added costs and complexity outweigh the benefits.

Pipelines clearly benefit from all instructions going through a similar sequence of steps. Processors with very complex instructions where every instruction behaves differently from the next are hard to pipeline. In 1980 the complex instruction set microprocessor of the day was not pipelined due to the limited silicon resource, the limited design resource and the high complexity of designing a pipeline for a complex instruction set.

## 1.6   The Reduced Instruction Set Computer

In 1980 Patterson and Ditzel published a paper entitled 'The Case for the Reduced Instruction Set Computer' (a full reference is given in the bibliography on page 406). In this seminal work they expounded the view that the optimal architecture for a single-chip processor need not be the same as the optimal architecture for a multi-chip processor. Their argument was subsequently supported by the results of a processor design project undertaken by a postgraduate class at Berkeley which incorporated a Reduced Instruction Set Computer (RISC) architecture. This design, the Berkeley RISC I, was much simpler than the commercial CISC processors of the day and had taken an order of magnitude less design effort to develop, but nevertheless delivered a very similar performance.

The RISC I instruction set differed from the minicomputer-like CISC instruction sets used on commercial microprocessors in a number of ways. It had the following key features:

**RISC architecture**
- A fixed (32-bit) instruction size with few formats; CISC processors typically had variable length instruction sets with many formats.

- A load-store architecture where instructions that process data operate only on registers and are separate from instructions that access memory; CISC processors typically allowed values in memory to be used as operands in data processing instructions.

- A large register bank of thirty-two 32-bit registers, all of which could be used for any purpose, to allow the load-store architecture to operate efficiently; CISC register sets were getting larger, but none was this large and most had different registers for different purposes (for example, the *data* and *address* registers on the Motorola MC68000).

These differences greatly simplified the design of the processor and allowed the designers to implement the architecture using organizational features that contributed to the performance of the prototype devices:

**RISC organization**
- Hard-wired instruction decode logic; CISC processors used large microcode ROMs to decode their instructions.

- Pipelined execution; CISC processors allowed little, if any, overlap between consecutive instructions (though they do now).

- Single-cycle execution; CISC processors typically took many clock cycles to complete a single instruction.

By incorporating all these architectural and organizational changes at once, the Berkeley RISC microprocessor effectively escaped from the problem that haunts progress by incremental improvement, which is the risk of getting stuck in a local maximum of the performance function.

**RISC advantages**

Patterson and Ditzel argued that RISC offered three principal advantages:

- A smaller die size.

  A simple processor should require fewer transistors and less silicon area. Therefore a whole CPU will fit on a chip at an earlier stage in process technology development, and once the technology has developed beyond the point where either CPU will fit on a chip, a RISC CPU leaves more die area free for performance-enhancing features such as cache memory, memory management functions, floating-point hardware, and so on.

- A shorter development time.

  A simple processor should take less design effort and therefore have a lower design cost and be better matched to the process technology when it is launched (since process technology developments need be predicted over a shorter development period).

- A higher performance.

  This is the tricky one! The previous two advantages are easy to accept, but in a world where higher performance had been sought through ever-increasing complexity, this was a bit hard to swallow.

  The argument goes something like this: smaller things have higher natural frequencies (insects flap their wings faster than small birds, small birds faster than large birds, and so on) so a simple processor ought to allow a high clock rate. So let's design our complex processor by starting with a simple one, then add complex instructions one at a time. When we add a complex instruction it will make some high-level function more efficient, but it will also slow the clock down a bit for all instructions. We can measure the overall benefit on typical programs, and when we do, all complex instructions make the program run slower. Hence we stick to the simple processor we started with.

These arguments were backed up by experimental results and the prototype processors (the Berkeley RISC II came shortly after RISC I). The commercial processor companies were sceptical at first, but most new companies designing processors for their own purposes saw an opportunity to reduce development costs and get ahead of the game. These commercial RISC designs, of which the ARM was the first, showed that the idea worked, and since 1980 all new general-purpose processor architectures have embraced the concepts of the RISC to a greater or lesser degree.

**RISC in retrospect**

Since the RISC is now well established in commercial use it is possible to look back and see more clearly what its contribution to the evolution of the microprocessor really was.

Early RISCs achieved their performance through:

- Pipelining.

  Pipelining is the simplest form of concurrency to implement in a processor and delivers around two to three times speed-up. A simple instruction set greatly simplifies the design of the pipeline.

- A high clock rate with single-cycle execution.

  In 1980 standard semiconductor memories (DRAMs – Dynamic Random Access Memories) could operate at around 3 MHz for random accesses and at 6 MHz for sequential (page mode) accesses. The CISC microprocessors of the time could access memory at most at 2 MHz, so memory bandwidth was not being exploited to the full. RISC processors, being rather simpler, could be designed to operate at clock rates that would use all the available memory bandwidth.

  Neither of these properties is a feature of the architecture, but both depend on the architecture being simple enough to allow the implementation to incorporate it. RISC architectures succeeded because they were simple enough to enable the designers to exploit these organizational techniques. It was entirely feasible to implement a fixed-length instruction load-store architecture using microcode, multi-cycle execution and no pipeline, but such an implementation would exhibit no advantage over an off-the-shelf CISC. It was *not* possible, at that time, to implement a hard-wired, single-cycle execution pipelined CISC. But it is now!

**Clock rates**

As footnotes to the above analysis, there are two aspects of the clock rate discussion that require further explanation:

- 1980s CISC processors often had higher clock rates than the early RISCs, but they took several clock cycles to perform a single memory access, so they had a lower memory access rate. Beware of evaluating processors on their clock rate alone!

- The mismatch between the CISC memory access rate and the available bandwidth appears to conflict with the comments in 'Complex Instruction Set Computers' on page 21 where microcode is justified in an early 1970s minicomputer on the grounds of the slow main memory speed relative to the processor speed. The resolution of the conflict lies in observing that in the intervening decade memory technology had become significantly faster while early CISC microprocessors were slower than typical minicomputer processors. This loss of processor speed was due to the necessity to switch from fast bipolar technologies to much slower NMOS technologies to achieve the logic density required to fit the complete processor onto a single chip.

## RISC drawbacks

RISC processors have clearly won the performance battle and should cost less to design, so is a RISC all good news? With the passage of time, two drawbacks have come to light:

- RISCs generally have poor code density compared with CISCs;
- RISCs don't execute x86 code.

The second of these is hard to fix, though PC emulation software is available for many RISC platforms. It is only a problem, however, if you want to build an IBM PC compatible; for other applications it can safely be ignored.

The poor code density is a consequence of the fixed-length instruction set and is rather more serious for a wide range of applications. In the absence of a cache, poor code density leads to more main memory bandwidth being used for instruction fetching, resulting in a higher memory power consumption. When the processor incorporates an on-chip cache of a particular size, poor code density results in a smaller proportion of the working set being held in the cache at any time, increasing the cache miss rate, resulting in an even greater increase in the main memory bandwidth requirement and consequent power consumption.

## ARM code density and Thumb

The ARM processor design is based on RISC principles, but for various reasons suffers less from poor code density than most other RISCs. Its code density is still, however, not as good as some CISC processors. Where code density is of prime importance, ARM Limited has incorporated a novel mechanism, called the **Thumb** architecture, into some versions of the ARM processor. The Thumb instruction set is a 16-bit compressed form of the original 32-bit ARM instruction set, and employs dynamic decompression hardware in the instruction pipeline. Thumb code density is better than that achieved by most CISC processors.

The Thumb architecture is described in Chapter 7.

## Beyond RISC

It seems unlikely that RISC represents the last word on computer architecture, so is there any sign of another breakthrough which will render the RISC approach obsolete?

There is no development visible at the time of writing which suggests a change on the same scale as RISC, but instruction sets continue to evolve to give better support for efficient implementations and for new applications such as multimedia.

## 1.7   Design for low power consumption

Since the introduction of digital computers 50 years ago there has been sustained improvement in their cost-effectiveness at a rate unparalleled in any other technical endeavour. As a side-effect of the route taken to increased performance, the power consumption of the machines has reduced equally dramatically. Only very recently, however, has the drive for minimum power consumption become as important as, and in some application areas more important than, the drive for increased performance. This change has come about as a result of the growing market for battery-powered portable equipment, such as digital mobile telephones and lap-top computers, which incorporate high-performance computing components.

Following the introduction of the integrated circuit the computer business has been driven by the win-win scenario whereby smaller transistors yield lower cost, higher performance and lower power consumption. Now, though, designers are beginning to design specifically for low power, even, in some cases, sacrificing performance to achieve it.

The ARM processor is at the centre of this drive for power-efficient processing. It therefore seems appropriate to consider the issues around design for low power.

**Where does the power go?**

The starting point for low-power design is to understand where the power goes in existing circuits. CMOS is the dominant technology for modern high-performance digital electronics, and has itself some good properties for low-power design, so we start by looking at where the power goes in a CMOS circuit.

A typical CMOS circuit is the static NAND gate, illustrated in Figure 1.2 on page 5. All signals swing between the voltages of the power and ground rails, *Vdd* and *Vss*. Until recently a 5 volt supply was standard, but many modern CMOS processes require a lower supply voltage of around 3 volts and this will reduce further in the future.

The gate operates by connecting the output either to *Vdd* through a pull-up network of p-type transistors, or to *Vss* through a pull-down network of n-type transistors. When the inputs are both close to one rail or the other, then one of these networks is conducting and the other is effectively not conducting, so there is no path through the gate from *Vdd* to *Vss*. Furthermore, the output is normally connected to the inputs of similar gates and therefore sees only capacitive load. Once the output has been driven close to either rail, it takes no current to hold it there. Therefore a short time after the gate has switched the circuit reaches a stable condition and no further current is taken from the supply.

This characteristic of consuming power only when switching is not shared by many other logic technologies and has been a major factor in making CMOS the technology of choice for high-density integrated circuits.

**CMOS power components**

The total power consumption of a CMOS circuit comprises three components:

- Switching power.

  This is the power dissipated by charging and discharging the gate output capacitance $C_L$, and represents the useful work performed by the gate.

  The energy per output transition is:

$$E_t = \frac{1}{2} \cdot C_L \cdot Vdd^2$$

$$\approx 1\,\text{picojoule}$$

Equation 2

- Short-circuit power.

  When the gate inputs are at an intermediate level both the p- and n-type networks can conduct. This results in a transitory conducting path from $Vdd$ to $Vss$. With a correctly designed circuit (which generally means one that avoids slow signal transitions) the short-circuit power should be a small fraction of the switching power.

- Leakage current.

  The transistor networks do conduct a very small current when they are in their 'off' state; though on a conventional process this current is very small (a small fraction of a nanoamp per gate), it is the only dissipation in a circuit that is powered but inactive, and can drain a supply battery over a long period of time. It is generally negligible in an active circuit.

  In a well-designed active circuit the switching power dominates, with the short-circuit power adding perhaps 10% to 20% to the total power, and the leakage current being significant only when the circuit is inactive.

**CMOS circuit power**

The total power dissipation, $P_C$, of a CMOS circuit, neglecting the short-circuit and leakage components, is therefore given by summing the dissipation of every gate $g$ in the circuit $C$:

$$P_C = \frac{1}{2} \cdot f \cdot Vdd^2 \cdot \sum_{g \in C} A_g \cdot C_L^g$$

Equation 3

where $f$ is the clock frequency, $A_g$ is the gate **activity factor** (reflecting the fact that not all gates switch every clock cycle) and $C_L^g$ is the gate load capacitance. Note that within this summation clock lines, which make two transitions per clock cycle, have an activity factor of 2.

**Low-power circuit design**

The typical gate load capacitance is a function of the process technology and therefore not under the direct control of the designer. The remaining parameters in Equation 3 suggest various approaches to low-power design. These are listed below with the most important first:

1. Minimize the power supply voltage, *Vdd.*

   The quadratic contribution of the supply voltage to the power dissipation makes this an obvious target. This is discussed further below.

2. Minimize the circuit activity, *A.*

   Techniques such as clock gating fall under this heading. Whenever a circuit function is not needed, activity should be eliminated.

3. Minimize the number of gates.

   Simple circuits use less power than complex ones, all other things being equal, since the sum is over a smaller number of gate contributions.

4. Minimize the clock frequency, *f.*

   Avoiding unnecessarily high clock rates is clearly desirable, but although a lower clock rate reduces the power consumption it also reduces performance, having a neutral effect on power-efficiency (measured, for example, in MIPS – Millions of Instructions Per Second – per watt). If, however, a reduced clock frequency allows operation at a reduced *Vdd*, this will be highly beneficial to the power-efficiency.

**Reducing Vdd**

As the feature size on CMOS processes gets smaller, there is pressure to reduce the supply voltage. This is because the materials used to form the transistors cannot withstand an electric field of unlimited strength, and as transistors get smaller the field strength increases if the supply voltage is held constant.

However, with increasing interest in design specifically for low power, it may be desirable for the supply voltage to be reduced faster than is necessary solely to prevent electrical breakdown. What prevents very low supply voltages from being used now?

The problem with reducing *Vdd* is that this also reduces the performance of the circuit. The saturated transistor current is given by:

$$I_{sat} \propto (Vdd - V_t)^2 \qquad \text{Equation 4}$$

where $V_t$ is the transistor threshold. The charge on a circuit node is proportional to *Vdd*, so the maximum operating frequency is given by:

$$f_{max} \propto \frac{(Vdd - V_t)^2}{Vdd} \qquad \text{Equation 5}$$

Therefore the maximum operating frequency is reduced as *Vdd* is reduced. The performance loss on a sub-micron process may not be as severe as Equation 5 suggests since the current at high voltage may be limited by velocity saturation effects, but performance will be lost to some extent. Equation 5 suggests that an obvious way to ameliorate the performance loss would be to reduce $V_t$. However the leakage current depends strongly on $V_t$:

$$I_{leak} \propto \exp\left(-\frac{V_t}{35\ mV}\right)$$  Equation 6

Even a small reduction in $V_t$ can significantly increase the leakage current, increasing the battery drain through an inactive circuit.

**Low-power strategies**

To conclude this introduction to design techniques for low power consumption, here are some suggested strategies for low-power applications.

- Minimize *Vdd*.

  Choose the lowest clock frequency that delivers the required performance, then set the power supply voltage as low as is practical given the clock frequency and the requirements of the various system components.

- Minimize off-chip activity.

  Off-chip capacitances are much higher than on-chip loads, so always minimize off-chip activity. Avoid allowing transients to drive off-chip loads and use caches to minimize accesses to off-chip memories.

- Minimize on-chip activity.

  Lower priority than minimizing off-chip activity, it is still important to avoid clocking unnecessary circuit functions (for example, by using gated clocks) and to employ sleep modes where possible.

- Exploit parallelism.

  Where the power supply voltage is a free variable parallelism can be exploited to improve power-efficiency. Duplicating a circuit allows the two circuits to sustain the same performance at half the clock frequency of the original circuit, which allows the required performance to be delivered with a lower supply voltage.

Design for low power is an active research area and one where new ideas are being generated at a high rate. It is expected that a combination of process and design technology improvements will yield two to three orders of magnitude improvement in the power-efficiency of high-speed digital circuits over the next five to ten years.

## 1.8   Examples and exercises

(The more practical exercises will require you to have access to some form of hardware simulation environment.)

**Example 1.1**     **Design a 4-bit binary counter using logic gates and a 4-bit register.**

If the register inputs are denoted by $D[0]$ to $D[3]$ and its outputs are denoted by $Q[0]$ to $Q[3]$, the counter may be implemented by building combinatorial logic that generates $D[3:0] = Q[3:0] + 1$. The logic equations for a binary adder are given in the Appendix (Equation 18 on page 391 gives the sum and Equation 19 the carry). When the second operand is a constant these equations simplify to:

$$D[0] \quad = \overline{Q[0]} \qquad\qquad\qquad\qquad\qquad\qquad\qquad \text{Equation 7}$$

$$D[i] \quad = Q[i] \cdot \overline{C[i\text{-}1]} + \overline{Q[i]} \cdot C[i\text{-}1] \qquad\qquad\qquad\qquad \text{Equation 8}$$

$$C[i] \quad = Q[i] \cdot C[i\text{-}1] \qquad\qquad\qquad\qquad\qquad\qquad \text{Equation 9}$$

for $1 \le i \le 3$, and $C[0] = 1$. ($C[3]$ is not needed.) These equations may be drawn as the logic circuit shown below, which also includes the register.

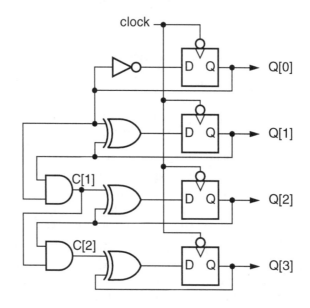

**Exercise 1.1.1** Modify the binary counter to count from 0 to 9, and then, on the next clock edge, to start again at zero. (This is a **modulo 10** counter.)

**Exercise 1.1.2** Modify the binary counter to include a **synchronous clear** function. This means adding a new input ('clear') which, if active, causes the counter output to be zero after the next clock edge whatever its current value is.

**Exercise 1.1.3** Modify the binary counter to include an **up/down** input. When this input is high the counter should behave as described in the example above; when it is low the counter should count down (in the reverse sequence to the *up* mode).

**Example 1.2** **Add indexed addressing to the MU0 instruction set.**

The minimum extension that is useful here is to introduce a new 12-bit index register (X) and some new instructions that allow it to be initialized and used in load and store instructions. Referring to Table 1.1 on page 9, there are eight unused opcodes in the original design, so we could add up to eight new instructions before we run out of space. The basic set of indexing operations is:

```
LDX S           ; X := mem₁₆[S]
LDA S, X        ; ACC := mem₁₆[S+X]
STA S, X        ; mem₁₆[S+X] := ACC
```

An index register is much more useful if there is some way to modify it, for instance to step through a table:

```
INX             ; X := X + 1
DEX             ; X := X - 1
```

This gives the basic functionality of an index register. It would increase the usefulness of X to include a way to store it in memory, then it could be used as a temporary register, but for simplicity we will stop here.

**Exercise 1.2.1** Modify the RTL organization shown in Figure 1.6 on page 12 to include the X register, indicating the new control signals required.

**Exercise 1.2.2** Modify the control logic in Table 1.2 on page 13 to support indexed addressing. If you have access to a hardware simulator, test your design. (This is non-trivial!)

**Example 1.3**     **Estimate the performance benefit of a single-cycle delayed branch.**

A delayed branch allows the instruction following the branch to be executed whether or not the branch is taken. The instruction after the branch is in the 'delay slot'. Assume the dynamic instruction frequencies shown in Table 1.3 on page 23 and the pipeline structure shown in Figure 1.13 on page 24; ignore register hazards; assume all delay slots can be filled (most single delay slots can be filled).

If there is a dedicated branch target adder in the decode stage, a branch has a 1-cycle delayed effect, so a single delay slot removes all wasted cycles. One instruction in four is a branch, so four instructions take five clock cycles without the delay slot and four with it, giving 25% higher performance.

If there is no dedicated branch target adder and the main ALU stage is used to compute the target, a branch will incur three wasted cycles. Therefore four instructions on average include one branch and take seven clock cycles, or six with a single delay slot. The delay slot therefore gives 17% higher performance (but the dedicated branch adder does better even without the delay slot).

**Exercise 1.3.1**    Estimate the performance benefit of a 2-cycle delayed branch assuming that all the first delay slots can be filled, but only 50% of the second delay slots can be filled.

Why is the 2-cycle delayed branch only relevant if there is no dedicated branch target adder?

**Exercise 1.3.2**    What is the effect on code size of the 1- and 2-cycle delayed branches suggested above? (All unfilled branch delay slots must be filled with no-ops.)

# 2 The ARM Architecture

**Summary of chapter contents**

The ARM processor is a *Reduced Instruction Set Computer* (RISC). The RISC concept, as we saw in the previous chapter, originated in processor research programmes at Stanford and Berkeley universities around 1980.

In this chapter we see how the RISC ideas helped shape the ARM processors. The ARM was originally developed at Acorn Computers Limited of Cambridge, England, between 1983 and 1985. It was the first RISC microprocessor developed for commercial use and has some significant differences from subsequent RISC architectures. The principal features of the ARM architecture are presented here in overview form; the details are postponed to subsequent chapters.

In 1990 Advanced RISC Machines Limited was established as a separate company specifically to widen the exploitation of ARM technology, since when the ARM has been licensed to many semiconductor manufacturers around the world. It has become established as a market-leader for low-power and cost-sensitive embedded applications.

No processor is particularly useful without the support of hardware and software development tools. The ARM is supported by a toolkit which includes an instruction set emulator for hardware modelling and software testing and benchmarking, an assembler, C and C++ compilers, a linker and a symbolic debugger.

## 2.1   The Acorn RISC Machine

The first ARM processor was developed at Acorn Computers Limited, of Cambridge, England, between October 1983 and April 1985. At that time, and until the formation of Advanced RISC Machines Limited in 1990, ARM stood for **Acorn RISC Machine**.

Acorn had developed a strong position in the UK personal computer market due to the success of the BBC (British Broadcasting Corporation) microcomputer, a 6502-powered machine that rapidly became established as the dominant machine in UK schools following its introduction in January 1982 in support of a series of television programmes broadcast by the BBC. The BBC micro also enjoyed enthusiastic support in the hobbyist market and found its way into a number of research laboratories and higher education establishments.

Following the success of the BBC micro, Acorn's engineers looked at various microprocessors to build a successor machine around, but found all the commercial offerings lacking. The 16-bit CISC microprocessors that were available in 1983 were slower than standard memory parts. They also had instructions that took many clock cycles to complete (in some cases, many hundreds of clock cycles), giving them very long interrupt latencies. The BBC micro benefited greatly from the 6502's rapid interrupt response, so Acorn's designers were unwilling to accept a retrograde step in this aspect of the processor's performance.

As a result of these frustrations with the commercial microprocessor offerings, the design of a proprietary microprocessor was considered. The major stumbling block was that the Acorn team knew that commercial microprocessor projects had absorbed hundreds of man-years of design effort. Acorn could not contemplate an investment on that scale since it was a company of only just over 400 employees in total. It had to produce a better design with a fraction of the design effort, and with no experience in custom chip design beyond a few small gate arrays designed for the BBC micro.

Into this apparently impossible scenario, the papers on the Berkeley RISC I fell like a bolt from the blue. Here was a processor which had been designed by a few postgraduate students in under a year, yet was competitive with the leading commercial offerings. It was inherently simple, so there were no complex instructions to ruin the interrupt latency. It also came with supporting arguments that suggested it could point the way to the future, though technical merit, however well supported by academic argument, is no guarantee of commercial success.

The ARM, then, was born through a serendipitous combination of factors, and became the core component in Acorn's product line. Later, after a judicious modification of the acronym expansion to **Advanced RISC Machine**, it lent its name to the company formed to broaden its market beyond Acorn's product range. Despite the change of name, the architecture still remains close to the original Acorn design.

## 2.2   Architectural inheritance

At the time the first ARM chip was designed, the only examples of RISC architectures were the Berkeley RISC I and II and the Stanford MIPS (which stands for **Microprocessor without Interlocking Pipeline Stages**), although some earlier machines such as the Digital PDP-8, the Cray-1 and the IBM 801, which predated the RISC concept, shared many of the characteristics which later came to be associated with RISCs.

**Features used**

The ARM architecture incorporated a number of features from the Berkeley RISC design, but a number of other features were rejected. Those that were used were:

- A load-store architecture.
- Fixed-length 32-bit instructions.
- 3-address instruction formats.

**Features rejected**

The features that were employed on the Berkeley RISC designs which were rejected by the ARM designers were:

- Register windows.

  The register banks on the Berkeley RISC processors incorporated a large number of registers, 32 of which were visible at any time. Procedure entry and exit instructions moved the visible 'window' to give each procedure access to new registers, thereby reducing the data traffic between the processor and memory resulting from register saving and restoring.

  The principal problem with register windows is the large chip area occupied by the large number of registers. This feature was therefore rejected on cost grounds, although the shadow registers used to handle exceptions on the ARM are not too different in concept.

  In the early days of RISC this mechanism was strongly associated with the RISC concept, due to its inclusion in the Berkeley prototypes, but subsequently only the Sun SPARC architecture has adopted it in its original form

- Delayed branches.

  Branches cause pipelines problems since they interrupt the smooth flow of instructions. Most RISC processors ameliorate the problem by using delayed branches where the branch takes effect *after* the following instruction has executed.

  The problem with delayed branches is that they remove the atomicity of individual instructions. They work well on single issue pipelined processors, but they do not scale well to super-scalar implementations and can interact badly with branch prediction mechanisms.

On the original ARM delayed branches were not used because they made exception handling more complex; in the long run this has turned out to be a good decision since it simplifies re-implementing the architecture with a different pipeline.

- Single-cycle execution of all instructions.

Although the ARM executes most data processing instructions in a single clock cycle, many other instructions take multiple clock cycles.

The rationale here was based on the observation that with a single memory for both data and instructions, even a simple load or store instruction requires at least two memory accesses (one for the instruction and one for the data). Therefore single cycle operation of all instructions is only possible with separate data and instruction memories, which were considered too expensive for the intended ARM application areas.

Instead of single-cycle execution of all instructions, the ARM was designed to use the minimum number of cycles required for memory accesses. Where this was greater than one, the extra cycles were used, where possible, to do something useful, such as support auto-indexing addressing modes. This reduces the total number of ARM instructions required to perform any sequence of operations, improving performance and code density.

**Simplicity**    An overriding concern of the original ARM design team was the need to keep the design simple. Before the first ARM chips, Acorn designers had experience only of gate arrays with complexities up to around 2,000 gates, so the full-custom CMOS design medium was approached with some respect. When venturing into unknown territory it is advisable to minimize those risks which are under your control, since this still leaves significant risks from those factors which are not well understood or are fundamentally not controllable.

The simplicity of the ARM may be more apparent in the hardware organization and implementation (described in Chapter 4) than it is in the instruction set architecture. From the programmer's perspective it is perhaps more visible as a conservatism in the ARM instruction set design which, while accepting the fundamental precepts of the RISC approach, is less radical than many subsequent RISC designs.

The combination of the simple hardware with an instruction set that is grounded in RISC ideas but retains a few key CISC features, and thereby achieves a significantly better code density than a pure RISC, has given the ARM its power-efficiency and its small core size.

## 2.3  The ARM programmer's model

A processor's instruction set defines the operations that the programmer can use to change the state of the system incorporating the processor. This state usually comprises the values of the data items in the processor's visible registers and the system's memory. Each instruction can be viewed as performing a defined transformation from the state before the instruction is executed to the state after it has completed. Note that although a processor will typically have many invisible registers involved in executing an instruction, the values of these registers before and after the instruction is executed are not significant; only the values in the visible registers have any significance. The visible registers in an ARM processor are shown in Figure 2.1.

When writing user-level programs, only the 15 general-purpose 32-bit registers (r0 to r14), the program counter (r15) and the current program status register (CPSR) need be considered. The remaining registers are used only for system-level programming and for handling exceptions (for example, interrupts).

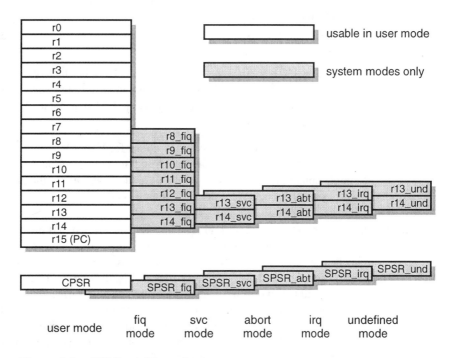

**Figure 2.1**  ARM's visible registers.

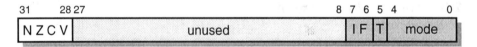

| 31 | 28 27 | | 8 7 6 5 4 | 0 |
| N Z C V | unused | | I F | T | mode |

**Figure 2.2**   ARM CPSR format.

**The Current Program Status Register (CPSR)**

The CPSR is used in user-level programs to store the condition code bits. These bits are used, for example, to record the result of a comparison operation and to control whether or not a conditional branch is taken. The user-level programmer need not usually be concerned with how this register is configured, but for completeness the register is illustrated in Figure 2.2. The bits at the bottom of the register control the processor mode (see Section 5.1 on page 110), instruction set ('T', see Section 7.1 on page 200) and interrupt enables ('I' and 'F', see Section 5.2 on page 113) and are protected from change by the user-level program. The condition code flags are in the top four bits of the register and have the following meanings:

- N: Negative; the last ALU operation which changed the flags produced a negative result (the top bit of the 32-bit result was a one).
- Z: Zero; the last ALU operation which changed the flags produced a zero result (every bit of the 32-bit result was zero).
- C: Carry; the last ALU operation which changed the flags generated a carry-out, either as a result of an arithmetic operation in the ALU or from the shifter.
- V: oVerflow; the last arithmetic ALU operation which changed the flags generated an overflow into the sign bit.

Note that although the above definitions for C and V look quite complex, their use does not require a detailed understanding of their operation. In most cases there is a simple condition test which gives the desired result without the programmer having to work out the precise values of the condition code bits.

**The memory system**

In addition to the processor register state, an ARM system has memory state. Memory may be viewed as a linear array of bytes numbered from zero up to $2^{32}$-1. Data items may be 8-bit bytes, 32-bit words, or, in some ARM systems, 16-bit half-words. Words are always aligned on 4-byte boundaries (that is, the two least significant address bits are zero) and half-words are aligned on even byte boundaries.

The memory organization is illustrated in Figure 2.3 on page 43. This shows a small area of memory where each byte location has a unique number. A byte may occupy any of these locations, and a few examples are shown in the figure. A word-sized data item must occupy a group of four byte locations starting at a byte address

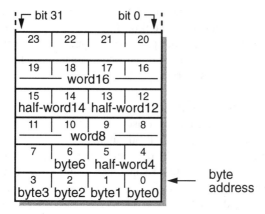

**Figure 2.3**    ARM memory organization.

which is a multiple of four, and again the figure contains a couple of examples. Half-words, where they are supported, occupy two byte locations starting at an even byte address.

(This is the standard, 'little-endian', memory organization used by the ARM. ARM can also be configured to work with a 'big-endian' memory organization; we will return to this issue in Chapter 5.)

**Load-store architecture**

In common with most RISC processors, ARM employs a load-store architecture. This means that the instruction set will only process (add, subtract, and so on) values which are in registers (or specified directly within the instruction itself), and will always place the results of such processing into a register. The only operations which apply to memory state are ones which copy memory values into registers (load instructions) or copy register values into memory (store instructions).

Older (CISC) processors would typically allow a value from memory to be added to a value in a register, and would sometimes allow a value in a register to be added to a value in memory. ARM does not support such 'memory-to-memory' operations. Therefore all ARM instructions fall into one of the following three categories:

1. Data processing instructions. These use and change only register values. For example, an instruction can add two registers and place the result in a register.

2. Data transfer instructions. These copy memory values into registers (load instructions) or copy register values into memory (store instructions). An additional form, useful only in systems code, exchanges a memory value with a register value.

3.  Control flow instructions. Normal instruction execution uses instructions stored at consecutive memory addresses. Control flow instructions cause execution to switch to a different address, either permanently (branch instructions) or saving a return address to resume the original sequence (branch and link instructions) or trapping into system code (supervisor calls).

**Supervisor mode**

The ARM processor supports a protected supervisor mode. The protection mechanism ensures that user code cannot gain supervisor privileges without appropriate checks being carried out to ensure that the code is not attempting illegal operations.

The upshot of this for the user-level programmer is that system-level functions can only be accessed through specified supervisor calls. These functions generally include any accesses to hardware peripheral registers, and to widely-used operations such as character input and output. User-level programmers are principally concerned with devising algorithms to operate on the data 'owned' by their programs, and rely on the operating system to handle all transactions with the world outside their programs. The instructions which request operating system functions are covered in 'Supervisor calls' on page 70.

**The ARM instruction set**

All ARM instructions are 32 bits wide (except the compressed 16-bit Thumb instructions which are described in Chapter 7) and are aligned on 4-byte boundaries in memory. Basic use of the instruction set is described in Chapter 3 and full details, including the binary instruction formats, are given in Chapter 5. The most notable features of the ARM instruction set are:

*   The load-store architecture.
*   3-address data processing instructions (that is, the two source operand registers and the result register are all independently specified).
*   Conditional execution of every instruction.
*   The inclusion of very powerful load and store multiple register instructions.
*   The ability to perform a general shift operation and a general ALU operation in a single instruction that executes in a single clock cycle.
*   Open instruction set extension through the coprocessor instruction set, including adding new registers and data types to the programmer's model.
*   A very dense 16-bit compressed representation of the instruction set in the Thumb architecture.

To those readers familiar with modern RISC instruction sets, the ARM instruction set may appear to have rather more formats than other commercial RISC processors. While this is certainly the case and it does lead to more complex instruction decoding, it also leads to higher code density. For the small embedded systems that most ARM processors are used in, this code density advantage outweighs the small performance penalty incurred by the decode complexity. Thumb code extends this advantage to give ARM better code density than most CISC processors.

**The I/O system**

The ARM handles **I/O** (input/output) peripherals (such as disk controllers, network interfaces, and so on) as memory-mapped devices with interrupt support. The internal registers in these devices appear as addressable locations within the ARM's memory map and may be read and written using the same (load-store) instructions as any other memory locations.

Peripherals may attract the processor's attention by making an interrupt request using either the normal interrupt (*IRQ*) or the fast interrupt (*FIQ*) input. Both interrupt inputs are level-sensitive and maskable. Normally most interrupt sources share the IRQ input, with just one or two time-critical sources connected to the higher-priority FIQ input.

Some systems may include direct memory access (**DMA**) hardware external to the processor to handle high-bandwidth I/O traffic. This is discussed further in Section 11.6 on page 304.

Interrupts are a form of *exception* and are handled as outlined below.

**ARM exceptions**

The ARM architecture supports a range of interrupts, traps and supervisor calls, all grouped under the general heading of exceptions. The general way these are handled is the same in all cases:

1. The current state is saved by copying the PC into r14_*exc* and the CPSR into SPSR_*exc* (where *exc* stands for the exception type).

2. The processor operating mode is changed to the appropriate exception mode.

3. The PC is forced to a value between $00_{16}$ and $1C_{16}$, the particular value depending on the type of exception.

The instruction at the location the PC is forced to (the *vector address*) will usually contain a branch to the exception handler. The exception handler will use r13_*exc*, which will normally have been initialized to point to a dedicated stack in memory, to save some user registers for use as work registers.

The return to the user program is achieved by restoring the user registers and then using an instruction to restore the PC and the CPSR atomically. This may involve some adjustment of the PC value saved in r14_*exc* to compensate for the state of the pipeline when the exception arose. This is described in more detail in Section 5.2 on page 113.

## 2.4    ARM development tools

Software development for the ARM is supported by a coherent range of tools developed by ARM Limited, and there are also some tools available in the public domain such as an ARM back-end for the *gcc* C compiler.

Since the ARM is widely used as an embedded controller where the target hardware will not make a good environment for software development, the tools are intended for **cross-development** (that is, they run on a different architecture from the one for which they produce code) from a platform such as a PC running Windows or a Sun, Digital Alpha AXP or Hewlett-Packard workstation. The overall structure of the ARM cross-development toolkit is shown in Figure 2.4. C or assembler source files are compiled or assembled into ARM object format (*.aof*) files, which are then linked into ARM image format (*.aif*) files. The image format files can be built to include the debug tables required by the ARM symbolic debugger (**ARMsd**) which can load, run

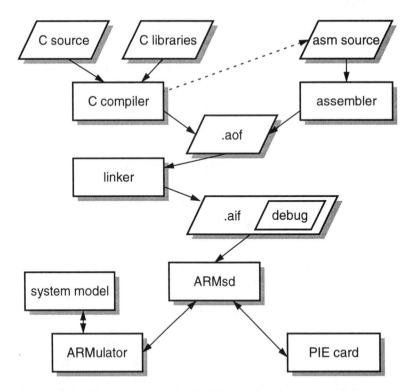

**Figure 2.4**    The structure of the ARM cross-development toolkit.

and debug programs either on hardware such as the ARM **PIE** (Platform Independent Evaluation) card or using a software emulation of the ARM (the **ARMulator**). The ARMulator has been designed to allow easy extension of the software model to include system features such as caches, particular memory timing characteristics, and so on.

**The ARM C compiler**

The ARM C compiler is compliant with the **ANSI** (American National Standards Institute) standard for C and is supported by the appropriate library of standard functions. It uses the ARM Procedure Call Standard (see Section 6.8 on page 185) for all externally available functions. It can be told to produce assembly source output instead of ARM object format, so the code can be inspected, or even hand optimized, and then assembled subsequently.

A version of the compiler can also produce Thumb code.

**The ARM assembler**

The ARM assembler is a full macro assembler which produces ARM object format output that can be linked with output from the C compiler.

Assembly source language is near machine-level, with most assembly instructions translating into single ARM (or Thumb) instructions. ARM assembly language programming is introduced in the next chapter, and the full details of the ARM instruction set, including assembly language formats, are given in Chapter 5. The Thumb instruction set and assembly language formats are given in Chapter 7.

**The linker**

The linker takes one or more object files and combines them into an executable program. It resolves symbolic references between the object files and extracts object modules from libraries as needed by the program. It can assemble the various components of the program in a number of different ways, depending on whether the code is to run in RAM (Random Access Memory, which can be read and written) or ROM (Read Only Memory), whether overlays are required, and so on.

Normally the linker includes debug tables in the output file. If the object files were compiled with full debug information, this will include full symbolic debug tables (so the program can be debugged using the variable names in the source program). The linker can also produce library modules that are not executable but are ready for efficient linking with object files in the future.

**ARMsd**

The ARM symbolic debugger is a front-end interface to assist in debugging programs running either under emulation (on the ARMulator) or remotely on a target system such as the PIE card. The remote system must support the appropriate remote debug protocols either via a serial line or through a JTAG test interface (see Section 8.2 on page 221). Debugging a system where the processor core is embedded within an application-specific system chip is a complex issue that we will return to in Chapter 8.

At its most basic, ARMsd allows an executable program to be loaded into the ARMulator or the PIE card and run. It allows the setting of breakpoints, which are addresses in the code which, if executed, cause execution to halt so that the processor state can be examined. In the ARMulator, or when running on hardware with appropriate support, it also allows the setting of watchpoints. These are memory addresses which, if accessed as data addresses, cause execution to halt in a similar way.

At a more sophisticated level ARMsd supports full source level debugging, allowing the C programmer who is not familiar with ARM machine or assembly code to debug a program using the source file to specify breakpoints and using variable names from the original program.

**ARMulator**

The ARMulator (*ARM emulator*) is a suite of programs that models the behaviour of various ARM processor cores in software on a host system. It can operate at various levels of accuracy:

- *Instruction-accurate* modelling gives the exact behaviour of the system state without regard to the precise timing characteristics of the processor.
- *Cycle-accurate* modelling gives the exact behaviour of the processor on a cycle-by-cycle basis, allowing the exact number of clock cycles that a program requires to be established.
- *Timing-accurate* modelling presents signals at the correct time within a cycle, allowing logic delays to be accounted for.

All these approaches run considerably slower than the real hardware, but the first incurs the smallest speed penalty and is best suited to software development.

At its simplest, the ARMulator allows an ARM program developed using the C compiler or assembler to be tested and debugged on a host machine with no ARM processor connected. It allows the number of clock cycles the program takes to execute to be measured exactly, so the performance of the target system can be evaluated.

At its most complex, the ARMulator can be used as the centre of a complete, timing-accurate, C model of the target system, with full details of the cache and memory management functions added, running an operating system.

In between these two extremes the ARMulator comes with a set of model prototyping modules including a rapid prototype memory model and coprocessor interfacing support. (There is more detail on this in Section 8.1 on page 220.)

The ARMulator can also be used as the core of a timing-accurate ARM behavioural model in a hardware simulation environment such as that offered by VHDL. (VHDL is a standard widely-supported hardware description language.) A VHDL 'wrapper' must be generated to interface the ARMulator C code to the VHDL environment.

**The PIE card**  The PIE card is a minimal ARM system which incorporates an ARM processor, some RAM, a ROM containing the 'Demon' debug monitor program which supports the ARM remote debug protocol and a serial link to a host machine.

The host normally runs ARMsd to load programs into the PIE card and to control their running and debugging.

The PIE card is a low-cost way to run programs on real ARM hardware. Its design is discussed further in Section 13.2 on page 350 where it is presented as an example of an ARM system.

**Toolkit**      ARM Limited supplies the complete set of tools described above, with some support
**version 2.0**  utility programs and documentation, as the 'ARM Software Development Toolkit'. The Toolkit version 2.0 CD-ROM includes a PC version of the toolset that runs under Windows 3.1, Windows 95 and Windows NT (and under Windows NT on a Digital Alpha AXP machine) and includes a full Windows-based project manager.

The ARM Project Manager is a graphical front-end for the tools described above. It supports the building of a single library or executable image from a list of files that make up a particular project. These files may be:

- Source files (C, assembler, and so on);
- Object files;
- Library files.

The source files may be edited within the Project Manager, a dependency list created and the output library or executable image built. There are many options which may be chosen for the build, such as:

- Whether the output should be optimized for code size or execution time.
- Whether the output should be in debug or release form.

  (Code compiled for source-level debugging cannot be fully optimized since the mapping from the source to fully-optimized output is too obscure for debugging purposes!)

- Which ARM processor is the target (and, particularly, whether it supports the Thumb instruction set).

The CD-ROM also contains versions of the tools that run on a Sun or HP UNIX host, where a command-line interface is used. All versions have on-line help available.

**JumpStart**    The JumpStart tools from VLSI Technology, Inc., include the same basic set of development tools, but present a full X-windows interface on a suitable workstation rather than the command-line interface of Toolkit version 2.0.

## 2.5   Example and exercises

**Example 2.1**   **Describe the principal features of the ARM architecture.**

The main features of the ARM architecture are:

- A large set of registers, all of which can be used for most purposes.
- A load-store architecture.
- 3-address instructions (that is, the two source operand registers and the result register are all independently specified).
- Conditional execution of every instruction.
- The inclusion of very powerful load and store multiple register instructions.
- The ability to perform a general shift operation and a general ALU operation in a single instruction that executes in a single clock cycle.
- Open instruction set extension through the coprocessor instruction set, including adding new registers and data types to the programmer's model.

If the Thumb instruction set is considered part of the ARM architecture, we could also add:

- A very dense 16-bit compressed representation of the instruction set in the Thumb architecture.

**Exercise 2.1.1**   Which features does ARM have in common with many other RISC architectures?

**Exercise 2.1.2**   Which features of the ARM architecture are not shared by most other RISCs?

**Exercise 2.1.3**   Which features of most other RISC architectures are not shared by the ARM?

# 3 ARM Assembly Language Programming

**Summary of chapter contents**

The ARM processor is very easy to program at the assembly level, though for most applications it is more appropriate to program in a high-level language such as C or C++.

Assembly language programming requires the programmer to think at the level of the individual machine instruction. An ARM instruction is 32 bits long, so there are around 4 billion different binary machine instructions. Fortunately there is considerable structure within the instruction space, so the programmer does not have to be familiar with each of the 4 billion binary encodings on an individual basis. Even so, there is a considerable amount of detail to be got right in each instruction. The assembler is a computer program which handles most of this detail for the programmer.

In this chapter we will look at ARM assembly language programming at the user level and see how to write simple programs which will run on the ARM PIE card or an ARM emulator (for example, the ARMulator which comes as part of the ARM development toolkit). Once the basic instruction set is familiar we will move on, in Chapter 5, to look at system-level programming and some of the finer details of the ARM instruction set, including the binary-level instruction encoding.

Some ARM processors support a form of the instruction set that has been compressed into 16-bit 'Thumb' instructions. These are discussed in Chapter 7.

## 3.1   Data processing instructions

ARM data processing instructions enable the programmer to perform arithmetic and logical operations on data values in registers. All other instructions just move data around and control the sequence of program execution, so the data processing instructions are the only instructions which modify data values. These instructions typically require two operands and produce a single result, though there are exceptions to both of these rules. A characteristic operation is to add two values together to produce a single result which is the sum.

Here are some rules which apply to ARM data processing instructions:

- All operands are 32 bits wide and come from registers or are specified as literals in the instruction itself.

- The result, if there is one, is 32 bits wide and is placed in a register.

  (There is an exception here: long multiply instructions, available on some versions of ARM, produce a 64-bit result; they are discussed in Section 5.8 on page 128.)

- Each of the operand registers and the result register are independently specified in the instruction. That is, the ARM uses a '3-address' format for these instructions.

**Simple register operands**

A typical ARM data processing instruction is written in assembly language as shown below:

```
ADD     r0, r1, r2          ; r0 := r1 + r2
```

The semicolon in this line indicates that everything to the right of it is a comment and should be ignored by the assembler. Comments are put into the assembly source code to make reading and understanding it easier.

This example simply takes the values in two registers (r1 and r2), adds them together, and places the result in a third register (r0). The values in the source registers are 32 bits wide and may be considered to be either unsigned integers or signed 2's-complement integers. The addition may produce a carry-out or, in the case of signed 2's-complement values, an internal overflow into the sign bit, but in either case this is ignored.

Note that in writing the assembly language source code, care must be taken to write the operands in the correct order, which is result register first, then the first operand and lastly the second operand (though for **commutative** operations the order of the first and second operands is not significant when they are both registers). When this instruction is executed the only change to the system state is the value of the destination register r0.

The different instructions available in this form are listed below in their classes:

- Arithmetic operations.

  These instructions perform binary arithmetic (addition, subtraction and reverse subtraction, which is subtraction with the operand order reversed) on two 32-bit operands. The operands may be unsigned or 2's-complement signed integers; the carry-in, when used, is the current value of the C bit in the CPSR.

  ```
  ADD    r0, r1, r2           ; r0 := r1 + r2
  ADC    r0, r1, r2           ; r0 := r1 + r2 + C
  SUB    r0, r1, r2           ; r0 := r1 - r2
  SBC    r0, r1, r2           ; r0 := r1 - r2 + C - 1
  RSB    r0, r1, r2           ; r0 := r2 - r1
  RSC    r0, r1, r2           ; r0 := r2 - r1 + C - 1
  ```

  'ADD' is simple addition, 'ADC' is add with carry, 'SUB' is subtract, 'SBC' is subtract with carry, 'RSB' is reverse subtraction and 'RSC' reverse subtract with carry.

- Bit-wise logical operations.

  These instructions perform the specified Boolean logic operation on each bit pair of the input operands, so in the first case $r0[i] := r1[i]$ AND $r2[i]$ for each value of $i$ from 0 to 31 inclusive, where $r0[i]$ is the $i$th bit of r0.

  ```
  AND    r0, r1, r2           ; r0 := r1 and r2
  ORR    r0, r1, r2           ; r0 := r1 or r2
  EOR    r0, r1, r2           ; r0 := r1 xor r2
  BIC    r0, r1, r2           ; r0 := r1 and not r2
  ```

  We have met AND, OR and XOR (here called EOR) logical operations at the hardware gate level in Section 1.2 on page 4; the final mnemonic, BIC, stands for 'bit clear' where every '1' in the second operand clears the corresponding bit in the first. (The 'not' operation in the assembly language comment inverts each bit of the following operand.)

- Register movement operations.

  These instructions ignore the first operand, which is omitted from the assembly language format, and simply move the second operand (possibly bit-wise inverted) to the destination.

  ```
  MOV    r0, r2               ; r0 := r2
  MVN    r0, r2               ; r0 := not r2
  ```

  The 'MVN' mnemonic stands for 'move negated'; it leaves the result register set to the value obtained by inverting every bit in the source operand.

- Comparison operations.

    These instructions do not produce a result (which is therefore omitted from the assembly language format) but just set the condition code bits (N, Z, C and V) in the CPSR according to the selected operation.

    ```
    CMP     r1, r2              ; set cc on r1 - r2
    CMN     r1, r2              ; set cc on r1 + r2
    TST     r1, r2              ; set cc on r1 and r2
    TEQ     r1, r2              ; set cc on r1 xor r2
    ```

    The mnemonics stand for 'compare' (CMP), 'compare negated' (CMN), '(bit) test' (TST) and 'test equal' (TEQ).

**Immediate operands**

If, instead of adding two registers, we simply wish to add a constant to a register, we can replace the second source operand with an immediate value, which is a literal constant, preceded by '#':

```
ADD     r3, r3, #1          ; r3 := r3 + 1
AND     r8, r7, #&ff        ; r8 := r7[7:0]
```

The first example also illustrates that although the 3-address format allows source and destination operands to be specified separately, they are not required to be distinct registers. The second example shows that the immediate value may be specified in hexadecimal (base 16) notation by putting '&' after the '#'.

Since the immediate value is coded within the 32 bits of the instruction, it is not possible to enter every possible 32-bit value as an immediate. The values which can be entered correspond to any 32-bit binary number where all the binary ones fall within a group of eight adjacent bit positions on a 2-bit boundary. Most valid immediate values are given by:

$$immediate = (0 \rightarrow 255) \times 2^{2n}$$ 
Equation 10

where $0 \le n \le 12$. The assembler will also replace MOV with MVN, ADD with SUB, and so on, where this can bring the immediate within range.

This may appear a complex constraint on the immediate values, but it does, in practice, cover all the most common cases such as a byte value at any of the four byte positions within a 32-bit word, any power of 2, and so on. In any case the assembler will report any value which is requested that it cannot encode.

(The reason for the constraint on immediate values is the way they are specified at the binary instruction level. This is described in the Chapter 5, and the reader who wishes to understand this issue fully should look there for the complete explanation.)

**Shifted register operands**

A third way to specify a data operation is similar to the first, but allows the second register operand to be subject to a shift operation before it is combined with the first operand. For example:

```
ADD     r3, r2, r1, LSL #3 ; r3 := r2 + 8 x r1
```

Note that this is still a single ARM instruction, executed in a single clock cycle. Most processors offer shift operations as separate instructions, but the ARM combines them with a general ALU operation in a single instruction.

Here 'LSL' indicates 'logical shift left by the specified number of bits', which in this example is 3. Any number from 0 to 31 may be specified, though using 0 is equivalent to omitting the shift altogether. As before, '#' indicates an immediate quantity. The available shift operations are:

- LSL: logical shift left by 0 to 31 places; fill the vacated bits at the least significant end of the word with zeros.

- LSR: logical shift right by 0 to 32 places; fill the vacated bits at the most significant end of the word with zeros.

- ASL: arithmetic shift left; this is a synonym for LSL.

- ASR: arithmetic shift right by 0 to 32 places; fill the vacated bits at the most significant end of the word with zeros if the source operand was positive, or with ones if the source operand was negative.

- ROR: rotate right by 0 to 32 places; the bits which fall off the least significant end of the word are used, in order, to fill the vacated bits at the most significant end of the word.

- RRX: rotate right extended by 1 place; the vacated bit (bit 31) is filled with the old value of the C flag and the operand is shifted one place to the right. With appropriate use of the condition codes (see below) a 33-bit rotate of the operand and the C flag is performed.

These shift operations are illustrated in Figure 3.1 on page 56.

It is also possible to use a register value to specify the number of bits the second operand should be shifted by:

```
ADD     r5, r5, r3, LSL r2 ; r5 := r5 + r3 x 2**r2
```

This is a 4-address instruction. Only the bottom eight bits of r2 are significant, but since shifts by more than 32 bits are not very useful this limitation is not important for most purposes.

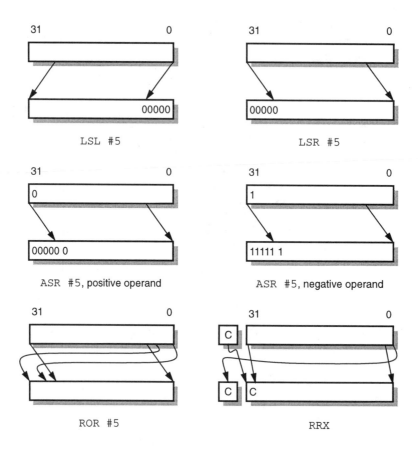

**Figure 3.1**   ARM shift operations

**Setting the condition codes**

Any data processing instruction can set the condition codes (N, Z, C and V) if the programmer wishes it to. The comparison operations only set the condition codes, so there is no option with them, but for all other data processing instructions a specific request must be made. At the assembly language level this request is indicated by adding an 's' to the opcode, standing for 'Set condition codes'. As an example, the following code performs a 64-bit addition of two numbers held in r0–r1 and r2–r3, using the C condition code flag to store the intermediate carry:

```
ADDS    r2, r2, r0 ; 32-bit carry out -> C..
ADC     r3, r3, r1 ; .. and added into high word
```

Since the s opcode extension gives the programmer control over whether or not an instruction modifies the condition codes, the codes can be preserved over long instruction sequences when it is appropriate to do so.

An arithmetic operation (which here includes CMP and CMN) sets all the flags according to the arithmetic result. A logical or move operation does not produce a meaningful value for C or V, so these operations set N and Z according to the result but preserve V, and either preserve C when there is no shift operation, or set C to the value of the last bit to fall off the end of the shift. This detail is not often significant.

## Use of the condition codes

We have already seen the C flag used as an input to an arithmetic data processing instruction. However we have not yet seen the most important use of the condition codes, which is to control the program flow through the conditional branch instructions. These will be described in Section 3.3 on page 66.

## Multiplies

A special form of the data processing instruction supports multiplication:

```
MUL     r4, r3, r2          ; r4 := (r3 x r2)[31:0]
```

There are some important differences from the other arithmetic instructions:

- Immediate second operands are not supported.
- The result register must not be the same as the second source register.
- If the 's' bit is set the V flag is preserved (as for a logical instruction) and the C flag is rendered meaningless.

Multiplying two 32-bit integers gives a 64-bit result, the least significant 32 bits of which are placed in the result register and the rest are ignored. This can be viewed as multiplication in modulo $2^{32}$ arithmetic and gives the correct result whether the operands are viewed as signed or unsigned integers. (Some ARMs also support long multiply instructions which place the most significant 32 bits into a second result register; these are described in Section 5.8 on page 128.)

An alternative form, subject to the same restrictions, adds the product to a running total. This is the multiply-accumulate instruction:

```
MLA     r4, r3, r2, r1     ; r4 := (r3 x r2 + r1)[31:0]
```

Multiplication by a constant can be implemented by loading the constant into a register and then using one of these instructions, but it is usually more efficient to use a short series of data processing instructions using shifts and adds or subtracts. For example, to multiply r0 by 35:

```
ADD     r0, r0, r0, LSL #2; r0':= 5 x r0
RSB     r0, r0, r0, LSL #3; r0":= 7 x r0' (= 35 x r0)
```

## 3.2  Data transfer instructions

Data transfer instructions move data between ARM registers and memory. There are three basic forms of data transfer instruction in the ARM instruction set:

- Single register load and store instructions.

  These instructions provide the most flexible way to transfer single data items between an ARM register and memory. The data item may be a byte, a 32-bit word, or, on some ARM chips, a 16-bit half-word.

- Multiple register load and store instructions.

  These instructions are less flexible than single register transfer instructions, but enable large quantities of data to be transferred more efficiently. They are used for procedure entry and exit, to save and restore workspace registers, and to copy blocks of data around memory.

- Single register swap instructions.

  These instructions allow a value in a register to be exchanged with a value in memory, effectively doing both a load and a store operation in one instruction. They are little used in user-level programs, so they will not be discussed further in this section. Their principal use is to implement semaphores to ensure mutual exclusion on accesses to shared data structures in multi-processor systems, but don't worry if this explanation has little meaning for you at the moment.

It is quite possible to write any program for the ARM using only the single register load and store instructions, but there are situations where the multiple register transfers are much more efficient, so the programmer should be familiar with them.

**Register-indirect addressing**

Towards the end of Section 1.4 on page 15 there was a discussion of memory addressing mechanisms that are available to the processor instruction set designer. The ARM data transfer instructions are all based around register-indirect addressing, with modes that include base-plus-offset and base-plus-index addressing.

Register-indirect addressing uses a value in one register (the **base** register) as a memory address and either **loads** the value from that address into another register or **stores** the value from another register into that memory address.

These instructions are written in assembly language as follows:

```
LDR    r0, [r1]          ; r0 := mem32[r1]
STR    r0, [r1]          ; mem32[r1] := r0
```

Other forms of addressing all build on this form, adding immediate or register offsets to the base address. In all cases it is necessary to have an ARM register loaded with an address which is near to the desired transfer address, so we will begin by look-ing at ways of getting memory addresses into a register.

**Initializing an address pointer**

To load or store from or to a particular memory location, an ARM register must usu-ally be initialized to contain the address of that location, or, in the case of single regis-ter transfer instructions, an address within 4 Kbytes of that location. If the location is close to the code being executed it is often possible to exploit the fact that the program counter, r15, is close to the desired address. A data processing instruction can be employed to add a small offset to r15, but calculating the appropriate offset may not be that straightforward. However, this is the sort of tricky calculation that assemblers are good at, and ARM assemblers have an inbuilt 'pseudo instruction', ADR, which makes this easy. A pseudo instruction looks like a normal instruction in the assembly source code but does not correspond directly to a particular ARM instruction. Instead, the assembler has a set of rules which enable it to select the most appropriate ARM instruction or short instruction sequence for the situation in which the pseudo instruc-tion is used. (ADR is always assembled into a single ADD or SUB instruction.)

As an example, consider a program which must copy data from TABLE1 to TABLE2, both of which are near to the code:

```
COPY    ADR     r1, TABLE1          ; r1 points to TABLE1
        ADR     r2, TABLE2          ; r2 points to TABLE2
        ..
TABLE1                              ; < source of data >
        ..
TABLE2                              ; < destination >
        ..
```

Of course any ARM instruction can be used to compute the address of a data item in memory, but for the purposes of small programs the ADR pseudo instruction will do what we require.

**Single register load and store instructions**

These instructions compute an address for the transfer using a base register, which should contain an address near to the target address, and an offset which may be another register or an immediate value.

We have just seen the simplest form of these instructions, which does not use an offset:

```
LDR     r0, [r1]           ; r0 := mem32[r1]
STR     r0, [r1]           ; mem32[r1] := r0
```

The notation used here indicates that the data quantity is the 32-bit memory word addressed by r1. The word address in r1 should be aligned on a 4-byte boundary,

so the two least significant bits of r1 should be zero. We can now copy the first word
from one table to the other:

```
COPY    ADR     r1, TABLE1              ; r1 points to TABLE1
        ADR     r2, TABLE2              ; r2 points to TABLE2
        LDR     r0, [r1]                ; load first value...
        STR     r0, [r2]                ; and store it in TABLE2
        ..
TABLE1                                  ; < source of data >
        ..
TABLE2                                  ; < destination >
        ..
```

We could now use data processing instructions to modify both base registers
ready for the next transfer:

```
COPY    ADR     r1, TABLE1              ; r1 points to TABLE1
        ADR     r2, TABLE2              ; r2 points to TABLE2
LOOP    LDR     r0, [r1]                ; get TABLE1 1st word
        STR     r0, [r2]                ; copy into TABLE2
        ADD     r1, r1, #4              ; step r1 on 1 word
        ADD     r2, r2, #4              ; step r2 on 1 word
        ???                             ; if more go back to LOOP
        ..
TABLE1                                  ; < source of data >
        ..
TABLE2                                  ; < destination >
        ..
```

Note that the base registers are incremented by 4 (bytes), since this is the size of
a word. If the base register was word-aligned before the increment, it will be word-
aligned afterwards too.

All load and store instructions could use just this simple form of register-indirect
addressing. However, the ARM instruction set includes more addressing modes that
can make the code more efficient.

**Base plus
offset
addressing**

If the base register does not contain exactly the right address, an offset of up to
4 Kbytes may be added (or subtracted) to the base to compute the transfer address:

```
        LDR     r0, [r1,#4]             ; r0 := mem32[r1 + 4]
```

This is a **pre-indexed** addressing mode. It allows one base register to be used to
access a number of memory locations which are in the same area of memory.

Sometimes it is useful to modify the base register to point to the transfer address. This can be achieved by using pre-indexed addressing with **auto-indexing**, and allows the program to walk through a table of values:

```
LDR     r0, [r1,#4]!        ; r0 := mem32[r1 + 4]
                            ; r1 := r1 + 4
```

The exclamation mark indicates that the instruction should update the base register after initiating the data transfer. On the ARM this auto-indexing costs no extra time since it is performed on the processor's datapath while the data is being fetched from memory. It is exactly equivalent to preceding a simple register-indirect load with a data processing instruction that adds the offset (4 bytes in this example) to the base register, but the time and code space cost of the extra instruction are avoided.

Another useful form of the instruction, called **post-indexed** addressing, allows the base to be used without an offset as the transfer address, after which it is auto-indexed:

```
LDR     r0, [r1], #4        ; r0 := mem32[r1]
                            ; r1 := r1 + 4
```

Here the exclamation mark is not needed, since the only use of the immediate offset is as a base register modifier. Again, this form of the instruction is exactly equivalent to a simple register-indirect load followed by a data processing instruction, but it is faster and occupies less code space.

Using the last of these forms we can now improve on the table copying program example introduced earlier:

```
COPY    ADR     r1, TABLE1        ; r1 points to TABLE1
        ADR     r2, TABLE2        ; r2 points to TABLE2
LOOP    LDR     r0, [r1], #4      ; get TABLE1 1st word
        STR     r0, [r2], #4      ; copy into TABLE2
        ???                       ; if more go back to LOOP
        ..
TABLE1                            ; < source of data >
        ..
TABLE2                            ; < destination for >
        ..
```

The load and store instructions are repeated until the required number of values has been copied into TABLE2, then the loop is exited. Control flow instructions are required to determine the loop exit; they will be introduced shortly.

In the above examples the address offset from the base register was always an immediate value. It can equally well be another register, which may be subject to a shift operation before being added to the base, but such forms of the instruction are less useful than the immediate offset form. They are described fully in Section 5.9 on page 130.

As a final variation, the size of the data item which is transferred may be a single unsigned 8-bit byte instead of a 32-bit word. This option is selected by adding a letter B onto the opcode:

```
LDRB    r0, [r1]                ; r0 := mem_8[r1]
```

In this case the transfer address can have any alignment and is not restricted to a 4-byte boundary, since bytes may be stored at any byte address. The loaded byte is placed in the bottom byte of r0 and the remaining bytes are filled with zeros.

(Some ARM processors also support **signed** bytes, where the top bit of the byte indicates whether the value should be treated as positive or negative, and signed and unsigned 16-bit half-words, but many do not so these variants will not be described until later.)

**Multiple register data transfers**

Where considerable quantities of data are to be transferred, it is preferable to move several registers at a time. These instructions allow any subset (or all) of the 16 registers to be transferred with a single instruction. The trade-off is that the available addressing modes are more restricted than with a single register transfer instruction.

A simple example of this instruction class is:

```
LDMIA   r1, {r0,r2,r5}          ; r0 := mem_32[r1]
                                ; r2 := mem_32[r1 + 4]
                                ; r5 := mem_32[r1 + 8]
```

Since the transferred data items are always 32-bit words, the base address (r1) should be word-aligned. The transfer list, within the curly brackets, may contain any or all of r0 to r15. Note, however, that including r15 in the list will cause a change in the control flow, since r15 is the PC. We will return to this case when we discuss control flow instructions and will not consider it further until then.

The above example illustrates a common feature of all forms of these instructions: the lowest register is transferred to or from the lowest address, and then the other registers are transferred in order of register number to or from consecutive word addresses above the first. However there are several variations on how the first address is formed, and auto-indexing is also available (again by adding a '!' after the base register).

**Stack addressing**

The addressing variations stem from the fact that one use of these instructions is to implement stacks within memory. A stack is a form of last-in-first-out store which supports simple dynamic memory allocation, that is, memory allocation where the address to be used to store a data value is not known at the time the program is compiled or assembled. An example would be a recursive function, where the depth of recursion depends on the value of the argument. A stack is usually implemented as a linear data structure which grows up (an **ascending** stack) or down (a **descending** stack) memory as data is added to it and shrinks back as data is removed. A **stack pointer** holds the address of the current top of the stack, either by pointing to the last valid data item pushed onto the stack (a **full** stack), or by pointing to the vacant slot where the next data item will be placed (an **empty** stack).

The above description suggests that there are four variations on a stack, representing all the combinations of ascending and descending full and empty stacks. The ARM multiple register transfer instructions support all four forms of stack:

- Full ascending: the stack grows up through increasing memory addresses and the base register points to the highest address containing a valid item.

- Empty ascending: the stack grows up through increasing memory addresses and the base register points to the first empty location above the stack.

- Full descending: the stacks grows down through decreasing memory addresses and the base register points to the lowest address containing a valid item.

- Empty descending: the stack grows down through decreasing memory addresses and the base register points to the first empty location below the stack.

**Block copy addressing**

Although the stack view of multiple register transfer instructions is useful, there are occasions when a different view is easier to understand. For example, when these instructions are used to copy a block of data from one place in memory to another a mechanistic view of the addressing process is more useful. Therefore the ARM assembler supports two different views of the addressing mechanism, both of which map onto the same basic instructions, and which can be used interchangeably. The block copy view is based on whether the data is to be stored above or below the address held in the base register and whether the address incrementing or decrementing begins before or after storing the first value. The mapping between the two views depends on whether the operation is a load or a store, and is detailed in Table 3.1 on page 65.

The block copy views are illustrated in Figure 3.2 on page 64, which shows how each variant stores three registers into memory and how the base register is modified if auto-indexing is enabled. The base register value before the instruction is r9, and after the auto-indexing it is r9'.

To illustrate the use of these instructions, here are two instructions which copy eight words from the location r0 points to to the location r1 points to:

```
LDMIA    r0!, {r2-r9}
STMIA    r1,  {r2-r9}
```

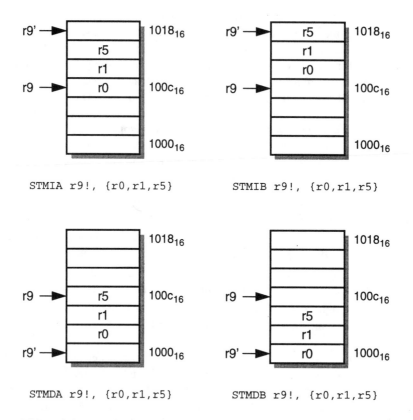

**Figure 3.2**   Multiple register transfer addressing modes.

After executing these instructions r0 has increased by 32 since the '!' causes it to auto-index across eight words, whereas r1 is unchanged. If r2 to r9 contained useful values, we could preserve them across this operation by pushing them onto a stack:

```
STMEA    r13!, {r2-r9}        ; save regs onto stack
LDMIA    r0!,  {r2-r9}
STMIA    r1,   {r2-r9}
LDMEA    r13!, {r2-r9}        ; restore from stack
```

Note that auto-indexing is almost always specified for stack operations in order to ensure that the stack pointer has a consistent behaviour.

**Table 3.1** The mapping between the stack and block copy views of the load and store multiple instructions.

| | | Ascending | | Descending | |
|---|---|---|---|---|---|
| | | **Full** | **Empty** | **Full** | **Empty** |
| **Increment** | **Before** | STMIB STMFA | | | LDMIB LDMED |
| | **After** | | STMIA STMEA | LDMIA LDMFD | |
| **Decrement** | **Before** | | LDMDB LDMEA | STMDB STMFD | |
| | **After** | LDMDA LDMFA | | | STMDA STMED |

The load and store multiple register instructions are an efficient way to save and restore processor state and to move blocks of data around in memory. They save code space and operate up to four times faster than the equivalent sequence of single register load or store instructions (a factor of two due to improved sequential behaviour and another factor of nearly two due to the reduced instruction count). This significant advantage suggests that it is worth thinking carefully about how data is organized in memory in order to maximize the potential for using multiple register data transfer instructions to access it.

These instructions are, perhaps, not pure 'RISC' since they cannot be executed in a single clock cycle even with separate instruction and data caches, but other RISC architectures are beginning to adopt multiple register transfer instructions in order to increase the data bandwidth between the processor's registers and the memory.

On the other side of the equation, load and store multiple instructions are complex to implement, as we shall see later.

The ARM multiple register transfer instructions are uniquely flexible in being able to transfer any subset of the 16 currently visible registers, and this feature is powerfully exploited by the ARM procedure call mechanism which is described in Section 6.8 on page 185.

## 3.3   Control flow instructions

This third category of instructions neither processes data nor moves it around; it simply determines which instructions get executed next.

**Branch instructions**

The normal way to switch program execution from one place to another is to use the branch instruction:

```
        B       LABEL
        ..
LABEL   ..
```

The processor normally executes instructions sequentially, but when it reaches the branch instruction it proceeds directly to the instruction at LABEL instead of executing the instruction immediately after the branch. In this example LABEL comes after the branch instruction in the program, so the instructions in between are skipped. However, LABEL could equally well come before the branch, in which case the processor goes back to it and possibly repeats some instructions it has already executed.

**Conditional branches**

Sometimes you will want the processor to take a decision whether or not to branch. For example, to implement a loop a branch back to the start of the loop is required, but this branch should only be taken until the loop has been executed the required number of times, then the branch should be skipped.

The mechanism used to control loop exit is conditional branching. Here the branch has a condition associated with it and it is only executed if the condition codes have the correct value. A typical loop control sequence might be:

```
        MOV     r0, #0              ; initialize counter
LOOP    ..
        ADD     r0, r0, #1          ; increment loop counter
        CMP     r0, #10             ; compare with limit
        BNE     LOOP                ; repeat if not equal
        ..                          ; else fall through
```

This example shows one sort of conditional branch, BNE, or 'branch if not equal'. There are many forms of the condition. All the forms are listed in Table 3.2 on page 67, along with their normal interpretations. The pairs of conditions which are listed in the same row of the table (for instance BCC and BLO) are synonyms which result in identical binary code, but both are available because each makes the interpretation of the assembly source code easier in particular circumstances. Where the table refers to signed or unsigned comparisons this does not reflect a choice in the comparison instruction itself but supports alternative interpretations of the operands.

**Table 3.2** Branch conditions.

| Branch | Interpretation | Normal uses |
|--------|---------------|-------------|
| B | Unconditional | Always take this branch |
| BAL | Always | Always take this branch |
| BEQ | Equal | Comparison equal or zero result |
| BNE | Not equal | Comparison not equal or non-zero result |
| BPL | Plus | Result positive or zero |
| BMI | Minus | Result minus or negative |
| BCC | Carry clear | Arithmetic operation did not give carry-out |
| BLO | Lower | Unsigned comparison gave lower |
| BCS | Carry set | Arithmetic operation gave carry-out |
| BHS | Higher or same | Unsigned comparison gave higher or same |
| BVC | Overflow clear | Signed integer operation; no overflow occurred |
| BVS | Overflow set | Signed integer operation; overflow occurred |
| BGT | Greater than | Signed integer comparison gave greater than |
| BGE | Greater or equal | Signed integer comparison gave greater or equal |
| BLT | Less than | Signed integer comparison gave less than |
| BLE | Less or equal | Signed integer comparison gave less than or equal |
| BHI | Higher | Unsigned comparison gave higher |
| BLS | Lower or same | Unsigned comparison gave lower or same |

**Conditional execution**

An unusual feature of the ARM instruction set is that conditional execution applies not only to branches but to all ARM instructions. A branch which is used to skip a small number of following instructions may be omitted altogether by giving those instructions the opposite condition. For example, consider the following sequence:

```
        CMP     r0, #5
        BEQ     BYPASS              ; if (r0 != 5) {
        ADD     r1, r1, r0          ;    r1 := r1 + r0 - r2
        SUB     r1, r1, r2          ; }
BYPASS  ..
```

This may be replaced by:

```
CMP     r0, #5              ; if (r0 != 5) {
ADDNE   r1, r1, r0          ;    r1 := r1 + r0 - r2
SUBNE   r1, r1, r2          ; }
..
```

The new sequence is both smaller and faster than the old one. Whenever the conditional sequence is three instructions or fewer it is better to exploit conditional execution than to use a branch, provided that the skipped sequence is not doing anything complicated with the condition codes within itself. Conditional execution is invoked by adding the 2-letter condition after the 3-letter opcode (and before any other instruction modifier letter such as the 'S' that controls setting the condition codes in a data processing instruction or the 'B' that specifies a byte load or store).

Just to emphasize the scope of this technique, note that every ARM instruction, including supervisor calls and coprocessor instructions, may have a condition appended which causes it to be skipped if the condition is not met.

It is sometimes possible to write very compact code by cunning use of conditionals, for example:

```
; if ((a==b) && (c==d)) e++;

CMP     r0, r1
CMPEQ   r2, r3
ADDEQ   r4, r4, #1
```

Note how if the first comparison finds unequal operands the second is skipped, causing the increment to be skipped also. The logical 'and' in the if clause is implemented by making the second comparison conditional.

**Branch and link instructions**

A common requirement in a program is to be able to branch to a subroutine in a way which makes it possible to resume the original code sequence when the subroutine has completed. This requires that a record is kept of the value of the program counter just before the branch is taken.

ARM offers this functionality through the branch and link instruction which, as well as performing a branch in exactly the same way as the branch instruction, also saves the address of the instruction following the branch in the link register, r14:

```
        BL      SUBR            ; branch to SUBR
        ..                      ; return to here
SUBR    ..                      ; subroutine entry point
        MOV     pc, r14         ; return
```

Note that since the return address is held is a register, the subroutine should not call a further, nested, subroutine without first saving r14, otherwise the new return address will overwrite the old one and it will not be possible to find the way back to the original caller. The normal mechanism used here is to push r14 onto a stack in memory. Since the subroutine will often also require some work registers, the old values in these registers can be saved at the same time using a store multiple instruction:

```
          BL      SUB1
          ..
SUB1      STMFA   r13, {r0-r2,r14}   ; save work & link regs
          BL      SUB2
          ..
SUB2      ..
```

A subroutine that does not call another subroutine (a **leaf** subroutine) need not save r14 since it will not be overwritten.

**Subroutine return instructions**

To get back to the calling routine, the value saved by the branch and link instruction in r14 must be copied back into the program counter. In the simplest case of a leaf subroutine (a subroutine that does not call another subroutine) a MOV instruction suffices, exploiting the visibility of the program counter as r15:

```
SUB2      ..
          MOV     pc, r14 ; copy r14 into r15 to return
```

In fact the availability of the program counter as r15 means that any of the data processing instructions can be used to compute a return address, though the 'MOV' form is by far the most commonly used.

Where the return address has been pushed onto a stack, it can be restored along with any saved work registers using a load multiple instruction:

```
SUB1      STMFA   r13, {r0-r2,r14}; save work regs & link
          BL      SUB2
          ..
          LDMFA   r13, {r0-r2,pc} ; restore work regs & return
```

Note here how the return address is restored directly to the program counter, not to the link register. This single restore and return instruction is very powerful. Note also the use of the stack view of the multiple register transfer addressing modes. The same stack model (in this case 'full ascending') is used for both the store and the load, ensuring that the correct values will be collected. It is important that for any particular stack the same addressing mode is used for every use of the stack, unless you really know what you are doing.

**Supervisor calls**

Whenever a program requires input or output, for instance to send some text to the display, it is normal to call a supervisor routine. The supervisor is a program which operates at a privileged level, which means that it can do things that a user-level program cannot do directly. The limitations on the capabilities of a user-level program vary from system to system, but in many systems the user cannot access hardware facilities directly.

The supervisor provides trusted ways to access system resources which appear to the user-level program rather like special subroutine accesses. The instruction set includes a special instruction, SWI, to call these functions. (SWI stands for 'SoftWare Interrupt', but is usually pronounced 'Supervisor Call'.)

Although the supervisor calls are implemented in system software, and could therefore be totally different from one ARM system to another, most ARM systems implement a common subset of calls in addition to any specific calls required by the particular application. The most useful of these is a routine which sends the character in the bottom byte of r0 to the user display device:

```
        SWI     SWI_WriteC          ; output r0[7:0]
```

Another useful call returns control from a user program back to the monitor program:

```
        SWI     SWI_Exit            ; return to monitor
```

The operation of SWIs is described in more detail in Section 5.6 on page 122.

**Jump tables**

Jump tables are not normally used by less experienced programmers, so you can ignore this section if you are relatively new to programming at the assembly level.

The idea of a jump table is that a programmer sometimes wants to call one of a set of subroutines, the choice depending on a value computed by the program. It is clearly possible to do this with the instructions we have seen already. Suppose the value is in r0. We can then write:

```
        BL      JUMPTAB
        ..
JUMPTAB CMP     r0, #0
        BEQ     SUB0
        CMP     r0, #1
        BEQ     SUB1
        CMP     r0, #2
        BEQ     SUB2
        ..
```

However, this solution becomes very slow when the list of subroutines is long unless there is some reason to think that the later choices will rarely be used. A solution which is more efficient in this case exploits the visibility of the program counter in the general register file:

```
            BL       JUMPTAB
            ..
JUMPTAB ADR r1, SUBTAB        ; r1 -> SUBTAB
        CMP  r0, #SUBMAX       ; check for overrun..
        LDRLS pc, [r1,r0,LSL #2] ; .. if OK, table jump
        B     ERROR            ; .. otherwise signal error
SUBTAB  DCD   SUB0             ; table of subroutine
        DCD   SUB1             ;          entry points
        DCD   SUB2
        ..
```

The 'DCD' directive instructs the assembler to reserve a word of store and to initialize it to the value of the expression to the right, which in these cases is just the address of the label.

This approach has a constant performance however many subroutines are in the table and independent of the distribution of frequency of use. Note, however, that the consequences of reading beyond the end of the table are likely to be dire, so checking for overrun is essential! Here, note how the overrun check is implemented by making the load into the PC conditional, so the overrun case skips the load and falls into the branch to the error handler. The only performance cost of checking for overrun is the comparison with the maximum value. More obvious code might have been:

```
        ..
        CMP  r0, #SUBMAX       ; check for overrun..
        BHI  ERROR            ; .. if overrun call error
        LDR  pc, [r1,r0,LSL #2] ; .. else table jump
        ..
```

but note that here the cost of conditionally skipping the branch is borne every time the jump table is used. The original version is more efficient except when overrun is detected, which should be infrequent and, since it represents an error, performance in that case is not of great concern.

An alternative, less obvious way to implement a jump table is discussed in 'switches' on page 181.

## 3.4   Writing simple assembly language programs

We now have all the basic tools for writing simply assembly language programs. As with any programming task, it is important to have a clear idea of your algorithm before beginning to type instructions into the computer. Large programs are almost certainly better written in C or C++, so we will only look at small examples of assembly language programs.

Even the most experienced programmers begin by checking that they can get a very simple program to run before moving on to whatever their real task is. There are so many complexities to do with learning to use a text editor, working out how to get the assembler to run, how to load the program into the machine, how to get it to start executing and so on. This sort of simple test program is often referred to as a *Hello World* program because all it does is print 'Hello World' on the display before terminating. Here is an ARM assembly language version:

```
          AREA      HelloW,CODE,READONLY ; declare code area
SWI_WriteC    EQU       &0          ; output character in r0
SWI_Exit      EQU       &11         ; finish program
          ENTRY                     ; code entry point
START     ADR       r1, TEXT        ; r1 -> "Hello World"
LOOP      LDRB      r0, [r1], #1    ; get the next byte
          CMP       r0, #0          ; check for text end
          SWINE     SWI_WriteC      ; if not end print ..
          BNE       LOOP            ;  .. and loop back
          SWI       SWI_Exit        ; end of execution
TEXT      =         "Hello World",&0a,&0d,0
          END                       ; end of program source
```

This program illustrates a number of the features of the ARM assembly language and instruction set:

- The declaration of the code 'AREA', with appropriate attributes.

- The definitions of the system calls which will be used in the routine. (In a larger program these would be defined in a file which other code files would reference.)

- The use of the ADR pseudo instruction to get an address into a base register.

- The use of auto-indexed addressing to move through a list of bytes.

- Conditional execution of the SWI instruction to avoid an extra branch.

Note also the use of a zero byte to mark the end of the string (following the linefeed and carriage return special characters). Whenever you use a looping structure, make sure it has a terminating condition.

In order to run this program you will need the following tools, all of which are available within the ARM software development toolkit:

- A text editor to type the program into.
- An assembler to turn the program into ARM binary code.
- An ARM system or emulator to execute the binary on. The ARM system must have some text output capability. (The ARM PIE card, for example, sends text output back up to the host for output onto the host's display.)

Once you have this program running you are ready to try something more useful. From now on, the only thing that changes is the program text. The use of the editor, the assembler, and the test system or emulator will remain pretty similar to what you have done already, at least up to the point where your program refuses to do what you want and you can't see why it refuses. Then you will need to use a debugger to see what is happening inside your program. This means learning how to use another complex tool, so we will put off that moment for as long as possible.

For the next example, we can now complete the block copy program developed partially earlier in the text. To ensure that we know it has worked properly, we will use a text source string so that we can output it from the destination address, and we will initialize the destination area to something different:

```
            AREA     BlkCpy,CODE,READONLY
SWI_WriteC  EQU      &0          ; output character in r0
SWI_Exit    EQU      &11         ; finish program
            ENTRY                ; code entry point
            ADR      r1, TABLE1   ; r1 -> TABLE1
            ADR      r2, TABLE2   ; r2 -> TABLE1
            ADR      r3, T1END    ; r3 -> T1END
LOOP1       LDR      r0, [r1], #4 ; get TABLE1 1st word
            STR      r0, [r2], #4 ; copy into TABLE2
            CMP      r1, r3       ; finished?
            BLT      LOOP1        ; if not, do more
            ADR      r1, TABLE2   ; r1 -> TABLE2
LOOP2       LDRB     r0, [r1], #1 ; get next byte
            CMP      r0, #0       ; check for text end
            SWINE    SWI_WriteC   ; if not end, print ..
            BNE      LOOP2        ;  .. and loop back
            SWI      SWI_Exit     ; finish
TABLE1      =        "This is the right string!", &0a, &0d, 0
T1END
            ALIGN                 ; ensure word alignment
TABLE2      =        "This is the wrong string!", 0
            END
```

This program uses word loads and stores to copy the table, which is why the tables must be word-aligned. It then uses byte loads to print out the result using a routine which is the same as that used in the 'Hello World' program.

Note the use of 'BLT' to control the loop termination. If TABLE1 contains a number of bytes which is not a multiple of four, there is a danger that r1 would step past T1END without ever exactly equalling it, so a termination condition based on 'BNE' might fail.

If you have succeeded in getting this program running, you are well on the way to understanding the basic operation of the ARM instruction set. The examples and exercises which follow should be studied to reinforce this understanding. As you attempt more complex programming tasks, questions of detail will arise. These should be answered by the full instruction set description given in Chapter 5.

## Program design

With a basic understanding of the instruction set, small programs can be written and debugged without too much trouble by just typing them into an editor and seeing if they work. However, it is dangerous to assume that this simple approach will scale to the successful development of complex programs which may be expected to work for many years, which may be changed by other programmers in the future, and which may end up in the hands of customers who will use use them in unexpected ways.

This book is not a text on program design, but having offered an introduction to programming it would be a serious omission not to point out that there is a lot more to writing a useful program than just sitting down and typing code.

Serious programming should start not with coding, but with careful design. The first step of the development process is to understand the requirements; it is surprising how often programs do not behave as expected because the requirements were not well understood by the programmer! Then the (often informal) requirements should be translated into an unambiguous specification. Now the design can begin, defining a program structure, the data structures that the program works with and the algorithms that are used to perform the required operations on the data. The algorithms may be expressed in **pseudo-code**, a program-like notation which does not follow the syntax of a particular programming language but which makes the meaning clear.

Only when the design is developed should the coding begin. Individual modules should be coded, tested thoroughly (which may require special programs to be designed as 'test-harnesses') and documented, and the program built piece by piece.

Today nearly all programming is based on high-level languages, so it is rare for large programs to be built using assembly programming as described here. Sometimes, however, it may be necessary to develop small software components in assembly language to get the best performance for a critical application, so it is useful to know how to write assembly code for these purposes.

## 3.5   Examples and exercises

Once you have the basic flavour of an instruction set the easiest way to learn to write programs is to look at some examples, then attempt to write your own program to do something slightly different. To see whether or not your program works you will need an ARM assembler and either an ARM emulator or hardware with an ARM processor in it. The following sections contain example ARM programs and suggestions for modifications to them. You should get the original program working first, then see if you can edit it to perform the modified function suggested in the exercises.

**Example 3.1**   **Print out r1 in hexadecimal.**

This is a useful little routine which dumps a register to the display in hexadecimal (base 16) notation; it can be used to help debug a program by writing out register values and checking that algorithms are producing the expected results, though in most cases using a debugger is a better way of seeing what is going on inside a program.

```
            AREA      Hex_Out,CODE,READONLY
SWI_WriteC  EQU       &0            ; output character in r0
SWI_Exit    EQU       &11           ; finish program
            ENTRY                   ; code entry point
            LDR       r1, VALUE     ; get value to print
            BL        HexOut        ; call hexadecimal output
            SWI       SWI_Exit      ; finish
VALUE       DCD       &12345678     ; test value
HexOut      MOV       r2, #8        ; nibble count = 8
LOOP        MOV       r0, r1, LSR #28   ; get top nibble
            CMP       r0, #9        ; 0-9 or A-F?
            ADDGT     r0, r0, #"A"-10   ; ASCII alphabetic
            ADDLE     r0, r0, #"0"      ; ASCII numeric
            SWI       SWI_WriteC    ; print character
            MOV       r1, r1, LSL #4    ; shift left one nibble
            SUBS      r2, r2, #1    ; decrement nibble count
            BNE       LOOP          ; if more do next nibble
            MOV       pc, r14       ; return
            END
```

**Exercise 3.1.1**   Modify the above program to output r1 in binary format. For the value loaded into r1 in the example program you should get:

00010010001101000101011001111000

**Exercise 3.1.2**   Use HEXOUT as the basis of a program to display the contents of an area of memory.

**Example 3.2**     **Write a subroutine to output a text string immediately following the call.**

It is often useful to be able to output a text string without having to set up a separate data area for the text (though this is inefficient if the processor has separate data and instruction caches, as does the StrongARM; in this case it is better to set up a separate data area). A call should look like:

```
BL        TextOut
=         "Test string",&0a,&0d,0
ALIGN
..                                ; return to here
```

The issue here is that the return from the subroutine must not go directly to the value put in the link register by the call, since this would land the program in the text string. Here is a suitable subroutine and test harness:

```
          AREA    Text_Out,CODE,READONLY
SWI_WriteC   EQU     &0           ; output character in r0
SWI_Exit     EQU     &11          ; finish program
          ENTRY   }              ; code entry point
          BL      TextOut        ; print following string
          =       "Test string",&0a,&0d,0
          ALIGN
          SWI     SWI_Exit       ; finish
TextOut LDRB    r0, [r14], #1  ; get next character
          CMP     r0, #0         ; test for end mark
          SWINE   SWI_WriteC     ; if not end, print..
          BNE     TextOut        ; .. and loop
          ADD     r14, r14, #3   ; pass next word boundary
          BIC     r14, r14, #3   ; round back to boundary
          MOV     pc, r14        ; return
          END
```

This example shows r14 incrementing along the text string and then being adjusted to the next word boundary prior to the return. If the adjustment (add 3, then clear the bottom two bits) looks like slight of hand, check it; there are only four cases.

**Exercise 3.2.1**   Using code from this and the previous examples, write a program to dump the ARM registers in hexadecimal with formatting such as:

```
r0 = 12345678
r1 = 9ABCDEF0
```

**Exercise 3.2.2**   Now try to save the registers you need to work with before they are changed, for instance by saving them near the code using PC-relative addressing.

# 4 ARM Organization and Implementation

**Summary of chapter contents**

The organization of the ARM integer processor core has changed very little from the first three micron devices developed at Acorn Computers between 1983 and 1985 to the ARM6 and ARM7 developed by ARM Limited between 1990 and 1995. The 3-stage pipeline has been steadily tightened up and CMOS process technology has reduced in feature size by almost an order of magnitude over this period, so the performance of the cores has improved dramatically, but the basic principles of operation have remained largely the same.

This chapter includes descriptions of the internal structure of these processor cores and covers the operation of the pipeline and a number of implementation details.

The development of any microprocessor is dependent on the availability of suitable computer-based tools to support physical design, simulation and verification. The tools used in the development of the ARM cores are described at the end of the chapter.

Recently a number of ARM cores have been announced which deviate from the 3-stage pipeline organization. The ARM8 and StrongARM use different pipeline structures and the asynchronous AMULET cores employ a radically different design style. The organizations of these cores are not discussed in this chapter; they are deferred to Chapter 9.

## 4.1   ARM organization

The organization of the ARM is illustrated in Figure 4.1 on page 79. The principal components are:

- The register bank, which stores the processor state. It has two read ports and one write port which can each be used to access any register, plus an additional read port and an additional write port that give special access to r15, the program counter. (The additional write port on r15 allows it to be updated as the instruction fetch address is incremented and the read port allows instruction fetch to resume after a data address has been issued.)

- The barrel shifter, which can shift or rotate one operand by any number of bits.

- The ALU, which performs the arithmetic and logic functions required by the instruction set.

- The address register and incrementer, which select and hold all memory addresses and generate sequential addresses when required.

- The data registers which hold data passing to and from memory.

- The instruction decoder and associated control logic.

In a single-cycle data processing instruction, two register operands are accessed, the value on the B bus is shifted and combined with the value on the A bus in the ALU, then the result is written back into the register bank. The program counter value is in the address register, from where it is fed into the incrementer, then the incremented value is copied back into r15 in the register bank and also into the address register to be used as the address for the next instruction fetch.

**The ARM pipeline**

ARM processors up to the ARM7 employ a simple 3-stage pipeline with the following pipeline stages:

- Fetch;

  the instruction is fetched from memory and placed in the instruction pipeline.

- Decode;

  the instruction is decoded and the datapath control signals prepared for the next cycle. In this stage the instruction 'owns' the decode logic but not the datapath.

- Execute;

  the instruction 'owns' the datapath; the register bank is read, an operand shifted, the ALU result generated and written back into a destination register.

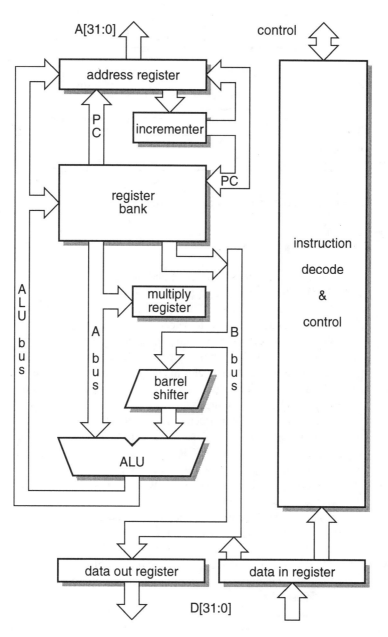

**Figure 4.1** ARM organization.

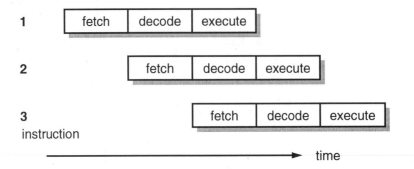

**Figure 4.2**    ARM single-cycle instruction pipeline operation.

(Note that ARM8, StrongARM and the AMULET asynchronous ARM processors all use different pipeline organizations.)

At any one time, three different instructions may occupy each of these stages, so the hardware in each stage has to be capable of independent operation.

When the processor is executing instructions that complete in a single cycle, the pipeline enables one instruction to be completed every clock cycle. An individual instruction takes three clock cycles to complete, so it has a three cycle **latency**, but the **throughput** is one instruction per cycle. The pipeline operation for single-cycle instructions is shown in Figure 4.2.

When a multi-cycle instruction is executed the flow is less regular, as illustrated in Figure 4.3 on page 81. This shows a sequence of single-cycle ADD instructions with a data store instruction, STR, occurring after the first ADD. The cycles that access main memory are shown with light shading so it can be seen that memory is used in every cycle. The datapath is likewise used in every cycle, being involved in all the execute cycles, the address calculation  and the data transfer. The decode logic is always generating the control signals for the datapath to use in the next cycle, so in addition to the explicit decode cycles it is also generating the control for the data transfer during the address calculation cycle of the STR.

Thus, in this instruction sequence, all parts of the processor are active in every cycle and the memory is the limiting factor, defining the number of cycles the sequence must take.

The simplest way to view breaks in the ARM pipeline is to observe that:

- All instructions occupy the datapath for one or more adjacent cycles.

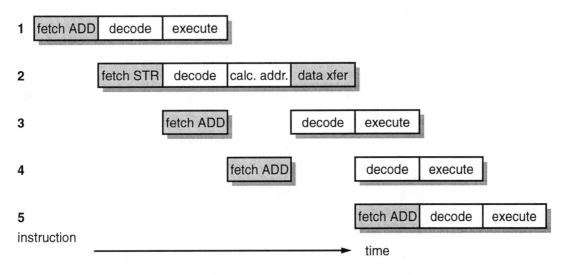

**Figure 4.3**   ARM multi-cycle instruction pipeline operation.

- For each cycle that an instruction occupies the datapath, it occupies the decode logic in the immediately preceding cycle.
- During the first datapath cycle each instruction issues a fetch for the next instruction but one.
- Branch instructions flush and refill the instruction pipeline.

**PC behaviour**

One consequence of the pipelined execution model used on the ARM is that the program counter, which is visible to the user as r15, must run ahead of the current instruction. If, as noted above, instructions fetch the next instruction but one during their first cycle, this suggests that the PC must point eight bytes (two instructions) ahead of the current instruction.

This is, indeed, what happens, and the programmer who attempts to access the PC directly through r15 must take account of the exposure of the pipeline here. However, for most normal purposes the assembler or compiler handles all the details.

Even more complex behaviour is exposed if r15 is used later than the first cycle of a instruction, since the instruction will itself have incremented the PC during its first cycle. Such use of the PC is not often beneficial so the ARM architecture definition specifies the result as 'unpredictable' and it should be avoided, especially since later ARMs do not have the same behaviour in these cases.

## 4.2  ARM instruction execution

The execution of an ARM instruction can best be understood by reference to the data-path organization as presented in Figure 4.1 on page 79. We will use an annotated version of this diagram, omitting the control logic section, and highlighting the active buses to show the movement of operands around the various units in the processor. We start with a simple data processing instruction.

**Data processing instructions**

A data processing instruction requires two operands, one of which is always a register and the other is either a second register or an immediate value. The second operand is passed through the barrel shifter where it is subject to a general shift operation, then it is combined with the first operand in the ALU using a general ALU operation. Finally, the result from the ALU is written back into the destination register (and the condition code register may be updated).

All these operations take place in a single clock cycle as shown in Figure 4.4 on page 83. Note also how the PC value in the address register is incremented and copied back into both the address register and r15 in the register bank, and the next instruction but one is loaded into the bottom of the instruction pipeline (*i. pipe*). The immediate value, when required, is extracted from the current instruction at the top of the instruction pipeline. For data processing instructions only the bottom eight bits (bits [7:0]) of the instruction are used in the immediate value.

**Data transfer instructions**

A data transfer (load or store) instruction computes a memory address in a manner very similar to the way a data processing instruction computes its result. A register is used as the base address, to which is added (or from which is subtracted) an offset which again may be another register or an immediate value. This time, however, a 12-bit immediate value is used without a shift operation rather than a shifted 8-bit value. The address is sent to the address register, and in a second cycle the data transfer takes place. Rather than leave the datapath largely idle during the data transfer cycle, the ALU holds the address components from the first cycle and is available to compute an auto-indexing modification to the base register if this is required. (If auto-indexing is not required the computed value is not written back to the base register in the second cycle.)

The datapath operation for the two cycles of a data store instruction (STR) with an immediate offset are shown in Figure 4.5 on page 84. Note how the incremented PC value is stored in the register bank at the end of the first cycle so that the address register is free to accept the data transfer address for the second cycle, then at the end of the second cycle the PC is fed back to the address register to allow instruction prefetching to continue.

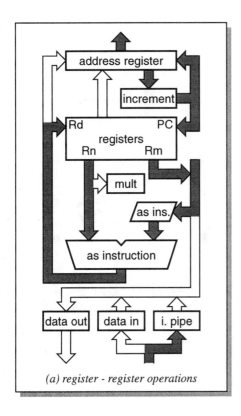

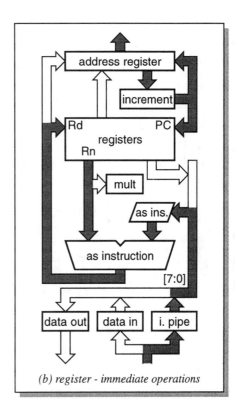

**Figure 4.4** Data processing instruction datapath activity.

It should, perhaps, be noted at this stage that the value sent to the address register in a cycle is the value used for the memory access in the *following* cycle. The address register is, in effect, a pipeline register between the processor datapath and the external memory.

(The address register can produce the memory address for the next cycle a little before the end of the current cycle, moving responsibility for the pipeline delay out into the memory when this is desired. This can enable some memory devices to operate at higher performance, but this detail can be postponed for the time being. For now we will view the address register as a pipeline register to memory.)

When the instruction specifies the store of a byte data type, the 'data out' block extracts the bottom byte from the register and replicates it four times across the 32-bit

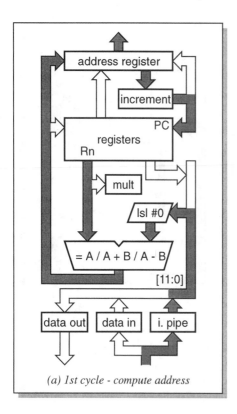
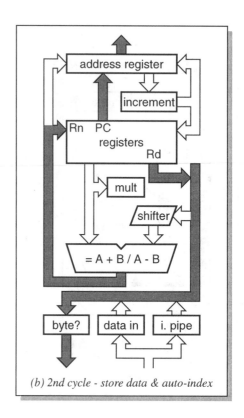

*(a) 1st cycle - compute address*          *(b) 2nd cycle - store data & auto-index*

**Figure 4.5**   STR (store register) datapath activity.

data bus. External memory control logic can then use the bottom two bits of the address bus to activate the appropriate byte within the memory system.

Load instructions follow a similar pattern except that the data from memory only gets as far as the 'data in' register on the second cycle and a third cycle is needed to transfer the data from there to the destination register.

**Branch instructions**

Branch instructions compute the target address in the first cycle as shown in Figure 4.6 on page 85. A 24-bit immediate field is extracted from the instruction and then shifted left two bit positions to give a word-aligned offset which is added to the PC. The result is issued as an instruction fetch address, and while the instruction pipeline refills the

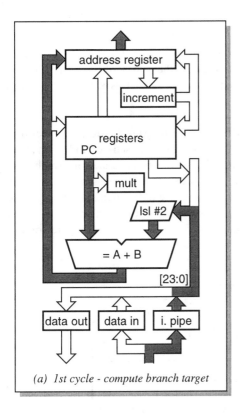
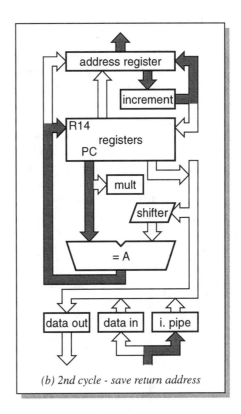

*(a) 1st cycle - compute branch target*   *(b) 2nd cycle - save return address*

**Figure 4.6**   The first two (of three) cycles of a branch instruction.

return address is copied into the link register (r14) if this is required (that is, if the instruction is a 'branch with link').

The third cycle, which is required to complete the pipeline refilling, is also used to make a small correction to the value stored in the link register in order that it points directly at the instruction which follows the branch. This is necessary because r15 contains pc + 8 whereas the address of the next instruction is pc + 4 (see 'PC behaviour' on page 81).

Other ARM instructions operate in a similar manner to those described above. We will now move on to look in more detail at how the datapath carries out these operations.

## 4.3  ARM implementation

The ARM implementation follows a similar approach to that outlined in Chapter 1 for MU0; the design is divided into a datapath section that is described in *register transfer level* (RTL) notation and a control section that is viewed as a *finite state machine* (FSM).

**Clocking scheme**

Unlike the MU0 example presented in Section 1.3 on page 8, ARM does not operate with edge-sensitive registers; instead the design is based around 2-phase non-overlapping clocks, as shown in Figure 4.7, which are generated internally from a single input clock signal. This scheme allows the use of level-sensitive transparent latches. Data movement is controlled by passing the data alternately through latches which are open during phase 1 and latches which are open during phase 2. The non-overlapping property of the phase 1 and phase 2 clocks ensures that there are no race conditions in the circuit.

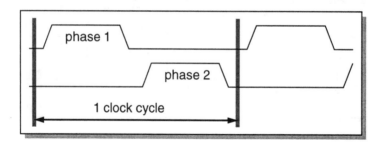

**Figure 4.7**   2-phase non-overlapping clock scheme.

**Datapath timing**

The normal timing of the datapath components is illustrated in Figure 4.8 on page 87. The register read buses are dynamic and are precharged during phase 2 (here 'dynamic' means that they are sometimes undriven and retain their logic values as electrical charge; charge-retention circuits are used to give pseudo-static behaviour so that data is not lost if the clock is stopped at any point in its cycle). When phase 1 goes high, the selected registers discharge the read buses which become valid early in phase 1. One operand is passed through the barrel shifter, which also uses dynamic techniques, and the shifter output becomes valid a little later in phase 1.

The ALU has input latches which are open during phase 1, allowing the operands to begin combining in the ALU as soon as they are valid, but they close at the end of phase 1 so that the phase 2 precharge does not get through to the ALU. The ALU

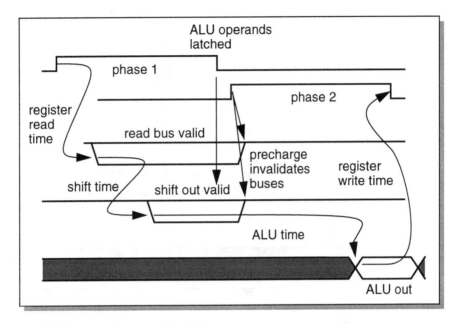

**Figure 4.8** ARM datapath timing.

then continues to process the operands through phase 2, producing a valid output towards the end of the phase which is latched in the destination register at the end of phase 2.

Note how, though the data passes through the ALU input latches, these do not affect the datapath timing since they are open when valid data arrives. This property of transparent latches is exploited in many places in the design of the ARM to ensure that clocks do not slow critical signals.

The minimum datapath cycle time is therefore the sum of:

- The register read time.
- The shifter delay.
- The ALU delay.
- The register write set-up time.
- The phase 2 to phase 1 non-overlap time.

Of these, the ALU delay dominates. The ALU delay is highly variable, depending on the operation it is performing. Logical operations are relatively fast, since they

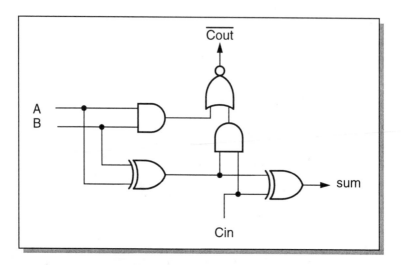

**Figure 4.9**    The original ARM1 ripple-carry adder circuit.

involve no carry propagation. Arithmetic operations (addition, subtraction and comparisons) involve longer logic paths as the carry can propagate across the word width.

**Adder design**

Since the 32-bit addition time has a significant effect on the datapath cycle time, and hence the maximum clock rate and the processor's performance, it has been the focus of considerable attention during the development of successive versions of the ARM processor.

The first ARM processor prototype used a simple ripple-carry adder as shown in Figure 4.9. Using a CMOS AND-OR-INVERT gate for the carry logic and alternating AND/OR logic so that even bits use the circuit shown and odd bits use the dual circuit with inverted inputs and outputs and AND and OR gates swapped around, the worst-case carry path is 32 gates long.

In order to allow a higher clock rate, ARM2 used a 4-bit carry look-ahead scheme to reduce the worst-case carry path length. The circuit is shown in Figure 4.10 on page 89. The logic produces carry generate (G) and propagate (P) signals which control the 4-bit carry-out. The carry propagate path length is reduced to eight gate delays, again using merged AND-OR-INVERT gates and alternating AND/OR logic.

**ALU functions**

The ALU does not only add its two inputs. It must perform the full set of data operations defined by the instruction set, including address computations for memory transfers, branch calculations, bit-wise logical functions, and so on.

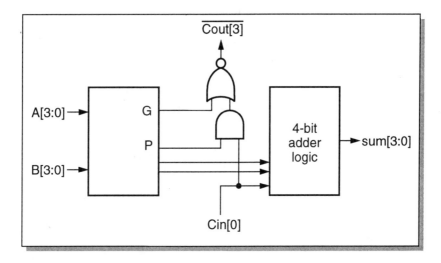

**Figure 4.10** The ARM2 4-bit carry look-ahead scheme.

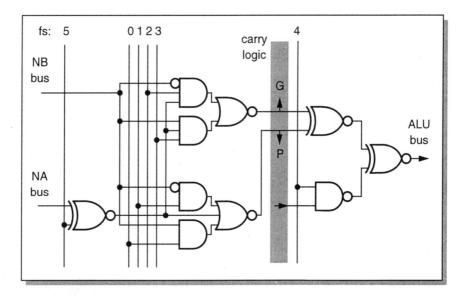

**Figure 4.11** The ARM2 ALU logic for one result bit.

**Table 4.1**   ARM2 ALU function codes.

| fs5 | fs4 | fs3 | fs2 | fs1 | fs0 | ALU output |
|-----|-----|-----|-----|-----|-----|------------|
| 0 | 0 | 0 | 1 | 0 | 0 | A and B |
| 0 | 0 | 1 | 0 | 0 | 0 | A and not B |
| 0 | 0 | 1 | 0 | 0 | 1 | A xor B |
| 0 | 1 | 1 | 0 | 0 | 1 | A plus not B plus carry |
| 0 | 1 | 0 | 1 | 1 | 0 | A plus B plus carry |
| 1 | 1 | 0 | 1 | 1 | 0 | not A plus B plus carry |
| 0 | 0 | 0 | 0 | 0 | 0 | A |
| 0 | 0 | 0 | 0 | 0 | 1 | A or B |
| 0 | 0 | 0 | 1 | 0 | 1 | B |
| 0 | 0 | 1 | 0 | 1 | 0 | not B |
| 0 | 0 | 1 | 1 | 0 | 0 | zero |

The full ARM2 ALU logic is illustrated in Figure 4.11 on page 89. The set of functions generated by this ALU and the associated values of the ALU function selects are listed in Table 4.1.

**The ARM6 carry-select adder**

A further improvement in the worst-case add time was introduced on the ARM6 by using a carry-select adder. This form of adder computes the sums of various fields of the word for a carry-in of both zero and one, and then the final result is selected by using the correct carry-in value to control a multiplexer. The overall scheme is illustrated in Figure 4.12 on page 91.

The critical path is now $O(\log_2[\text{word width}])$ gates long, though direct comparison with previous schemes is difficult since the fan-out on some of these gates is high. However, the worst-case addition time is significantly faster than the 4-bit carry look-ahead adder at the cost of significantly increased silicon area.

**ARM6 ALU structure**

The ARM6 carry-select adder does not easily lead to a merging of the arithmetic and logic functions into a single structure as was used on ARM2. Instead, a separate logic unit runs in parallel with the adder, and a multiplexer selects the output from the adder or from the logic unit as required.

The overall ALU structure is shown in Figure 4.13 on page 92. The input operands are each selectively inverted, then added and combined in the logic unit, and finally the required result is selected and issued on the ALU result bus.

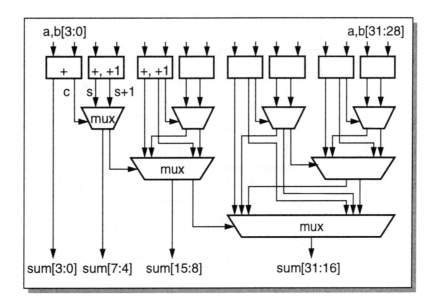

**Figure 4.12** The ARM6 carry-select adder scheme.

The $C$ and $V$ flags are generated in the adder (they have no meaning for logical operations), the $N$ flag is copied from bit 31 of the result and the $Z$ flag is evaluated from the whole result bus. Note that producing the $Z$ flag requires a 32-input NOR gate and this can easily become a critical path signal.

**The barrel shifter**

The ARM architecture supports instructions which perform a shift operation in series with an ALU operation, leading to the organization shown in Figure 4.1 on page 79. The shifter performance is therefore critical since the shift time contributes directly to the datapath cycle time as shown in in the datapath timing diagram in Figure 4.8 on page 87.

(Other processor architectures tend to have the shifter in parallel with the ALU, so as long as the shifter is no slower than the ALU it does not affect the datapath cycle time.)

In order to minimize the delay through the shifter, a cross-bar switch matrix is used to steer each input to the appropriate output. The principle of the cross-bar switch is illustrated in Figure 4.14 on page 93, where a $4 \times 4$ matrix is shown. (The ARM processors use a $32 \times 32$ matrix.) Each input is connected to each output through a

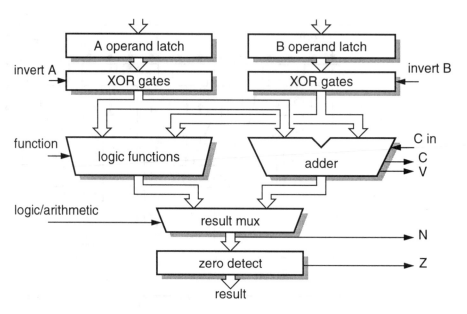

**Figure 4.13**   The ARM6 ALU organization.

switch. If precharged dynamic logic is used, as it is on the ARM datapaths, each switch can be implemented as a single NMOS transistor.

   The shifting functions are implemented by wiring switches along diagonals to a common control input:

- For a left or right shift function, one diagonal is turned on. This connects all the input bits to their respective outputs where they are used. (Not all are used, since some bits 'fall off the end'.) In the ARM the barrel shifter operates in negative logic where a '1' is represented as a potential near ground and a '0' by a potential near the supply. Precharging sets all the outputs to a logic '0', so those outputs that are not connected to any input during a particular switching operation remain at '0' giving the zero filling required by the shift semantics.

- For a rotate right function, the right shift diagonal is enabled together with the complementary left shift diagonal. For example, on the 4-bit matrix rotate right one bit is implemented using the 'right 1' and the 'left 3' (3 = 4 - 1) diagonals.

- Arithmetic shift right uses sign-extension rather than zero-fill for the unconnected output bits. Separate logic is used to decode the shift amount and discharge those outputs appropriately.

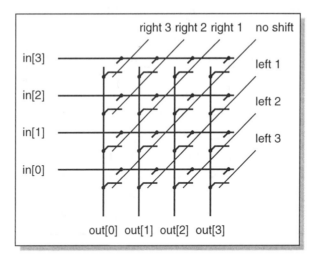

**Figure 4.14**   The cross-bar switch barrel shifter principle.

**Multiplier design**

All ARM processors apart from the first prototype have included hardware support for integer multiplication. Two styles of multiplier have been used:

- Most ARM cores include low-cost multiplication hardware that supports only the 32-bit result multiply and multiply-accumulate instructions.
- ARM cores with an 'M' in their name (for example the ARM7DM) and recent higher performance ARMs (the ARM8 and StrongARM) have high-performance multiplication hardware and support the 64-bit result multiply and multiply-accumulate instructions.

The low-cost support uses the main datapath iteratively, employing the barrel shifter and ALU to generate a 2-bit product in each clock cycle. Early-termination logic stops the iterations when there are no more ones in the multiply register.

The multiplier employs a modified Booth's algorithm to produce the 2-bit product, exploiting the fact that $\times 3$ can be implemented as $\times (-1) + \times 4$. This allows all four values of the 2-bit multiplier to be implemented by a simple shift and add or subtract, possibly carrying the $\times 4$ over to the next cycle.

The control settings for the Nth cycle of the multiplication are shown in Table 4.2 on page 94. (Note that the $\times 2$ case is also implemented with a subtract and carry; it could equally well use an add with no carry, but the control logic is slightly simplified with this choice.)

**Table 4.2**  The 2-bit multiplication algorithm, Nth cycle.

| Carry-in | Multiplier | Shift | ALU | Carry-out |
|----------|-----------|-------|-----|-----------|
| 0 | × 0 | LSL #2N | A + 0 | 0 |
|   | × 1 | LSL #2N | A + B | 0 |
|   | × 2 | LSL #(2N + 1) | A − B | 1 |
|   | × 3 | LSL #2N | A − B | 1 |
| 1 | × 0 | LSL #2N | A + B | 0 |
|   | × 1 | LSL #(2N + 1) | A + B | 0 |
|   | × 2 | LSL #2N | A − B | 1 |
|   | × 3 | LSL #2N | A + 0 | 1 |

Since this multiplication uses the existing shifter and ALU, the additional hardware it requires is limited to a dedicated two-bits-per-cycle shift register for the multiplier and a few gates for the Booth's algorithm control logic. In total this amounts to an overhead of a few per cent on the area of the ARM core.

**High-speed multiplier**

Where multiplication performance is very important, more hardware resource must be dedicated to it. In some embedded systems the ARM core is used to perform real-time digital signal processing (DSP) in addition to general control functions. DSP programs are typically multiplication intensive and the performance of the multiplication hardware can be critical to meeting the real-time constraints.

The high-performance multiplication used in some ARM cores employs a widely-used redundant binary representation to avoid the carry-propagate delays associated with adding partial products together. Intermediate results are held as partial sums and partial carries where the true binary result is obtained by adding these two together in a carry-propagate adder such as the adder in the main ALU, but this is only done once at the end of the multiplication. During the multiplication the partial sums and carries are combined in **carry-save** adders where the carries only propagate across one bit per addition stage. This gives the carry-save adder a much shorter logic path than the carry-propagate adder, which may have to propagate a carry across all 32 bits. Therefore several carry-save operations may be performed in a single clock cycle which can only accommodate one carry-propagate operation.

There are many ways to construct carry-save adders, but the simplest is the 3-input 2-output form. This accepts as inputs a partial sum, a partial carry and a partial product, all of the same binary weight, and produces as outputs a new partial sum and a new partial carry where the carry has twice the weight of the sum. The logic function for each bit is identical to a conventional full adder as used in a ripple-carry carry-propagate adder (see Figure 4.9 on page 88), but the structure is different. Figure 4.15 on page 96 illustrates the two structures. The carry-propagate adder takes two conventional (irredundant) binary numbers as inputs and produces a binary sum; the carry-save adder takes one binary and one redundant (partial sum and partial carry) input and produces a sum in redundant binary representation.

During the iterative multiplication stages, the sum is fed back and combined with one new partial product in each iteration. When all the partial products have been added, the redundant representation is converted into a conventional binary number by adding the partial sum and partial carry in the carry-propagate adder in the ALU.

High-speed multipliers have several layers of carry-save adder in series, each handling one partial product. If the partial product is produced following a modified Booth's algorithm similar to the one described in Table 4.2 on page 94, each stage of carry-save adder handles two bits of the multiplier in each cycle.

The overall structure of the high-performance multiplier used on some ARM cores is shown in Figure 4.16 on page 96. The register names refer to the instruction fields described in Section 5.8 on page 128. The carry-save array has four layers of adders, each handling two multiplier bits, so the array can multiply eight bits per clock cycle. The partial sum and carry registers are cleared at the start of the instruction, or the partial sum register may be initialized to the accumulate value. As the multiplier is shifted right eight bits per cycle in the 'Rs' register, the partial sum and carry are rotated right eight bits per cycle. The array is cycled up to four times, using early termination to complete the instruction in fewer cycles where the multiplier has sufficient zeros in the top bits, and the partial sum and carry are combined 32 bits at a time and written back into the register bank. (When the multiply terminates early some realignment of the partial sum and carry is required; this is not shown in Figure 4.16.)

The high-speed multiplier requires considerably more dedicated hardware than the low-cost solution employed on other ARM cores. There are 160 bits of shift register and 128 bits of carry-save adder logic. The incremental area cost is around 10% of the simpler processor cores, though a rather smaller proportion of the higher-performance cores such as ARM8 and StrongARM. Its benefits are that it speeds up multiplication by a factor of around 3 and it supports the added functionality of the 64-bit result forms of the multiply instruction.

**The register bank**

The last major block on the ARM datapath is the register bank. This is where all the user-visible state is stored in 31 general-purpose 32-bit registers, amounting to around 1 Kbits of data altogether. Since the basic 1-bit register cell is repeated so many times in the design, it is worth putting considerable effort into minimizing its size.

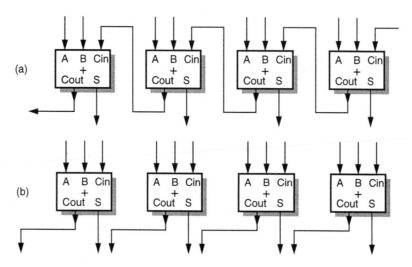

**Figure 4.15**   Carry-propagate (a) and carry-save (b) adder structures.

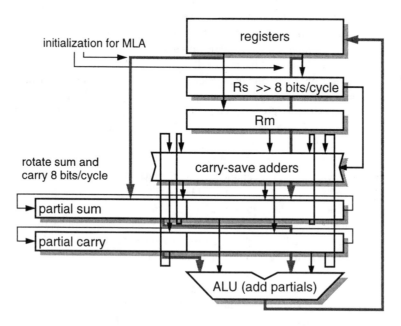

**Figure 4.16**   ARM high-speed multiplier organization.

The transistor circuit of the register cell used in ARM cores up to the ARM6 is shown in Figure 4.17. The storage cell is an asymmetric cross-coupled pair of CMOS inverters which is overdriven by a strong signal from the ALU bus when the register contents are changed. The feedback inverter is made weak in order to minimize the cell's resistance to the new value. The *A* and *B* read buses are precharged to *Vdd* during phase 2 of the clock cycle, so the register cell need only discharge the read buses, which it does through n-type pass transistors when the read-lines are enabled.

This register cell design works well with a 5 volt supply, but writing a '1' through the n-type pass transistor becomes difficult at lower supply voltages. Since a low supply voltage gives good power-efficiency, ARM cores since the ARM6 have either used a full CMOS transmission gate (with a p-type transistor in parallel with the n-type pass transistor in the write circuit, requiring complementary write enable control lines) or a more sophisticated register circuit.

These register cells are arranged in columns to form a 32-bit register, and the columns are packed together to form the complete register bank. The decoders for the read and write enable lines are then packed above the columns as shown in Figure 4.18 on page 98, so the enables run vertically and the data buses horizontally across the array of register cells. Since a decoder is logically more complex than the register cell itself, but the horizontal pitch is chosen to suit the cell, the decoder layout can become very tight and the decoders themselves have to be tall and thin.

The ARM program counter register is physically part of the register bank in the simpler cores, but it has two write and three read ports whereas the other registers have one write and two read ports. The symmetry of the register array is preserved by putting the PC at one end where it is accessible to the additional ports and it can be allowed to have a 'fatter' profile.

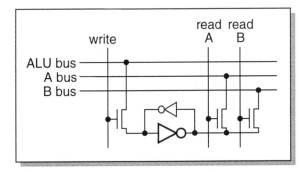

**Figure 4.17**   ARM2 register cell circuit.

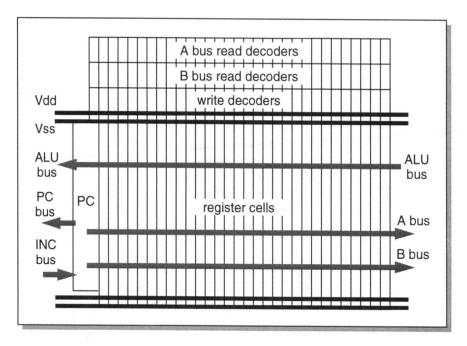

**Figure 4.18**   ARM register bank floorplan.

The register bank accounts for around one-third of the total transistor count of the simpler ARM cores, but takes a proportionately much smaller share of the silicon area by virtue of its very dense, memory-like structure. It does not match the transistor density of a block of SRAM since it has two read ports and fits on a datapath pitch that is optimized for more complex logic functions such as the ALU. However, it is much denser than those logic functions due to its higher regularity.

**Datapath layout**

The ARM datapath is laid out to a constant pitch per bit. The pitch will be a compromise between the optimum for the complex functions (such as the ALU) which are best suited to a wide pitch and the simple functions (such as the barrel shifter) which are most efficient when laid out on a narrow pitch.

Each function is then laid out to this pitch, remembering that there may also be buses passing over a function (for example the B bus passes through the ALU but is not used by it); space must be allowed for these. It is a good idea to produce a floorplan for the datapath noting the 'passenger' buses through each block, as illustrated in

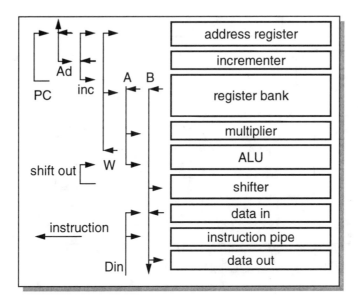

**Figure 4.19**   ARM core datapath buses.

Figure 4.19. The order of the function blocks is chosen to minimize the number of additional buses passing over the more complex functions.

Modern CMOS processes allow wiring in several metal layers (the early ARM cores used two metal layers.) The wiring layers used for power and ground, bus signals along the datapath and control signals across the datapath must be chosen carefully (for example on ARM2 *Vdd* and *Vss* run along both sides of the datapath in metal 2, control wires pass across the datapath in metal 1 and buses run along it in metal 2.)

**Control structures**

The control logic on the simpler ARM cores has three structural components which relate to each other as shown in Figure 4.20 on page 100.

1. An instruction decoder **PLA** (programmable logic array). This unit uses some of the instruction bits and an internal cycle counter to define the class of operation to be performed on the datapath in the next cycle.

2. Distributed secondary control associated with each of the major datapath function blocks. This logic uses the class information from the main decoder PLA to select other instruction bits and/or processor state information to control the datapath.

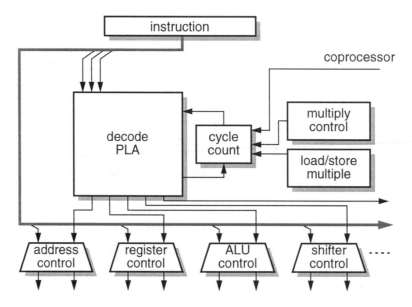

**Figure 4.20**    ARM control logic structure.

3. Decentralized control units for specific instructions that take a variable number of cycles to complete (load and store multiple, multiply and coprocessor operations). Here the main decoder PLA locks into a fixed state until the remote control unit indicates completion.

The main decoder PLA has around 14 inputs, 40 product terms and 40 outputs, the precise number varying slightly between the different cores. On recent ARM cores it is implemented as two PLAs: a small, fast PLA which generates the time critical outputs and a larger, slower PLA which generates all the other outputs. Functionally, however, it can be viewed as a single PLA unit.

The 'cycle count' block distinguishes the different cycles of multi-cycle instructions so that the decode PLA can generate different control outputs for each cycle. It is, in fact, not simply a counter but a more general finite state machine capable of skipping unneeded cycles and of locking into a fixed state. It determines when the current instruction is about to complete and initiates the transfer of the next instruction from the instruction pipeline, including aborting instructions at the end of their first cycle if they fail their condition test. However, much of the time its behaviour is like that of a simple counter so it is not *too* misleading to think of it as an instruction cycle counter.

## 4.4   The ARM coprocessor interface

The ARM supports a general-purpose extension of its instruction set through the addition of hardware coprocessors, and it also supports the software emulation of these coprocessors through the undefined instruction trap.

**Coprocessor architecture**

The coprocessor architecture is described in Section 5.15 on page 141. Its most important features are:

- Support for up to 16 logical coprocessors.
- Each coprocessor can have up to 16 private registers of any reasonable size; they are not limited to 32 bits.
- Coprocessors use a load-store architecture, with instructions to perform internal operations on registers, instructions to load and save registers from and to memory, and instructions to move data to or from an ARM register.

The simpler ARM cores offer the coprocessor interface at board level, so a coprocessor may be introduced as a separate component. High clock speeds make board-level interfacing very difficult, so the higher-performance ARMs restrict the coprocessor interface to on-chip use for cache and memory management control functions.

**Coprocessor interface**

The ARM coprocessor interface is based on 'bus watching'. The coprocessor is attached to a bus where the ARM instruction stream flows into the ARM, and the coprocessor copies the instructions into an internal pipeline that mimics the behaviour of the ARM instruction pipeline.

As each coprocessor instruction begins execution there is a 'hand-shake' between the ARM and the coprocessor to confirm that they are both ready to execute it. The hand-shake uses three signals:

1. $\overline{cpi}$ (from ARM to all coprocessors).

   This signal, which stands for 'CoProcessor Instruction', indicates that the ARM has identified a coprocessor instruction and wishes to execute it.

2. $cpa$ (from the coprocessors to ARM).

   This is the 'CoProcessor Absent' signal which tells the ARM that there is no coprocessor present that is able to execute the current instruction.

3. $cpb$ (from the coprocessors to ARM).

   This is the 'CoProcessor Busy' signal which tells the ARM that the coprocessor cannot begin executing the instruction yet.

The timing is such that both the ARM and the coprocessor must generate their respective signals autonomously. The coprocessor cannot wait until it sees $\overline{cpi}$ before generating *cpa* and *cpb*.

**Hand-shake outcomes**

Once a coprocessor instruction has entered the ARM and coprocessor pipelines, there are four possible ways it may be handled depending on the hand-shake signals:

1. The ARM may decide not to execute it, either because it falls in a branch shadow or because it fails its condition code test. (All ARM instructions are conditionally executed, including coprocessor instructions.) ARM will not assert $\overline{cpi}$, and the instruction will be discarded by all parties.

2. The ARM may decide to execute it (and signal this by asserting $\overline{cpi}$), but no present coprocessor can take it so *cpa* stays active. ARM will take the undefined instruction trap and use software to recover, possibly by emulating the trapped instruction.

3. ARM decides to execute the instruction and a coprocessor accepts it, but cannot execute it yet. The coprocessor takes *cpa* low but leaves *cpb* high. The ARM will 'busy-wait' until the coprocessor takes *cpb* low, stalling the instruction stream at this point. If an enabled interrupt request arrives while the coprocessor is busy, ARM will break off to handle the interrupt, probably returning to retry the coprocessor instruction later.

4. ARM decides to execute the instruction and a coprocessor accepts it for immediate execution. $\overline{cpi}$, *cpa* and *cpb* are all taken low and both sides commit to complete the instruction.

**Data transfers**

If the instruction is a coprocessor data transfer instruction the ARM is responsible for generating an initial memory address (the coprocessor does not require any connection to the address bus) but the coprocessor determines the length of the transfer; ARM will continue incrementing the address until the coprocessor signals completion. The *cpa* and *cpb* hand-shake signals are also used for this purpose.

Since the data transfer is not interruptible once it has started, coprocessors should limit the maximum transfer length to 16 words (the same as a maximum length load or store multiple instruction) so as not to compromise the ARM's interrupt response.

**Pre-emptive execution**

A coprocessor may begin executing an instruction as soon as it enters its pipeline so long as it can recover its state if the hand-shake does not ultimately complete. All activity must be **idempotent** (repeatable with identical results) up to the point of commitment.

## 4.5 Design tools

The design flow used to develop the early ARM processor cores (but not ARM8 or StrongARM) is a conventional VLSI design flow with a few specialist point tools. The specification is converted into a design which is modelled at the behavioural level using 'ASim', an ARM Limited proprietary simulator (originally developed at Acorn) which is broadly equivalent in its capabilities to commercially available simulators such as Verilog. Recently ARM has begun using VHDL-based tools in place of ASim.

Once the design is stable it is converted into schematics within a Compass Design Automation environment. The schematics can be checked against test vectors generated from the behavioural model and then converted into layout, either manually or automatically. The layout is *design rule checked* (**DRC**) and manual layout is *netlist*

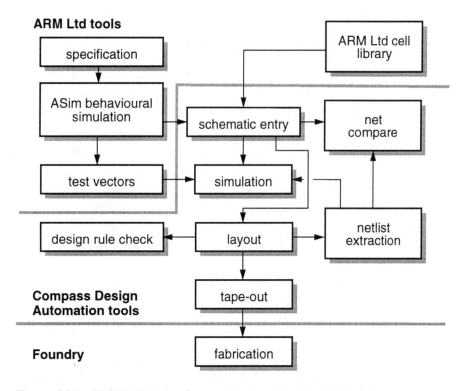

**Figure 4.21** The VLSI design flow used to develop early ARM chips.

*compared* against the schematic (this is called **LVS** – *layout versus schematic* – in some design systems). The netlist extracted from the layout contains all the layout capacitance values, so it is re-simulated to ensure that the test vectors still operate correctly.

Test vectors are generated for design blocks at the level of the ALU or the barrel shifter to ensure that these components are correct before they are assembled into the complete chip; smaller blocks are much easier to debug than complete chips. The fully assembled chip is also checked against test vectors, but here the expectation is that it will work first time.

Finally the design is 'taped-out' and shipped for prototype fabrication by one of ARM's semiconductor partners.

## Critical paths

A clocked chip will normally operate correctly over a range of clock frequencies. The lowest frequency is determined by the dynamic storage time of the circuits used in the design, and most low-power designs are constructed using static or pseudo-static circuit techniques that allow operation down to arbitrarily slow clock rates so that the clock can be stopped to save power without the circuit losing state. The highest clock frequency is determined, in principle, by increasing the clock rate until some circuit malfunctions. The **critical path** in a digital design is the path through the logic which stops working first as the clock speed is increased. The folklore in processor design suggests that the critical path is always where least expected, because that is where the designer focused least effort.

A lot of design work typically goes into making the datapath cycle very fast. The ALU carry path is optimized, the register read transistors are carefully sized for best performance, and so on, but all this effort is wasted if the clock rate is limited by the speed of some part of the control logic that only comes into play under an infrequent exception condition. Therefore a methodology is needed to analyse all of the design to identify the critical path.

In a design based on edge-triggered latches, such as MU0, critical path analysis is a simple matter of following all the logic paths from any register output to any register input and identifying the longest. On designs which use transparent latches, such as the ARM, the signals are not retimed at each register since they may pass through a latch which is already open, so the critical path may be several cycles long.

An approach used on the ARM6 core starts from a directed graph of timing dependencies similar to the simple example shown in Figure 4.22 on page 105. The graph comprises *nodes*, which represent the time in a clock cycle when a particular signal becomes valid, and *arcs*, which represent the causal links from one signal to another and are marked with the delay through the logic linking the signals.

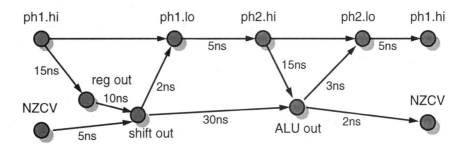

**Figure 4.22** Directed graph of timing dependencies.

Initially the delay numbers are guesses, but as the design develops they can be refined to use nominal gate path delays from schematics and then accurate timing figures based on extracted layout characteristics.

Note in Figure 4.22 that some nodes appear at both the left- and the right-hand ends of the graph; these are called the 'cyclic' nodes. The full graph is an infinite repetition of this subgraph, and the subgraph is selected by cutting a section one clock cycle long from the full graph. The cut is arbitrary, though the cut which results in the minimum number of cyclic nodes will be most efficient.

**Critical path algorithm**

The algorithm to identify the critical path begins by reducing the graph to one with just the cyclic nodes, removing all the inner detail by recursively searching the graph for the longest path from each input to each output. Then the reduced graph is repeated to form graphs of length 1 to $N$ clock cycles, where $N$ is the number of cyclic nodes. Finally each of these graphs is searched for the longest route from any input to its corresponding output, and the longest of these over all the repeated graphs, scaled by the number of clock cycles the graph represents, gives the minimum clock period for the design. Tracing this path back to the original graph yields the critical path.

(The reason why the search can be limited to at most $N$ cycles is that at the start of each cycle the path must pass through a cyclic node, so the maximum length before passing through the same node twice is $N$ cycles.)

This rather complex procedure has successfully identified critical paths on ARM cores which turned out to be three clock cycles long, starting from the register read, following the barrel shifter and ALU out to a condition code flag, then through the instruction decoder to affect the instruction pipeline behaviour in the following cycle. This knowledge can be used to identify and remove obscure critical paths which would otherwise have unnecessarily restricted the processor's performance.

**Validation**     A microprocessor is a complex piece of logic and there is plenty of scope for making design errors. Some of these may manifest themselves in obscure ways and be very hard to find with simple test programs running on the schematic. Extensive testing is required to generate an acceptable level of confidence that the design is correct before the tape is shipped for manufacture.

One approach to validation is to run large 'real' programs on the design to check it operates correctly. Another approach is to use random testing, where the response of the design is compared against a trusted reference design. A third approach is to use carefully designed test programs to carry out exhaustive self-testing of areas of the instruction set. The third approach is the one favoured by ARM designers, combined perhaps with some 'real' program testing.

In 1984 a validation suite was developed for the original ARM prototypes; this has been updated and augmented to keep track with subsequent architecture developments. Each validation program checks the operation of an area of the instruction set and prints a 'go/no-go' result. Some programs check interrupts and exceptions, so the ASim model must be built to produce these under program control. This is achieved using special coprocessor models that fire off interrupts at programmed times.

The ARM validation suite requires several million simulated processor cycles to execute. This is generally too many to run on a transistor-level simulator (although today it is possible, given enough time and enough machines, and was done as part of the final verification of the StrongARM); normally, therefore, the ASim reference model is checked using the validation suite and the VLSI design is checked at the block level using test patterns extracted automatically from the ASim model.

A benefit of having the validation suite written as several independent programs rather than one monolithic test is that the programs can be run concurrently on several machines. In the late stages of design it is common to want to run the entire suite several times after minor changes. Standard UNIX techniques allow the test programs to be scheduled overnight on otherwise idle workstations to give the full results, which together require many CPU-days of processing time, by the following morning.

As core designs get more sophisticated validation techniques must improve. New approaches, such as extended testing using random instruction sequences, play an increasing role in ensuring 'right first time' designs.

## 4.6 Examples and exercises

**Example 4.1** **Why does r15 give pc + 8 in the first cycle of an instruction and pc + 12 in subsequent cycles on an ARM6?**

This is the ARM pipeline being exposed to the programmer. Referring back to Figure 4.2 on page 80, we can see that the pc value was incremented once when the current instruction ('1' in the figure below) was fetched and once when its successor ('2') was fetched, giving pc + 8 at the start of the first execute cycle. During the first execute cycle a third instruction ('3') is fetched, giving pc + 12 in all subsequent execute cycles.

While multi-cycle instructions interrupt the pipeline flow they do not affect this aspect of the behaviour. An instruction always fetches the next-instruction-but-one during its first execute cycle, so r15 always progresses from pc + 8 at the start of the first execute cycle to pc + 12 at the start of the second (and subsequent) execute cycle(s).

(Note that other ARM processors do not share this behaviour, so it should never be relied upon when writing ARM programs.)

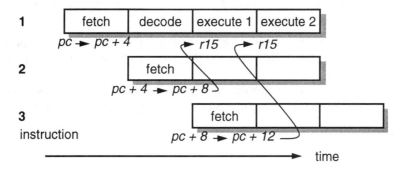

**Exercise 4.1.1** Draw a pipeline flow diagram along the lines of the one above to illustrate the timing of an ARM branch instruction. (The branch target is computed in the first execute cycle of the instruction and issued to memory in the following cycle.)

**Exercise 4.1.2** How many execute cycles are there after the branch target calculation and before the instruction at the branch target is ready to execute?

What does the processor use these execute cycles for?

**Example 4.2**     **Complete the ARM2 4-bit carry logic circuit outlined in Figures 4.10 and 4.11 on page 89.**

The 4-bit carry look-ahead scheme uses the individual bit carry generate and propagate signals produced by the logic shown in Figure 4.11. Denoting these by G[3:0] and P[3:0], the carry-out from the top bit of a 4-bit group is given by:

Cout = G[3] + P[3].(G[2] + P[2].(G[1] + P[1].(G[0] + P[0].Cin)))

Therefore the group generate and propagate signals, G4 and P4, as used in Figure 4.10 are given by:

G4    = G[3] + P[3].(G[2] + P[2].(G[1] + P[1].G[0]))

P4    = P[3].P[2].P[1].P[0]

These two signals are independent of the carry-in signal and therefore can be set up ready for its arrival, allowing the carry to propagate across the 4-bit group in just one AND-OR-INVERT gate delay.

**Exercise 4.2.1**     Write a logic expression for one bit of the ALU output generated by the circuit shown in Figure 4.11 in terms of the inputs and the function select lines, and hence show how all the ALU functions listed in Table 4.1 on page 90 are generated.

**Exercise 4.2.2**     Estimate the gate count for the ripple-carry adder and for the 4-bit carry look-ahead adder, basing both designs on the circuit in Figure 4.11 and varying only the carry scheme.
         How much does the extra speed of the carry look-ahead scheme cost in terms of gate count? How does it affect the regularity, and hence the design cost, of the adder?

# 5 The ARM Instruction Set

**Summary of chapter contents**

In Chapter 3 we looked at user-level ARM assembly language programming and got the general flavour of the ARM instruction set. In this chapter we will look in finer detail at the instruction set to see the full range of instructions that are available in the standard ARM instruction set.

Some ARM chips will also execute a compressed form of the instruction set where a subset of the full ARM instruction set is encoded into 16-bit instructions. These instructions are 'Thumb' instructions, and are discussed more fully in Chapter 7. The only aspects of the Thumb architecture we will see in this chapter are the instructions available in the ARM instruction set which cause the processor to switch to executing Thumb instructions.

As with any processor's full instruction set, the ARM instruction set has corners which conceal complex behaviour. Often these corners are not at all useful to programmers, in which case ARM Limited does not define the behaviour of the processor in the corner cases and the corresponding instructions should not be used. The fact that a particular implementation of the ARM behaves in a particular way in such a case should not be taken as meaning that future implementations will behave the same way. Programs should only use instructions with defined semantics!

Some ARM instructions are not available on all ARM chips; these will be highlighted as they arise.

## 5.1  Introduction

The ARM programmers' model was introduced in Figure 2.1 on page 41. In this chapter we will consider the supervisor and exception modes, so now the shaded registers will also come into play.

**Data types**      All ARM processors support two data types:

- 8-bit unsigned bytes;
- 32-bit words; these are aligned on 4-byte boundaries.

    Later ARM processors also support:

- 8-bit signed bytes;
- 16-bit signed and unsigned half-words; these are aligned on 2-byte boundaries.

    ARM instructions are all 32-bit words and must be word-aligned. Thumb instructions are half-words and must be aligned on 2-byte boundaries.

    Internally all ARM operations are on 32-bit operands; the shorter data types are only supported by data transfer instructions. When a byte is loaded from memory it is zero- or sign-extended to 32 bits and then treated as a 32-bit value for internal processing.

    ARM coprocessors may support other data types, and in particular there is a defined set of types to represent floating-point values. There is no explicit support for these types within the ARM core, however, and in the absence of a floating-point coprocessor these types are interpreted by software which uses the standard types listed above.

**Memory**          There are two ways to store words in a byte-addressed memory, depending on whether
**organization**    the least significant byte is stored at a lower or higher address than the next most significant byte. Since there is no good reason for choosing one approach over the other the argument as to which is better is more a matter of religion than reason. The two schemes are illustrated in Figure 5.1 on page 111, which shows how an assortment of data types would be stored under the two schemes. ('half-word12' is found at address 12, and so on.)

    The 'little-endian' and 'big-endian' terminology which is used to denote the two approaches is derived from Swift's *Gulliver's Travels*. The inhabitants of Lilliput, who are well known for being rather small are, in addition, constrained by law to break their eggs only at the little end. When this law is imposed, those of their fellow citizens who prefer to break their eggs at the big end take exception to the new rule and

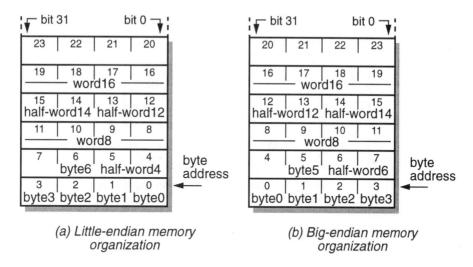

(a) Little-endian memory
organization

(b) Big-endian memory
organization

**Figure 5.1**   Little- and big-endian memory organizations.

civil war breaks out. The big-endians eventually take refuge on a nearby island, which is the kingdom of Blefuscu. The civil war results in many casualties.

The application of the 'big-endian' and 'little-endian' terms to the two ways to organize computer memory comes from 'On Holy Wars and a Plea for Peace' by Danny Cohen in the October 1981 issue of *Computer*.

To my knowledge, no one has yet been mortally wounded in an argument over byte ordering. However the issue causes significant practical difficulties when datasets are transferred between machines of opposite orderings.

Most ARM chips remain strictly neutral in the dispute and can be configured to work with either memory arrangement. Despite this, throughout this book we will assume a little-endian ordering where bytes of increasing significance are stored at increasing addresses in memory. ARM may be neutral, but I am not!

**Privileged modes**

Most programs operate in user mode as described in Chapter 3. However ARM has other **privileged** operating modes which are used to handle exceptions and supervisor calls (which are sometimes called **software interrupts**).

The current operating mode is defined by the bottom five bits of the CPSR (see Figure 2.2 on page 42). The interpretation of these bits is summarized in Table 5.1 on page 112. Where the register set is not the user registers, the relevant shaded registers

**Table 5.1**   ARM operating modes and register usage.

| CPSR[4:0] | Mode | Use | Registers |
|-----------|------|-----|-----------|
| 10000 | User | Normal user code | user |
| 10001 | FIQ | Processing fast interrupts | _fiq |
| 10010 | IRQ | Processing standard interrupts | _irq |
| 10011 | SVC | Processing software interrupts (SWIs) | _svc |
| 10111 | Abort | Processing memory faults | _abt |
| 11011 | Undef | Handling undefined instruction traps | _und |
| 11111 | System | Running privileged operating system tasks | user |

shown in Figure 2.1 on page 41 replace the corresponding user registers and the current SPSR (**Saved Program Status Register**; see below) also becomes accessible.

Some ARM processors do not support all of the above operating modes, and some also support '26-bit' modes for backwards compatibility with older ARMs; these will be discussed further in Section 5.21 on page 153.

The privileged modes can only be entered through controlled mechanisms; with suitable memory protection they allow a fully protected operating system to be built. This issue will be discussed further in Chapter 11.

Most ARMs are used in embedded systems where such protection is inappropriate, but the privileged modes can still be used to give a weaker level of protection that is useful for trapping errant software.

**The SPSRs**      Each privileged mode (except system mode) has associated with it a Saved Program Status Register, or SPSR. This register is used to save the state of the CPSR (Current Program Status Register) when the privileged mode is entered in order that the user state can be fully restored when the user process is resumed.

Often the SPSR may be untouched from the time the privileged mode is entered to the time it is used to restore the CPSR, but if the privileged software is to be re-entrant (for example, if supervisor code makes supervisor calls to itself) then the SPSR must be copied into a general register and saved.

## 5.2    Exceptions

Exceptions are usually used to handle unexpected events which arise during the execution of a program, such as interrupts or memory faults. In the ARM architecture the term is also used to cover software interrupts and undefined instruction traps (which do not really qualify as 'unexpected') and the system reset function which logically arises before rather than during the execution of a program (although the processor may be reset again while running). These events are all grouped under the 'exception' heading because they all use the same basic mechanism within the processor.

ARM exceptions may be considered in three groups:

1.  Exceptions generated as the direct effect of executing an instruction.

    Software interrupts, undefined instructions (including coprocessor instructions where the requested coprocessor is absent) and prefetch aborts (instructions that are invalid due to a memory fault occurring during fetch) come under this heading.

2.  Exceptions generated as a side-effect of an instruction.

    Data aborts (a memory fault during a load or store data access) are in this class.

3.  Exceptions generated externally, unrelated to the instruction flow.

    Reset, IRQ and FIQ fall into this category.

**Exception entry**

When an exception arises, ARM completes the current instruction as best it can (except that *reset* exceptions terminate the current instruction immediately) and then departs from the current instruction sequence to handle the exception. Exception entry caused by a side-effect or an external event usurps the next instruction in the current sequence; direct-effect exceptions are handled in sequence as they arise. The processor performs the following sequence of actions:

*   It changes to the operating mode corresponding to the particular exception.

*   It saves the address of the instruction following the exception entry instruction in r14 of the new mode.

*   It saves the old value of the CPSR in the SPSR of the new mode.

*   It disables IRQs by setting bit 7 of the CPSR and, if the exception is a fast interrupt, disables further fast interrupts by setting bit 6 of the CPSR.

*   It forces the PC to begin executing at the relevant vector address given in Table 5.2 on page 114.

    Normally the vector address will contain a branch to the relevant routine, though the FIQ code can start immediately since it occupies the highest vector address.

**Table 5.2**   Exception vector addresses.

| Exception | Mode | Vector address |
|---|---|---|
| Reset | SVC | 0x00000000 |
| Undefined instruction | UND | 0x00000004 |
| Software interrupt (SWI) | SVC | 0x00000008 |
| Prefetch abort (instruction fetch memory fault) | Abort | 0x0000000C |
| Data abort (data access memory fault) | Abort | 0x00000010 |
| IRQ (normal interrupt) | IRQ | 0x00000018 |
| FIQ (fast interrupt) | FIQ | 0x0000001C |

The two banked registers in each of the privileged modes are used to hold the return address and a stack pointer; the stack pointer may be used to save other user registers so that they can be used by the exception handler. FIQ mode has additional private registers to give better performance by avoiding the need to save user registers in most cases where it is used.

**Exception return**

Once the exception has been handled the user task is normally resumed. This requires the handler code to restore the user state exactly as it was when the exception first arose:

- Any modified user registers must be restored from the handler's stack.
- The CPSR must be restored from the appropriate SPSR.
- The PC must be changed back to the relevant instruction address in the user instruction stream.

Note that the last two of these steps cannot be carried out independently. If the CPSR is restored first, the banked r14 holding the return address is no longer accessible; if the PC is restored first, the exception handler loses control of the instruction stream and cannot cause the restoration of the CPSR to take place. There are also more subtle difficulties to do with ensuring that instructions are always fetched in the correct operating mode to ensure that memory protection schemes are not bypassed. Therefore ARM provides two mechanisms which cause both steps to happen atomically as part of a single instruction. One of these is used when the return address has been kept in the banked r14 and the other when the return address has been saved onto a stack. First we look at the case where the return address is in r14.

- To return from a SWI or undefined instruction trap use:

```
MOVS    pc, r14
```

- To return from an IRQ, FIQ or prefetch abort use:

```
SUBS    pc, r14, #4
```

- To return from a data abort to retry the data access use:

```
SUBS    pc, r14, #8
```

The 's' modifier after the opcode signifies the special form of the instruction when the destination register is the PC. Note how the return instruction incorporates an adjustment to the return address where necessary:

- IRQ and FIQ must return one instruction early in order to execute the instruction that was 'usurped' for the exception entry.

- Prefetch abort must return one instruction early to execute the instruction that had caused a memory fault when first requested.

- Data abort must return two instructions early to retry the data transfer instruction, which was the instruction *before* the one usurped for exception entry.

If the handler has copied the return address out onto a stack (in order, for example, to allow re-entrant behaviour, though note that in this case the SPSR must be saved as well as the PC) the restoration of the user registers and the return may be implemented with a single multiple register transfer instruction such as:

```
LDMIA   r13!, {r0-r3,pc}^ ; restore and return
```

Here the '^' after the register list (which must include the PC) indicates that this is a special form of the instruction. The CPSR is restored at the same time that the PC is loaded from memory, which will always be the last item transferred from memory since the registers are loaded in increasing order.

The stack pointer (r13) used here is the banked register belonging to the privileged operating mode; each privileged mode can have its own stack pointer which must be initialized during system start-up.

Clearly the stack return mechanism can only be employed if the value in r14 was adjusted, where necessary, before being saved onto the stack.

**Exception priorities**

Since multiple exceptions can arise at the same time it is necessary to define a priority order to determine the order in which the exceptions are handled. On ARM this is:

1. Reset (highest priority).
2. Data abort.
3. FIQ.
4. IRQ.
5. Prefetch abort.
6. SWI, undefined instruction (including absent coprocessor). These are mutually exclusive instruction encodings and therefore cannot occur simultaneously.

Reset starts the processor from a known state and renders all other pending exceptions irrelevant.

The most complex exception scenario is where an FIQ, an IRQ and a third exception (which is not Reset) happen simultaneously. FIQ has higher priority than IRQ and also masks it out, so the IRQ will be ignored until the FIQ handler explicitly enables IRQ or returns to the user code.

If the third exception is a data abort, the processor will enter the data abort handler and then immediately enter the FIQ handler, since data abort entry does not mask FIQs out. The data abort is 'remembered' in the return path and will be processed when the FIQ handler returns.

If the third exception is not a data abort, the FIQ handler will be entered immediately. When FIQ and IRQ have both completed, the program returns to the instruction which generated the third exception, and in all the remaining cases the exception will recur and be handled accordingly.

**Address exceptions**

The observant reader will have noticed that Table 5.2 on page 114 shows the use of all of the first eight word locations in memory as exception vector addresses apart from address 0x00000014. This location *was* used on earlier ARM processors which operated within a 26-bit address space (see 'ARM 26-bit architecture' on page 154) to trap load or store addresses which fell outside the address space. These traps were referred to as 'address exceptions'.

Since 32-bit ARMs are unable to generate addresses which fall outside their 32-bit address space, address exceptions have no role in the current architecture and the vector address at 0x00000014 is unused.

## 5.3   Conditional execution

An unusual feature of the ARM instruction set is that every instruction is conditionally executed. Conditional branches are a standard feature of most instruction sets, but ARM extends the conditional execution to all of its instructions, including supervisor calls and coprocessor instructions. The condition field occupies the top four bits of the 32-bit instruction field:

31        28 27                                                                                         0

cond

**Figure 5.2**   The ARM condition code field.

Each of the 16 values of the condition field causes the instruction to be executed or skipped according to the values of the N, Z, C and V flags in the CPSR. The conditions are given in Table 5.3 on page 118. Every ARM instruction mnemonic may be extended by appending the two letters defined in this table, though the 'always' condition (AL) may be omitted since it is the default condition that is assumed if no other condition is specified.

**The 'never' condition**

The 'never' condition (NV) should not be used – there are plenty of other ways to write no-ops (instructions that have no effect on the processor state) in ARM code. The reason to avoid the 'never' condition is that ARM Limited have indicated that they may use this area of the instruction space for other purposes in the future, so although current ARMs may behave as expected, there is no guarantee that future variants will behave the same way.

**Alternative mnemonics**

Where alternative mnemonics are shown in the same row in the condition table this indicates that there is more than one way to interpret the condition field. For instance, in row 3 the same condition field value can be invoked by the mnemonic extension CS or HS. Both cause the instruction to be executed only if the C bit in the CPSR is set. The alternatives are available because the same test is used in different circumstances. If you have previously added two unsigned integers and want to test whether there was

**Table 5.3**   ARM condition codes.

| Opcode [31:28] | Mnemonic extension | Interpretation | Status flag state for execution |
|---|---|---|---|
| 0000 | EQ | Equal / equals zero | Z set |
| 0001 | NE | Not equal | Z clear |
| 0010 | CS/HS | Carry set / unsigned higher or same | C set |
| 0011 | CC/LO | Carry clear / unsigned lower | C clear |
| 0100 | MI | Minus / negative | N set |
| 0101 | PL | Plus / positive or zero | N clear |
| 0110 | VS | Overflow | V set |
| 0111 | VC | No overflow | V clear |
| 1000 | HI | Unsigned higher | C set and Z clear |
| 1001 | LS | Unsigned lower or same | C clear or Z set |
| 1010 | GE | Signed greater than or equal | N equals V |
| 1011 | LT | Signed less than | N is not equal to V |
| 1100 | GT | Signed greater than | Z clear and N equals V |
| 1101 | LE | Signed less than or equal | Z set or N is not equal to V |
| 1110 | AL | Always | any |
| 1111 | NV | Never (do not use!) | none |

a carry-out from the addition, you should use CS. If you have compared two unsigned integers and want to test whether the first was higher or the same as the second, use HS. The alternative mnemonic removes the need for the programmer to remember that an unsigned comparison sets the carry on higher or the same.

The observant reader will note that the conditions are in pairs where the second condition is the inverse of the first, so for any condition the opposite condition is also available (with the exception of 'always', since 'never' should not be used). Therefore whenever *if...then...* can be implemented with conditional instructions, *...else...* can be added using instructions with the opposite condition.

## 5.4   Branch and Branch with Link (B, BL)

Branch and Branch with Link instructions are the standard way to cause a switch in the sequence of instruction execution. The ARM normally executes instructions from sequential word addresses in memory, using conditional execution to skip over individual instructions where required. Whenever the program must deviate from sequential execution a control flow instruction is used to modify the program counter. Although there are several ways to achieve this in special circumstances, Branch and Branch with Link instructions are the standard way.

**Binary
encoding**

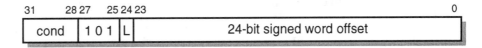

**Figure 5.3**   Branch and Branch with Link binary encoding.

**Description**
Branch and Branch with Link instructions cause the processor to begin executing instructions from an address computed by sign extending the 24-bit offset specified in the instruction, shifting it left two places to form a word offset, then adding it to the program counter which contains the address of the branch instruction plus eight bytes. (See 'PC behaviour' on page 81 for an explanation of the PC offset.) The assembler will compute the correct offset under normal circumstances.

The range of the branch instruction is +/- 32 Mbytes.

The Branch with Link variant, which has the L bit (bit 24) set, also moves the address of the instruction following the branch into the link register (r14) of the current processor mode. This is normally used to perform a subroutine call, with the return being caused by copying the link register back into the PC.

Both forms of the instruction may be executed conditionally or unconditionally.

**Assembler
format**

B{L}{<cond>}     <target address>

'L' specifies the branch and link variant; if 'L' is not included a branch without link is generated.'<cond>' should be one of the mnemonic extensions given in Table 5.3 on page 118 or, if omitted, 'AL' is assumed.'<target address>' is normally a label in the assembler code; the assembler will generate the offset (which will be the difference between the address of the target and the address of the branch instruction plus 8).

**Examples**          An unconditional jump:

```
            B         LABEL   ; unconditional jump ..
            ..
LABEL       ..                ; .. to here
```

To execute a loop ten times:

```
            MOV       r0, #10 ; initialize loop counter
LOOP        ..
            SUBS      r0, #1  ; decrement counter setting CCs
            BNE       LOOP    ; if counter <> 0 repeat loop ..
            ..                ; .. else drop through
```

To call a subroutine:

```
            ..
            BL        SUB     ; branch and link to subroutine SUB
            ..                ; return to here
            ..
SUB         ..                ; subroutine entry point
            MOV       PC, r14 ; return
```

Conditional subroutine call:

```
            ..
            CMP       r0, #5  ; if r0 < 5
            BLLT      SUB1    ; then call SUB1
            BLGE      SUB2    ; else call SUB2
            ..
```

(Note that this example will only work correctly if SUB1 does not change the condition codes, since if the BLLT is taken it will return to the BLGE. If the condition codes are changed by SUB1, SUB2 may be executed as well.)

**Notes**          1. If you are familiar with other RISC processors you might expect ARM to execute the instruction after the branch before moving to LABEL in the first example above, following the *delayed branch* model employed by many other RISCs. This expectation will not be fulfilled, however, since ARM does not employ a delayed branch mechanism.

2. Branches which attempt to go past the beginning or the end of the 32-bit address space should be avoided since they may have unpredictable results.

## 5.5   Branch and eXchange instructions (BX)

This is an instruction available only on very recent ARM chips and has been added as a mechanism for switching the processor to execute Thumb (16-bit) instructions. A similar Thumb instruction causes the processor to switch back to 32-bit ARM instructions. The Thumb instruction set is described in Chapter 7.

**Binary encoding**

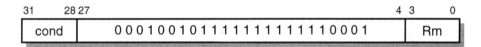

| 31 | 28 27 | | 4 3 | 0 |

| cond | 0 0 0 1 0 0 1 0 1 1 1 1 1 1 1 1 1 1 1 1 0 0 0 1 | Rm |

**Figure 5.4**   Branch and exchange instruction binary encoding.

**Description**   Bit[0] of Rm is copied into the T bit in the CPSR and bits[31:1] or [31:2] are moved into the PC:

- If Rm[0] is 1, the processor switches to execute Thumb instructions and begins executing at the address in Rm aligned to a half-word boundary by clearing the bottom bit.
- If Rm[0] is 0, the processor continues executing ARM instructions and begins executing at the address in Rm aligned to a word boundary by clearing Rm[1:0].

Note that when used as a subroutine return mechanism, this instruction allows the instruction set (ARM or Thumb) of the calling routine to be saved along with the return address, so the same return mechanism can be used to return to either an ARM or a Thumb caller.

**Assembler format**

```
BX{<cond>} Rm
```

**Example**

```
BX      r0      ; branch to address in r0,
                ; enter Thumb state if r0[0] = 1
```

**Notes**   1. Some recent ARM processors which do not support the Thumb instruction set will trap this instruction, allowing software emulation of Thumb.

## 5.6   Software Interrupt (SWI)

The software interrupt instruction is used for calls to the operating system and is often called a 'supervisor call'. It puts the processor into supervisor mode and begins executing instructions from address 0x08.

If this area of memory is suitably protected it is possible to build an operating system on the ARM that is fully protected from a malicious user, though since ARM is rarely used in multi-user applications this level of protection is not often sought.

**Binary encoding**

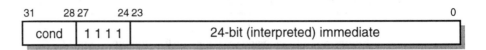

**Figure 5.5**   Software interrupt binary encoding.

**Description**

The 24-bit immediate field does not influence the operation of the instruction but may be interpreted by the system code.

If the condition is passed the instruction enters supervisor mode using the standard ARM exception entry sequence. In detail, the processor actions are:

1.  Save the address of the instruction after the SWI in r14_svc.

2.  Save the CPSR in SPSR_svc.

3.  Enter supervisor mode and disable IRQs (but not FIQs) by setting CPSR[4:0] to $10011_2$ and CPSR[7] to 1.

4.  Set the PC to $08_{16}$ and begin executing the instructions there.

To return to the instruction after the SWI the system routine must not only copy r14_svc back into the PC, but it must also restore the CPSR from SPSR_svc. This requires the use of one of the special forms of the data processing instruction described in the next section.

**Assembler format**

```
SWI{<cond>}      <24-bit immediate>
```

**Examples**       To output the character 'A':

```
            MOV     r0, #'A'              ; get 'A' into r0..
            SWI     SWI_WriteC            ; .. and print it
```

A subroutine to output a text string following the call:

```
            ..
            BL      STROUT                ; output following message
            =       "Hello World",&0a,&0d,0
            ..                            ; return to here
            ..
STROUT      LDRB    r0, [r14], #1         ; get character
            CMP     r0, #0                ; check for end marker
            SWINE   SWI_WriteC            ; if not end, print ..
            BNE     STROUT                ; .. and loop
            ADD     r14, #3               ; align to next word
            BIC     r14, #3
            MOV     pc, r14               ; return
```

To finish executing the user program and return to the monitor program:

```
            SWI     SWI_Exit              ; return to monitor
```

**Notes**      1. An SWI may be executed when the processor is already in supervisor mode pro-
                  vided the original return address (in r14_svc) and SPSR_svc have been saved;
                  otherwise these registers will be overwritten when the SWI is executed.

               2. The interpretation of the 24-bit immediate is system dependent, but most systems
                  support a standard subset for character I/O and similar basic functions.

                  The immediates can be specified as constant expressions, but it is usually better to
                  declare names for the required calls (and set their values) at the start of the pro-
                  gram (or import a file which declares their values for the local operating system)
                  and then use these names in the code.

                  To see how to declare names and give them values look at the 'Examples and exer-
                  cises' on page 75.

               3. The first instruction executed in supervisor mode, which is at $08_{16}$, is normally a
                  branch to the SWI handler which resides somewhere nearby in memory. Writing
                  the SWI handler to start at $08_{16}$ is not possible because the next memory word, at
                  $0C_{16}$, is the entry point for the prefetch abort handler.

## 5.7   Data processing instructions

The ARM data processing instructions are used to modify data values in registers. The operations that are supported include arithmetic and bit-wise logical combinations of 32-bit data types. One operand may be shifted or rotated *en route* to the ALU, allowing, for example, shift and add in a single instruction.

Multiply instructions use different formats, so these are considered separately in the next section.

**Binary encoding**

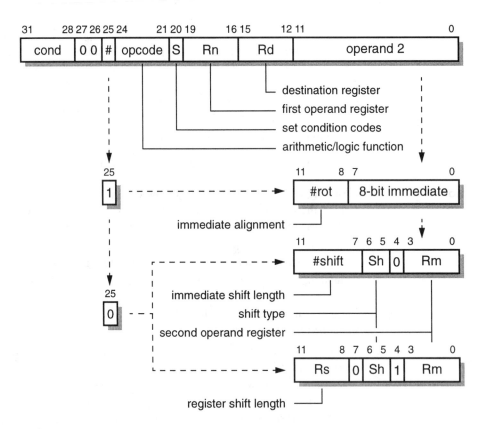

**Figure 5.6**   Data processing instruction binary encoding.

**Description**  The ARM data processing instructions employ a 3-address format, which means that the two source operands and the destination register are specified independently. One source operand is always a register; the second may be a register, a shifted register or an immediate value. The shift applied to the second operand, if it is a register, may be a logical or arithmetic shift or a rotate (see Figure 3.1 on page 56), and it may be by an amount specified either as an immediate quantity or by a fourth register.

The operations that may be specified are listed in Table 5.4 on page 126.

When the instruction does not require all the available operands (for instance MOV ignores Rn and CMP ignores Rd) the unused register field should be set to zero. The assembler will do this automatically.

These instructions allow direct control of whether or not the processor's condition codes are affected by their execution through the S bit (bit 20). When clear, the condition codes will be unchanged; when set (and Rd is not r15; see below):

- The N flag is set if the result is negative, otherwise it is cleared (that is, N equals bit 31 of the result).
- The Z flag is set if the result is zero, otherwise it is cleared.
- The C flag is set to the carry-out from the ALU when the operation is arithmetic (ADD, ADC, SUB, SBC, RSB, RSC, CMP, CMN) or to the carry-out from the shifter otherwise. If no shift is required, C is preserved.
- The V flag is preserved in non-arithmetic operations. It is set in an arithmetic operation if there is an overflow from bit 30 to bit 31 and cleared if no overflow occurs. It has significance only when an arithmetic operation has operands that are viewed as 2's complement signed values, and indicates a result that is out of range.

**Multiply by a constant**  These instructions may be used to multiply a register by a small constant much more efficiently than can be achieved using the multiply instructions described in the next section. Examples are given below.

**Use of r15**  The PC may be used as a source operand except when a register-specified shift amount is used, in which case none of the three source registers should be r15. When r15 is used as a source operand, the value supplied is the address of the instruction plus eight bytes. (The 8-byte offset exposes the pipelined operation of the processor; see 'PC behaviour' on page 81.)

The PC may also be specified as the destination for the result, in which case the instruction is a form of branch. This is exploited as a standard way to return from a subroutine.

**Table 5.4**    ARM data processing instructions.

| Opcode [24:21] | Mnemonic | Meaning | Effect |
|---|---|---|---|
| 0000 | AND | Logical bit-wise AND | Rd := Rn AND Op2 |
| 0001 | EOR | Logical bit-wise exclusive OR | Rd := Rn EOR Op2 |
| 0010 | SUB | Subtract | Rd := Rn - Op2 |
| 0011 | RSB | Reverse subtract | Rd := Op2 - Rn |
| 0100 | ADD | Add | Rd := Rn + Op2 |
| 0101 | ADC | Add with carry | Rd := Rn + Op2 + C |
| 0110 | SBC | Subtract with carry | Rd := Rn - Op2 + C - 1 |
| 0111 | RSC | Reverse subtract with carry | Rd := Op2 - Rn + C - 1 |
| 1000 | TST | Test | Scc on Rn AND Op2 |
| 1001 | TEQ | Test equivalence | Scc on Rn EOR Op2 |
| 1010 | CMP | Compare | Scc on Rn - Op2 |
| 1011 | CMN | Compare negated | Scc on Rn + Op2 |
| 1100 | ORR | Logical bit-wise OR | Rd := Rn OR Op2 |
| 1101 | MOV | Move | Rd := Op2 |
| 1110 | BIC | Bit clear | Rd := Rn AND NOT Op2 |
| 1111 | MVN | Move negated | Rd := NOT Op2 |

When the PC is specified as the destination register Rd, the S bit still controls the effect of the instruction on the CPSR, but in a rather different way. Instead of updating the flags according to the ALU output as described above, when the S bit is set the SPSR of the current mode is copied into the CPSR, possibly affecting the interrupt enable flags and the processor operating mode. This mechanism restores the PC and the CPSR atomically, and is the standard way to return from an exception. Since there is no SPSR in user and system modes, this form of the instruction should not be used in those modes.

**Assembler format**

The assembler representation is one of the following, omitting Rn when the instruction is monadic (MOV, MVN) or Rd when the instruction is a comparison producing only condition code outputs (CMP, CMN, TST, TEQ):

```
<op>{<cond>}{S} Rd, Rn, #<32-bit immediate>
<op>{<cond>}{S} Rd, Rn, Rm, {<shift>}
```

where <shift> specifies the shift type (LSL, LSR, ASL, ASR, ROR or RRX) and, in all cases but RRX, the shift amount which may be a 5-bit immediate (#<#shift>) or a register (Rs).

**Examples**

To add r1 to r3 and place the result in r5:

```
ADD     r5, r1, r3
```

To decrement r2 and check for zero:

```
SUBS    r2, r2, #1          ; dec r2 and set cc
BEQ     LABEL               ; branch if r2 zero
..                          ; .. else fall through
```

To multiply r0 by 5:

```
ADD     r0, r0, r0, LSL #2
```

A subroutine to multiply r0 by 10:

```
        MOV     r0, #3
        BL      TIMES10
        ..
TIMES10 MOV     r0, r0, LSL #1     ; x 2
        ADD     r0, r0, r0, LSL #2 ; x 5
        MOV     pc, r14            ; return
```

To add a 64-bit integer in r0, r1 to one in r2, r3:

```
ADDS    r2, r2, r0          ; add lower, save carry
ADC     r3, r3, r1          ; add higher and carry
```

**Notes**

1. Since the immediate field must be encoded within a subset of a 32-bit instruction, not all 32-bit immediate values can be represented. The binary encoding shown in Figure 5.6 on page 124 shows how the immediate values are encoded. The immediate value is generated by rotating an 8-bit immediate field through an even number of bit positions.

## 5.8   Multiply instructions

ARM multiply instructions produce the product of two 32-bit binary numbers held in
registers. The result of multiplying two 32-bit binary numbers is a 64-bit product.
Some forms of the instruction, available only on certain versions of the processor,
store the full result into two independently specified registers; other forms store only
the least significant 32 bits into a single register.

In all cases there is a multiply-accumulate variant that adds the product to a running total and both signed and unsigned operands may be used. The least significant
32 bits of the result are the same for signed and unsigned operands, so there is no need
for separate signed and unsigned versions of the 32-bit result instructions.

**Binary
encoding**

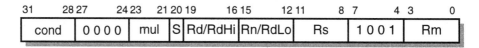

**Figure 5.7**   Multiply instruction binary encoding.

**Description**       The functions of the various forms of multiply are listed in Table 5.5 on page 129. The
notation used in the table is as follows:

- 'RdHi:RdLo' is the 64-bit number formed by concatenating RdHi (the most
  significant 32 bits) and RdLo (the least significant 32 bits).

- '[31:0]' selects only the least significant 32 bits of the result.

- Simple assignment is denoted by ':='.

- Accumulation (adding the right-hand side to the left) is denoted by '+='.

The S bit controls the setting of the condition codes as with the other data
processing instructions. When it is set in the instruction:

- The N flag is set to the value of bit 31 of Rd for the variants which produce a 32-bit
  result, and bit 31 of RdHi for the long forms.

- The Z flag is set if Rd or RdHi and RdLo are zero.

- The C flag is set to a meaningless value.

- The V flag is unchanged.

**Table 5.5**   Multiply instructions.

| Opcode [23:21] | Mnemonic | Meaning | Effect |
|---|---|---|---|
| 000 | MUL | Multiply (32-bit result) | Rd := (Rm * Rs) [31:0] |
| 001 | MLA | Multiply-accumulate (32-bit result) | Rd := (Rm * Rs + Rn) [31:0] |
| 100 | UMULL | Unsigned multiply long | RdHi:RdLo := Rm * Rs |
| 101 | UMLAL | Unsigned multiply-accumulate long | RdHi:RdLo += Rm * Rs |
| 110 | SMULL | Signed multiply long | RdHi:RdLo := Rm * Rs |
| 111 | SMLAL | Signed multiply-accumulate long | RdHi:RdLo += Rm * Rs |

**Assembler formats**

Instructions that produce the least significant 32 bits of the product:

```
MUL{<cond>}{S}  Rd, Rm, Rs
MLA{<cond>}{S}  Rd, Rm, Rs, Rn
```

The following instructions produce the full 64-bit result:

```
<mul>{<cond>}{S}RdHi, RdLo, Rm, Rs
```

where <mul> is one of the 64-bit multiply types (UMULL, UMLAL, SMULL, SMLAL).

**Examples**

To form a scalar product of two vectors:

```
        MOV   r11, #20          ; initialize loop counter
        MOV   r10, #0           ; initialize total
LOOP    LDR   r0, [r8], #4      ; get first component..
        LDR   r1, [r9], #4      ; ..and second
        MLA   r10, r0, r1, r10  ; accumulate product
        SUBS  r11, r11, #1      ; decrement loop counter
        BNE   LOOP
```

**Notes**

1. Specifying r15 for any of the operand or result registers should be avoided as it produces unpredictable results.

2. Rd, RdHi and RdLo should be distinct from Rm, and RdHi and RdLo should not be the same register.

3. Some ARM processors only support the 32-bit multiply instructions (MUL and MLA). The 64-bit multiplies are available only on ARM7 versions with an 'M' in their name (ARM7DM, ARM7TM, and so on) and subsequent processors.

## 5.9    Single word and unsigned byte data transfer instructions

These instructions are the most flexible way to transfer single bytes or words of data between ARM's registers and memory. Transferring large blocks of data is usually better done using the multiple register transfer instructions, and some ARM processors also support instructions for transferring half-words and signed bytes.

Provided that a register has been initialized to point somewhere near (usually within 4 Kbytes of) the required memory address, these instructions provide an efficient load and store mechanism with a relatively rich set of addressing modes which include immediate and register offsets, auto-indexing and PC-relative.

**Binary encoding**

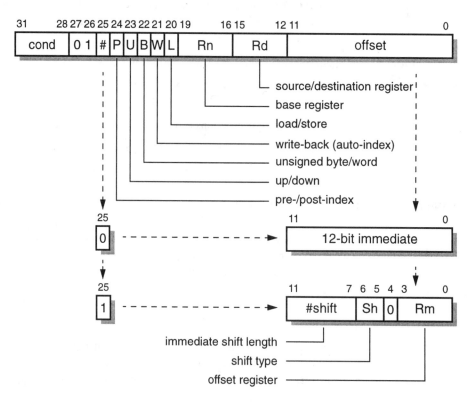

**Figure 5.8**    Single word and unsigned byte data transfer instruction binary encoding.

**Description**  These instructions construct an address starting from a base register (Rn), then adding (U = 1) or subtracting (U = 0) an unsigned immediate or (possibly scaled) register offset. The base or computed address is used to load (L = 1) or store (L = 0) an unsigned byte (B = 1) or word (B = 0) quantity to or from a register (Rd), from or to memory. When a byte is loaded into a register it is zero extended to 32 bits. When a byte is stored into memory, the bottom eight bits of the register are stored into the addressed location.

A pre-indexed (P = 1) addressing mode uses the computed address for the load or store operation, and then, when write-back is requested (W = 1), updates the base register to the computed value.

A post-indexed (P = 0) addressing mode uses the unmodified base register for the transfer and then updates the base register to the computed address irrespective of the W bit (since the offset has no significance other than as a base register modifier, and can always be set to immediate zero if no change is desired). Since the W bit is unused in this case, it has an alternative function which is only relevant in code which is not running in user mode: setting W = 1 causes the processor to request a user mode access to memory, allowing the operating system to adopt a user view of the memory translation and protection scheme.

**Assembler format**  The pre-indexed form of the instruction:

    LDR|STR{<cond>}{B} Rd, [Rn, <offset>]{!}

The post-indexed form:

    LDR|STR{<cond>}{B}{T} Rd, [Rn], <offset>

A useful PC-relative form that leaves the assembler to do all the work:

    LDR|STR{<cond>}{B} Rd, LABEL

LDR is 'load register', STR is 'store register'; the optional 'B' selects an unsigned byte transfer, the default is word; <offset> may be #+/-<12-bit immediate> or +/-Rm {, shift} where the shift specifier is the same as for data processing instructions except that register specified shift amounts are not available; ! selects write-back (auto-indexing) in the pre-indexed form.

The T flag selects the user view of the memory translation and protection system and should only be used in non-user modes. The user should fully understand the memory management environment in which the processor is being used, so this is really only a facility for operating system experts.

**Examples**        To store a byte in r0 to a peripheral:

```
        LDR      r1, UARTADD          ; UART address into r1
        STRB     r0, [r1]             ; store data to UART
          ..
UARTADD &        &1000000             ; address literal
```

   The assembler will use a pre-indexed, PC-relative addressing mode to load the address into r1. The literal must be within range (that is, within 4 Kbytes of the load instruction) for this to be possible.

**Notes**        1. Using the PC as the base address delivers the address of the instruction plus eight bytes; it should not be used as the offset register, nor with any auto-indexing addressing mode (including any post-indexed mode).

   2. Loading a word into the PC causes a branch to the loaded address and is a recognized way of implementing jump tables. Loading a byte into the PC should be avoided.

   3. Storing the PC to memory gives different results on different implementations of the processor and should therefore be avoided if possible.

   4. In general Rd, Rn and Rm should be distinct registers, though loading into the base register (Rd = Rn) is acceptable provided auto-indexing is not used in the same instruction.

   5. When a word is loaded from a non-word-aligned address the loaded data is the word-aligned word containing the addressed byte, rotated so that the addressed byte is in the least significant byte of the destination register. Some ARM systems may raise an exception under these circumstances (controlled by the A flag in bit 1 of CP15 register 1, described in Section 11.2 on page 291).

   6. When a word is stored to a non-word-aligned address the bottom two bits of the address are ignored and the word is stored as though they had been zero. Some ARM systems may raise an exception under these circumstances (again controlled by the A flag in CP15 register 1).

## 5.10   Half-word and signed byte data transfer instructions

These instructions were a fairly late addition to the ARM instruction set and are not supported by all ARM processors. As a result of their late arrival they are somewhat 'shoe-horned' into the instruction space as indicated by the split immediate field.

The addressing modes available with these instructions are a subset of those available with the unsigned byte and word forms.

**Binary encoding**

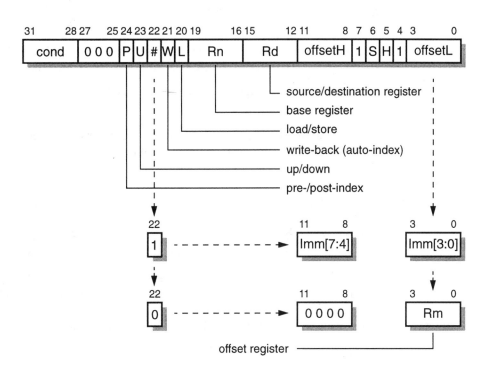

**Figure 5.9**   Half-word and signed byte data transfer instruction binary encoding.

**Description**   These instructions are very similar to the word and unsigned byte forms described in the previous section, but here the immediate offset is limited to eight bits and the scaled register offset is no longer available.

The S and H bits define the type of the operand to be transferred as listed in Table 5.6 on page 134. Note that the fourth combination of these bits, corresponding to an unsigned byte type, is not available in this format. The format described in the

**Table 5.6**  Data type encoding.

| S | H | Data type |
|---|---|---|
| 1 | 0 | Signed byte |
| 0 | 1 | Unsigned half-word |
| 1 | 1 | Signed half-word |

previous section should be used instead. Since there is no difference between storing signed and unsigned data, the only relevant forms of this instruction format are:

- Load signed byte, signed half-word or unsigned half-word.
- Store half-word.

An unsigned value is zero-extended to 32 bits when loaded; a signed value is extended to 32 bits the most significant bit of the data.

**Assembler formats**

The pre-indexed form:

    LDR|STR{<cond>}H|SH|SB Rd, [Rn, <offset>]{!}

The post-indexed form:

    LDR|STR{<cond>}H|SH|SB Rd, [Rn], <offset>

where <offset> is #+/-<8-bit immediate> or +/-Rm and H|SH|SB selects the data type; otherwise the assembler format is as for words and unsigned byte transfers.

**Examples**

To expand an array of signed half-words into an array of words:

```
          ADR     r1, ARRAY1        ; half-word array start
          ADR     r2, ARRAY2        ; word array start
          ADR     r3, ENDARR1       ; ARRAY1 end + 2
LOOP      LDRSH   r0, [r1], #2      ; get signed half-word
          STR     r0, [r2], #4      ; save word
          CMP     r1, r3            ; check for end of array
          BLT     LOOP              ; if not finished, loop
```

**Notes**

1. Similar limitations to those on the word and unsigned byte transfers described in the previous section apply on the use of r15 and the register operands.

2. All half-word transfers should use half-word aligned addresses.

## 5.11 Multiple register transfer instructions

The ARM multiple register transfer instructions allow any subset (or all) of the 16 registers visible in the current operating mode to be loaded from or stored to memory. A form of the instruction also allows the operating system to load or store the user-mode registers to save or restore the user process state, and another form allows the CPSR to be restored from the SPSR as part of a return from an exception handler.

These instructions are used on procedure entry and return to save and restore workspace registers and are useful for high-bandwidth memory block copy routines.

**Binary encoding**

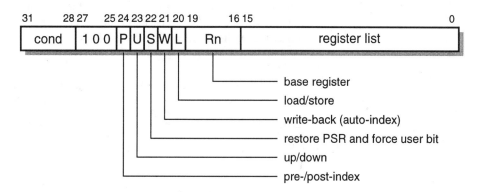

**Figure 5.10**   Multiple register data transfer instruction binary encoding.

**Description**

The register list in the bottom 16 bits of the instruction includes a bit for each visible register, with bit 0 controlling whether or not r0 is transferred, bit 1 controls r1, and so on up to bit 15 which controls the transfer of the PC.

The registers are loaded from or stored to a contiguous block of memory words defined by the base register and the addressing mode. The base address will be incremented (U = 1) or decremented (U = 0) before (P = 1) or after (P = 0) each word transfer. Auto-indexing is supported; if W = 1 the base register will be increased (U = 1) or decreased (U = 0) by the number of bytes transferred when the instruction completes.

Special forms of the instruction allow it to be used to restore the CPSR: if the PC is in the register list of a load multiple and the S bit is set, the SPSR of the current mode will be copied into the CPSR, giving an atomic return and restore state instruction. This form should not be used in user mode code since there is no SPSR in user mode.

If the PC is not in the register list and the S bit is set, both load and store multiple instructions executed in non-user modes will transfer the user mode registers (while using the current mode base register). This allows an operating system to save and restore user process state.

**Assembler format**

The normal form of the instruction is:

```
LDM|STM{<cond>}<add mode> Rn{!}, <registers>
```

where `<add mode>` specifies one of the addressing modes detailed in Table 3.1 on page 65. The instruction bits correspond closely to the mechanistic view described in this table, with 'increment' corresponding to U = 1 and 'before' corresponding to P = 1. '!' specifies auto-indexing (W = 1), and `<registers>` is a list of registers and register ranges enclosed in curly brackets, for example: {r0, r3-r7, pc}.

In a non-user mode, the CPSR may be restored by:

```
LDM{<cond>}<add mode> Rn{!}, <registers + pc>^
```

The register list must contain the PC. In a non-user mode, the user registers may be saved or restored by:

```
LDM|STM{<cond>}<add mode> Rn, <registers - pc>^
```

In this case the register list must not contain the PC and write-back should not be specified.

**Examples**

To save three work registers and the return address upon entering a subroutine:

```
STMEA   r13!, {r0-r2, r14}
```

This assumes that r13 has been initialized for use as a stack pointer. To restore the work registers and return:

```
LDMEA   r13!, {r0-r2, pc}
```

**Notes**

1. If the PC is specified in the register list in a store multiple instruction, the value saved is implementation dependent. Normally, therefore, specifying the PC in an STM should be avoided. (Loading the PC has the expected result and is a standard way of returning from a procedure.)

2. The base register may be specified in the transfer list of either a load or store multiple, but write-back should not be specified in the same instruction since the result of doing so is unpredictable.

3. If the base register contains an address that is not word-aligned, the bottom two bits will be ignored. Some ARM systems may generate an exception.

## 5.12 Swap memory and register instructions (SWP)

Swap instructions combine a load and a store of a word or an unsigned byte in a single instruction. Normally the two transfers are combined into an atomic memory operation that cannot be split by an external memory access (for instance from a DMA controller), and therefore the instruction can be used as the basis of a semaphore mechanism to give mutually exclusive access to data structures that are shared between multiple processes, processors, or a processor and a DMA controller. These instructions are little used outside their role in the construction of semaphores.

**Binary encoding**

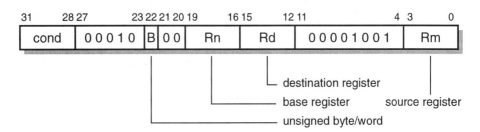

**Figure 5.11**  Swap memory and register instruction binary encoding.

**Description**  The instruction loads the word (B = 0) or unsigned byte (B = 1) at the memory location addressed by Rn into Rd, and stores the same data type from Rm into the same memory location. Rd and Rm may be the same register (but should both be distinct from Rn), in which case the register and memory values are exchanged. The ARM executes separate memory read and then memory write cycles, but asserts a 'lock' signal to indicate to the memory system that the two cycles should not be separated.

**Assembler format**

```
SWP{<cond>}{B} Rd, Rm, [Rn]
```

**Examples**

```
ADR     r0, SEMAPHORE
SWPB    r1, r1, [r0]        ; exchange byte
```

**Notes**  1.  The PC should not be used as any of the registers in this instruction.

2.  The base register (Rn) should not be the same as either the source (Rm) or the destination (Rd) registers.

## 5.13   Status register to general register transfer instructions

When it is necessary to save or modify the contents of the CPSR or the SPSR of the current mode, those contents must first be transferred into a general register, the selected bits modified and then the value returned to the status register. These instructions perform the first step in this sequence.

**Binary encoding**

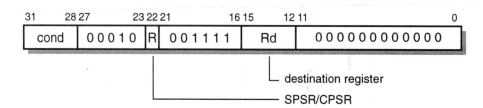

**Figure 5.12**   Status register to general register transfer instruction binary encoding.

**Description**   The CPSR (R = 0) or the current mode SPSR (R = 1) is copied into the destination register (Rd). All 32 bits are copied.

**Assembler format**

```
MRS{<cond>} Rd, CPSR|SPSR
```

**Examples**

```
MRS     r0, CPSR          ; move the CPSR to r0
MRS     r3, SPSR          ; move the SPSR to r3
```

**Notes**   1. The SPSR form should not be used in user or system mode since there is no accessible SPSR in those modes.

2. When modifying the CPSR or SPSR care should be taken to preserve the values of all the unused bits; this will maximize the probability of compatibility with future uses of those bits. This is best achieved by moving the status register to a general register (using these instructions), modifying only the necessary bits and then moving the result back to the status register.

## 5.14  General register to status register transfer instructions

When it is necessary to save or modify the contents of the CPSR or the SPSR of the current mode, those contents must first be transferred into a general register, the selected bits modified and then the value returned to the status register. These instructions perform the last step in this sequence.

**Binary encoding**

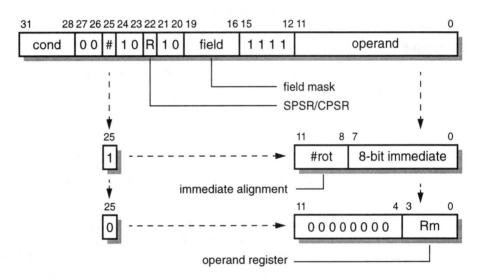

**Figure 5.13**   Transfer to status register instruction binary encoding.

**Description**   The operand, which may be a register (Rm) or a rotated 8-bit immediate (specified in the same way as the immediate form of operand2 in the data processing instructions), is moved under a field mask to the CPSR (R = 0) or current mode SPSR (R = 1).

The field mask controls the update of the four byte fields within the PSR register. Instruction bit 16 determines whether PSR[7:0] is updated, bit 17 controls PSR[15:8], bit 18 controls PSR[23:16] and bit 19 controls PSR[31:24].

When an immediate operand is used only the flags (PSR[31:24]) may be selected for update. (These are the only bits that may be updated by user-mode code.)

**Assembler format**

```
MSR{<cond>} CPSR_f|SPSR_f, #<32-bit immediate>
MSR{<cond>} CPSR_<field>|SPSR_<field>, Rm
```

where <field> is one of:

- c – the control field – PSR[7:0].
- x – the extension field – PSR[15:8] (unused on current ARMs).
- s – the status field – PSR[23:16] (unused on current ARMs).
- f – the flags field – PSR[31:24].

**Examples**

To set the N, Z, C and V flags:

```
MSR     CPSR_f, #&f0000000; set all the flags
```

To set just the C flag, preserving N, Z and V:

```
MRS     r0, CPSR            ; move the CPSR to r0
ORR     r0, r0, #&20000000; set bit 29 of r0
MSR     CPSR_f, r0          ; move back to CPSR
```

To switch from supervisor mode into IRQ mode (for instance, to intialize the IRQ stack pointer at start up):

```
MRS     r0, CPSR            ; move the CPSR to r0
BIC     r0, r0, #&1f        ; clear the bottom 5 bits
ORR     r0, r0, #&12        ; set the bits to IRQ mode
MSR     CPSR_c, r0          ; move back to CPSR
```

In this case it is necessary to copy the original CPSR value in order not to change the interrupt enable settings. The particular case illustrated could be simplified since IRQ mode just requires one bit cleared from supervisor mode (see Table 5.1 on page 112), but the code above can be used to move between any two non-user modes or from a non-user mode into user mode.

The mode change takes effect only after the MSR has been executed; the intermediate working has no effect on the mode until the result is copied back into the CPSR.

**Notes**

1. Attempts to modify any of CPSR[23:0] whilst in user mode have no effect.

2. Attempts to access the SPSR whilst in user or system mode should be avoided, since they have unpredictable results as there is no SPSR in these modes.

## 5.15   Coprocessor instructions

The ARM architecture supports a general mechanism for extending the instruction set through the addition of coprocessors. The most common use of a coprocessor is the system coprocessor used to control on-chip functions such as the cache and memory management unit on the ARM610. A floating-point ARM coprocessor has also been developed, and application specific coprocessors are a possibility.

**Coprocessor registers**

ARM coprocessors have their own private register sets and their state is controlled by instructions that mirror the instructions that control ARM registers.

The ARM has sole responsibility for control flow, so the coprocessor instructions are concerned with data processing and data transfer. Following RISC load-store architectural principles, these categories are cleanly separated. The instruction formats reflect this:

**Coprocessor data operations**

- Coprocessor data operations are completely internal to the coprocessor and cause a state change in the coprocessor registers. An example would be floating-point addition, where two registers in the floating-point coprocessor are added together and the result placed into a third register.

**Coprocessor data transfers**

- Coprocessor data transfer instructions load or store the values in coprocessor registers from or to memory. Since coprocessors may support their own data types, the number of words transferred for each register is coprocessor dependent. The ARM generates the memory address, but the coprocessor controls the number of words transferred. A coprocessor may perform some type conversion as part of the transfer (for instance the floating-point coprocessor converts all loaded values into its 80-bit internal representation).

**Coprocessor register transfers**

- In addition to the above, it is sometimes useful to move values between ARM and coprocessor registers. Again taking the floating-point coprocessor as an illustration, a 'FIX' instruction takes a floating-point value from a coprocessor register, converts it to an integer, and moves the integer into an ARM register. A floating-point comparison produces a result which is often needed to affect control flow, so the result of the compare must be moved to the ARM CPSR.

Taken together these instructions support a generalized extension of the ARM instruction set to support application-specific data types and functions.

## 5.16 Coprocessor data operations

These instructions are used to control internal operations on data in coprocessor registers. The standard format follows the 3-address form of ARM's integer data processing instructions, but other interpretations of all the coprocessor fields are possible.

**Binary encoding**

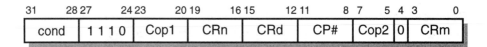

| 31 | 28 27 | 24 23 | 20 19 | 16 15 | 12 11 | 8 7 | 5 4 3 | 0 |
|----|-------|-------|-------|-------|-------|-----|-------|---|
| cond | 1 1 1 0 | Cop1 | CRn | CRd | CP# | Cop2 | 0 | CRm |

**Figure 5.14** Coprocessor data processing instruction binary encoding.

**Description**

The ARM offers this instruction to any coprocessors that may be present. If it is accepted by one of them the ARM proceeds to the next instruction; if it is not accepted the ARM takes the undefined instruction trap (which may be used to implement a software emulation of the missing coprocessor).

Normally the coprocessor identified with the coprocessor number CP# will accept the instruction and perform the operation defined by the Cop1 and Cop2 fields, using CRn and CRm as the source operands and placing the result in CRd.

**Assembler format**

```
CDP{<cond>} <CP#>, <Cop1>, CRd, CRn, CRm{, <Cop2>}
```

**Examples**

```
CDP    p2, 3, Cr0, Cr1, Cr2
CDPEQ  p3, 6, Cr1, Cr5, Cr7, 4
```

**Notes**

1. The interpretation of the Cop1, CRn, CRd, Cop2 and CRm fields is coprocessor-dependent. The above interpretation is recommended and will maximize compatibility with ARM development tools.

## 5.17  Coprocessor data transfers

The coprocessor data transfer instructions are similar to the immediate offset forms of the word and unsigned byte data transfer instructions described earlier, but with the offset limited to eight bits rather than 12.

Auto-indexed forms are available, with pre- and post-indexed addressing.

**Binary encoding**

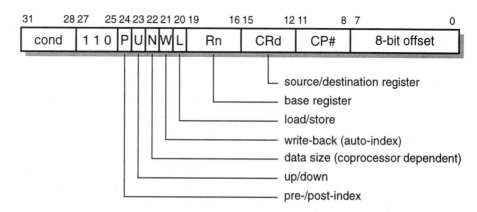

**Figure 5.15**  Coprocessor data transfer instruction binary encoding.

**Description**  The instruction is offered to any coprocessors which may be present; if none accept it ARM takes the undefined instruction trap and may use software to emulate the coprocessor. Normally the coprocessor with coprocessor number CP#, if present, will accept the instruction.

The address calculation takes place within the ARM, using an ARM base register (Rn) and an 8-bit immediate offset which is scaled to a word offset by shifting it left two bit positions. The addressing mode and auto-indexing are controlled in the same way as the ARM word and unsigned byte transfer instructions. This defines the first transfer address; subsequent words are transferred to or from incrementing word addresses.

The data is supplied by or received into a coprocessor register (CRd), with the number of words transferred being controlled by the coprocessor and the N bit selecting one of two possible lengths.

**Assembler format**

The pre-indexed form:

    LDC|STC{<cond>}{L} <CP#>, CRd, [Rn, <offset>]{!}

The post-indexed form:

    LDC|STC{<cond>}{L} <CP#>, CRd, [Rn], <offset>

In both cases LDC selects a load from memory into the coprocessor register, STC selects a store from the coprocessor register into memory. The L flag, if present, selects the long data type (N = 1). <offset> is #+/-<8-bit immediate>.

**Examples**

    LDC     p6, Cr0, [r1]
    STCEQL  p5, Cr1, [r0], #4

**Notes**

1. The interpretation of the N and CRd fields is coprocessor-dependent. The use shown above is recommended and will maximize compatibility with ARM development tools.

2. If the address is not word-aligned the two least significant bits will be ignored, though some ARM systems may raise an exception.

3. The number of words transferred is controlled by the coprocessor and the ARM will continue to generate sequential addresses until the coprocessor indicates that the transfer should complete (see 'Data transfers' on page 102). During the data transfer the ARM will not respond to interrupt requests, so coprocessor designers should be careful not to compromise the system interrupt response time by allowing very long data transfers.

   Limiting the maximum transfer length to 16 words will ensure that coprocessor data transfers take no longer than worst-case load and store multiple register instructions.

## 5.18   Coprocessor register transfers

These instructions allow an integer generated in a coprocessor to be transferred directly into a ARM register or the ARM condition code flags.

Typical uses are:

- A floating-point FIX operation which returns the integer to an ARM register;
- A floating-point comparison which returns the result of the comparison directly to the ARM condition code flags where it can determine the control flow;
- A FLOAT operation which takes an integer value from an ARM register and sends it to the coprocessor where it is converted to floating-point representation and placed in a coprocessor register.

The system control coprocessors used to control the cache and memory management functions on the more complex ARM CPUs (Central Processing Units) generally use these instructions to access and modify the on-chip control registers.

**Binary encoding**

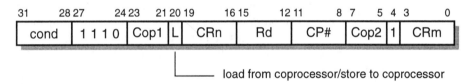

**Figure 5.16**   Coprocessor register transfer instruction binary encoding.

**Description**   The instruction is offered to any coprocessors present; normally the coprocessor with coprocessor number CP# will accept the instruction. If no coprocessor accepts the instruction ARM raises an undefined instruction trap.

If a coprocessor accepts a load from coprocessor instruction, it will normally perform an operation defined by Cop1 and Cop2 on source operands CRn and CRm and return a 32-bit integer result to the ARM which will place it in Rd.

If a coprocessor accepts a store to coprocessor instruction, it will accept a 32-bit integer from the ARM register Rd and do something with it.

If the PC is specified as the destination register Rd in a load from coprocessor instruction, the top four bits of the 32-bit integer generated by the coprocessor are placed into the N, Z, C and V flags in the CPSR.

**Assembler
format**

Move to ARM register from coprocessor:

    MRC{<cond>} <CP#>, <Cop1>, Rd, CRn, CRm{, <Cop2>}

Move to coprocessor from ARM register:

    MCR{<cond>} <CP#>, <Cop1>, Rd, CRn, CRm{, <Cop2>}

**Examples**
    MCR     p14, 3, r0, Cr1, Cr2
    MRCCS   p2, 4, r3, Cr3, Cr4, 6

**Notes**

1. The Cop1, CRn, Cop2 and CRm fields are interpreted by the coprocessor. The above interpretations are recommended to maximize compatibility with ARM development tools.

2. Where the coprocessor must perform some internal work to prepare a 32-bit value for transfer to the ARM (for example, a floating-point FIX operation has to convert the floating-point value into its equivalent fixed-point value), this must take place before the coprocessor commits to the transfer. Therefore it will often be necessary for the coprocessor hand-shake to 'busy-wait' while the data is prepared.

   The ARM can take interrupts during the busy-wait period, and if it does get interrupted it will break off from the hand-shake to service the interrupt. It will probably retry the coprocessor instruction when it returns from the interrupt service routine, but it may not; the interrupt may cause a task switch, for example.

   In either case, the coprocessor must give consistent results. Therefore the preparation work carried out before the hand-shake commit phase must not change the coprocessor's visible state.

3. Transfers from the ARM to the coprocessor are generally simpler since any data conversion work can take place in the coprocessor after the transfer has completed.

## 5.19   Unused instruction space

Not all of the $2^{32}$ instruction bit encodings have been assigned meanings; the encodings that have not been used so far are available for future instruction set extensions.

The unused instruction encodings each fall into particular gaps left in the used encodings, and their likely future use can be inferred from where they lie.

**Unused arithmetic instructions**

These instructions look very like the multiply instructions described in Section 5.8 on page 128. This would be a likely encoding, for example, for an integer divide instruction.

| 31   28 | 27         22 | 21 20 | 19    16 | 15    12 | 11    8 | 7    4 | 3    0 |
|---------|---------------|-------|----------|----------|---------|--------|--------|
| cond    | 0 0 0 0 0 1   | op    | Rn       | Rd       | Rs      | 1 0 0 1| Rm     |

**Figure 5.17**   Arithmetic instruction extension space.

**Unused control instructions**

These instructions include the branch and exchange instructions described in Section 5.5 on page 121 and the status register transfer instructions described in Sections 5.13 and 5.14 on pages 138 and 139. The gaps here could be used to encode other instructions that affect the processor operating mode.

| 31   28 | 27       23 | 22 21 | 20 | 19    16 | 15    12 | 11    8 | 7 | 6 | 4 | 3    0 |
|---------|-------------|-------|----|----------|----------|---------|---|---|---|--------|
| cond    | 0 0 0 1 0   | op1   | 0  | Rn       | Rd       | Rs      | op2 | | 0 | Rm |
| cond    | 0 0 0 1 0   | op1   | 0  | Rn       | Rd       | Rs      | 0 | op2 | 1 | Rm |
| cond    | 0 0 1 1 0   | op1   | 0  | Rn       | Rd       | #rot    | 8-bit immediate | | | |

**Figure 5.18**   Control instruction extension space.

**Unused load/store instructions**

There are unused encodings in the areas occupied by the swap instructions described in Section 5.12 on page 137 and the load and store half-word and signed byte instructions described in Section 5.10 on page 133. These are likely to be used to support additional data transfer instructions, should these be required in the future.

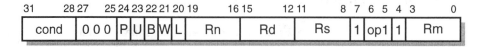

**Figure 5.19**   Data transfer instruction extension space.

**Unused coprocessor instructions**

The following instruction format is similar to the coprocessor data transfer instruction described in Section 5.17 on page 143, and is likely to be used to support any additional coprocessor instructions that may be required:

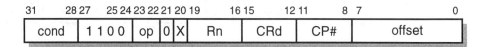

**Figure 5.20**   Coprocessor instruction extension space.

**Undefined instruction space**

The largest area of undefined instructions looks like the word and unsigned byte data transfer instruction described in Section 5.9 on page 130. However the future options on this space are being kept completely open.

**Figure 5.21**   Undefined instruction space.

**Behaviour of unused instructions**

All current ARM processors will take the undefined instruction trap if an attempt is made to execute an instruction that matches the encoding shown in Figure 5.21, in the undefined instruction space.

   The latest ARM processors should take the undefined instruction trap if any unused opcode is executed, but previous versions (including ARM6 and ARM7) will behave unpredictably. Therefore these instructions should be avoided!

## 5.20    Memory faults

ARM processors allow the memory system (or, more usually, the memory management unit) to fault on any memory access. What this means is that instead of returning the requested value from memory, the memory system returns a signal that indicates that the memory access has failed to complete correctly. The processor will then enter an exception handler and the system software will attempt to recover from the problem. The most common sources of a memory fault in a general-purpose machine are:

**Page absent**
- The addressed memory location has been paged out to disk.

    In a virtual memory system infrequently used pages are held on disk. An attempt to access instructions or data on such a page will fail, causing the MMU to abort the access. The system software must identify the cause of the abort, fetch the required page into memory from disk, change the translation tables in the MMU accordingly and retry the aborted access.

    Since fetching a page from disk is a slow process, the operating system will often switch out the faulted process and schedule another task while the transfer takes place.

**Page protected**
- The addressed memory location is temporarily inaccessible.

    When a page is loaded into memory, the operating system may initially make it read only. An attempt to write the page will fault, alerting the operating system to the fact that the page has been modified and must be saved when it is swapped out to disk again. (An unmodified page need not be written to disk again if the old copy is still there.)

    Some operating systems will periodically make pages inaccessible in order to generate statistics about their use for the paging algorithm.

**Soft memory errors**
- A soft error has been detected in the memory.

    A large memory system has a not-insignificant error rate due to alpha particle radiation changing the state of a dynamic RAM storage cell. Where the memory system has simple error detection (such as a parity check) the fault is not recoverable so the faulting process must be terminated. Where the memory system has full error check and correct (ECC) hardware the processor will usually be unaware of the error, though a fault could still be generated in order that the operating system can accumulate statistics on the memory error rate. In the intermediate case, where the memory has a hardware error detector but relies on software error correction, the fault, correct and retry sequence is followed.

**Embedded systems**

In a typical small embedded ARM application, a hard disk is usually unavailable, and in any case paging to disk is usually incompatible with the real-time constraints that the system must meet. Furthermore the memory system is usually small (a few megabytes at most, comprising a handful of memory chips) so the soft error rate is negligible and error detection is rarely incorporated. Therefore many embedded systems will not use memory faults at all.

A typical use in an embedded system might be to store a library of routines in compressed form in ROM and to use the virtual memory technique to trap calls to individual routines, expanding them as required into RAM for execution. The benefit of storing them in compressed form is the reduction in the size and cost of the ROM; the penalty is the time taken for decompression.

An additional use in an embedded system might be to offer some protection for processes running under a real-time operating system.

**Memory faults**

The ARM handles memory faults detected during instruction fetches (*prefetch aborts*) and those detected during data transfers (*data aborts*) separately.

**Prefetch aborts**

If an instruction fetch faults, the memory system raises the abort signal (a dedicated input to the processor) and returns a meaningless instruction word. Internally ARM puts the meaningless instruction into the instruction pipeline along with the abort flag, and then continues with business as usual until the instruction enters the decode stage, whereupon the abort flag overrides the instruction and causes the decoder to generate an exception entry sequence using the prefetch abort vector.

If the aborted instruction does not get executed, for instance because it was fetched immediately after a branch instruction that was ultimately taken, then no exception is raised and the fault is ignored.

**Data aborts**

Memory faults which arise during an access to memory for a data value are far more complex to handle. The memory system need not differentiate the instruction and data cases; it simply raises the abort input when it sees an address that it can't handle. The processor has to work much harder in response to a data abort, however, since this is a problem with the instruction that is currently executing whereas a prefetch abort is a problem with an instruction that has not yet entered decode.

Since the objective, in some cases, is to retry the instruction when the cause of the fault has been resolved, the instruction should do its best to ensure that its state (that is, its register values) after an abort is unchanged from its state before it started executing. Failing that, it should at least ensure that enough state can be recovered so that after the instruction has been executed a second time its state is the same as it would have been had the instruction completed the first time.

**LDM data abort**

To see just how hard this can get, consider a load multiple instruction with 16 registers in the register list using r0 as the base register. Initially the addresses are fine, so the loading begins. The first data value to arrive overwrites r0, then successive registers get written until the final address (destined for the PC) crosses a page boundary and faults. Most of the processor state has been lost. How can the processor recover?

The abort signal is just in time to prevent the PC from being overwritten, so at least we have an address for the instruction that caused the fault. But we appear to have lost the base register a long time back, so how can the instruction be retried? Fortunately the processor has kept a copy of the base register value (possibly after auto-indexing) in a dark corner while the instruction was proceeding, so the last act of the instruction, when it should have been changing the PC to the new value had the PC access not faulted, is instead to copy this preserved value back into the base register.

So we have preserved the PC and the (modified) base register, but we have over-written several other registers in the meantime. The base register modification can be reversed by software, since we can inspect the instruction and determine the number of registers in the list and the addressing mode. The overwritten registers are exactly those that we will load again with the correct values when we retry the instruction, so all is well (just!).

**An historical note**

The requirement to recover from data aborts was added fairly late in the development of the first ARM processor chip. Up to that point, the various load and store multiple addressing modes had been implemented starting from the base address and incre-menting up or decrementing down memory according to the mode. The chip was therefore designed with an address incrementer/decrementer unit.

When it became clear that support for virtual memory was needed it was rapidly seen that the decrementing mode made abort recovery much harder, since the PC could be overwritten before the abort was signalled. Therefore the implementation was changed always to increment the address. The memory addresses used were the same, and the mapping of register to memory was unchanged (see Figure 3.2 on page 64); just the order of the transfer was changed to lowest address first, PC last.

This change was implemented too late to affect the layout of the address generat-ing logic, so the first ARM silicon has an address incrementer/decrementer hard-wired always to increment. Needless to say, this redundancy was not carried forward to sub-sequent implementations.

**Abort timing**

The earlier a processor gets an indication of a fault from the memory system, the bet-ter placed it is to preserve state. The earlier a processor requires the fault signal, the harder the memory system is to design. There is therefore a tension between the archi-tectural simplicity of the processor's fault handling and the engineering efficiency of the memory system.

This tension doesn't affect just the memory management unit. Where the processor has a cache memory, the cache design can also be affected by the abort timing.

Early ARM processors required the abort signal by the end of phase 1 of the clock cycle (see Figure 4.7 on page 86), before half-way through the memory access. A fully associative cache with a CAM-RAM (CAM is Content Addressable Memory) organization can be designed to generate its hit/miss signal from the CAM access only, in time either to confirm a satisfactory access or to halt the processor in phase 1. Once the processor is halted, the MMU has time to control the generation of the abort signal. A set-associative cache, on the other hand, will usually produce its hit/miss signal at the end of the cycle, too late to defer a miss to the MMU (which may generate an abort) without a significant performance loss. (The ARM710, which has a set-associative RAM-RAM cache, does not follow this rule, and the cache still generates its hit/ miss signal and the MMU its protection information before the end of phase 1.)

In order to ease the constraints on the cache and MMU designs, later ARMs were redesigned to allow aborts to be flagged at the end of the cycle, with a similar timing to the read data. The compromise that had to be accepted was that now the processor state has changed further so there is more work for the abort recovery software to do.

Some ARM processors may be configured (by external hard-wiring or using the L bit, bit 6 of CP15 register 1, see Section 11.2 on page 291) to work with either early or late abort timing.

**ARM data aborts**

The state of the ARM after a data abort depends on the particular processor and, with some processors, on the early/late abort configuration:

- In all cases the PC is preserved (so on data abort exception entry r14_abt contains the address of the faulting instruction plus eight bytes).
- The base register will either be unmodified, or will contain a value modified by auto-indexing (it will not be overwritten by a loaded value).
- Other load destination registers may have been overwritten, but the correct value will be loaded when the instruction is retried.

Because the base register may be modified by auto-indexing, certain (not very useful) auto-indexing modes should be avoided. For example:

```
LDR     r0, [r1], r1
```

This instruction uses r1 as the address for the load, then uses post-indexing to add r1 to itself, losing the top bit in the process. If, following a data abort, only the modified value of r1 is available, it is not possible to recover the original transfer address. In general, using the same register for the base and the index in an addressing mode should be avoided.

## 5.21 ARM architecture variants

The ARM architecture has undergone a number of revisions in the course of its development.

**Version 1**
ARM architecture version 1 describes the first ARM processor, developed at Acorn Computers Limited between 1983 and 1985. These first ARM chips supported only 26-bit addressing (see below) and had no multiply or coprocessor support. Their only use in a product was in the ARM second processor attachments to the BBC microcomputer; these were made in very small numbers, but established the ARM as the first commercially exploited single-chip RISC microprocessor. They were also used internally within Acorn in prototypes of the Archimedes personal workstation.

**Version 2**
The ARM2 chip was sold in volume in the Acorn Archimedes and A3000 products. It was still a 26-bit address machine, but included the 32-bit result multiply instructions and coprocessor support. ARM2 employs the architecture that ARM Limited now calls ARM architecture version 2.

**Version 2a**
The ARM3 chip was the first ARM with an on-chip cache. The architecture was very similar to version 2, but added the atomic load and store (SWP) instruction and introduced the use of coprocessor 15 as the system control coprocessor to manage the cache.

**Version 3**
The first ARM processor designed by ARM Limited following their establishment as a separate company in 1990 was the ARM6, sold as a macrocell, a stand-alone processor (the ARM60) and as an integrated CPU with an on-chip cache, MMU and write buffer (the ARM600, and the ARM610 used in the Apple Newton). The ARM6 introduced ARM architecture version 3, which had 32-bit addressing, separate CPSR and SPSRs, and added the undefined and abort modes to allow coprocessor emulation and virtual memory support in supervisor mode.

ARM architecture version 3 is backwards compatible with version 2a, allowing either hard-wired 26-bit operation or process-by-process mixed 26- and 32-bit operation.

**Version 3G**
ARM architecture version 3G is version 3 without backwards compatibility to version 2a.

**Version 3M**
ARM architecture version 3M introduces the signed and unsigned multiply and multiply-accumulate instructions that generate the full 64-bit result.

**Version 4**     Version 4 of the architecture adds the signed and unsigned half-word and signed byte load and store instructions and reserves some of the SWI space for architecturally defined operations. The system mode (a privileged mode that uses the user registers) is introduced, and several unused corners of the instruction space are trapped as undefined instructions.

At this stage those uses of r15 which yielded 'pc + 12' in earlier ARMs are declared to give unpredictable results (so architecture version 4 compliant implementations need not reproduce the 'pc + 12' behaviour). This is the first architecture version to have a full formal definition.

**Version 4T**     The 16-bit Thumb compressed form of the instruction set is introduced in version 4T of the architecture.

**ARM 26-bit architecture**     The original ARM chip, designed at Acorn Computers Limited in 1984, had a slightly different architecture from the one described so far in this chapter. The biggest difference was that the address bus was limited to 26 bits rather than the 32 bits supported by current ARMs.

Although ARM Limited emphasizes the 32-bit capabilities of their current designs, many of their products also have backwards compatibility modes that enable them to be configured to support 26-bit operation.

**26-bit architecture differences**     The major differences between the 26-bit architecture and the 32-bit architecture are:

- The 26-bit architecture PC uses a 24-bit (word) address, supporting a 64 Mbyte address space.
- Only four operating modes are supported (user, supervisor, FIQ and IRQ).
- The condition codes (N, Z, C and V), the interrupt disable flags (I and F) and the two mode bits (M[1:0]) required to select one of the four modes use the remaining eight bits of r15, sharing r15 with the PC.
- The processor therefore requires no CPSR or any SPSR.
- An 'address exception' is raised if a data transfer is attempted with an address outside the 64 Mbyte space (that is, with any of the top six bits set).

Since r15 contains both the PC and the PSR state, the problem of returning to a user process from an exception handler is greatly simplified. Where the 32-bit architecture requires a special form of instruction to restore the CPSR from the SPSR as a side-effect to the return instruction, the 26-bit architecture can simply copy the link register (r14) to r15, thereby restoring the PC and the PSR directly. This elegant mechanism had to be abandoned to allow the processor to operate in a 32-bit address space.

The merged PC and PSR also gives rise to some instruction set differences, particularly where the instruction directly modifies the PSR.

**The 26-bit format of register 15**

The 26-bit architecture format of register 15 is illustrated in Figure 5.22. Bits [25:2] are the program counter (PC), and bits [31:26] and [1:0] are referred to as the Program Status Register, or PSR.

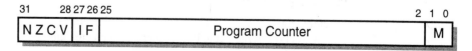

**Figure 5.22**  The 26-bit architecture format of register 15.

The N, Z, C, V, I and F flags have the same meaning in the 26-bit and 32-bit architectures, and the mode bits (bits [1:0]) correspond to the bottom two bits of the 32-bit CPSR described in Table 5.1 on page 112. Note how the abort, undefined and system modes collapse onto supervisor mode when only the bottom two bits in this table are used. Address exceptions (which cannot arise in the 32-bit architecture) are also handled in supervisor mode.

**Mode protection**

The I, F and M[1:0] bits are protected from modification by user-mode code.

**Use of r15**

When r15 is used as an operand in a 26-bit mode, the value presented may be just the PC or the PC with the PSR:

- When used as the base register for a word or unsigned byte load or store, the value delivered is the PC. PC-relative addressing is straightforward. (r15 should not be used as the base register for a multiple register transfer instruction).

- The value saved in the link register (r14) in a branch and link or exception entry is the PC together with the PSR.

- In a data processing instruction, r15 delivers just the PC when used in the first operand (Rn) position, and it delivers the PC with the PSR when used in the second operand (Rm) position.

This may appear complex, but the implementation is remarkably simple. Referring to Figure 4.1 on page 79, whenever the PC is read onto the A bus its value is delivered without the PSR, but on the B bus it comes with the PSR.

**Writing to r15**

When r15 is specified as the destination in a 26-bit mode, normally only the PC is modified. Exceptions to this rule are:

- Data processing instructions with the S bit set.

  If r15 is the destination and the S bit is set, the 32-bit result is written into the PC plus PSR (except that the interrupt and mode bits are protected in user mode).

- Load multiple instructions with restore PSR copy the last memory word into the PC plus PSR (excepting protected bits).

- Special variants (not available in the 32-bit architecture) of the CMP, CMN, TST and TEQ instructions write to the PSR (excepting protected bits) but not the PC.

**Writing to the PSR**

The special variants of the CMP, CMN, TST and TEQ instructions have the form:

```
<op>{<cond>}P Rn, #<32-bit immediate>
<op>{<cond>}P Rn, Rm, {<shift>}
```

where <op> is one of CMP, CMN, TST or TEQ. The 'P' indicates that the destination (Rd) should be set to r15 rather than the default r0. The instruction carries out the function specified in Table 5.4 on page 126, and the ALU result bits (note: not the normal ALU flag outputs) are written to the corresponding PSR bits.

As an example, here is a 26-bit architecture instruction to take the processor from any privileged (that is, non-user) mode into FIQ mode:

```
TEQP    pc, #1  ; go into FIQ mode
```

This illustration highlights a number of tricky points. The PC is used as the first operand, which means that r15 supplies only the PC and the PSR bits are zero. Therefore TEQ exclusive-ORs the immediate operand with zero in all the relevant bit positions, so the immediate operand is written unchanged into the PSR, putting the processor into FIQ mode (and enabling both interrupts and clearing the condition code flags).

Note also that since the 32-bit immediate is generated by rotating a byte right through an even number of bit positions, any PSR value can be generated. A byte rotated right six bit positions exactly covers all the PSR bits.

**26-bit support**

The ARM 26-bit architecture should be viewed as obsolete, even though processors which support it are still manufactured.

All new system designs should therefore conform to one of the 32-bit architectures.

## 5.22    Example and exercises

(See also Sections 3.4 and 3.5 on pages 72 and 75.)

**Example 5.1**    **Write a scalar product program which is significanty faster than that given in Section 5.8 on page 129.**

The original program takes ten cycles plus the (data dependent) multiply time for each pair of data values. Each data value costs three cycles to load and the branch costs three cycles per loop.

The load costs may be reduced by using multiple register loads and the branch cost by 'loop unrolling'. Combining these two techniques gives a program such as:

```
        MOV     r11, #20            ; initialize loop counter
        MOV     r10, #0             ; initialize total
LOOP    LDMIA   r8!, {r0-r3}        ; load 4 1st vector values..
        LDMIA   r9!, {r4-r7}        ; ..and 4 2nd vector values
        MLA     r10, r0, r4, r10    ; accumulate 1st product
        MLA     r10, r1, r5, r10    ; accumulate 2nd product
        MLA     r10, r2, r6, r10    ; accumulate 3rd product
        MLA     r10, r3, r7, r10    ; accumulate 4th product
        SUBS    r11, r11, #4        ; decrement loop count by 4
        BNE     LOOP                ; loop if not finished
```

Now the loop overhead is 16 cycles plus the multiply time for four pairs of data values, or four cycles for each pair.

**Exercise 5.1.1**    Write a subprogram which copies a string of bytes from one memory location to another. The start of the source string will be passed in r1, the length (in bytes) in r2 and the start of the destination string in r3.

**Exercise 5.1.2**    Repeat the previous exercise using the technique demonstrated in the above example to improve the performance. Assume that both source and destination strings are word-aligned and the string is a multiple of 16 bytes long.

**Exercise 5.1.3**    Now assume that the source string is word-aligned but the destination string may have any byte alignment. The string is still a multiple of 16 bytes long. Write a program which handles 16 byte blocks at a time, using multiple register transfers for the bulk of the storing but byte stores for the end conditions.

# 6 Architectural Support for High-Level Languages

**Summary of chapter contents**

High-level languages allow a program to be expressed in terms of abstractions such as data types, structures, procedures, functions, and so on. Since the RISC approach represents a movement away from instruction sets that attempt to support these high-level concepts directly, we need to be satisfied that the more primitive RISC instruction set still offers building blocks that can be assembled to give the necessary support.

In this chapter we will look at the requirements that a high-level language imposes on an architecture and see how those requirements may be met. We will use C as the example high-level language (though some might debate its qualification for this role!) and the ARM instruction set as the architecture that the language is compiled onto.

In the course of this analysis, it will become apparent that a RISC architecture such as that of the ARM has a vanilla flavour and leaves a number of important decisions open for the compiler writer to take according to taste. Some of these decisions will affect the ease with which a program can be built up from routines generated from different source languages. Since this is an important issue, there is a defined *ARM Procedure Call Standard* that compiler writers should use to ensure the consistency of entry and exit conditions.

Another area that benefits from agreement across compilers is the support for floating-point operations, which use data types that are not defined in the ARM hardware instruction set.

## 6.1    Abstraction in software design

We have already met a level of abstraction that is important to software design. The essence of an ARM processor is captured in the ARM instruction set which was described in Chapter 5. We shall see in Chapter 9 that there are many ways to implement the ARM architecture, but the whole point of an architecture is to ensure that the programmer need not be concerned with particular implementation details. If a program works correctly on one implementation it should work correctly on them all (with certain provisos).

**Assembly-level abstraction**

A programmer who writes at the assembly programming level works (almost) directly with the raw machine instruction set, expressing the program in terms of instructions, addresses, registers, bytes and words.

A good programmer, faced with a non-trivial task, will begin by determining higher levels of abstraction that simplify the program design; for instance a graphics program may do a lot of line drawing, so a subroutine that will draw a line given the end coordinates will be useful. The rest of the program can then work just in terms of these end coordinates.

Abstraction is important, then, at the assembly programming level, but all the responsibility for supporting the abstraction and expressing it in terms of the machine primitives rests with the programmer, who must therefore have a good understanding of those primitives and be prepared to return frequently to think at the level of the machine.

**High-level languages**

A high-level language allows the programmer to think in terms of abstractions that are above the machine level; indeed, the programmer may not even know on which machine the program will ultimately run. Parameters such as the number of registers vary from architecture to architecture, so clearly these must not be reflected in the design of the language.

The job of supporting the abstractions used in the high-level language on the target architecture falls upon the *compiler*. Compilers are themselves extremely complex pieces of software, and the efficiency of the code they produce depends to a considerable extent on the support that the target architecture offers them to do their job.

At one time, the conventional wisdom was that the best way to support a compiler was to raise the complexity of the instruction set to implement the high-level operations of the language directly. The introduction of the RISC philosophy reversed that approach, focusing instruction set design on flexible primitive operations from which the compiler can build its high-level operations.

This chapter describes the requirements of high-level languages and shows how they are met by the ARM architecture, which is based on this RISC philosophy.

## 6.2 Data types

It is possible, though not very convenient, to express any computer program in terms of the basic Boolean logic variables 'true' (1) and 'false' (0). We can see that this is possible, since at the gate level that is all that the hardware can handle.

The definition of the ARM instruction set already introduces an abstraction away from logic variables when it expresses the functions of the processor in terms of instructions, bytes, words, addresses, and so on. Each of these terms describes a collection of logic variables viewed in a particular way. Note, for example, that an instruction, a data word and an address are all 32 bits long and a 32-bit memory location which contains one of these is indistinguishable from one that contains another of a different type. The difference is not in the way the information is stored but in the way it is used. A computer data type can therefore be characterized by:

- The number of bits it requires.

- The ordering of those bits.

- The uses to which the group of bits is put.

Some data types, such as addresses and instructions, exist principally to serve the purposes of the computer, whereas others exist to represent information in a way that is accessible to human users. The most basic of the latter category, in the context of computation, is the number.

**Numbers**

What started as a simple concept, presumably as a means of checking that no sheep had been stolen overnight, has evolved over the ages into a very complex mechanism capable of computing the behaviour of transistors a thousandth of a millimetre wide switching a hundred million times a second.

**Roman numerals**

Here is a number written by a human:

MCMXCV

**Decimal numbers**

The interpretation of this **Roman** numeral is complex; the value of a symbol depends on the symbol and its positional relationship to its neighbours. This way of writing a number has largely (but not entirely; see the page numbers in the front matter of this book) been replaced by the **decimal** scheme where the same number appears as:

1995

Here we understand that the right-hand digit represents the number of units, the digit to its left the number of tens, then hundreds, thousands, and so on. Each time we move left one place the value of the digit is increased by a factor of 10.

**Binary coded decimal**

To represent such a number as a group of Boolean variables, the simplest thing appears to be to find a representation for each digit and then use four of these to represent the whole number. We need four Boolean variables to be able to represent each digit from 0 to 9 differently, so the first form of this number that could easily be handled by logic gates is:

0001 1001 1001 0101

This is the binary coded decimal scheme which is supported by some computers and is commonly used in pocket calculators.

**Binary notation**

Most computers, most of the time, abandon the human-oriented decimal scheme altogether in favour of a pure binary notation where the same number becomes:

11111001011

Here the right-hand digit represents units, the next one 2, then 4, and so on. Each time we move left one place the value of the digit doubles. Since a value of 2 in one column can be represented by a value of 1 in the next column left, we never need a digit to have any value other than 0 or 1, and hence each binary digit (**bit**) can be represented by a single Boolean variable.

**Hexadecimal notation**

Although machines use binary numbers extensively internally, a typical 32-bit binary number is fairly unmemorable, but rather than convert it to the familiar decimal form (which is quite hard work and error-prone), computer users often describe the number in **hexadecimal** (base 16) notation. This is easy because the binary number can be split into groups of four binary digits and each group replaced by a hexadecimal number. Because, in base 16, we need symbols for numbers from 0 to 15, the early letters of the alphabet have been pressed into service where the decimal symbols run out: we use 0 to 9 as themselves and A to F to represent 10 to 15. Our number becomes:

7CB

(At one time it was common to use octal, base 8, notation in a similar role. This avoids the need to use alphabetic characters, but groups of three bits are less convenient to work with than groups of four, so the use of octal has largely been abandoned.)

**Number ranges**

When writing on paper, we use the number of decimal digits that are required to represent the number we want to write. A computer usually reserves a fixed number of bits for a number, so if the number gets too big it cannot be represented. The ARM deals efficiently with 32-bit quantities, so the first data type that the architecture supports is the 32-bit (unsigned) integer, which has a value in the range:

$$0 \text{ to } 4\,294\,976\,295_{10} = 0 \text{ to } FFFFFFFF_{16}$$

(The subscript indicates the number base, so the range above is expressed in decimal first and in hexadecimal second. Note how the hexadecimal value 'F' represents a binary number of all '1's.)

This looks like a large range, and indeed is adequate for most purposes, though the programmer must be aware of its limitations. Adding two unsigned numbers near the maximum value within the range will give the wrong answer, since the correct answer cannot be represented within 32 bits. The C flag in the program status register gives the only indication that something has gone wrong and the answer is not to be trusted.

If a large number is subtracted from a small number, the result will be negative and cannot be represented by an unsigned integer of any size.

**Signed integers**

In many cases it is useful to be able to represent negative numbers as well as positive ones. Here the ARM supports a 2's complement binary notation where the value of the top bit is made negative; in a 32-bit signed integer all the bits have the same value as they have in the unsigned case apart from bit 31, which has the value $-2^{31}$ instead of $+2^{31}$. Now the range of numbers is:

$$-2\ 147\ 488\ 148_{10} \text{ to } +2\ 147\ 488\ 147_{10} = 80000000_{16} \text{ to } 7FFFFFFF_{16}$$

Note that the sign of the number is determined by bit 31 alone, and the positive integer values have exactly the same representation as their unsigned equivalents.

The ARM, in common with most processors, uses the 2's complement notation for signed integers because adding or subtracting them requires exactly the same Boolean logic functions as are needed for unsigned integers, so there is no need to have separate instructions (the exception being multiplication with a full 64-bit result; here ARM *does* have separate signed and unsigned instructions).

The 'architectural support' for signed integers is the V flag in the program status registers which has no use when the operands are unsigned but indicates an **overflow** (out of range) error when signed operands are combined. The source operands cannot be out of range since they are represented as 32-bit values, but when two numbers near the extremes of the range are added or subtracted, the result could fall outside the range; its 32-bit representation will be an in-range number of the wrong value and sign.

**Other number sizes**

The natural representation of a number in the ARM is as a signed or unsigned 32-bit integer; indeed, internally to the processor that is all that there is. However, all ARM processors will perform unsigned 8-bit (byte) loads and stores, allowing small positive numbers to occupy a smaller space in memory than a 32-bit word, and some versions of the processor also support signed byte and signed and unsigned 16-bit transfers, also principally to reduce the memory required to store small values.

Where a 32-bit integer is too small, larger numbers can be handled using multiple words and multiple registers. A 64-bit addition can be performed with two 32-bit additions, using the C flag in the status register to propagate the carry from the lower word to the higher word:

```
; 64-bit addition of [r1,r0] to [r3,r2]
ADDS    r2, r2, r0        ; add low, save carry
ADC     r3, r3, r1        ; add high with carry
```

**Real
numbers**

So far we have just considered integers, or whole numbers. 'Real' numbers are used to represent fractions and transcendental values that are useful when dealing with physical quantities.

The representation of real numbers in computers is a big issue that is deferred to the next section. An ARM core has no support for real data types, though ARM Limited has defined a set of types and instructions that operate on them. These instructions are either executed on a floating-point coprocessor or emulated in software.

**Printable
characters**

After the number, the next most basic data type is the printable character. To control a standard printer we need a way to represent all the normal characters such as the upper and lower case alphabet, decimal digits from 0 to 9, punctuation marks and a number of special characters such as £, $, %, and so on.

**ASCII**

Counting all these different characters, the total rapidly approaches a hundred or so. Some time ago the binary representation of these characters was standardized in the 7-bit ASCII (American Standard for Computer Information Interchange) code, which includes these printable characters and a number of control codes whose names reflect the teletype origins of the code, such as 'carriage return', 'line feed', and 'bell'.

The normal way to store an ASCII character in a computer is to put the 7-bit binary code into an 8-bit byte. Many systems extend the code using, for example, the 8-bit ISO character set where the other 128 binary codes within the byte represent special characters (for instance, characters with accents). The most flexible way to represent characters is the 16-bit 'Unicode' which incorporates many such 8-bit character sets within a single encoding.

'1995' encoded as 8-bit printable characters is:

$$00110001\ 00111001\ 00111001\ 00110101 = 31\ 39\ 39\ 35_{16}$$

**ARM
support for
characters**

The support in the ARM architecture for handling characters is the unsigned byte load and store instructions; these have already been mentioned as being available to support small unsigned integers, but that role is rare compared with their frequency of use for transferring ASCII characters.

There is nothing in the ARM architecture that reflects the particular codes defined by ASCII; any other encoding is equally well supported provided it uses no more than eight bits. However, it would be perverse these days to choose a different code for characters without having a very good reason.

**Byte ordering**

The above ASCII example highlights an area of some potential difficulty. It is written to be read from left to right, but if it is read as a 32-bit word, the least significant byte is at the right. A character output routine might print characters at successive increasing byte addresses, in which case, with 'little-endian' addressing, it will print '5991'. We clearly need to be careful about the order of bytes within words in memory.

(ARMs can operate with either little- or big-endian addressing. See 'Memory organization' on page 110.)

**High-level languages**

A high-level language defines the data types that it needs in its specification, usually without reference to any particular architecture that it may run on. Sometimes the number of bits used to represent a particular data type is architecture-dependent in order to allow a machine to use its most efficient size.

**ANSI C basic data types**

The dialect of the 'C' language defined by the American National Standards Institute (ANSI), and therefore known as 'ANSI standard C' or simply 'ANSI C', defines the following basic data types:

- Signed and unsigned **characters** of at least eight bits.
- Signed and unsigned **short integers** of at least 16 bits.
- Signed and unsigned **integers** of at least 16 bits.
- Signed and unsigned **long integers** of at least 32 bits.
- **Floating-point, double** and **long double** floating-point numbers.
- **Enumerated** types.
- **Bitfields**.

The ARM C compiler adopts the minimum sizes for each of these types except the standard integer, where it uses 32-bit values since this is the most frequently used data type and the ARM supports 32-bit operations more efficiently than 16-bit operations.

Enumerated types (where variables have one value out of a specified set of possible values) are implemented as the smallest integer type with the necessary range of values. Bitfield types (sets of Boolean variables) are implemented within integers; several may share one integer, with the first declared holding the lowest bit positions, but may not straddle word boundaries.

**ANSI C derived data types**

In addition, the ANSI C standard defines derived data types:

- **Arrays** of several objects of the same type.
- **Functions** which return an object of a given type.
- **Structures** containing a sequence of objects of various types.
- **Pointers** (which are usually machine addresses) to objects of a given type.
- **Unions** which allow objects of different types to occupy the same space at different times.

ARM pointers are 32 bits long (the size of ARM native addresses) and resemble unsigned integers, though note that they obey different arithmetic rules.

The ARM C compiler aligns characters on byte boundaries (that is, at the next available address), short integers at even addresses and all other types on word boundaries. A structure always starts on a word boundary with the first-named component, then subsequent components are packed as closely as possible consistent with these alignment rules. (**Packed** structures violate the alignment rules; use of memory is discussed more extensively in Section 6.9 on page 191.)

**ARM architectural support for C data types**

We have seen above that the ARM integer core provides native support for signed and unsigned 32-bit integers and for unsigned bytes, covering the C integer (given the decision to implement these as 32-bit values), long integer and unsigned character types. Pointers are implemented as native ARM addresses and are therefore supported directly.

The ARM addressing modes provide reasonable support for arrays and structures: base plus scaled index addressing allows an array of objects of a size which is $2^n$ bytes to be scanned using a pointer to the start of the array and a loop variable as the index; base plus immediate offset addressing gives access to an object within a structure. However additional address calculation instructions will be necessary for more complex accesses.

Versions of the ARM that include signed byte and signed and unsigned 16-bit loads and stores can also be considered to provide native support for short integer and signed character types.

Floating-point types are discussed in the next section, however here we can note that the basic ARM core offers little direct support for them. These types (and the instructions that manipulate them) are, in the absence of specific floating-point support hardware, handled by complex software emulation routines.

## 6.3    Floating-point data types

Floating-point numbers attempt to represent real numbers with uniform accuracy. A generic way to represent a real number is in the form:

$$R = a \times b^n$$                                                    Equation 11

where $n$ is chosen so that $a$ falls within a defined range of values; $b$ is usually implicit in the data type and is often equal to 2.

**IEEE 754**

There are many complex issues to resolve with the handling of floating-point numbers in computers to ensure that the results are consistent when the same program is run on different machines. The consistency problem was greatly aided by the introduction in 1985 of the IEEE Standard for Binary Floating-Point Arithmetic (ANSI/IEEE Standard 754-1985, sometimes referred to simply as IEEE 754) which defines in considerable detail how floating-point numbers should be represented, the accuracy with which calculations should be performed, how errors should be detected and returned, and so on.

The most compact representation of a floating-point number defined by IEEE 754 is the 32-bit 'single precision' format:

**Single precision**

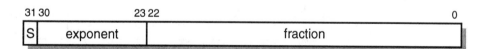

**Figure 6.1**    IEEE 754 single precision floating-point number format.

The number is made up from a **sign bit** ('S'), an **exponent** which is an unsigned integer value with a 'bias' of +127 (for normalized numbers) and a **fractional** component. A number of terms in the previous sentence may be unfamiliar. To explain them, let us look at how a number we recognize, '1995', is converted into this format.

We start from the binary representation of 1995, which has already been presented:

11111001011

This is a positive number, so the S bit will be zero.

**Normalized numbers**

The first step is to **normalize** the number, which means convert it into the form shown in Equation 11 on page 167 where $1 \leq a < 2$ and $b = 2$. Looking at the binary form of the number, $a$ can be constrained within this range by inserting a 'binary point' (similar in interpretation to the more familiar decimal point) after the first '1'. The implicit position of the binary point in the binary integer representation is to the right of the right-most digit, so here we have to move it left ten places. Hence the normalized representation of 1995 is:

$$1995 = 1.1111001011 \times 2^{1010} \qquad \text{Equation 12}$$

where $a$ and $n$ are both in binary notation.

When any number is normalized, the bit in front of the binary point in $a$ will be a '1' (otherwise the number is not normalized). Therefore there is no need to store this bit.

**Exponent bias**

Finally, since the format is required to represent very small numbers as well as very large ones, some numbers may require negative exponents in their normalized form. Rather than use a signed exponent, the standard specifies a 'bias'. This bias (+127 for single precision normalized numbers) is added to the exponent value. Hence 1995 is represented as:

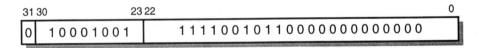

**Figure 6.2**    IEEE 754 single precision representation of '1995'.

The exponent is 127+10 = 137; the fraction is zero-extended to the right to fill the 23-bit field.

**Normalized value**

In general, the value of a 32-bit normalized number is given by:

$$\text{value (norm)} = (-1)^{S} \times 1.\text{fraction} \times 2^{(\text{exponent} - 127)} \qquad \text{Equation 13}$$

Although this format represents a wide range of values efficiently, it has one rather glaring problem: there is no way to represent zero. Therefore the IEEE 754 standard reserves numbers where the exponent is either zero or 255 to represent special values:

- Zero is represented by a zero exponent and fraction (but either sign value, so positive and negative zeros can be represented).

- Plus or minus infinity are represented by the maximum exponent value with a zero fraction and the appropriate sign bit.

- NaN (**Not a Number**) is indicated by the maximum exponent and a non-zero fraction; 'quiet' NaNs have a '1' in the most significant fraction bit position and 'signalling' NaNs have a '0' in that bit (but a '1' somewhere else, otherwise they look like infinity).

- **Denormalized** numbers, which are numbers that are just too small to normalize within this format, have a zero exponent, a non-zero fraction and a value given by:

$$\text{value (denorm)} = (-1)^{S} \times 0.\text{fraction} \times 2^{(-126)} \qquad \text{Equation 14}$$

The 'NaN' format is used to represent the results of invalid floating-point operations, such as taking the logarithm of a negative number, and prevents a series of operations from producing an apparently valid result when an intermediate error condition was not checked.

**Double precision**

For many purposes the accuracy offered by the single precision format is inadequate. Greater accuracy may be achieved by using the double precision format which uses 64 bits to store each floating-point value.

The interpretation is similar to that for single precision values, but now the exponent bias for normalized numbers is +1023:

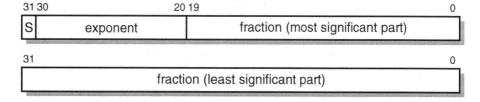

**Figure 6.3** IEEE 754 double precision floating-point number format.

**Double
extended
precision**

Even greater accuracy is available from the double extended precision format, which uses 80 bits of information spread across three words. The exponent bias is 16383, and the J bit is the bit to the left of the binary point (and is a '1' for all normalized numbers):

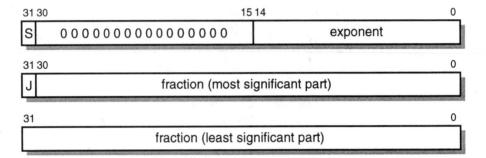

**Figure 6.4**    IEEE 754 double extended precision floating-point number format.

**Packed
decimal**

In addition to the binary floating-point representations detailed above, the IEEE 754 standard also specifies packed decimal formats. Referring back to Equation 11 on page 167, in these packed formats $b$ is 10 and $a$ and $n$ are stored in a binary coded decimal format as described in 'Binary coded decimal' on page 162. The number is normalized so that $1 \le a < 10$. The packed decimal format is shown below:

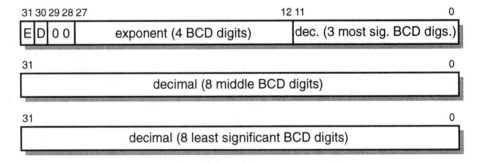

**Figure 6.5**    IEEE 754 packed decimal floating-point number format.

The sign of the exponent is held in bit 31 of the first word ('E') and the sign of the decimal in bit 30 ('D'). The value of the number is:

$$\text{value (packed)} = (-1)^{D} \times \text{decimal} \times 10^{((-1)^{E} \times \text{exponent})} \qquad \text{Equation 15}$$

**Extended packed decimal**

The extended packed decimal format occupies four words to give higher precision. The value is still as given by Equation 15 above and the format is:

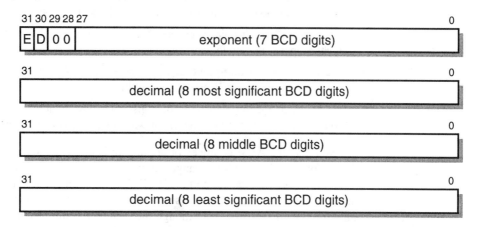

**Figure 6.6** IEEE 754 extended packed decimal floating-point number format.

**ARM floating-point instructions**

Although there is no direct support for any of these floating-point data types in a standard ARM integer core, ARM Limited has defined a set of floating point instructions within the coprocessor instruction space. These instructions are normally implemented entirely in software through the undefined instruction trap (which collects any coprocessor instructions that are not accepted by a hardware coprocessor), but a subset may be handled in hardware by the FPA10 floating-point coprocessor.

**ARM floating-point library**

As an alternative to the ARM floating-point instruction set (and the only option for Thumb code), ARM Limited also supplies a C floating-point library which supports IEEE single and double precision formats. The C compiler has a flag to select this route which produces code that is both faster (by avoiding the need to intercept, decode and emulate the floating-point instructions) and more compact (since only the functions which are used need be included in the image) than software emulation.

## 6.4   The ARM floating-point architecture

Where full floating-point support is required, the ARM floating-point architecture provides extensive support for the data types described in the previous section either entirely in software or using a combined software/hardware solution based around the FPA10 floating-point accelerator.

The ARM floating-point architecture presents:

- An interpretation of the coprocessor instruction set when the coprocessor number is 1 or 2. (The floating-point system uses two logical coprocessor numbers.)

- Eight 80-bit floating-point registers in coprocessors 1 and 2 (the same physical registers appear in both logical coprocessors).

- A user-visible floating-point status register (FPSR) which controls various operating options and indicates error conditions.

- Optionally, a floating-point control register (FPCR) which is user-invisible and should be used only by the support software specific to the hardware accelerator.

Note that the ARM coprocessor architecture allows the floating-point emulator (FPE) software to be used interchangeably with the combination of the FPA10 and the floating-point accelerator support code (FPASC), or any other hardware-software combination that supports the same set of instructions. Application binaries will work with either support environment, though the compiler optimization strategy is different (the FPE software works best with grouped floating-point instructions whereas the FPA10/FPASC works best with distributed instructions).

**FPA10 data types**

The ARM FPA10 hardware floating-point accelerator supports single, double and extended double precision formats. Packed decimal formats are supported only by software.

The coprocessor registers are all extended double precision, and all internal calculations are carried out in this, the highest precision format, except that there are faster versions of some instructions which do not produce the full 80-bit accuracy. However loads and stores between memory and these registers can convert the precision as required.

This is similar to the treatment of integers in the ARM integer architecture, where all internal operations are on 32-bit quantities, but memory transfers can specify bytes and, in some cases, half-words.

**Load and store floating instructions**

Since there are only eight floating-point registers, the register specifier field in the coprocessor data transfer instruction (shown in Figure 5.15 on page 143) has a spare bit which is used here as an additional data size specifier:

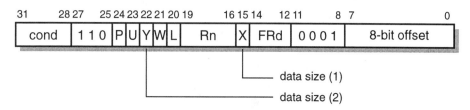

**Figure 6.7**   Load and store floating binary encoding.

The other fields in this format are described in Section 5.17 on page 143. The X and Y bits allow one of four precisions to be specified, choosing between single, double, double extended and packed decimal. (The choice between packed decimal and extended packed decimal is controlled by a bit in the FPSR.)

**Load and store multiple floating**

The load and store multiple floating-point registers instructions are used to save and restore the floating-point register state. Each register is saved using three memory words, and the precise format is not defined; it is intended that the only use for the saved values will be to reload them using the equivalent load multiple floating instruction to restore the context. 'FRd' specifies the first register to be transferred, and 'X' and 'Y' encode the number of registers transferred which can be from one to four. Note that these instructions use coprocessor number 2, whereas the other floating-point instructions use coprocessor number 1.

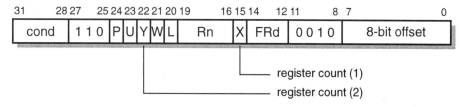

**Figure 6.8**   Load and store multiple floating binary encoding.

**Floating-point data operations**

The floating-point data operations perform arithmetic functions on values in the floating-point registers; their only interaction with the outside world is to confirm that they should complete through the ARM coprocessor handshake. (Indeed, a floating-point coprocessor may begin executing one of these instructions before the handshake begins so long as it waits for confirmation from the ARM before committing a state change.)

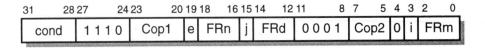

**Figure 6.9**   Floating-point data processing binary encoding.

The instruction format has a number of opcode bits, augmented by extra bits from each of the three register specifier fields since only three bits are required to specify one of the eight floating-point registers:

- 'i' selects between a register ('FRm') or one of eight constants for the second operand.
- 'e' and 'Cop2' control the destination size and the rounding mode.
- 'j' selects between monadic (single operand) and dyadic (two operand) operations.

The instructions include simple arithmetic operations (add, subtract, multiply, divide, remainder, power), transcendental functions (log, exponential, sin, cos, tan, arcsin, arccos, arctan) and assorted others (square root, move, absolute value, round).

**Floating-point register transfers**

The register transfer instructions accept a value from or return a value to an ARM register. This is generally combined with a floating-point processing function.

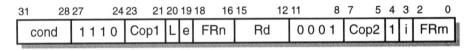

**Figure 6.10**   Floating-point register transfer binary encoding.

Transfers from ARM to the floating-point unit include 'float' (convert an integer in an ARM register to a real in a floating-point register) and writes to the floating-point status and control registers; going the other way there is 'fix' (convert a real in a floating-point register to an integer in an ARM register) and reads of the status and control registers.

The floating-point compare instructions are special cases of this instruction type, where Rd is r15. Two floating-registers are compared and the result of the comparison is returned to the N, Z, C and V flags in the ARM CPSR where they can directly control the execution of conditional instructions:

- N indicates 'less than'.

- Z indicates equality.

- C and V indicate more complex conditions, including 'unordered' comparison results which can arise when an operand is a 'NaN' (not a number).

**Floating-point instruction frequencies**

The design of the FPA10 is guided by the typical frequencies of the various floating-point instructions. These were measured running compiled programs using the floating-point emulator software and are summarized in Table 6.1.

The statistics are dominated by the number of load and store operations that take place. As a result, the FPA10 has been designed to allow these to operate concurrently with internal arithmetic operations.

**Table 6.1**  Floating-point instruction frequencies.

| Instruction | Frequency |
|-------------|-----------|
| Load/store | 67% |
| Add | 13% |
| Multiply | 10.5% |
| Compare | 3% |
| Fix and float | 2% |
| Divide | 1.5% |
| Others | 3% |

**FPA10**
**organization**

The internal organization of the FPA10 is illustrated in Figure 6.11. Its external inter-face is to the ARM data bus and the coprocessor hand-shake signals, so it has a modest pin-count requirement. The major components are:

- The coprocessor pipeline follower (see Section 4.4 on page 101).

- The load/store unit that carries out format conversion on floating-point data types as they are loaded from and stored to memory.

- The register bank which stores eight 80-bit extended precision floating-point operands.

- The arithmetic unit which incorporates an adder, a multiplier and a divider, together with rounding and normalizing hardware.

The load/store unit operates concurrently with the arithmetic unit, enabling new operands to be loaded from memory while previously loaded operands are being proc-essed. Hardware interlocks protect against data hazards.

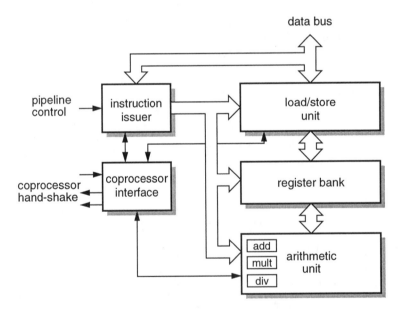

**Figure 6.11**   FPA10 internal organization.

**FPA10 pipeline**

The FPA10 arithmetic unit operates in four pipeline stages:

1. Prepare: align operands.
2. Calculate: add, multiply or divide.
3. Align: normalize the result.
4. Round: apply appropriate rounding to the result.

A floating-point operation can begin as soon as it is detected in the instruction pipeline (that is, before the ARM hand-shake has occurred), but the result write-back must await the hand-shake.

**Floating-point context switches**

The FPA registers represent additional process state which must be saved and restored across context switches. However, typically only a small number of active processes use floating-point instructions. Therefore saving and restoring the FPA registers on every switch is an unnecessary overhead. Instead, the software minimizes the number of saves and restores by the following algorithm:

- When a process using the FPA is switched out, the FPA registers are not saved but the FPA is turned off.
- If a subsequent process executes a floating-point instruction this will trap; the trap code will save the FPA state and enable the FPA.

Thus the FPA state saving and restoring overhead is only incurred for processes which use the FPA; in a typical system with only one process using the FPA, the overhead is avoided altogether.

**Summary of FPA10 features**

The design of the FPA10 reflects a careful choice of hardware functions based on an analysis of the typical frequencies of various floating-point functions. The ARM coprocessor architecture allows a flexible combination of hardware and software functions, giving the designer a free choice of which operations to implement in hardware. The FPA10 implements the most important functions in hardware but falls back on support software for rarer and more complex functions. Its main features are:

- IEEE 754 floating-point standard compliance.
- Support for 32-, 64- and 80-bit binary floating-point data types, with packed decimal types supported by software.
- Low power consumption (250 mW at 5 V, 4 MFLOPS).
- Concurrent load/store and arithmetic activity.
- Small die size: 134k transistors, 67 mm$^2$ (on 1 μm CMOS).

## 6.5  Expressions

Unsigned arithmetic on an n-bit integer is defined in ANSI C to be modulo $2^n$, so over-flow cannot occur. Therefore the basic ARM integer data processing instructions implement most of the C integer arithmetic, bit-wise and shift primitives directly. Exceptions are division and remainder which require several ARM instructions.

**Register use**    Since all data processing instructions operate only on values in register, the key to the efficient evaluation of a complex expression is to get the required values into the registers in the right order and to ensure that frequently used values are normally resident in registers. There is clearly a trade-off between the number of values that can be held in registers and the number of registers remaining for intermediate results during expression evaluation (remembering that registers are also needed to hold the addresses of operands that must be fetched from memory). Optimizing this trade-off is a major task for the compiler, as is sorting out the right order to load and combine operands to achieve the result prescribed by the operator precedence defined in the language.

**ARM**
**support**    The 3-address instruction format used by the ARM gives the compiler the maximum flexibility in how it preserves or re-uses registers during expression evaluation.

Thumb instructions are generally 2-address, which restricts the compiler's freedom to some extent, and the smaller number of general registers also makes its job harder (and will result in less efficient code).

**Accessing**
**operands**    A procedure will normally work with operands that are presented in one of the following ways, and can be accessed as indicated:

1. As an argument passed through a register.

   The value is already in a register, so no further work is necessary.

2. As an argument passed on the stack.

   Stack pointer (r13) relative addressing with an immediate offset known at compile-time allows the operand to be collected with a single LDR.

3. As a constant in the procedure's literal pool.

   PC-relative addressing, again with an immediate offset known at compile-time, gives access with a single LDR.

4. As a local variable.

   Local variables are allocated space on the stack and are accessed by a stack pointer relative LDR.

5. As a global variable.

   Global (and static) variables are allocated space in the static area and are accessed by static base relative addressing. The static base is usually in r9 (see the 'ARM Procedure Call Standard' on page 187).

   If the value that is passed is a pointer, an additional LDR (with an immediate offset) may be required to access an operand within the structure that it points to.

**Pointer arithmetic**

Arithmetic on pointers depends on the size of the data type that the pointers are pointing to. If a pointer is incremented it changes in units of the size of the data item in bytes.

Thus:

```
int *p;
p = p+1;
```

will increase the value of p by 4 bytes. Since the size of a data type is known at compile-time, the compiler can scale constants by an appropriate amount. If a variable is used as an offset it must be scaled at run-time:

```
int i= 4;
p = p + i;
```

If p is held in r0 and i in r1, the change to p may be compiled as:

```
ADD     r0, r0, r1, LSL #2 ; scale r1 to int
```

Where the data type is a structure with a size which is not a power of 2 bytes, a multiplication by a small constant is required. The shift and add instructions can usually produce the desired product in a small number of operations, using a temporary register where necessary.

**Arrays**

Arrays in C are little more than a shorthand notation for pointer operations, so the above comments apply here too. The declaration:

```
int a[10];
```

establishes a name, a, for the array which is just a pointer to the first element, and a reference to a[i] is equivalent to the pointer-plus-offset form *(a+i); the two may be used interchangeably.

## 6.6  Conditional statements

Conditional statements are executed if the Boolean result of a test is true (or false); in C these include if...else statements and switches (C 'case' statements).

**if...else**     The ARM architecture offers unusually efficient support for conditional expressions when the conditionally executed statement is small.

For example, here is a C statement to find the maximum of two integers:

```
if (a>b) c=a; else c=b;
```

If the variables a, b and c are in registers r0, r1 and r2, the compiled code could be as simple as:

```
CMP     r0, r1              ; if (a>b)...
MOVGT   r2, r0              ; ..c=a..
MOVLE   r2, r1              ; ...else c=b
```

(In this particular case the C compiler can produce a rather more obvious sequence:

```
MOV     r2, r0              ; c=a
CMP     r0, r1              ; if (a>b)...
MOVLE   r2, r1              ; ...c=b
```

However, this doesn't scale well to more complex 'if' statements so we will ignore it in this general discussion.)

The 'if' and 'else' sequences may be a few instructions long with the same condition on each instruction (provided none of the conditionally executed instructions changes the condition codes), but beyond two or three instructions it is generally better to fall back on the more conventional solution:

```
        CMP     r0, r1              ; if (a>b)...
        BLE     ELSE                ; skip clause if false
        MOV     r2, r0              ; ..c=a..
        B       ENDIF               ; skip else clause
ELSE    MOV     r2, r1              ; ...else c=b
ENDIF   ..
```

Here the 'if' and 'else' sequences may be any length and may use the condition codes freely (including, for example, for nested if statements) since they are not required beyond the branch immediately following the compare instruction.

Note, however, that whichever branch is taken, this second code sequence will take approximately twice as long to execute as the first for this simple example.

Branches are expensive on the ARM, so the absence of them from the first sequence makes it very efficient.

**switches** A switch, or case, statement extends the two-way decision of an if...else statement to many ways. The standard C form of a switch statement is:

```
switch (expression) {
    case constant-expression₁: statements₁
    case constant-expression₂: statements₂
    ...
    case constant-expressionₙ: statementsₙ
    default: statementsₒ
}
```

Normally each group of statements ends with a 'break' (or a 'return') to cause the switch statement to terminate, otherwise the C semantics cause execution to fall through to the next group of statements. A switch statement with 'breaks' can always be translated into an equivalent series of if...else statements:

```
temp = expression;
if (temp==constant-expression₁) {statements₁}
else ...
else if (temp==constant-expressionₙ) {statementsₙ}
else {statementsₒ}
```

However this can result in slow code if the switch statement has many cases. An alternative is to use a *jump table*. In its simplest form a jump table contains a target address for each possible value of the switch expression:

```
        ; r0 contains value of expression
        ADR    r1, JUMPTABLE       ; get base of jump table
        CMP    r0, #TABLEMAX       ; check for overrun..
        LDRLS  pc, [r1,r0,LSL #2] ;  .. if OK get pc
        ; statementsₒ              ;  .. otherwise default
        B      EXIT                ; break
L1      ..     ; statements₁
        B      EXIT                ; break
        ..
LN      ..     ; statementsₙ
EXIT    ..
```

Clearly it is not possible for the jump table to contain an address for every possible value of a 32-bit integer, and equally clearly it is vital that the jump table look-up does not fall past the end of the table, so some checking is necessary.

Another way of compiling a switch statement is illustrated by a procedure in the 'Dhrystone' benchmark program which ends (effectively) as follows:

```
switch (a) {
    case 0: *b = 0; break;
    case 1: if (c>100) *b = 0; else *b = 3; break;
    case 2: *b = 1; break
    case 3: break;
    case 4: *b = 2; break;
} /* end of switch */
} /* end of procedure */
```

The code which is generated highlights a number of aspects of the ARM instruction set. The switch statement is implemented by adding the value of the expression (in v2; the register naming convention follows the ARM Procedure Call Standard which will be described in Section 6.8 on page 187) to the PC after scaling it to a word offset. The overrun case falls through the add instruction into the slot left free by the PC offset. Any cases which require a single instruction (such as case 3), and the last case whatever its length, can be completed in line; others require a branch. This example also illustrates an if...then...else implemented using condition instructions.

```
                ; on entry a1 = 0, a2 = 3, v2 = switch expression
        CMP     v2,#4                   ; check value for overrun..
        ADDLS   pc,pc,v2,LSL #2     ;   .. if OK, add to pc (+8)
        LDMDB   fp,{v1,v2,fp,sp,pc} ;   .. if not OK, return
        B       L0                      ; case 0
        B       L1                      ; case 1
        B       L2                      ; case 2
        LDMDB   fp,{v1,v2,fp,sp,pc} ; case 3 (return)
        MOV     a1,#2                   ; case 4
        STR     a1,[v1]
        LDMDB   fp,{v1,v2,fp,sp,pc} ; return
L0      STR     a1,[v1]
        LDMDB   fp,{v1,v2,fp,sp,pc} ; return
L1      LDR     a3,c_ADDR               ; get address of c
        LDR     a3,[a3]                 ; get c
        CMP     a3,#&64                 ; c>100?..
        STRLE   a2,[v1]                 ;   .. No:  *b = 3
        STRGT   a1,[v1]                 ;   .. Yes: *b = 0
        LDMDB   fp,{v1,v2,fp,sp,pc} ; return
c_ADDR  DCD     <address of c>
L2      MOV     a1,#1
        STR     a1,[v1]                 ; *b = 1
        LDMDB   fp,{v1,v2,fp,sp,pc} ; return
```

## 6.7  Loops

The C language supports three forms of loop control structure:

- for (e1; e2; e3) {..}
- while (e1) {..}
- do {..} while (e1)

Here e1, e2 and e3 are expressions which evaluate to 'true' or 'false' and {..} is the body of the loop which is executed a number of times determined by the control structure. Often the body of a loop is very simple, which puts the onus on the compiler to minimize the overhead of the control structure. Each loop must have at least one branch instruction, but any more would be wasteful.

**for loops**     A typical 'for' loop uses the control expressions to manage an index:

```
for (i=0; i<10; i++) {a[i] = 0}
```

The first control expression is executed once before the loop begins, the second is tested each time the loop is entered and controls whether the loop is executed, and the third is executed at the end of each pass through the loop to prepare for the next pass. This loop could be compiled as:

```
          MOV     r1, #0               ; value to store in a[i]
          ADR     r2, a[0]             ; r2 points to a[0]
          MOV     r0, #0               ; i=0
LOOP      CMP     r0, #10              ; i<10 ?
          BGE     EXIT                 ; if i >= 10 finish
          STR     r1, [r2,r0,LSL #2]; a[i] = 0
          ADD     r0, r0, #1           ; i++
          B       LOOP
EXIT      ..
```

(This example illustrates the optimization technique of *strength reduction*, which means moving fixed operations outside the loop. The first two instructions are logically inside the loop in the C program, but have been moved outside since they are initializing registers to the same constants each time round the loop.)

This code may be improved by omitting the conditional branch to EXIT and applying the opposite condition to the following instructions, causing the program to fall through rather than branch round them when the terminating condition is met. However, it can be further improved by moving the test to the bottom of the loop (which is possible here since the initialization and test are with constants, so the compiler can be sure that the loop will be executed at least once).

**while loops**     A 'while' loop has a simpler structure and generally controls loops where the number of iterations is not a constant or clearly defined by a variable at run-time. The standard conceptual arrangement of a 'while' loop is as follows:

```
LOOP    ..                  ; evaluate expression
        BEQ     EXIT
        ..                  ; loop body
        B       LOOP
EXIT    ..
```

The two branches appear to be necessary since the code must allow for the case where the body is not executed at all. A little re-ordering produces more efficient code:

```
        B       TEST
LOOP    ..                  ; loop body
TEST    ..                  ; evaluate expression
        BNE     LOOP
EXIT    ..
```

This second code sequence executes the loop body and evaluates the control expression exactly the same way as the original version and has the same code size, but it executes one fewer (untaken) branch per iteration, so the second branch has been removed from the loop overhead. An even more efficient code sequence can be produced by the compiler:

```
        ..                  ; evaluate expression
        BEQ     EXIT        ; skip loop if necessary
LOOP    ..                  ; loop body
TEST    ..                  ; evaluate expression
        BNE     LOOP
EXIT    ..
```

The saving here is that one fewer branch is executed each time the complete 'while' structure is encountered (assuming that the body is executed at least once). This is a modest gain and costs extra instructions, so it is worthwhile only if performance matters much more than code size.

**do..while loops**     The conceptual arrangement of a 'do..while' loop is similar to the improved 'while' loop above, but without the initial branch since the loop body is executed before the test (and is therefore always executed at least once):

```
LOOP    ..                  ; loop body
        ..                  ; evaluate expression
        BNE     LOOP
EXIT    ..
```

## 6.8   Functions and procedures

**Program
design**

Good programming practice requires that large programs are broken down into components that are small enough to be thoroughly tested; a large, monolithic program is too complex to test fully and is likely to have 'bugs' in hidden corners that do not emerge early enough in the program's life to be fixed before the program is shipped to users.

Each small software component should perform a specified operation using a well-defined interface. How it performs this operation should be of no significance to the rest of the program (this is the principle of **abstraction**; see Section 6.1 on page 160).

**Program
hierarchy**

Furthermore, the full program should be designed as a **hierarchy** of components, not simply a flat list.

A typical hierarchy is illustrated in Figure 6.12. The top of the hierarchy is the program called *main*. The remaining hierarchy is fairly informal; lower-level routines may be shared by higher-level routines, calls may skip levels, and the depth may vary across the hierarchy.

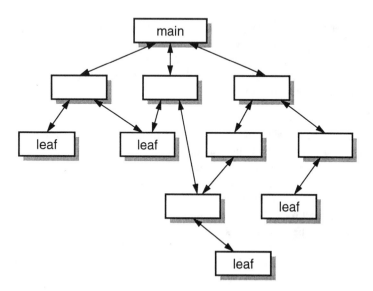

**Figure 6.12**   Typical hierarchical program structure.

**Leaf routines**

At the lowest level of the hierarchy there are **leaf** routines; these are routines which do not themselves call any lower-level routines. In a typical program some of the bottom-level routines will be **library** or **system** functions; these are predefined operations which may or may not be leaf routines (that is, they may or may not have internal structure).

**Terminology**

There are several terms that are used to describe components of this program structure, often imprecisely. We shall attempt to apply terms as follows:

- **Subroutine**: a generic term for a routine that is called by a higher-level routine, particularly when viewing a program at the assembly language level.

- **Function**: a subroutine which returns a value through its name. A typical invocation looks like:

```
c = max (a, b);
```

- **Procedure**: a subroutine which is called to carry out some operation on specified data item(s). A typical invocation looks like:

```
printf ("Hello World\n");
```

**C functions**

Some programming languages make a clear distinction between functions and procedures, but C does not. In C all subroutines are functions, but they can have side-effects in addition to returning a value, and when the returned value is of type 'void' it is effectively suppressed and only the side-effects remain, giving a behaviour which looks just like a procedure.

**Arguments and parameters**

An **argument** is an expression passed to a function call; a value received by the function is a **parameter**. C uses a strict 'call by value' semantics, so a copy is made of each argument when a function is called and, though the function may change the values of its parameters, since these are only copies of the arguments the arguments themselves are not affected.

(A **call by reference** semantics would cause any change to a parameter within a function to be passed back to the calling program, which clearly only makes sense when the argument is a simple variable, but C does not support this.)

The way a C function can change data within the calling program, other than by returning a single value, is when it is passed a pointer to the data as an argument. The function can then use the pointer to access and modify the data structure.

**ARM
Procedure
Call
Standard**

In order to support flexible mixing of routines generated by different compilers and written in assembly language, ARM Limited has defined a set of rules for procedure entry and exit. The ARM Procedure Call Standard (**APCS**) is employed by the ARM C compiler, though this is of significance to the C programmer only when the assembly-level output must be understood in detail.

The APCS imposes a number of conventions on the otherwise 'vanilla' flavour of the ARM architecture:

- It defines particular uses for the 'general-purpose' registers.
- It defines which form of stack is used from the full/empty, ascending/descending choices supported by the ARM instruction set.
- It defines the format of a stack-based data structure used for back-tracing when debugging programs.
- It defines the function argument and result passing mechanism to be used by all externally visible functions and procedures. ('Externally visible' means that the procedure interface is offered outside the current programming module. A function which is used only within the current module may be optimized by deviating from this convention.)
- It supports the ARM shared library mechanism, which means it supports a standard way for shared (re-entrant) code to access static data.

**APCS
register
usage**

The convention for the use of the 16 currently visible ARM registers is summarized in Table 6.2 on page 188. The registers are divided into three sets:

1. Four argument registers which pass values into the function.

   The function need not preserve these so it can use them as scratch registers once it has used or saved its parameter values. Since they will not be preserved across any calls this function makes to other functions, they must be saved across such calls if they contain values that are needed again. Hence, they are **caller-saved** register variables when so used.

2. Five (to seven) register variables which the function must return with unchanged values.

   These are **callee-saved** register variables. This function must save them if it wishes to use the registers, but it can rely on functions it calls not changing them.

3. Seven (to five) registers which have a dedicated role, at least some of the time.

   The link register (lr), for example, carries the return address on function entry, but if it is saved (as it must be if the function calls subfunctions) it may then be used as a scratch register.

**Table 6.2** APCS register use convention.

| Register | APCS name | APCS role |
|---|---|---|
| 0 | a1 | Argument 1 / integer result / scratch register |
| 1 | a2 | Argument 2 / scratch register |
| 2 | a3 | Argument 3 / scratch register |
| 3 | a4 | Argument 4 / scratch register |
| 4 | v1 | Register variable 1 |
| 5 | v2 | Register variable 2 |
| 6 | v3 | Register variable 3 |
| 7 | v4 | Register variable 4 |
| 8 | v5 | Register variable 5 |
| 9 | sb/v6 | Static base / register variable 6 |
| 10 | sl/v7 | Stack limit / register variable 7 |
| 11 | fp | Frame pointer |
| 12 | ip | Scratch reg. / new sb in inter-link-unit calls |
| 13 | sp | Lower end of current stack frame |
| 14 | lr | Link address / scratch register |
| 15 | pc | Program counter |

**APCS variants**

There are several (16) different variants of the APCS which are used to generate code for a range of different systems. They support:

- 32- or 26-bit PCs.

  Older ARM processors operated in a 26-bit address space (see Section 5.21, page 154) and some later versions continue to support this for backwards compatibility reasons.

- Implicit or explicit stack-limit checking.

  Stack overflow must be detected if code is to operate reliably. The compiler can insert instructions to perform explicit checks for overflow.

Where memory management hardware is available, an ARM system can allocate memory to the stack in units of a page. If the next logical page is mapped out, a stack overflow will cause a data abort and be detected. Therefore the memory management unit can perform stack-limit checking and there is no need for the compiler to insert instructions to perform explicit checks.

- Two ways to pass floating-point arguments.

  The ARM floating-point architecture (see Section 6.4 on page 172) specifies a set of eight floating-point registers. The APCS can use these to pass floating-point arguments into functions, and this is the most efficient solution when the system makes extensive use of floating-point variables. If, however, the system makes little or no use of floating-point types (and many ARM systems do not) this approach incurs a small overhead which is avoided by passing floating-point arguments in the integer registers and/or on the stack.

- Re-entrant or non re-entrant code.

  Code specified as re-entrant is position-independent and addresses all data indirectly through the static base register (sb). This code can be placed in a ROM and can be shared by several client processes. Generally, code to be placed in a ROM or a shared library should be re-entrant whereas application code will not be.

**Argument passing**

A C function may have many (or even a variable number of) arguments. The APCS organizes the arguments as follows:

1. If floating-point values are passed through floating-point registers, the first four floating-point arguments are loaded into the first four floating-point registers.

2. All remaining arguments are organized into a list of words; the first four words are loaded into a1 to a4, then the remaining words are pushed onto the stack in reverse order.

   Note that multi-word arguments, including double precision floating-point values, may be passed in integer registers, on the stack, or even split across the registers and the stack.

**Result return**

A simple result (such as an integer) is returned through a1. A more complex result is returned in memory to a location specified by an address which is effectively passed as an additional first argument to the function through a1.

**Function entry and exit**

A simple leaf function which can perform all its functions using only a1 to a4 can be compiled into code with a minimal calling overhead:

```
          BL      leaf1
          ..
leaf1     ..
          MOV     pc, lr  ; return
```

In typical programs somewhere around 50% of all function calls are to leaf functions, and these are often quite simple.

Where registers must be saved, the function must create a stack frame. This can be compiled efficiently using ARM's load and store multiple instructions:

```
          BL      leaf2
          ..
leaf2     STMFD   sp!, {regs, lr}   ; save registers
          ..
          LDMFD   sp!, {regs, pc}   ; restore and return
```

Here the number of registers which are saved and restored will be the minimum required to implement the function. Note the value saved from the link register (lr) is returned directly to the program counter (pc), and therefore lr is available as a scratch register in the body of the function (which it was not in the simple case above).

More complex function entry sequences are used where needed to create stack backtrace data structures, handle floating-point arguments passed in floating-point registers, check for stack overflow, and so on.

**Tail continued functions**

Simple functions that call another function immediately before returning often do not incur any significant call overhead; the compiler will cause the code to return directly from the continuing function. This makes veneer functions (functions that simply re-order arguments, change their type or add an extra argument) particularly efficient.

**ARM efficiency**

Overall the ARM supports functions and procedures efficiently and flexibly. The various flavours of the procedure call standard match different application requirements well, and all result in efficient code. The load and store multiple register instructions are exploited to good effect by the compiler in this context; without them calls to non-leaf functions would be much more costly.

The compiler is also able to make effective optimizations for leaf and tail continued functions, thereby encouraging good programming styles. Programmers can use better structured design when leaf function calls are efficient and can exploit abstraction better when veneer functions are efficient.

## 6.9 Use of memory

An ARM system, like most computer systems, has its memory arranged as a linear set of logical addresses. A C program expects to have access to a fixed area of program memory (where the application image resides) and to memory to support two data areas that grow dynamically and where the compiler often cannot work out a maximum size. These dynamic data areas are:

- The stack.

  Whenever a (non-trivial) function is called, a new activation frame is created on the stack containing a backtrace record, local (non-static) variables, and so on. When a function returns its stack space is automatically recovered and will be reused for the next function call.

- The heap.

  The heap is an area of memory used to satisfy program requests (malloc()) for more memory for new data structures. A program which continues to request memory over a long period of time should be careful to free up *all* sections that are no longer needed, otherwise the heap will grow until memory runs out.

**Address space model**   The normal use of memory is illustrated in Figure 6.13 on page 192. Where an application can use the entire memory space (or where a memory management unit can allow an application to think it has the entire memory space), the application image is loaded into the lowest address, the heap grows upwards from the top of the application and the stack grows downwards from the top of memory. The unused memory between the top of the heap and the bottom of the stack is allocated on demand to the heap or the stack, and if it runs out the program stops due to lack of memory.

In a typical memory managed ARM system the logical space allocated to a single application will be very large, in the range of 1 to 4 Gbytes. The memory management unit will allocate additional pages, on demand, to the heap or the stack, until it runs out of pages to allocate (either due to having allocated all the physical memory pages, or, in a system with virtual memory, due to running out of swap space on the hard disk). This will usually be a long time before the top of the heap meets the bottom of the stack.

In a system with no memory management support the application will be allocated all (if it is the only application to run at the time) or part (if more than one application is to run) of the physical memory address space remaining once the operating system has had its requirements met, and then the application runs out of memory precisely when the top of the heap meets the bottom of the stack.

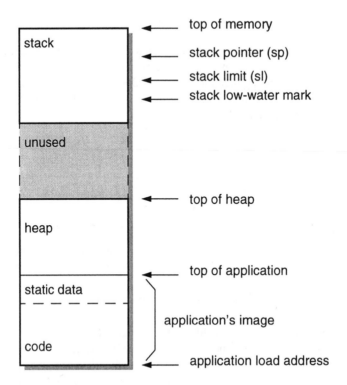

**Figure 6.13**    The standard ARM C program address space model.

**Chunked stack model**

Other address space models are possible, including implementing a 'chunked' stack where the stack is a series of chained chunks within the heap. This causes the application to occupy a single contiguous area of memory, which grows in one direction as required, and may be more convenient where memory is very tight.

**Stack behaviour**

It is important to understand the dynamic behaviour of the stack while a program is running, since it sheds some light on the scoping rules for local variables (which are allocated space on the stack).

Consider this simple program structure:

```
main () {
    ..                      /* t1 */
    func1 ();
    ..                      /* t5 */
```

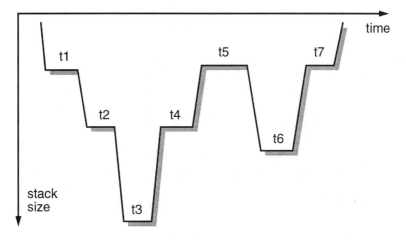

**Figure 6.14**  Example stack behaviour.

```
        func2 ();
        ..                      /* t7 */
} /* end of main */

func1 () {
        ..                      /* t2 */
        func2 ();
        ..                      /* t4 */
} /* end of func1 */

func2 () {
        ..                      /* t3, t6 */
} /* end of func2 */
```

Assuming that the compiler allocates stack space for each function call, the stack behaviour will be as shown in Figure 6.14. At each function call, stack space is allocated for arguments (if they cannot all be passed in registers), to save registers for use within the function, to save the return address and the old stack pointer, and to allocate memory on the stack for local variables.

Note how all the stack space is recovered on function exit and re-used for subsequent calls, and how the two calls to func2 () are allocated different memory areas (at times t3 and t6 in Figure 6.14), so even if the memory used for a local variable in the first call had not been overwritten in an intervening call to another function, the old value cannot be accessed in the second call since its address is not known. Once a procedure has exited, local variable values are lost forever.

**Data storage**    The various data types supported in C require differing amounts of memory to store their binary representations. The basic data types occupy a byte (chars), a half-word (short ints), a word (ints, single precision float) or multiple words (double precision floats). Derived data types (structs, arrays, unions, and so on) are defined in terms of multiple basic data types.

The ARM instruction set, in common with many other RISC processors, is most efficient at loading and storing data items when they are appropriately aligned in memory. A byte access can be made to any byte address with equal efficiency, but storing a word to a non word-aligned address is very inefficient, taking up to seven ARM instructions and requiring temporary work registers.

**Data alignment**    Therefore the ARM C compiler generally aligns data items on appropriate boundaries:

- Bytes are stored at any byte address.
- Half-words are stored at even byte addresses.
- Words are stored on four-byte boundaries.

Where several data items of different types are declared at the same time, the compiler will introduce **padding** where necessary to achieve this alignment:

                  struct S1 {char c; int x; short s;} example1;

This structure will occupy three words of memory as shown in Figure 6.15. (Note that structures are also padded to end on a word boundary.)

Arrays are laid out in memory by repeating the appropriate basic data item, obeying the alignment rules for each item.

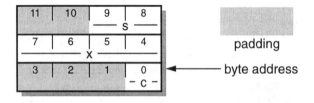

**Figure 6.15**   An example of normal struct memory allocation.

**Memory efficiency**

Given the data alignment rules outlined above, the programmer can help the compiler to minimize memory wastage by organizing structures appropriately. A structure with the same contents as above, but re-ordered as below, occupies only two memory words instead of the original three:

```
struct S2 {char c; short s; int x;} example2;
```

This will result in the memory occupancy illustrated in Figure 6.15. In general, ordering structure elements so that types smaller than a word can be grouped within a word will minimize the amount of padding that the compiler has to insert to maintain efficient alignment.

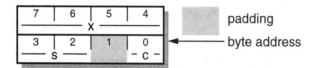

**Figure 6.16**    An example of more efficient struct memory allocation.

**Packed structs**

Sometimes it is necessary to exchange data with other computers that follow different alignment conventions, or to pack data tightly to minimize memory use even though this will reduce performance. For such purposes the ARM C compiler can produce code that works with packed data structures where all the padding is removed:

```
__packed struct S3 {char c; int x; short s;} example3;
```

A packed struct gives precise control of the alignment of all the fields but incurs the overhead of the ARM's relatively inefficient access to non-aligned operands, and therefore should only be used when strictly necessary. The memory occupancy of the packed structure declared above is illustrated in Figure 6.15.

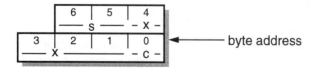

**Figure 6.17**    An example of packed struct memory allocation.

## 6.10   Run-time environment

A C program requires an environment in which to operate; this is usually provided through a library of functions that the C program can call. In a PC or workstation a C programmer can expect to find the full ANSI C library, giving access to a broad range of functions such as file management, input and output (printf()), the real-time clock, and so on.

**Minimal run-time library**

In a small embedded system such as a mobile telephone, most of these functions are irrelevant. ARM Limited supplies a minimal stand-alone run-time library which, once ported to the target environment, allows basic C programs to run. This library therefore reflects the minimal requirements of a C program. It comprises:

- Division and remainder functions.

  Since the ARM instruction set does not include divide instructions, these are implemented as library functions.

- Stack-limit checking functions.

  A minimal embedded system is unlikely to have memory management hardware available for stack overflow detection; therefore these library functions are needed to ensure programs operate safely.

- Stack and heap management.

  All C programs use the stack for (many) function calls, and all but the most trivial create data structures on the heap.

- Program start up.

  Once the stack and heap are initialized, the program starts with a call to main().

- Program termination.

  Most programs terminate by calling _exit(); even a program which runs forever should terminate if an error is detected.

The total size of the code generated for this minimal library is 736 bytes, and it is implemented in a way that allows the linker to omit any unreferenced sections to reduce the library image to around half a kilobyte in many cases. This is a great deal smaller than the full ANSI C library.

## 6.11   Examples and exercises

**Example 6.1**   **Write, compile and run a 'Hello World' program written in C.**

The following program has the required function:

```
/* Hello World in C */
#include <stdio.h>

int main()
{
  printf( "Hello World\n" );
  return( 0 );
}
```

The principal things to note from this example are:

- The '#include' directive which allows this program to use all the standard input and output functions available in C.

- The declaration of the 'main' procedure. Every C program must have exactly one of these as the program is run by calling it.

- The 'printf(..)' statement calls a function provided in stdio which sends output to the standard output device. By default this is the display terminal.

As with the assembly programming exercises, the major challenge is to establish the flow through the tools from editing the text to compiling, linking and running the program. Once this program is working, generating more complex programs is fairly straightforward (at least until the complexity reaches the point where the design of the program becomes a challenge in itself).

Using the ARM software development tools, the above program should be saved as 'HelloW.c'. Then a new project should be created using the Project Manager and this file added (as the only file in the project). A click on the 'Build' button will cause the program to be compiled and linked, then the 'Go' button will run it on the ARMulator, hopefully giving the expected output in the terminal window.

**Exercise 6.1.1**   Generate an assembly listing from the compiler (using the '-s' option) and look at the code which is produced.

**Exercise 6.1.2**   Run the program under the debugger, using single-stepping to observe the progress of the processor through the code.

**Example 6.2**    **Write the number 2001 in 32-bit binary, binary-coded decimal, ASCII and single-precision floating-point notation.**

```
Binary: 2001    = 1024 + 512 + 256 + 128 + 64 + 16 + 1
                = 00000000000000000000011111010001₂
BCD:    2001    = 0010 0000 0000 0001
ASCII:  2001    = 00110010 00110000 00110000 00110001
F-P:    2001    = 1.1111010001 x 2¹⁰¹⁰
                = 01001001 11110100 01000000 00000000
```

where the binary and floating-point values read:
$$= 00000000000000000000011111010001_2$$
$$= 1.1111010001 \times 2^{1010}$$

**Exercise 6.2.1**    Write a C program to convert a date presented in Roman numerals into decimal form.

**Example 6.3**    **Show how the following data is organized in memory:**

```
struct S1 {char c; int x;};
struct S2 {
  char c2[5];
  S1   s1[2];
} example;
```

The first structure statement only declares a type, so no memory is allocated. The second establishes a structure called 'example' comprising an array of five characters followed by an array of two structures of type S1. The structures must start on a word boundary, so the character array will be padded out to fill two words and each structure will also occupy two words. The memory organization is therefore as shown below:

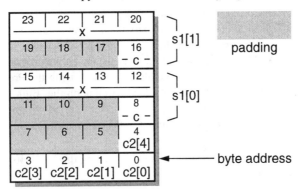

**Exercise 6.3.1**    Show how the same structure would be organized in memory if it were packed.

# 7 The Thumb Instruction Set

**Summary of chapter contents**

The Thumb instruction set addresses the issue of code density. It may be viewed as a compressed form of a subset of the ARM instruction set. Thumb instructions map onto ARM instructions, and the Thumb programmer's model maps onto the ARM programmer's model. Implementations of Thumb use dynamic decompression in an ARM instruction pipeline and then instructions execute as standard ARM instructions within the processor.

Thumb is not a complete architecture; it is not anticipated that a processor would execute Thumb instructions without also supporting the ARM instruction set. Therefore the Thumb instruction set need only support common application functions, allowing  recourse to the full ARM instruction set where necessary (for instance, all exceptions automatically enter ARM mode).

Thumb is fully supported by ARM development tools, and an application can mix ARM and Thumb subroutines flexibly to optimize performance or code density on a routine-by-routine basis.

This chapter covers the Thumb architecture and implementation, and suggests the characteristics of applications that are likely to benefit from using Thumb. In the right application, use of the Thumb instruction set can improve power-efficiency, save cost and enhance performance all at once.

## 7.1   The Thumb bit in the CPSR

ARM processors which support the Thumb instruction set can also execute the standard 32-bit ARM instruction set, and the interpretation of the instruction stream at any particular time is determined by bit 5 of the CPSR, the T bit (see Figure 2.2 on page 42). If T is set the processor interprets the instruction stream as 16-bit Thumb instructions, otherwise it interprets it as standard ARM instructions.

Not all ARM processors are capable of executing Thumb instructions; those that are have a T in their name, such as the ARM7TDMI described in Section 9.2 on page 249.

**Thumb entry**   ARM cores start up, after reset, executing ARM instructions. The normal way they switch to execute Thumb instructions is by executing a Branch and Exchange instruction (BX, see Section 5.5 on page 121). This instruction sets the T bit if the bottom bit of the specified register was set, and switches the program counter to the address given in the remainder of the register. Note that since the instruction causes a branch it flushes the instruction pipeline, removing any ambiguity over the interpretation of any instructions already in the pipeline (they are simply not executed).

Other instructions which change from ARM to Thumb code include exception returns, either using a special form of data processing instruction or a special form of load multiple register instruction (see 'Exception return' on page 114). Both of these instructions are generally used to return to whatever instruction stream was being executed before the exception was entered and are not intended for a deliberate switch to Thumb mode. Like BX, they also change the program counter and therefore flush the instruction pipeline.

**Thumb exit**   An explicit switch back to an ARM instruction stream can be caused by executing a Thumb BX instruction as described in Section 7.3 on page 203.

An implicit return to an ARM instruction stream takes place whenever an exception is taken, since exception entry is always handled in ARM code.

**Thumb systems**   It should be clear from the above that all Thumb systems include some ARM code, if only to handle initialization and exception entry.

It is likely, however, that most Thumb applications will make more than this minimal use of ARM code. A typical embedded system will include a small amount of fast 32-bit memory on the same chip as the ARM core and will execute speed-critical routines (such as digital signal processing algorithms) in ARM code from this memory. The bulk of the code will not be speed critical and may execute from a 16-bit off-chip ROM. This is discussed further at the end of the chapter.

## 7.2   The Thumb programmer's model

The Thumb instruction set is a subset of the ARM instruction set and the instructions
operate on a restricted view of the ARM registers. The programmer's model is illustrated in Figure 7.1. The instruction set gives full access to the eight 'Lo' general purpose registers r0 to r7, and makes extensive use of r13 to r15 for special purposes:

- r13 is used as a stack pointer.
- r14 is used as the link register.
- r15 is the program counter (PC).

These uses follow very closely the way these registers are used by the ARM
instruction set, though the use of r13 as a stack pointer in ARM code is purely a software convention, whereas in Thumb code it is somewhat hard-wired. The remaining
registers (r8 to r12 and the CPSR) have only restricted access:

- A few instructions allow the 'Hi' registers (r8 to r15) to be specified.
- The CPSR condition code flags are set by arithmetic and logical operations and
  control conditional branching.

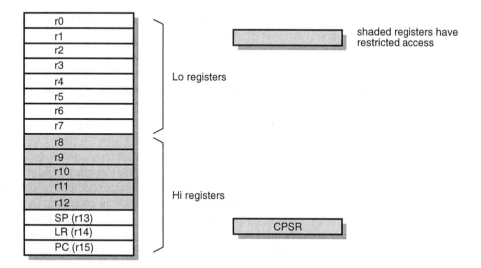

**Figure 7.1**   Thumb accessible registers.

| **Thumb-ARM similarities** | All Thumb instructions are 16 bits long. They map onto ARM instructions so they inherit many properties of the ARM instruction set: |

- The load-store architecture with data processing, data transfer and control flow instructions.

- Support for 8-bit byte, 16-bit half-word and 32-bit word data types where half-words are aligned on 2-byte boundaries and words are aligned on 4-byte boundaries.

- A 32-bit unsegmented memory.

| **Thumb-ARM differences** | However, in order to achieve a 16-bit instruction length a number of characteristic features of the ARM instruction set have been abandoned: |

- Most Thumb instructions are executed unconditionally.

  (*All* ARM instructions are executed conditionally.)

- Many Thumb data processing instructions use a 2-address format (the destination register is the same as one of the source registers).

  (ARM data processing instructions, with the exception of the 64-bit multiplies, use a 3-address format.)

- Thumb instruction formats are less regular than ARM instruction formats, as a result of the dense encoding.

| **Thumb exceptions** | All exceptions return the processor to ARM execution and are handled within the ARM programmer's model. Since the T bit resides in the CPSR, it is saved on exception entry in the appropriate SPSR, and the same return from exception instruction will restore the state of the processor and leave it executing ARM or Thumb instructions according to the state when the exception arose. |

Note that the ARM exception return instructions, described in 'Exception return' on page 114, involve return address adjustments to compensate for the ARM pipeline behaviour. Since Thumb instructions are two bytes rather than four bytes long, the natural offset should be different when an exception is entered from Thumb execution, since the PC value copied into the exception-mode link register will have incremented by a multiple of two rather than four bytes. However the Thumb architecture requires that the link register value be automatically adjusted to match the ARM return offset, allowing the same return instruction to work in both cases, rather than have the return sequence made more complex.

## 7.3 Thumb branch instructions

These control flow instructions include the various forms of PC-relative branch and branch-and-link instruction seen in the ARM instructions set, and the branch-and-exchange instruction for switching between the ARM and Thumb instruction sets.

The ARM instructions have a large (24-bit) offset field which clearly will not fit in a 16-bit instruction format. Therefore the Thumb instruction set includes various ways of subsetting the functionality.

**Binary encodings**

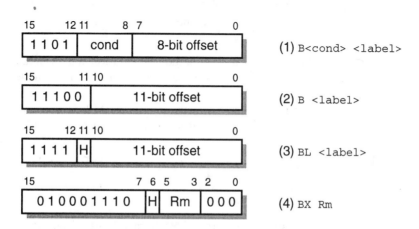

**Figure 7.2** Thumb branch instruction binary encodings.

**Description**

Typical uses of branch instructions include:

1. Short conditional branches to control (for example) loop exit.

2. Medium-range unconditional branches to 'goto' sections of code.

3. Long-range subroutine calls.

ARM handles all these with the same instruction, typically wasting many bits of the 24-bit offset in the first two cases. Thumb has to be more efficient, using different formats for each of these cases, numbered respectively in Figure 7.2.

The first two formats show how the condition field is traded-off against the offset length. The condition field in the first format is the same as that in all ARM instructions (see Section 5.3 on page 117); in both cases the offset is shifted left one bit (to give half-word alignment) and sign-extended to 32 bits.

The third format is more subtle. The branch and link subroutine mechanism often needs to have a long range, which is difficult within a 16-bit instruction format. Therefore Thumb uses two instructions, both with this format, to give a combined 22-bit half-word offset (which is sign-extended to 32 bits). The range of the instruction is therefore +/- 4 Mbytes. In order to make the two instructions independent, so that, for example, an interrupt can be taken between them, the link register is used as temporary storage. It will be overwritten at the end of the instruction pair anyway, so it can't contain anything useful. The operation of the instruction pair is:

1. (H=0)     LR := PC + (sign-extended offset shifted left 12 places);
2. (H=1)     PC := LR + (offset shifted left 1 place);
             LR := oldPC + 3.

Here 'oldPC' is the address of the second instruction; the return address has two bytes added to point to the next instruction and the bottom bit set to indicate that the caller is a Thumb routine.

The fourth format maps directly onto the ARM BX instruction (see Section 5.5 on page 121); here 'H' can be set to select a 'Hi' register (r8 to r15).

**Assembler format**

```
B<cond> <label>          ; format 1
B       <label>          ; format 2
BL      <label>          ; format 3
BX      Rm               ; format 4
```

A branch and link generates both format 3 instructions. It is not intended that format 3 instructions are used individually; they should always appear in pairs.

The assembler will compute the relevant offset to insert into the instruction from the current instruction address, the address of the target label, and a small correction for the pipeline behaviour. If the target is out of range an error message will be output.

**Equivalent ARM instruction**

Although formats 1 to 3 are very similar to the ARM branch and branch-with-link instructions, the ARM instructions only support word (4-byte) offsets whereas the Thumb instructions require half-word (2-byte) offsets. Therefore there is no direct mapping from these Thumb instructions into the ARM instruction set. The ARM cores which support Thumb are slightly modified to support half-word branch offsets, with ARM branch instructions being mapped to even half-word offsets.

Format 4 is equivalent to the ARM instruction with the same assembler syntax.

## 7.4   Thumb software interrupt instruction

The Thumb software interrupt instruction behaves exactly like the ARM equivalent and the exception entry sequence causes the processor to switch to ARM execution.

**Binary encoding**

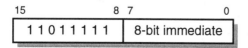

**Figure 7.3**   Thumb software interrupt binary encoding.

**Description**

This instruction causes the following actions:

- The address of the next Thumb instruction is saved in r14_svc.

- The CPSR is saved in SPSR_svc.

- The processor disables IRQ, clears the Thumb bit and enters supervisor mode by modifying the relevant bits in the CPSR.

- The PC is forced to address 0x08.

The ARM instruction SWI handler is then entered. The normal return instruction restores the Thumb execution state.

**Assembler format**

```
SWI     <8-bit immediate>
```

**Equivalent ARM instruction**

The equivalent ARM instruction has an identical assembler syntax; the 8-bit immediate is zero-extended to fill the 24-bit field in the ARM instruction.

Clearly, this limits the SWIs available to Thumb code to the first 256 of the 16 million potential ARM SWIs.

## 7.5  Thumb data processing instructions

Thumb data processing instructions comprise a highly optimized set of fairly complex formats covering the operations most commonly required by a compiler.

The functions of these instructions are clear enough. The selection of those to include and those to leave out is far less obvious, but is based on a detailed understanding of the needs of typical application programs.

**Binary encodings**

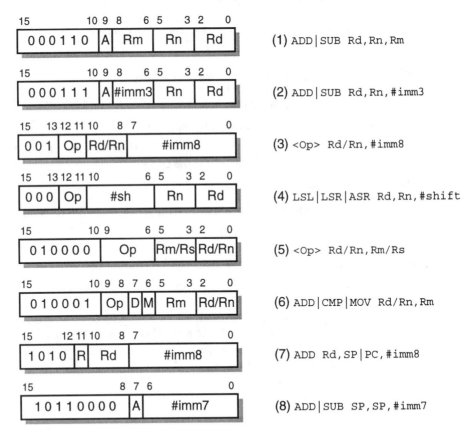

**Figure 7.4**  Thumb data processing instruction binary encodings.

**Description**    These instructions all map onto ARM data processing (including multiply) instructions. Although ARM supports a generalized shift on one operand together with an ALU operation in a single instruction, the Thumb instruction set separates shift and ALU operations into separate instructions, so here the shift operation is presented as an opcode rather than as an operand modifier.

**Assembler format**    The various instruction formats are:

```
1:      <op>    Rd, Rn, Rm          ; <op> = ADD|SUB
2:      <op>    Rd, Rn, #<#imm3>    ; <op> = ADD|SUB
3:      <op>    Rd|Rn, #<#imm8>     ; <op> = ADD|SUB|MOV|CMP
4:      <op>    Rd, Rn, #<#sh>      ; <op> = LSL|LSR|ASR
5:      <op>    Rd|Rn, Rm|Rs        ; <op> = MVN|CMP|CMN|..
    ; ..TST|ADC|SBC|NEG|MUL|LSL|LSR|ASR|ROR|AND|EOR|ORR|BIC
6:      <op>    Rd|Rn, Rm           ; <op> = ADD|CMP|MOV
    ;                                         (Hi regs)
7:      ADD     Rd, SP|PC, #<#imm8>
8:      <op>    SP, SP, #<#imm7>    ; <op> = ADD|SUB
```

**Equivalent ARM instructions**    The ARM data processing instructions that have equivalents in the Thumb instruction set are listed below, with their Thumb equivalents in the comment field.

Instructions which use the 'Lo', general-purpose registers (r0 to r7):

```
;  ARM instruction                  Thumb instruction

   MOVS    Rd, #<#imm8>         ; MOV    Rd, #<#imm8>
   MVNS    Rd, Rm               ; MVN    Rd, Rm
   CMP     Rn, #<#imm8>         ; CMP    Rn, #<#imm8>
   CMP     Rn, Rm               ; CMP    Rn, Rm
   CMN     Rn, Rm               ; CMN    Rn, Rm
   TST     Rn, Rm               ; TST    Rn, Rm
   ADDS    Rd, Rn, #<#imm3>     ; ADD    Rd, Rn, #<#imm3>
   ADDS    Rd, Rd, #<#imm8>     ; ADD    Rd, #<#imm8>
   ADDS    Rd, Rn, Rm           ; ADD    Rd, Rn, Rm
   ADCS    Rd, Rd, Rm           ; ADC    Rd, Rm
   SUBS    Rd, Rn, #<#imm3>     ; SUB    Rd, Rn, #<#imm3>
   SUBS    Rd, Rd, #<#imm8>     ; SUB    Rd, #<#imm8>
   SUBS    Rd, Rn, Rm           ; SUB    Rd, Rn, Rm
   SBCS    Rd, Rd, Rm           ; SBC    Rd, Rm
   RSBS    Rd, Rn, #0           ; NEG    Rd, Rn
   MOVS    Rd, Rm, LSL #<#sh>   ; LSL    Rd, Rm, #<#sh>
```

```
;  ARM instruction                    Thumb instruction

   MOVS    Rd, Rd, LSL Rs       ; LSL    Rd, Rs
   MOVS    Rd, Rm, LSR #<#sh> ; LSR    Rd, Rm, #<#sh>
   MOVS    Rd, Rd, LSR Rs       ; LSR    Rd, Rs
   MOVS    Rd, Rm, ASR #<#sh> ; ASR    Rd, Rm, #<#sh>
   MOVS    Rd, Rd, ASR Rs       ; ASR    Rd, Rs
   MOVS    Rd, Rd, ROR Rs       ; ROR    Rd, Rs
   ANDS    Rd, Rd, Rm           ; AND    Rd, Rm
   EORS    Rd, Rd, Rm           ; EOR    Rd, Rm
   ORRS    Rd, Rd, Rm           ; ORR    Rd, Rm
   BICS    Rd, Rd, Rm           ; BIC    Rd, Rm
   MULS    Rd, Rm, Rd           ; MUL    Rd, Rm
```

Instructions which operate with or on the 'Hi' registers (r8 to r15), in some cases in combination with a 'Lo' register:

```
;  ARM instruction                    Thumb instruction

   ADD     Rd, Rd, Rm           ; ADD    Rd, Rm (1/2 Hi regs)
   CMP     Rn, Rm               ; CMP    Rn, Rm (1/2 Hi regs)
   MOV     Rd, Rm               ; MOV    Rd, Rm (1/2 Hi regs)
   ADD     Rd, PC, #<#imm8>     ; ADD    Rd, PC, #<#imm8>
   ADD     Rd, SP, #<#imm8>     ; ADD    Rd, SP, #<#imm8>
   ADD     SP, SP, #<#imm7>     ; ADD    SP, SP, #<#imm7>
   SUB     SP, SP, #<#imm7>     ; SUB    SP, SP, #<#imm7>
```

**Notes**

1. *All* the data processing instructions that operate with and on the 'Lo' registers update the condition code bits (the S bit is set in the equivalent ARM instruction).

2. The instructions that operate with and on the 'Hi' registers do *not* change the condition code bits, with the exception of CMP which only changes the condition codes.

3. The instructions that are indicated above as requiring '1 or 2 Hi regs' must have one or both register operands specified in the 'Hi' register area.

4. #imm3, #imm7 and #imm8 denote 3-, 7- and 8-bit immediate fields respectively. #sh denotes a 5-bit shift amount field.

## 7.6 Thumb single register data transfer instructions

Again the choice of ARM instructions which are represented in the Thumb instruction set appears complex, but is based on the sort of things that compilers like to do frequently.

Note the larger offsets for accesses to the literal pool (PC-relative) and to the stack (SP-relative), and the restricted support given to signed operands (base plus register addressing only) compared with unsigned operands (base plus offset or register).

**Binary encodings**

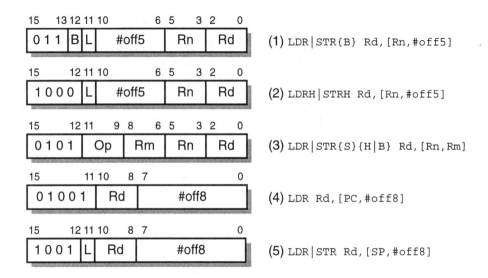

**Figure 7.5**   Thumb single register data transfer binary encodings.

**Description**   These instructions are a carefully derived subset of the ARM single register transfer instructions, and have exactly the same semantics as the ARM equivalent.

In all cases the offset is scaled to the size of the data type, so, for instance, the range of the 5-bit offset is 32 bytes in a load or store byte instruction, 64 bytes in a load or store half-word instruction and 128 bytes in a load or store word instruction.

**Assembler format**

The various assembler formats are:

```
1:      <op>    Rd, [Rn, #<#off5>] ; <op> = LDR|LDRB|STR|STRB
2:      <op>    Rd, [Rn, #<#off5>] ; <op> = LDRH|STRH
3:      <op>    Rd, [Rn, Rm]       ; <op> = ..
                ; .. LDR|LDRH|LDRSH|LDRB|LDRSB|STR|STRH|STRB
4:      LDR     Rd, [PC, #<#off8>]
5:      <op>    Rd, [SP, #<#off8>] ; <op> = LDR|STR
```

**Equivalent ARM instruction**

The ARM equivalents to these Thumb instructions have identical assembler formats.

**Notes**

1. #off5 and #off8 denote 5- and 8-bit immediate offsets respectively. The assembler format specifies the offset in bytes in all cases. The 5- or 8-bit offset in the instruction binary is scaled by the size of the data type.

2. As with the ARM instructions, the signed variants are only supported by the load instructions since store signed and store unsigned have exactly the same effect.

## 7.7 Thumb multiple register data transfer instructions

As in the ARM instruction set, the Thumb multiple register transfer instructions are useful both for procedure entry and return and for memory block copy. Here, however, the tighter encoding means that the two uses must be separated and the number of addressing modes restricted. Otherwise these instructions very much follow the spirit of their ARM equivalents.

**Binary encodings**

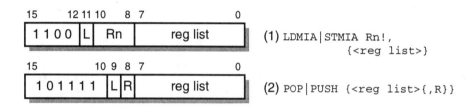

**Figure 7.6**  Thumb multiple register data transfer binary encodings.

**Description**   The block copy forms of the instruction use the LDMIA and STMIA addressing modes (see Figure 3.2 on page 64). The base register may be any of the 'Lo' registers (r0 to r7), and the register list may include any subset of these registers but should not include the base register itself since write-back is always selected (and the result of a load or store multiple register with the base register in the list and write-back selected is unpredictable).

The stack forms use SP (r13) as the base register and again always use write-back. The stack model is fixed as full-descending. In addition to the eight registers which may be specified in the register list, the link register (LR, or r14) may be included in the 'PUSH' instruction and the PC (r15) may be included in the 'POP' form, optimizing procedure entry and exit sequences as is often done in ARM code.

**Assembler format**   `<reg list>` is a list of registers and register ranges from r0 to r7.

```
LDMIA    Rn!, {<reg list>}
STMIA    Rn!, {<reg list>}
POP      {<reg list>{, PC}}
PUSH     {<reg list>{, LR}}
```

**Equivalent ARM instruction**

The equivalent ARM instructions have the same assembler format in the first two cases, and replace POP and PUSH with the appropriate addressing mode in the second two cases.

Block copy:

```
LDMIA    Rn!, {<reg list>}
STMIA    Rn!, {<reg list>}
```

Pop:

```
LDMFD    SP!, {<reg list>{, PC}}
```

Push:

```
STMFD    SP!, {<reg list>{, LR}}
```

**Notes**

1. The base register should be word-aligned. If it is not, some systems will ignore the bottom two address bits but others may generate an alignment exception.

2. Since all these instructions use base write-back, the base register should not be included in the register list.

3. The register list is encoded with one bit for each register; bit 0 indicates whether r0 will be transferred, bit 1 controls r1, etc. The R bit controls the PC and LR options in the POP and PUSH instructions.

## 7.8  Thumb implementation

The Thumb instruction set can be incorporated into an ARM processor macrocell with relatively minor changes to most of the processor logic. The biggest addition is the Thumb instruction decompressor in the instruction pipeline; this logic translates a Thumb instruction into its equivalent ARM instruction. The organization of this logic is shown in Figure 7.7.

The addition of the decompressor logic in series with the instruction decoder might be expected to increase the decode latency, but in fact the ARM7 pipeline does relatively little work in phase 1 of the decode cycle. Therefore the decompression logic can be accommodated here without compromising the cycle time or increasing the pipeline latency, and the Thumb pipeline operates in exactly the way as described in 'The ARM pipeline' on page 78.

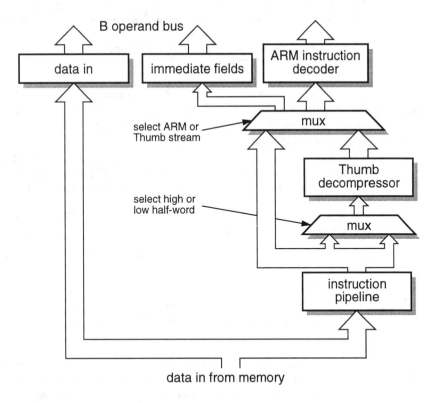

**Figure 7.7**  The Thumb instruction decompressor organization.

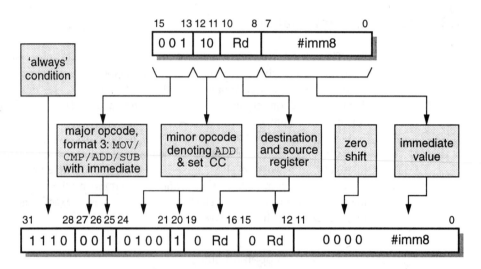

**Figure 7.8**    Thumb to ARM instruction mapping.

**Instruction mapping**

The Thumb decompressor performs a static translation from the 16-bit Thumb instruction into the equivalent 32-bit ARM instruction. This involves performing a look-up to translate the major and minor opcodes, zero-extending the 3-bit register specifiers to give 4-bit specifiers and mapping other fields across as required.

As an example, the mapping of a Thumb 'ADD Rd,#imm8' instruction (see Section 7.5 on page 206) to the corresponding ARM 'ADDS Rd,Rd,#imm8' instruction (described in Section 5.7 on page 124) is shown in Figure 7.8. Note that:

- Since the only conditional Thumb instructions are branches, the condition 'always' is used in translating all other Thumb instructions.

- Whether or not a Thumb data processing instruction should modify the condition codes in the CPSR is implicit in the Thumb opcode; this must be made explicit in the ARM instruction.

- The Thumb 2-address format can always be mapped into the ARM 3-address format by replicating a register specifier. (Going the other way is not, in general, possible.)

The simplicity of the decompression logic is crucial to the efficiency of the Thumb instruction set. There would be little merit in the Thumb architecture if it resulted in complex, slow and power-hungry decompression logic.

# 7.9   Thumb applications

To see where Thumb offers a benefit we need to review its properties. Thumb instructions are 16 bits long and encode the functionality of an ARM instruction in half the number of bits,  but since a Thumb instruction typically has less semantic content than an ARM instruction, a particular program will require more Thumb instructions than it would have needed ARM instructions. The ratio will vary from program to program, but in a typical example Thumb code may require 70% of the space of ARM code. Therefore if we compare the Thumb solution with the pure ARM code solution, the following characteristics emerge:

**Thumb
properties**

- The Thumb code requires 70% of the space of the ARM code.
- The Thumb code uses 40% more instructions than the ARM code.
- With 32-bit memory, the ARM code is 40% faster than the Thumb code.
- With 16-bit memory, the Thumb code is 45% faster than the ARM code.
- Thumb code uses 30% less external memory power than ARM code.

So where performance is all-important, a system should use 32-bit memory and run ARM code. Where cost and power consumption are more important, a 16-bit memory system and Thumb code may be a better choice. However there are intermediate positions which may give the best of both worlds:

**Thumb
systems**

- A high-end 32-bit ARM system may use Thumb code for certain non-critical routines to save power or memory requirements.
- A low-end 16-bit system may have a small amount of on-chip 32-bit RAM for critical routines running ARM code, but use off-chip Thumb code for all non-critical routines.

The second of these examples is perhaps closer to the sort of application for which Thumb was developed. Mobile telephone and pager applications incorporate real-time digital signal processing (DSP) functions that may require the full power of the ARM, but these are tightly coded routines that can fit in a small amount of on-chip memory. The more complex and much larger code that controls the user-interface, battery management system, and so on, is less time-critical, and the use of Thumb code will enable off-chip ROMs to give good performance on an 8- or 16-bit bus, saving cost and improving battery life.

## 7.10   Example and exercises

**Example 7.1**   **Rewrite the 'Hello World' program in Section 3.4 on page 72 to use Thumb instructions. How do the ARM and Thumb code sizes compare?**

Here is the original ARM program:

```
            AREA      HelloW,CODE,READONLY
SWI_WriteC  EQU       &0            ; output character in r0
SWI_Exit    EQU       &11           ; finish program
            ENTRY                   ; code entry point
START       ADR       r1, TEXT      ; r1 -> "Hello World"
LOOP        LDRB      r0, [r1], #1  ; get the next byte
            CMP       r0, #0        ; check for text end
            SWINE     SWI_WriteC    ; if not end print ..
            BNE       LOOP          ; .. and loop back
            SWI       SWI_Exit      ; end of execution
TEXT        =         "Hello World",&0a,&0d,0
            END                     ; end of program source
```

Most of these instructions have direct Thumb equivalents, however some do not. The load byte instruction does not support auto-indexing and the supervisor call cannot be conditionally executed. Hence the Thumb code needs to be slightly modified:

```
            AREA      HelloW_Thumb,CODE,READONLY
SWI_WriteC  EQU       &0            ; output character in r0
SWI_Exit    EQU       &11           ; finish program
            ENTRY                   ; code entry point
            CODE32                  ; enter in ARM state
            ADR       r0, START+1   ; get Thumb entry address
            BX        r0            ; enter Thumb area
            CODE16                  ; Thumb code follows..
START       ADR       r1, TEXT      ; r1 -> "Hello World"
LOOP        LDRB      r0, [r1]      ; get the next byte
            ADD       r1, r1, #1    ; increment pointer    **T
            CMP       r0, #0        ; check for text end
            BEQ       DONE          ; finished?            **T
            SWI       SWI_WriteC    ; if not end print ..
            B         LOOP          ; .. and loop back
DONE        SWI       SWI_Exit      ; end of execution
            ALIGN                   ; to ensure ADR works
TEXT        DATA
            =         "Hello World",&0a,&0d,&00
            END
```

The two additional instructions required to compensate for the features absent from the Thumb instruction set are marked with '**T' in the above listing. The ARM code size is six instructions plus 14 bytes of data, 38 bytes in all. The Thumb code size is eight instructions plus 14 bytes of data (ignoring the preamble required to switch the processor to executing Thumb instructions), making 30 bytes in all.

This example illustrates a number of important points to bear in mind when writing Thumb code:

- The assembler needs to know when to produce ARM code and when to produce Thumb code. The 'CODE32' and 'CODE16' directives provide this information. (These are instructions to the assembler and do not themselves cause any code to be generated.)

- Since the processor is executing ARM instructions when it calls the code, explicit provision must be made to instruct it to execute the Thumb instructions. The 'BX r0' instruction achieves this, provided that r0 has been initialized appropriately. Note particularly that the bottom bit of r0 is set to cause the processor to execute Thumb instructions at the branch target.

- In Thumb code 'ADR' can only generate word-aligned addresses. As Thumb instructions are half-words, there is no guarantee that a location following an arbitrary number of Thumb instructions will be word-aligned. Therefore the example program has an explicit 'ALIGN' before the text string.

In order to assemble and run this program on the ARM software development toolkit, an assembler which can generate Thumb code must be invoked and the ARMulator must emulate a 'Thumb-aware' processor core. The default setting of the Project Manager targets an ARM6 core and generates only 32-bit ARM code. This may be changed by choosing 'Project' from the 'Options' menu within the Project Manager and selecting 'TCC/TASM' in the 'Tools' dialogue box before generating the code. The 'Target Processor' will automatically switch to the Thumb-aware ARM7t when this is done.

Otherwise, assembling and running Thumb code is just like using ARM code.

**Exercise 7.1.1**   Convert the other programs in Sections 3.4 and 3.5 on pages 72 and 75 into Thumb code and compare their sizes with the original ARM code.

**Exercise 7.1.2**   Use TCC to generate Thumb code from C source programs (starting, as usual, with a 'Hello World' program). Look at the assembly code generated by the C compiler (using the '-s' option). Compare the code size and the execution time with the same programs compiled into ARM code.

# 8 Architectural Support for System Development

**Summary of chapter contents**

Designing any computer system is a complex task; designing an embedded 'system on a chip' is a daunting one. The development often takes place entirely within a CAD environment, and the first silicon must not only function but it must deliver the necessary performance and be manufacturable. The only scope for fixing design flaws is in the software; to modify the chip in order to correct errors takes too long.

For the last two decades the principal approach to microprocessor system development has been based upon the *In-Circuit Emulator* (ICE). The system itself was a printed circuit board incorporating a microprocessor chip and various memory and peripheral devices. To use the ICE, the microprocessor was removed from its socket and replaced by a header plug with an umbilical connection to the ICE equipment. The ICE emulated the function of the microprocessor and gave the user an inside view on the internal state of the system, giving access to read and modify processor registers and memory values, to set breakpoints, and so on.

Now that the microprocessor itself has become just a cell on a larger chip, this whole approach has collapsed. It is not possible to unplug part of a chip! There is, as yet, no approach that has replaced the ICE in all its roles, but there are several techniques that contribute, some of which require explicit support in the processor's architecture. This chapter covers the techniques available to support the development of system chips based on ARM cores and the architectural features built into the cores to assist in this process.

## 8.1   The ARMulator

The ARMulator is part of the cross-development toolkit described in Section 2.4 on page 46. It is a software emulator of the ARM processor which supports the debugging and evaluation of ARM code without requiring an ARM processor chip.

The ARMulator has a role in embedded system design. It supports the high-level prototyping of various parts of the system to support the development of software and the evaluation of architectural alternatives. It is made up of four components:

- The processor core model, which can emulate any current ARM core, including the Thumb instruction set.

- A memory interface which allows the characteristics of the target memory system to be modelled. Various models are supplied to support rapid prototyping, but the interface is fully customizable to incorporate the level of detail required.

- A coprocessor interface that supports custom coprocessor models.

- An operating system interface that allows individual system calls to be handled by the host or emulated on the ARM model.

The processor core model incorporates the remote debug interface, so the processor and system state are visible from ARMsd, the ARM symbolic debugger. Programs can be loaded, run and debugged through this interface.

**System modelling**

Using the ARMulator it is possible to build a complete, clock-cycle accurate software model of a system including a cache, MMU, physical memory, peripheral devices, operating system and software. Since this is likely to be the highest-level model of the system, it is the best place to perform the initial evaluation of design alternatives.

Once the design is reasonably stable, hardware development will probably move into a timing-accurate CAD environment, but software development can continue using the ARMulator-based model (probably moving up from cycle- to instruction-accurate timing for higher performance).

In the course of the detailed hardware design it is likely that some of the timing assumptions built into the original software model prove impossible to meet. As the design evolves it is important to keep the software model in step so that the software development is based on the most accurate estimates of timing that are available.

It is now common for complex systems development to be supported by multiple computer models of the target system built upon different levels of abstraction. Unless the lower-level models are synthesized automatically from the more abstract models, maintaining consistency between the models always takes considerable care and effort.

## 8.2   The JTAG boundary scan test architecture

Two difficult areas in the development of a product based around an application specific embedded system chip are the production testing of the VLSI component and the
production testing of the assembled printed circuit board.

    The second of these is addressed by the IEEE standard number 1149, 'Standard
Test Access Port and Boundary-Scan Architecture'. This standard describes a 5-pin
serial protocol for accessing and controlling the signal levels on the pins of a digital
circuit, and has extensions for testing the circuitry on the chip itself. The standard was
developed by the *Joint Test Action Group* (hence JTAG), and the architecture
described by the standard is known either as 'JTAG boundary scan' or as 'IEEE 1149'.

    The general structure of the JTAG boundary scan test interface is shown in
Figure 8.1. All the signals between the core logic and the pins are intercepted by the

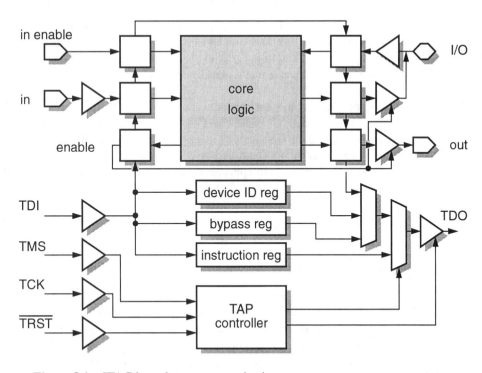

**Figure 8.1**   JTAG boundary scan organization.

serial scan path which can connect the core logic to the pins in normal operating mode, or can read out the original value and replace it with a new value in test mode.

**Test signals**　　The interface works with five dedicated signals which must be provided on each chip that supports the test standard:

- $\overline{TRST}$ is a test reset input which initializes the test interface.
- *TCK* is the test clock which controls the timing of the test interface independently from any system clocks.
- *TMS* is the test mode select which controls the operation of the test interface state machine.
- *TDI* is the test data input line which supplies the data to the boundary scan or instruction registers.
- *TDO* is the test data output line which carries the sampled values from the boundary scan chain and propagates data to the next chip in the serial test circuit.

The normal organization of the test circuit on a board that incorporates several chips with JTAG support is to connect $\overline{TRST}$, *TCK* and *TMS* to every chip in parallel and to connect *TDO* from one chip to *TDI* of the next in a single loop, so the board test interface has the same five signals listed above.

**TAP controller**　　The operation of the test interface is controlled by the Test Access Port (**TAP**) controller. This is a state machine whose state transitions are controlled by *TMS*; the state transition diagram is shown in Figure 8.2 on page 223. All the states have two exits so the transitions can be controlled by one signal, *TMS*. The two main paths in the state transition diagram control the operation of a data register (**DR**) and the instruction register (**IR**).

**Data registers**　　The behaviour of a particular chip is determined by the contents of the test instruction register, which can select between various different data registers:

- The **device ID** register reads out an identification number which is hard-wired into the chip.
- The **bypass** register connects *TDI* to *TDO* with a 1-clock delay to give the tester rapid access to another device in the test loop on the same board.
- The **boundary scan** register intercepts all the signals between the core logic and the pins and comprises the individual register bits which are shown as the squares connected to the core logic in Figure 8.1 on page 221.
- Other registers may be employed on the chip to test other functions as required.

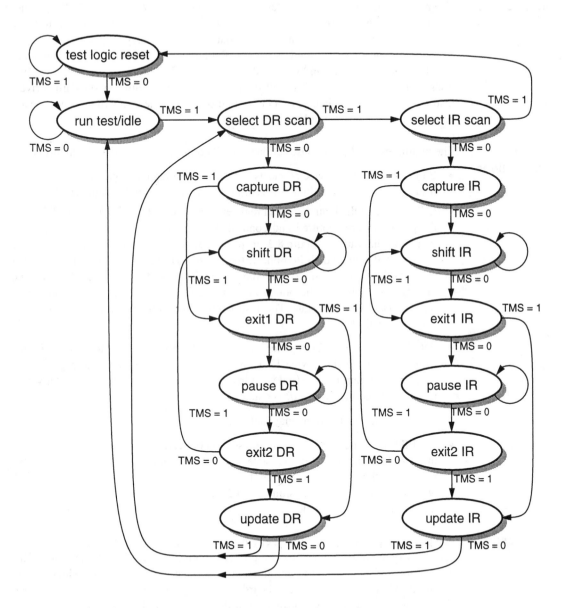

**Figure 8.2**    Test Access Port (TAP) controller state transition diagram.

**Instructions**

The normal operation of a JTAG test system is to enter an instruction which specifies the sort of test to be carried out next and the data register to be used for that test into the *instruction* register, and then to use the data register to carry out the test.

Instructions may be public or private. Public instructions are declared and available for general test use, and the standard specifies a minimum set of public instructions that must be supported by all devices that comply with the standard. Private instructions are for specialized on-chip test purposes and the standard does not specify how these should operate or how they should be used.

**Public instructions**

The minimum set of public instructions that all compliant devices must support is:

- BYPASS: here the device connects *TDI* to *TDO* though a single clock delay. This instruction exists to facilitate the testing of other devices in the same test loop.

- EXTEST: here the boundary scan register is connected between *TDI* and *TDO* and the pin states are captured and controlled by the register. Referring to the state transition diagram in Figure 8.2 on page 223, the pin states are captured in the *Capture DR* state and shifted out of the register via the *TDO* pin in the *Shift DR* state. As the captured data is shifted out, new data is shifted in via the *TDI* pin, and this data is applied to the boundary scan register outputs (and hence the output pins) in the *Update DR* state. This instruction exists to support the testing of board-level connectivity.

- IDCODE: here the ID register is connected between *TDI* and *TDO*. In the *Capture DR* state the device ID (a hard-wired identification number giving the manufacturer, part number and version of the part) is copied into the register which is then shifted out in the *Shift DR* state.

    Other public instructions may include:

- INTEST: here the boundary scan register is connected between *TDI* and *TDO* and the core logic input and output states are captured and controlled by the register. Note that the inputs are driven to the complement of the values supplied. Otherwise the operation is similar to EXTEST. This instruction exists to support the testing of the core logic.

**PCB testing**

The principal goal of the JTAG test circuit is to enable the continuity of tracks and the connectivity of solder connections on printed circuit boards (*PCBs*) to be tested. This has become difficult since the introduction of surface mount packages which do not require through-holes in the circuit board. Previously 'bed of nails' testers could contact all the pins on each IC package from the back of the PCB to check continuity;

surface mount packages typically have the pins closer together and the tracks accessible only on the component side of the board, making the 'bed of nails' approach inapplicable.

When the surface mount components have a JTAG test interface, this can be used (using the EXTEST instruction) to control outputs and observe inputs independently of the normal function of the chip, so board-level connectivity can readily be checked from chip to chip. If the board also contains components which do not have a JTAG interface these will require 'bed of nails' contacts, but these can be used together with the JTAG interfaces where available to minimize the cost and difficulty of building the production test equipment.

**VLSI testing**

High-complexity integrated circuits require extensive production testing to identify faulty devices before they get built into product. A production IC tester is a very expensive piece of equipment, and the time each device spends on the tester is an important factor in its manufacturing cost. Since the JTAG test circuitry operates through serial access, it is not a high-speed way to apply test vectors to the core logic. Furthermore it is not possible to apply test vectors through the JTAG port at the normal operating speed of the device to check its performance.

Therefore the JTAG architecture is not a generic solution to all the problems of VLSI production testing. However it can solve a number of problems:

- The JTAG port can be used for in-circuit functional testing of an IC (provided that the INTEST instruction is supported).

- It gives good control of the IC pins for parametric testing (checking the drive of the output buffers, leakage, input thresholds, and so on). This uses only the EXTEST instruction which is required on all JTAG compliant devices.

- It can be used to access internal scan paths to improve the controllability and observability of internal nodes that are hard to access from the pins.

- It can be used to give access to on-chip debug functions with no additional pins and without interfering with the system functions. This is exploited by the ARM EmbeddedICE debug architecture described briefly below and in detail in Section 8.3 on page 228.

- It offers an approach to the functional testing of macrocell-based designs as described below.

These uses are all in addition to its principal purpose, which is in the production testing of printed circuit boards.

**Embedded-ICE**

The ARM debug architecture, described in Section 8.3 on page 228, is based on an extension of the JTAG test port. The EmbeddedICE module introduces breakpoint and watchpoint registers which are accessed as additional data registers using special JTAG instructions, and a trace buffer which is similarly accessed. The scan path around the ARM core macrocell is used to introduce instructions into the ARM pipeline without interfering with other parts of the system and these instructions can be used to access and modify the ARM and system state.

The debug architecture gives most of the functionality of a conventional In-Circuit Emulation system to debug an ARM macrocell on a complex system chip, and since the JTAG test access port is used to control the debug hardware, no additional pins are required on the chip.

**Macrocell testing**

A growing trend in the design of complex system chips is to incorporate a number of complex, pre-designed macrocells, together with some application specific custom logic. The ARM processor core is itself one such macrocell; the others may come from ARM Limited, a semiconductor partner or some third party supplier. In such cases the designer of the system chip will have limited knowledge of the macrocells and will depend on the macrocell suppliers for the production test patterns for each macrocell.

Since the macrocells are buried within the system chip, the designer is faced with the problem of devising a way to apply the supplied test vectors to each of the macrocells in turn. Test patterns must also be generated for the custom logic part of the design, but the designer is assumed to understand that part of the logic.

There are various approaches to getting the test patterns onto the edges of the macrocells:

- Test modes may be provided which multiplex the signals from each macrocell in turn onto the pins of the system chip.

- An on-chip bus may support direct test access to each macrocell which is attached to it (see Section 8.5 on page 234).

- Each macrocell may have a boundary scan path through which the test patterns may be applied using an extension of the JTAG architecture.

This last approach is illustrated in Figure 8.3 on page 227. The chip has a peripheral boundary scan path to support the public EXTEST operation and additional paths around each macrocell, designed into the macrocell, for applying functional tests as supplied. The custom logic designed specifically for this chip may have its own scan path or, as shown in the figure, rely on the fact that all its interface signals must intercept one of the existing scan paths.

It should be recognized that although perfectly feasible for functional testing, the scan path approach to macrocell testing has the same drawbacks as using the JTAG

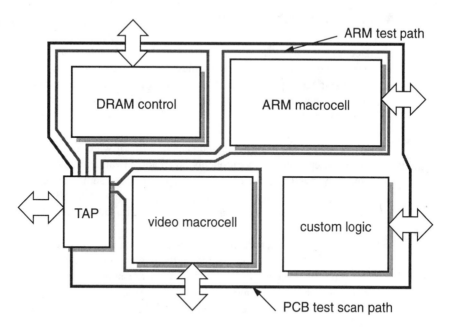

**Figure 8.3**   A possible JTAG extension for macrocell testing.

boundary scan path to test the core logic on a chip. The serial access is much slower than parallel access through the pins and performance testing at speed is not possible.

The most promising production test methodology for macrocell based system chips appears to be to exploit the on-chip bus to give parallel access to the macrocell's periphery (especially where the macrocell has been designed specifically to give good access through this route). Multiplexing is used to give external access to peripheral macrocell signals that are important for performance testing and cannot conveniently be accessed via the on-chip bus, and the JTAG port is used to access other signals and internal state where necessary via scan chains. We will return to this approach as it is supported by ARM's 'Advanced Microcontroller Bus Architecture' (AMBA) which is described in Section 8.5 on page 234; the AMBA testing methodology is described on page 238.

The JTAG system continues to be very important for board-level testing, and can also be used for in-circuit testing of the core logic and to access on-chip debug facilities. It is incorporated into most ARM designs and is an important component of their test and debug methodologies.

## 8.3   The ARM debug architecture

Debugging any computer system can be a complex task. There are two basic approaches to debugging, the simplest being based on watching a system from the outside using test equipment such as a logic analyser, and the more powerful being based on viewing a system from the inside with tools that support single stepping, the setting of breakpoints, and so on.

**Desktop debugging**

When the system to be debugged is a piece of software running on a desktop machine, all the user interface components are readily available and the debugger may itself simply be another piece of software running on the same machine. Breakpoints are set by replacing an instruction in the object program with a call to the debugger, remembering the original instruction so that it can be replaced when execution continues past the breakpoint.

Often compilers have compile-time options to generate extensive debug information such as symbol tables which the debugger can use to allow the user to debug the program from a source-level view, addressing variables by their source names rather than by their memory address. This 'source-level debugging' is more powerful and requires less detailed knowledge of the machine environment than object-level debugging.

A common weakness in software debuggers is the lack of a 'watchpoint' facility. A watchpoint is a memory address which halts execution if it is accessed as a data transfer address. Since many processors have no support for trapping on a particular address (apart, perhaps, from a memory management page fault, which is rather coarse for this purpose) this functionality is often omitted. This is a pity, since a very common source of error in a C program is corrupted data caused by an errant pointer in some unrelated part of the program, and this can be very hard to track down without a watchpoint facility.

**Embedded debugging**

Debugging becomes significantly more difficult when the target system is embedded. Now there is probably no user interface in the system, so the debugger must run on a remote host through some sort of communication link to the target. If the code is in ROM, instructions cannot simply be replaced by calls to the debugger since the locations are not writeable.

The standard solution here is the *In-Circuit Emulator* (**ICE**). The processor in the target system is removed and replaced by a connection to an emulator. The emulator may be based around the same processor chip, or a variant with more pins (and more visibility of its internal state), but it will also incorporate buffers to copy the bus activity off to a 'trace buffer' (which stores the signals on all the pins in each clock cycle for some number of cycles) and various hardware resources which can watch for particular events, such as execution passing through a breakpoint. The trace buffer and hardware resources are managed by software running on a host desktop system.

When a 'trigger' event occurs, the trace buffer is frozen so the user can observe activity around the point of interest. The host software will present the trace buffer data, give a view on the processor and system state and allow it to be modified, and generally attempt to appear as similar to a debugger in a desktop system as possible.

**Debugging processor cores**

The ICE approach depends on the system having an identifiable processor chip which can be removed and replaced by the ICE. Clearly, once the processor has become just one macrocell of many on a complex system chip, this is no longer possible.

Although simulation using software models such as the ARMulator should remove many of the design bugs before the physical system is built, it is often impossible to run the full software system under emulation, and it can be difficult to model all the real-time constraints accurately. Therefore it is likely that some debugging of the complete hardware and software system will be necessary. How can this be achieved? This is still an area of active research to identify the best overall strategy with acceptable hardware overhead costs, but considerable progress has been over the last few years in developing practical approaches, and the rest of this section presents the approach developed by ARM Limited.

**ARM debug hardware**

To provide debug facilities comparable with those offered by a typical ICE, the user must be able to set breakpoints and watchpoints (for code running in ROM as well as RAM), to inspect and modify the processor and system state, to see a trace of processor activity around the point of interest, and to do all this from the comfort of a desktop system with a good user interface.

The communication between the target system and the host is achieved by extending the functionality of the JTAG test port. Since the JTAG test pins are included in most designs for board testing, accessing the debug hardware through this port requires no additional dedicated pins, sparing the most precious resource on the chip from further pressure. JTAG scan chains are used to access the breakpoint and watchpoint registers and the trace buffer (where used), and also to force instructions into the processor to access processor and system state.

The breakpoint and watchpoint registers represent a fairly small hardware overhead that can often be accepted on production parts, but the trace buffer is a different matter. An ARM core has 80 or so interface signals, so ten bytes of trace memory are required for every clock cycle. This has to be on chip, so storing only 100 cycles takes of the order of a kilobyte of on-chip memory, which is a high overhead. Where a system chip has significant quantities of on-chip memory already, it may just be possible to partition this between system and debug use for debug purposes, whilst retaining real-time performance similar to that required in the production system, though this is unlikely since most such systems have little slack in their designs. (Where there are no real-time constraints, the trace buffer can be supplanted by single stepping.)

Typically, debuggable systems with ARM cores forego the trace buffer and just implement the breakpoint and watchpoint registers which are accessed through the JTAG port. The host system runs the standard ARM development tools, communicating with the target through a serial port. Special protocol conversion hardware sits between the host serial line and the target JTAG port.

In addition to the breakpoint and watchpoint events, it may also be desirable to halt the processor when a system-level event occurs. The debug architecture includes external inputs for this purpose.

The on-chip cell containing these facilities is called the *EmbeddedICE* module.

**Embedded-ICE**

The EmbeddedICE module consists of two watchpoint registers and control and status registers. The watchpoint registers can halt the ARM core when the address, data and control signals match the value programmed into the watchpoint register. Since the comparison is performed under a mask, either watchpoint register can be configured to operate as a breakpoint register capable of halting the processor when an instruction in either ROM or RAM is executed.

The comparison and mask logic is illustrated in Figure 8.4.

**Chaining**

Each watchpoint can look for a particular combination of values on the ARM address bus, data bus, $\overline{trans}$, $\overline{opc}$, $\overline{mas}[1:0]$ and $\overline{r/w}$ control signals, and if either combination is matched the processor is stopped. Alternatively, the two watchpoints may be chained to halt the processor when the second watchpoint is matched only after the first has previously been matched.

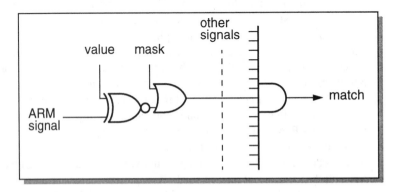

**Figure 8.4**   EmbeddedICE signal comparison logic.

**Registers**

EmbeddedICE registers are programmed via the JTAG test port, using a dedicated scan chain. The scan chain is 38 bits long, with 32 data bits, 5 address bits and a $\overline{r/w}$ bit which controls whether the register is read or written. The address bits specify the particular register following the mapping detailed in Table 8.1.

The use of the JTAG scan chain is illustrated in Figure 8.5 on page 232. The read or write takes place when the TAP controller enters the 'update DR' state (see Figure 8.2 on page 223).

**Accessing state**

The EmbeddedICE module allows a program to be halted at specific points, but it does not directly allow the processor or system state to be inspected or modified. This is achieved via further scan paths which are also accessed through the JTAG port.

The mechanism employed to access the processor state is to halt the processor, then to force an instruction such as a store multiple of all the registers into the processor's instruction queue. Then clocks are applied to the processor, again via the scan

**Table 8.1**   EmbeddedICE register mapping.

| Address | Width | Function |
|---------|-------|----------|
| 00000 | 3 | Debug control |
| 00001 | 5 | Debug status |
| 00100 | 6 | Debug comms control register |
| 00101 | 32 | Debug comms data register |
| 01000 | 32 | Watchpoint 0 address value |
| 01001 | 32 | Watchpoint 0 address mask |
| 01010 | 32 | Watchpoint 0 data value |
| 01011 | 32 | Watchpoint 0 data mask |
| 01100 | 9 | Watchpoint 0 control value |
| 01101 | 8 | Watchpoint 0 control mask |
| 10000 | 32 | Watchpoint 1 address value |
| 10001 | 32 | Watchpoint 1 address mask |
| 10010 | 32 | Watchpoint 1 data value |
| 10011 | 32 | Watchpoint 1 data mask |
| 10100 | 9 | Watchpoint 1 control value |
| 10101 | 8 | Watchpoint 1 control mask |

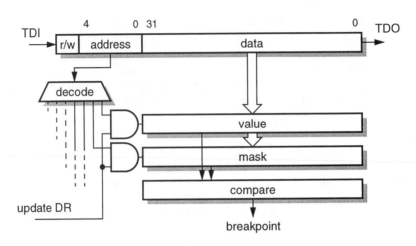

**Figure 8.5**   EmbeddedICE register read and write structure.

chain, causing it to write the registers out through its data port. Each register is collected by the scan chain and shifted out.

System state is harder to glean, since there may be system locations that cannot be read at the very low speeds that the scan path can generate. Here the processor is pre-loaded with a suitable instruction, then allowed to access the system location at system speed. This transfers the required system state into a processor register, whereupon it may be passed to the external debugger through the JTAG port as described above.

**Debug comms**

In additions to the breakpoint and watchpoint registers, the EmbeddedICE module also includes a **debug comms** port whereby the software running on the target system can communicate with the host. The software in the target system sees the comms port as a 6-bit control register and 32-bit data read and write registers which are accessed using MRC and MCR instructions to coprocessor 14. The host sees these registers in the EmbeddedICE register map as shown in Table 8.1 on page 231.

**Debugging**

An ARM-based system chip which includes the EmbeddedICE module connects to a host computer through the JTAG port and a protocol converter. This configuration supports the normal breakpoint, watchpoint and processor and system state access that the programmer is accustomed to using for native or ICE-based debugging (in addition to the comms port described above), and with suitable host software gives a full source-level debugging capability with low hardware overhead.

## 8.4 The Partner-ET ROM-ICE

We started considering the problem of debugging systems which incorporate on-chip processor cores by observing that the established approach to embedded system debugging, based on in-circuit emulation, is not applicable since it depends on the processor being an identifiable chip which can be removed from the board and replaced by the ICE module.

Now although the processor core is often inaccessible inside an embedded system chip, most embedded systems still use off-chip ROMs. Therefore an alternative debugging approach to the ARM on-chip EmbeddedICE is to exploit the off-chip ROM. This is the basis of the ROM-ICE ROM-based in-circuit emulator developed by Partner-ET and offered by VLSI Technology to support their ARM customers.

A ROM is usually connected to the processor address and data buses, so most of the signals used to set breakpoints and trace program execution are available at the ROM socket. ROM-ICE has additional inputs which are connected individually to the necessary ARM signals which are not available at the ROM socket.

**ROM-ICE functions**

The ROM-ICE supports hardware breakpointing, real-time program tracing, and memory and register inspection and modification. Higher-level functions are implemented in software to support program profiling.

The software support includes C and assembler source-level debugging and can be run from a PC or a UNIX workstation (the latter requiring a network adaptor kit to connect the ROM-ICE to an Ethernet).

Note that the ROM-ICE can work with a system with a 32-, 16- or 8-bit off-chip data bus and with two or four ROM.

**ROM-ICE pros and cons**

Clearly, if an embedded system chip runs from on-chip ROM, or loads software into an on-chip RAM and then executes it without broadcasting the memory traffic to the external bus, there is no way the ROM-ICE can trace or halt the program. An on-chip scheme such as EmbeddedICE can continue to operate under these conditions.

However, EmbeddedICE incurs a small cost for its on-chip support logic, and a much higher cost if an on-chip trace buffer is included. ROM-ICE has no such overhead and provides a trace facility. On-chip RAM is often so small that only very simple programs can run in it, and the large, complex control programs that cause many of the debugging difficulties in real systems are fully visible at the ROM.

ROM-ICE illustrates that there is more than one approach to debugging a system based around an embedded processor core, and this is an area that continues to attract new ideas.

## 8.5   The Advanced Microcontroller Bus Architecture (AMBA)

ARM processor cores have bus interfaces that are optimized for high-speed cache interfacing. Where a core is used, with or without a cache, as a component on a complex system chip, some interfacing is required to allow the ARM to communicate with other on-chip macrocells.

Although this interfacing is not particularly difficult to design, there are many potential solutions. Making an *ad hoc* choice in every case consumes design resource and inhibits the re-use of peripheral macrocells. To avoid this waste, ARM Limited specified an *Embedded Module Bus* (**EMB**) to standardize the on-chip connection of different macrocells. Macrocells designed to this bus interface can be viewed as a kit of parts for future system chips, and ultimately designing a complex chip based on a new combination of existing macrocells could become a straightforward task. ARM Limited built on its experience with EMB to develop the Advanced Microcontroller Bus Architecture, **AMBA**, which is described below.

GEC Plessey Semiconductors (GPS) defined a similar bus, BµILD, which is used in the Butterfly microcontroller described in Section 14.1 on page 370. ARM and GPS are working to converge AMBA and BµILD towards a common open standard.

**AMBA buses**   Two buses are defined within the AMBA specification:

- The *Advanced System Bus* (**ASB**) is used to connect high-performance system modules. This bus supports separate or multiplexed address and data and burst mode data transfers.

- The *Advanced Peripheral Bus* (**APB**) offers a simpler interface for low-performance peripherals.

The APB generally appears as a local secondary bus which appears as a single slave module on the ASB. A typical AMBA-based microcontroller will incorporate both buses as illustrated in Figure 8.6 on page 235.

**Arbitration**   A bus transaction is initiated by a bus master which requests access from a central arbiter. The arbiter decides priorities when there are conflicting requests, and its design is a system specific issue. The ASB only specifies the protocol which must be followed:

- The master issues a request (*A_REQ*) to the central arbiter.

- When the bus is available, the arbiter issues a grant (*A_GNT*) to the master. (The arbitration must take account of the bus lock signal (*B_LOCK*) when deciding which grant to issue to ensure that atomic bus transactions are not violated.)

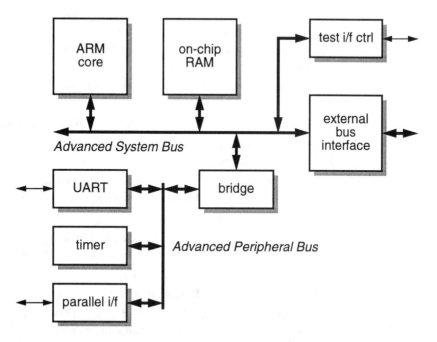

**Figure 8.6**  A typical AMBA-based system.

**Bus transfers**

When a master has been granted access to the bus, it issues address and control information to indicate the type of the transfer and the slave device which should respond. The following signals are centrally generated, for example by the Reset Controller or the Central Decoder:

- The bus clock, *B_CLK*. This will usually be the same as *mclk*, the ARM processor clock.

- Bus mode, *B_RES[2:0]*, conveys the clock, reset and system mode information (see 'Bus modes' on page 236).

The bus master which holds the grant then proceeds with the bus transaction using the following signals:

- Bus transaction, *B_TRAN[1:0]*, indicates whether the next bus cycle will be address-only, sequential or non-sequential. It is enabled by the grant signal and is ahead of the bus cycle to which it refers.

- The address bus, *B_A[31:0]*. (Not all address lines need be implemented in systems with modest address-space requirements, and in a multiplexed implementation the address is sent down the data bus.)
- Bus transfer direction, *B_WRITE*.
- Bus protection signals, *B_PROT[1:0]*, which indicate instruction or data fetches and supervisor or user access.
- The transfer size, *B_SIZE[1:0]*, specifies a byte, half-word or word transfer.
- Bus lock, *B_LOCK*, allows a master to retain the bus to complete an atomic read-modify-write transaction.
- The data bus, *B_D[31:0]*, used to transmit write data and to receive read data. In an implementation with multiplexed address and data, the address is also transmitted down this bus.

A slave unit may process the requested transaction immediately, accepting write data or issuing read data on *B_D[31:0]*, or signal one of the following responses:

- Bus wait, *B_WAIT*, allows a slave module to insert wait states when it cannot complete the transaction in the current cycle.
- Bus last, *B_LAST*, allows a slave to terminate a sequential burst to force the bus master to issue a new bus transaction request to continue.
- Bus error, *B_ERROR*, indicates a transaction that cannot be completed. If the master is a processor it should abort the transfer.

**Bus modes**    The ASB supports a number of independent on-chip modules, many of which may be able to drive the data bus (and some control lines). Provided all the modules obey the bus protocols, there will only be one module driving any bus line at any time. Immediately after power-on, however, all the modules come up in unknown states. It takes some time for a clock oscillator to stabilize after power-up, so there may be no reliable clock available to sequence all the modules into a known state. In any case, if two or more modules power-up trying to drive bus lines in opposite directions, the output drive clashes may cause power supply crow-bar problems which may prevent the chip from powering up properly at all.

Correct ASB power-up is ensured by imposing an asynchronous reset mode that forces all drivers off the bus independently of the clock.

Once the chip is operating stably, the ASB supports a number of operating modes which are listed below with their encodings on *B_RES[2:0]*:

1. POR, '000', Power On Reset. This is the asynchronous state which forces all modules off the bus.

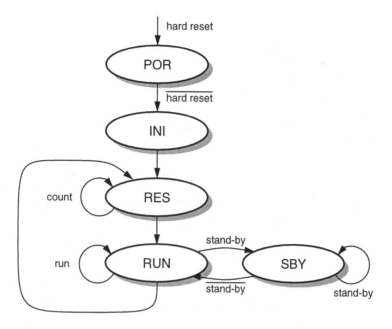

**Figure 8.7** ASB bus mode state transition graph.

2. INI, '100', Initialize. In this mode, all the internal state machines in the various modules are cleared down synchronously to an initial state.

3. RES, '101', Reset. The soft reset mode allows modules to recover (without losing their configuration) following a bus timeout or other protocol error.

4. RUN, '111', the normal operating mode.

5. SBY, '011', Stand-by. This is an optional low-power mode where the clock may be stopped, but the chip is ready to wake up (and return to RUN mode) in response to an external event.

Transitions between these bus modes follow the state transition diagram shown in Figure 8.7. Note that since the POR mode must be observed asynchronously by all modules, the corresponding mode value must not appear, even transiently, on *B_RES[2:0]*. Therefore the mode encodings have been chosen carefully to ensure that all legal transitions cannot produce this output as a logic hazard condition.

**Test interface**

A possible use of the AMBA is to provide support for a modular testing methodology through the *Test Interface Controller*. This approach allows each module on the AMBA to be tested independently by allowing an external tester to appear as a bus master on the ASB.

The only requirement for test mode to be supported is that the tester has access to the ASB through a 32-bit bidirectional port. Where a 32-bit bidirectional data bus interface to external memory or peripheral devices exists, this suffices. Where the off-chip data interface is only 16 or 8 bits wide other signals such as address lines are required to give 32 lines for test access.

The test interface allows control of the ASB address and data buses using protocols defined on the two test request inputs ($T\_RQA$ and $T\_RQB$) and an address latch and incrementer in the controller. A suitably designed macrocell module can then allow access to all of its interface signals in groups of up to 32 bits. For example, the ARM7 macrocell has a 13-bit control and configuration input, a 32-bit data input, a 15-bit status output and 32-bit address and data outputs. The test vectors are applied and the responses sensed following a sequence defined by a finite state automata whose state transitions are controlled by $T\_RQA$ and $T\_RQB$.

The AMBA macrocell test methodology may be compared with the JTAG-based methodology proposed in 'Macrocell testing' on page 226. Although perhaps less general, the AMBA approach will reduce test cost due its parallel tester interface.

**Advanced Peripheral Bus**

The ASB offers a relatively high-performance on-chip interconnect which suits processor, memory and peripheral macrocells with some built-in interface sophistication. For very simple, low-performance peripherals, the overhead of the interface is too high. The **Advanced Peripheral Bus** is a simple, static bus which operates as a stub on an ASB to offer a minimalist interface to very simple peripheral macrocells.

The bus includes address ($P\_A[n:0]$; the full 32 bits are not usually required) and data ($P\_D[m:0]$, where $m$ is 7, 15 or 31) buses which are no wider than necessary for the connected peripherals, a read/write direction indicator ($P\_WRITE$), individual peripheral select strobes ($P\_SELx$) and a peripheral timing strobe ($P\_STB$). APB peripherals may also make use of common ASB signals such as $B\_CLK$ and $B\_RES[2:0]$.

The address and control signals are all set-up and held with respect to the timing strobe to allow time for local decoding with the select acting as the local enable. Peripherals which are slave devices based around simple register mapping may be interfaced directly with minimal logic overhead.

## 8.6   The ARM reference microcontroller

The support for system development described so far in this chapter is principally aimed at testing and providing low-level access to processor and system state. AMBA offers a systematic way to connect hardware components together on a chip, but software development must still start from first principles on each new chip.

If a system developer wishes to start from a higher baseline, for example to base the software on a particular real-time operating system, then a number of components must be available to support the basic operating system functions. The **ARM reference microcontroller** specifies such a basic set of components, providing a framework within which an operating system can run but leaving full scope for application-specific system extensions.

The objective of the reference microcontroller is to ease the porting of software between compliant implementations and thereby raise the level from which software development begins on a new system.

**Base components**

The reference microcontroller specifies the following components:

- A memory map which allows the base address of the interrupt controller, the counter timers and the reset controller to vary but defines the offsets of the various registers from these base addresses.
- An interrupt controller with a defined set of functions, including a defined interrupt mechanism for a transmit and receive communications channel (though the mechanism of the channel itself is not defined).
- A counter timer with various defined functions.
- A reset controller with defined boot behaviour, power-on reset detection, a 'wait for interrupt' pause mode and an identification register.

The particular ARM core used with these components is not specified since this does not affect the system programmer's model.

**Memory map**

The system must define the base addresses of the interrupt controller (**ICBase**), the counter-timer (**CTBase**) and the reset and pause controller (**RPCBase**).

These addresses are not defined by the reference microcontroller specification, but all the addresses of the registers are defined relative to one or other of these base addresses.

**Interrupt controller**

The interrupt controller provides a uniform way of enabling, disabling and examining the status of up to 32 level-sensitive IRQ sources and one FIQ source. Each interrupt source has a mask bit which enables that source. Memory locations are defined with fixed offsets from *ICBase* to examine the unmasked, mask and masked interrupt status and to set or clear interrupt sources.

Five IRQ sources are defined by the reference microcontroller, corresponding to the communication receive and transmit functions, one for each counter-timer and one which can be generated directly by software (principally to enable an FIQ handler to generate an IRQ).

**Counter-timers**

Two 16-bit counter-timers are required, though more may be added. These are controlled by registers with fixed offsets relative to *CTBase*. The counters operate from the system clock with selectable pre-scaling of 0, 4 or 8 bits (so the input frequency is the system clock frequency divided by 1, 16 or 256).

Each counter-timer has a control register which selects the pre-scaling, enables or disables the counter and specifies the mode of operation as free-running or periodic, and a load register which specifies the value that the count starts from. A write to the 'load' register initializes the count value, which is then decremented to zero when an interrupt is generated. A write to the 'clear' register clears the interrupt. In free-running mode the counter continues to decrement past zero, whereas in periodic mode it is reloaded with the value in the 'load' register and decrements from there.

The current count value may be read from the 'value' register at any time.

**Reset and pause controller**

The reset and pause controller includes registers which are addressed at fixed offsets from *RPCBase*. The readable registers give identification and reset status information, including whether or not a power-on reset has occurred. The writeable registers can set or clear the reset status (though not the power-on reset status bit; this can only be set by a hardware power-on reset), clear the reset map (for instance to switch the ROM from location zero, where it is needed after power-on for the ARM reset vector, to the the normal memory map), and put the system into pause mode where it uses minimal power until an interrupt wakes it up again.

**System design**

Any ARM system which incorporates this basic set of components can support a suitably-configured operating system kernel. System design then consists of adding further application-specific peripherals and software, building upwards from a functional base.

Since most applications require these components there is little overhead incurred in using the reference microcontroller as the starting point for system development, and there is considerable benefit in starting from a functional system.

## 8.7    Example and exercises

**Example 8.1**    **Estimate the proportion of the number of test vectors required to test an ARM core via the JTAG and AMBA interfaces.**

An ARM core has in the region of 100 interface connections (32 data, 32 address, control, clock, bus, mode, and so on). The JTAG interface is serial. If the tester allows one vector to specify a pulse on *TCK* it will take 100 vectors to apply a parallel pattern to the ARM core. The AMBA test interface accesses the ARM periphery in five sections (see 'Test interface' on page 238), requiring five vectors on a standard tester.

The JTAG interface therefore appears to require 20 times the number of vectors. (Remember that JTAG is intended for PCB testing, not production VLSI testing.) In fact both the JTAG-based EmbeddedICE and AMBA interfaces include optimizations to improve the efficiency of getting instructions into the ARM core, which is the dominant requirement in testing it, but a very detailed analysis would be required to take these into account in the estimate.

**Exercise 8.1.1**    Summarize the problem areas in the production VLSI testing of complex macrocell-based system chips and discuss the relative merits of the various solutions.

**Exercise 8.1.2**    Describe and differentiate between production VLSI testing, printed circuit board testing and system debugging, and describe how a JTAG test port may be used to address each of these. Where is the JTAG approach most effective and where is it least effective?

**Exercise 8.1.3**    What problem does the Advanced Microprocessor Bus Architecture address and what problem does the ARM reference microcontroller address? How might they be related?

**Exercise 8.1.4**    Sketch a system development plan for an embedded system chip showing at which stage the ARMulator, AMBA, the reference microcontroller, EmbeddedICE and JTAG are (i) designed into the chip, and/or (ii) used to assist in the development process.

# 9 ARM Processor Cores

**Summary of chapter contents**

An ARM integer processor requires only a few square millimetres of silicon area, and as such can be used as a small cell in the corner of a large chip along with other cells chosen to suit the application for which the chip is designed.

One use for the 'spare' silicon area is to add performance enhancing features such as a cache memory and a write buffer, together with features such as memory management to support sophisticated operating systems. The resulting chip is a high-performance general-purpose CPU; chips which incorporate ARM processor cores in this way are described in Chapter 12.

An alternative way to exploit the rest of the chip area is to build application specific functions onto the chip, possibly including some memory, signal processing hardware, external memory controllers, serial interfaces, and so on. This 'system on a chip' use of processor macrocells represents the way of the future for many embedded systems and the small size of the ARM cores has given them a trail-blazing role in the development of such systems. Chapter 14 describes just a few of these embedded ARM systems.

This chapter looks at the processor cores themselves and the range of performance and functionality that is available. It also includes a description of the AMULET asynchronous ARM cores, which are research prototypes rather than commercial products, but they help to illustrate the breadth of design styles which have been used to implement the ARM architecture.

## 9.1 ARM6

The ARM6 core was the first implementation of the 32-bit ARM architecture (all previous ARM processors generated a 26-bit address) and formed the principal basis of the description of the ARM organization and implementation presented in Chapter 4. It implements ARM architecture version 3 (see Section 5.21 on page 153 for a full description of the ARM architecture variants), so it has backwards compatibility modes to support the older 26-bit architecture but does not incorporate 64-bit result multiplies or support for half-words, signed bytes, system mode or the Thumb instruction set.

The internal organization of the ARM6 was shown in Figure 4.1 on page 79 and the operation of its pipeline was covered in the same chapter. The only aspect of the device that has not been covered so far is the external hardware interface.

**Hardware interface**

The interface signals are shown in Figure 9.1. They are shown grouped by function, and the role of each group is described below with, where appropriate, information on the interface timing.

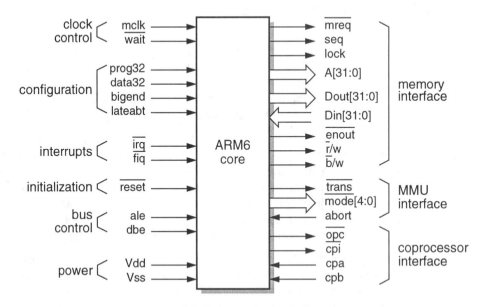

**Figure 9.1**   The ARM6 core interface signals.

**Clock control**

All state changes within the processor are controlled by *mclk*, the memory clock. Although this clock may be manipulated externally to cause the processor to wait for a slow access, is is often simpler to supply a free-running clock and to use $\overline{wait}$ to skip clock cycles. The internal clock is effectively just a logical AND of *mclk* and $\overline{wait}$, so $\overline{wait}$ must only change when *mclk* is low.

**Configuration**

These inputs configure the way the processor operates and are not expected to change dynamically, although they can be changed during phase 2 of the clock if necessary:

- *prog32* and *data32* can be used to force the processor into a backwards compatibility mode where the program and data space may be restricted to use 26-bit addressing. The 26-bit ARM architecture easily extends to support 32-bit data addressing; a 32-bit program space should not be used with a 26-bit data space. Where the full 32-bit architecture is selected, there is still support for 26-bit processes through software selectable 26-bit operating modes.

- *bigend* switches the byte ordering between little- and big-endian (see 'Memory organization' on page 110 for an explanation of endianness).

- *lateabt* switches the memory abort timing between two possible settings which trade off the amount of state recovery required against the time available for the MMU to validate the address (see 'Abort timing' on page 151).

**Interrupts**

The two interrupt inputs may be asynchronous to the processor clock since they pass through synchronizing latches before entering the processor's control logic. The fast interrupt request, $\overline{fiq}$, has higher priority than the normal interrupt request, $\overline{irq}$.

**Initialization**

$\overline{reset}$ starts the processor from a known state, executing from address $00000000_{16}$.

**Bus control**

Normally, the ARM6 core issues a new address as soon as it is available to maximize the time the MMU or memory controller has to process it. However, in simple systems where the address bus is connected directly to ROM or SRAM it is necessary to hold the old address to the end of the cycle. The core incorporates a transparent latch controlled by *ale*, which can re-time the address as required by external logic.

The ARM6 core indicates when it is performing a write cycle by signalling on $\overline{enout}$. Where the external data bus is bidirectional, $\overline{enout}$ is used to enable *dout[31:0]* onto it. Sometimes it is desirable to defer the write operation so that another device can drive the bus. The data bus enable signal, *dbe*, can be used to ensure that $\overline{enout}$ remains inactive in such circumstances. The core must be stopped (using $\overline{wait}$ or clock stretching) until the bus is available.

Both *ale* and *dbe* are externally timed as required by the external logic.

**Power**            The ARM6 core is designed to operate with a nominal 5 volt supply.

**Memory**           The memory interface comprises the 32-bit address ($A[31:0]$), data out ($Dout[31:0]$)
**interface**        and data in ($Din[31:0]$) buses together with six control signals.

- $\overline{mreq}$ indicates a processor cycle which requires a memory access.

- $seq$ indicates that the memory address will be sequential to (or possibly the same as) that used in the previous cycle.

- $lock$ indicates that the processor should keep the bus to ensure the atomicity of the read and write phases of a SWAP instruction.

- $\overline{enout}$ indicates that the processor is outputting data.

- $\overline{r}/w$ indicates whether the processor is performing a read or a write cycle.

- $\overline{b}/w$ indicates whether the access is for a byte or word quantity.

Although $\overline{enout}$ and $\overline{r}/w$ are indicating related information, $\overline{enout}$ is intended to control a driver onto a bidirectional data bus and is affected by $dbe$ whereas $\overline{r}/w$ is intended to prepare the memory system or MMU for a write cycle and is unaffected by $dbe$.

The signals which indicate the type of the memory cycle, $\overline{mreq}$ and $seq$, are issued early to give the memory control logic as long as possible to decide how to handle the memory access. The interpretation of the four possible combinations of values on these two signals is given in Table 9.1. When a sequential cycle follows a non-sequential cycle, the address will be that of the non-sequential cycle plus one word (four bytes); where the sequential cycle follows an internal or coprocessor register transfer cycle, the address will be unchanged from the preceding cycle. In a typical memory organization the incrementing case can be used, together with information about the preceding address, to prepare the memory for a fast sequential access, and

**Table 9.1**   ARM6 cycle types.

| $\overline{mreq}$ | $seq$ | Cycle | Use |
| --- | --- | --- | --- |
| 0 | 0 | N | Non-sequential memory access |
| 0 | 1 | S | Sequential memory access |
| 1 | 0 | I | Internal cycle – bus and memory inactive |
| 1 | 1 | C | Coprocessor register transfer – memory inactive |

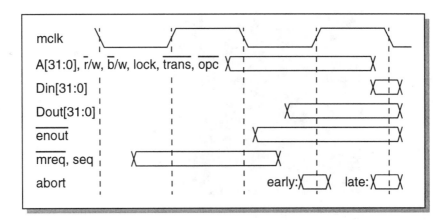

**Figure 9.2**    ARM6 core memory and MMU interface timing.

where the address remains the same this can be exploited to start a full memory access in the preceding cycle (since neither the internal nor the coprocessor register transfer cycles use the memory).

The timing of the critical interface signals is illustrated in Figure 9.2. The use of these signals and the design of the memory interface logic is discussed further in Section 13.1 on page 340, where specific examples are given.

**MMU interface**

The interface signals to the MMU provide information which is used to control access to areas of memory. The $\overline{trans}$ (translation control) signal indicates whether the processor is in a user ($\overline{trans}$ = 0) or privileged ($\overline{trans}$ = 1) mode so that some areas of memory can be restricted to supervisor-only access and, where appropriate, different translation tables can be used for user and supervisor code (though this is rarely done). Where more detailed information about the operating mode is required, $\overline{mode[4:0]}$ reflects the bottom five bits of the CPSR (inverted), though memory management at this level is rarely used; the detailed mode information is probably of most use when debugging.

Where an access is disallowed, this is signalled on the *abort* input. The timing of *abort* may be configured (using *lateabt*) to choose between *early abort* where the input must be valid half-way through the memory cycle and *late abort* where the input must be valid at the end of the cycle, with the data. Both timings are illustrated in Figure 9.2.

An aborted memory access causes the processor to take a prefetch or data abort, depending on the value of $\overline{opc}$ during the access.

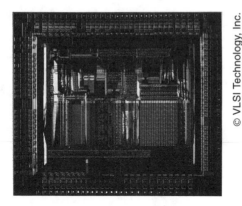

**Figure 9.3**   ARM60 die photograph.

The MMU may also use the $\overline{opc}$ signal where it is desired to support execute-only areas of memory, but it should be noted that this precludes the use of literal pools held in the code area for PC-relative access. For this reason execute-only protection is not widely used in ARM systems (and, in particular, is not supported in the ARM MMU architecture described in Section 11.3 on page 294).

**Coprocessor interface**

The $\overline{cpi}$, cpa and cpb coprocessor interface signals were described in Section 4.4 on page 101. The additional signal provided to the coprocessors is $\overline{opc}$, which indicates whether a memory access is to fetch an instruction or a data item. This is used by the coprocessor pipeline follower to track the ARM instruction execution. Where there is no requirement to connect a coprocessor, cpa and cpb should be tied high. This will cause all coprocessor instructions to take the undefined instruction trap.

**The ARM60 chip**

The ARM60 processor is an ARM6 core on a chip with JTAG boundary scan test logic and a pad ring. A photograph of a 0.8 μm ARM60 chip is shown in Figure 9.3 and the characteristics of the 0.6 μm part are summarized in Table 9.2.

**Table 9.2**   ARM60 characteristics.

| Process | 0.6 μm | Transistors | 42,748 | MIPS | 36 |
|---|---|---|---|---|---|
| Metal layers | 2 | Die area | 16 mm$^2$ | Power | 360 mW |
| Vdd | 5 V | Clock | 0 to 40 MHz | MIPS/W | 100 |

## 9.2 ARM7TDMI

The organization of the ARM7TDMI is illustrated in Figure 9.4. The ARM7TDMI core is functionally very similar to the ARM6 core, with a number of important extensions:

- It implements ARM architecture version 4T, with support for 64-bit result multiplies, half-word and signed byte loads and stores and the Thumb instruction set.
- It includes the EmbeddedICE module to support embedded system debugging.
- It is designed to operate from a 3 volt or a 5 volt power supply.

A number of backwards compatibility features have been left out:

- 26-bit modes are not supported, so the *prog32* and *data32* configuration inputs are not needed.
- Early abort timing is not supported, so the *lateabt* configuration input is omitted.

As the debug hardware is accessed via the JTAG test access port, the JTAG control logic is considered part of the processor macrocell. (An ARM6 application will usually include a JTAG test port, but it is external to the ARM6 core.)

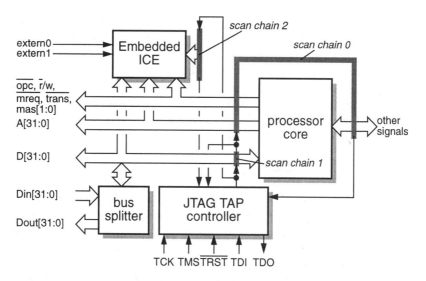

**Figure 9.4** ARM7TDMI organization.

**Hardware interface**

The hardware interface signals are shown in Figure 9.5 on page 251. Apart from the addition of the boundary scan and debug interfaces and the omission of the configuration signals mentioned above, there are several detailed differences from the ARM6:

- The *eclk* clock output reflects the clock used by the core, so it normally reflects the behaviour of *mclk* after $\overline{wait}$ has been gated in, but it also reflects the behaviour of the debug clock when in debugging mode.

- The *isync* input allows the interrupt synchronizers to be bypassed when the environment supplies inputs that are already synchronous to *mclk*; this removes the synchronizing delay from the interrupt latency.

- The *Tbit* output tells the environment whether the processor is currently executing ARM or Thumb instructions.

- The *mas[1:0]* (memory access size) outputs replace $\overline{b}/w$, allowing the processor to select half-word (and Thumb instruction) transfers in addition to bytes and words.

- The separate input (*Din[31:0]*) and output (*Dout[31:0]*) data buses are joined by a single bidirectional data bus (*D[31:0]*), with additional bus control signals ($\overline{enin}$, $\overline{enout}$) to ease the avoidance of on-chip bus clashes. Byte latch signals (*bl[3:0]*) make interfacing memories which are less than 32 bits wide easier.

**Data bus control**

Any bus which may be driven from different sources at different times requires very careful control to ensure that at most one source is driving at any time. Even if two sources are only on together transiently (due, for example, to slightly different delays in their enabling logic paths), the short-circuit current can waste significant power and generate significant electrical noise. Bus drivers tend to be among the most powerful devices on a chip, so their short-circuit currents can be high.

One way to avoid overlap is to use a clock to enforce a period when no source is driving the bus, and then to enable only one source in the active period. An illustration of this technique as applied to a simple board-level ARM system is given in Section 13.1 on page 340. However, in many cases no suitable clock is available, since to enforce an off period of half of an *mclk* cycle would seriously compromise performance. In such cases, some form of self-timing is required.

As a simple example of how a self-timed circuit can be employed, consider building an ARM7TDMI core into a chip where the data bus goes directly from the core to the pad ring. The connection from the core to the pad ring is bidirectional, and will be driven either by the core or by the pad input drivers, but never by both (and never by neither, except perhaps transiently, since a floating bus can cause avoidable power dissipation).

A suitable circuit is shown in Figure 9.6 on page 252. The non-overlapping drive is ensured by the cross-coupled NOR gates. This is a standard way of generating non-

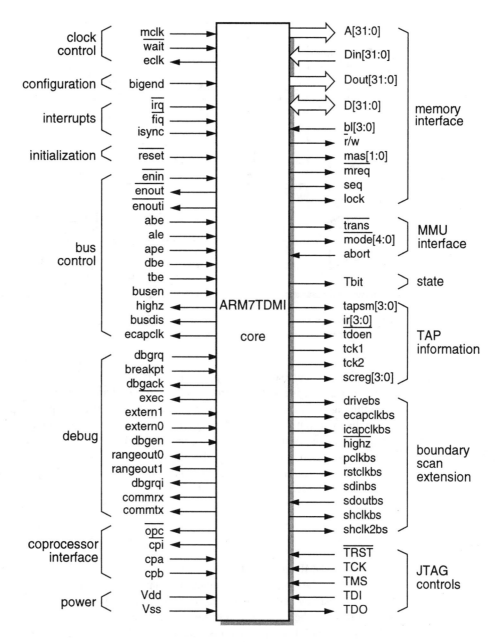

**Figure 9.5** The ARM7TDMI core interface signals.

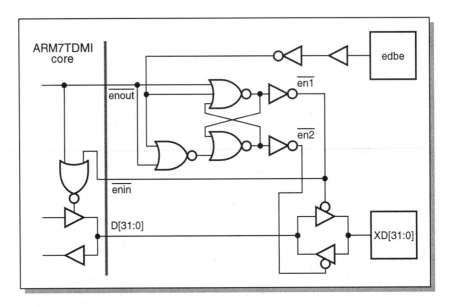

**Figure 9.6**    Data bus control circuit.

overlapping signals, such as the phase 1 and phase 2 clocks used in the ARM core itself, and here it prevents $\overline{en1}$ from rising until $\overline{en2}$ has fallen, and *vice versa*. Note that although as a Boolean logic circuit the cross-coupled NOR gates appear to guarantee that their outputs will not be high at the same time, this circuit actually requires careful analogue design to ensure that the signal rise and fall times and the varying gate thresholds do not compromise the non-overlap property at the bus drivers.

This circuit illustrates the role of $\overline{enin}$ and $\overline{enout}$ in controlling the bus, and also shows how an external data bus enable signal (*edbe*) can hold the processor off the external bus when there is other traffic requiring access to it. It should also be clear why these signals are not necessary on the ARM6 core, which has separate data in and data out buses.

**Debug support**

The ARM7TDMI implements the ARM debug architecture described in Section 8.3 on page 228. The EmbeddedICE module contains the breakpoint and watchpoint registers which allow code to be halted for debugging purposes. These registers are controlled through the JTAG test port using scan chain 2 (see Figure 9.4 on page 249). When a breakpoint or watchpoint is encountered, the processor halts and enters debug state. Once in debug state, the processor registers may be inspected by forcing

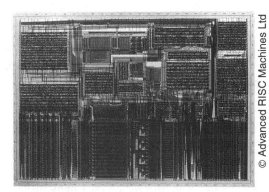

© Advanced RISC Machines Ltd

**Figure 9.7**    The ARM7TDMI processor core.

instructions into the instruction pipeline using scan chain 1. A store multiple of all the registers will present the register values on the data bus, where they can be sampled and shifted out again using scan chain 1. Accessing the banked registers requires instructions to be forced in to cause a mode change (note that in debug state the usual bar against switching into a privileged mode from user mode is removed).

Inspecting system state is achieved by causing the ARM to access memory locations at system speed and then switch immediately back into debug state.

**JTAG
extensions**

Since the JTAG Test Access Port (TAP) controller is included in the ARM7TDMI cell, several interface signals are made available to allow additional boundary scan paths to be added easily to any system chip which incorporates the cell. The 'boundary scan extension' signals shown in Figure 9.5 on page 251 allow an external scan path to be connected with minimal additional circuitry, and the 'TAP information' signals support more sophisticated extensions of the test system.

**ARM7TDMI
core**

A plot of the ARM7TDMI processor core is shown in Figure 9.7. The characteristics of the core when executing 32-bit ARM code are summarized in Table 9.3.

**Table 9.3**    ARM7TDMI characteristics.

| Process | 0.6 μm | Transistors | 74,209 | MIPS | 36 |
|---|---|---|---|---|---|
| Metal layers | 3 | Core area | 5 mm$^2$ | Power | 80 mW |
| Vdd | 3.3 V | Clock | 0 to 40 MHz | MIPS/W | 450 |

## 9.3    ARM8

The ARM8 core was developed at ARM Limited from 1993 to 1996 to supply the demand for an ARM core with a higher performance than was achievable with the ARM6/7 3-stage pipeline. The performance is improved by:

- Increasing the clock rate.

    This requires the logic in each pipeline stage to be simplified and, therefore, the number of pipeline stages to be increased.

- Reducing the CPI (clock cycles per instruction).

    This requires either that instructions which occupy more than one pipeline slot in an ARM6/7 are re-implemented to occupy fewer slots, or that pipeline stalls caused by dependencies between instructions are reduced, or a combination of both.

**Reducing the CPI**

The fundamental problem with reducing the CPI relative to an ARM7 core is related to the von Neumann bottleneck – any stored-program computer with a single instruction and data memory will have its performance limited by the available memory bandwidth. An ARM7 core accesses memory on (almost) every clock cycle either to fetch an instruction or to transfer data. Simply tightening-up on the few cycles where the memory is not used will yield only a small performance gain. To get a significantly better CPI than ARM7 the memory system must deliver more than one value in each clock cycle either by delivering more than 32 bits per cycle from a single memory or by having separate memories for instruction and data accesses.

**Double-bandwidth memory**

ARM8 retains a unified memory (either in the form of cache or on-chip RAM) but exploits the sequential nature of most memory accesses to achieve *double-bandwidth* from a single memory. It assumes that the memory it is connected to can deliver one word in a clock cycle and deliver the next sequential word half a cycle later concurrently with starting the next access. Typical memory organizations are quite capable of supplying the extra data with only a little extra hardware cost. Restricting the extra bandwidth to sequential accesses may seem to limit its usefulness, but instruction fetches are highly sequential and ARM's load multiple instructions generate sequential addresses (as do the store multiple instructions, though these do not exploit the double-bandwidth memory on ARM8), so the occurrence of sequential accesses is quite high in typical ARM code.

A 64-bit wide memory has the required characteristics, but delaying the arrival of the second word by half a clock cycle allows a 32-bit bus to be used and can save power in the memory itself since the sense-amplifiers for the second word need not be as sensitive as those for the first. As the first-level memory is likely to be on the same chip as the core at these performance levels it is possible to exploit this advantage.

**Core organization**

The ARM8 processor consists of a prefetch unit and an integer datapath. The prefetch unit is responsible for fetching instructions from memory and buffering them (in order to exploit the double-bandwidth memory). It then supplies up to one instruction per clock cycle to the integer unit, along with its PC value. The prefetch unit is responsible for branch prediction and can use any technique it wishes to attempt to guess where the instruction stream will go; the integer unit will compute the exact stream and issue corrections to the prefetch unit where necessary.

The first ARM8 cores incorporate a prefetch unit which uses static branch prediction based on the branch direction (backwards branches are predicted 'taken', whereas forwards branches are predicted 'not taken'), but the core is organized in such a way as to make the future incorporation of a more sophisticated prediction scheme straightforward.

The overall organization of the core is shown in Figure 9.8. The double-bandwidth memory will normally be on-chip, in the form of a cache memory on a general-purpose device such as the ARM810 (described in Section 12.3 on page 326) or as addressable RAM in an embedded application. The remaining memory may comprise conventional, single-bandwidth devices, but without some fast memory in the system the ARM8 core will show little benefit over the simpler ARM cores.

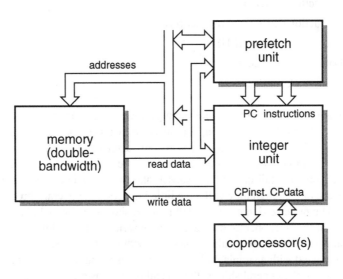

**Figure 9.8**    ARM8 processor core organization.

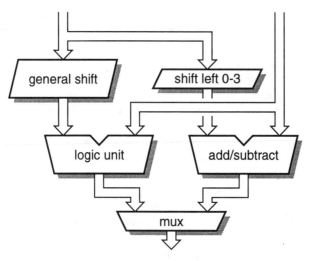

**Figure 9.9**    ARM8 ALU/Shifter organization.

**Pipeline organization**

The processor uses a 5-stage pipeline with the prefetch unit occupying the first stage and the integer unit using the remaining four stages:

1. Instruction prefetch.
2. Instruction decode and register read.
3. Execute (shift and ALU).
4. Data memory access.
5. Write-back results.

**ARM8 ALU/ Shifter**

Although the ARM architecture includes instructions that perform a general shift in series with any ALU operation, compilers rarely make good use of this feature. Therefore the ARM8 execution unit supports only a subset of the ARM combined shift and ALU operations in order to reduce the worst case delay through this pipeline stage. Instructions that fall outside this subset take two clock cycles in the execute stage; if these are rare enough they will have little impact on the overall throughput.

The organization of the ALU/Shifter is shown in Figure 9.9. A carefully chosen subset of the shift operations is available in series with an addition or subtraction, and all shift operations are available in series with a logical operation. The shift subset is implemented with a simple multiplexer which is much faster than the cross-bar switch structure of the general shifter; the logical operations are much faster than addition or subtraction since they do not require carry-propagate logic.

**Integer unit organization**

The organization of the ARM8 integer unit is illustrated in Figure 9.10 on page 258. The instruction stream and associated PC values are supplied by the prefetch unit through the interface shown at the top of the figure; the system control coprocessor connects through the dedicated coprocessor instruction and data buses to the left of the figure; the interface to the data memory is to the right of the figure and comprises an address bus, a write data bus and a read data bus.

Note that the read memory data bus supports double-bandwidth transfers on load multiple instructions, and both register write ports are used in load multiple instructions to store the double-bandwidth data stream. Since load multiple instructions transfer word quantities only, it does not matter that half of the data stream bypasses the byte alignment and sign extension logic.

**ARM8 applications**

ARM8 has been designed as a general-purpose processor core that can readily be manufactured by ARM Limited's many licensees, so it is not highly optimized for a particular process technology. It offers significantly (two to three times) higher performance than the simpler ARM cores for a similar increase in silicon area, and requires the support of double-bandwidth on-chip memory if it is to realize its full potential.

One application of the ARM8 core is to build a high-performance CPU such as the ARM810, described in Section 12.3 on page 326. There the double-bandwidth memory is in the form of a cache, and the chip also incorporates a memory management unit and system control coprocessor CP15.

Embedded applications of ARM8 would probably include some directly mapped on-chip double-bandwidth memory used as a software controlled cache for speed-critical routines, although they could, as an alternative, include a cache memory similar to but smaller than that on the ARM810. The application specific macrocells occupy the remaining silicon area. The application must require the extra performance available from the ARM8 core in order to justify the additional costs incurred in the larger core and higher performance support memory.

Where embedded applications require critical sections of code to remain in fast memory, a cache may not be adequate since items get flushed from the cache in a way that is rather hard to control. The ARM810 cache design recognizes this problem, however, and allows sections to be 'locked down' to ensure that they will not be flushed.

**ARM8 silicon**

The ARM8 core has been incorporated into the ARM810 which is described in Section 12.3 on page 326. The core uses 124,554 transistors and operates at speeds up to 72 MHz on a 0.5 μm CMOS process with three metal layers.

The core layout can be seen in the ARM810 die photograph in Figure 12.12 on page 328 in the upper left-hand area of the die.

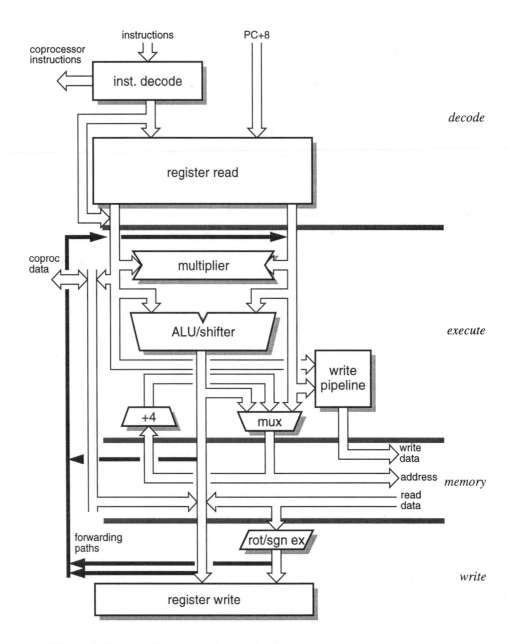

**Figure 9.10**   ARM8 integer unit organization.

## 9.4   AMULET1&2

The AMULET processor cores are fully asynchronous implementations of the ARM architecture, which means that they are self-timed and operate without any externally supplied clock. At the time of writing they are unique; no other commercial microprocessor architecture has been implemented in this style.

At present these processor cores are research prototypes, developed at the University of Manchester in England, and their commercial future is not yet clear. There is insufficient space in this book to present complete descriptions of them, but they are outlined here since they represent another, very different, way to implement the ARM instruction set. The bibliography at the back of the book includes a reference where further details on AMULET1 may be found, and fuller details on AMULET2 (and AMULET2e) will be published in due course.

**Motivation for self-timed design**

Since there are, at the time of writing, no other examples of asynchronous VLSI implementations of commercial microprocessors, it is perhaps necessary to give some reasons why such an implementation style may be advantageous.

The principal motivation for re-examining asynchronous design is its potential for power-efficiency. The clock in a synchronous circuit runs all the time, causing transitions in the circuit that dissipate electrical power. The clock frequency must be set so that the processor can cope with the peak workload, and although the clock rate can be adjusted under software control to varying demands, this can only be done relatively crudely at a coarse granularity. Therefore most of the time the clock is running faster than is necessary to support the current workload, resulting in wasted power. An asynchronous design, on the other hand, only causes transitions in the circuit in response to a request to carry out useful work. It can switch instantaneously between zero power dissipation and maximum performance upon demand.

Since many embedded applications have rapidly varying workloads, an asynchronous processor appears to offer the potential of significant power savings.

Additional reasons for looking at asynchronous design include its lower emission of electromagnetic radiation due to less coherent internal activity, and its potential to deliver typical rather than worst-case performance since its timing adjusts to actual conditions whereas a clocked circuit must be toleranced for worst-case conditions.

**Self-timed signalling**

Asynchronous design is a complex discipline with many different facets and many different approaches. It is outside the scope of this book to offer any general introduction to asynchronous design, but a few basic concepts should enable the reader to come to grips with the most important features of the AMULET cores. The foremost of these concepts is the idea of asynchronous communication. How is the flow of data controlled in the absence of any reference clock?

The AMULET designs both use forms of the *Request-Acknowledge* hand-shake to control the flow of data. The sequence of actions comprising the communication of data from the *Sender* to the *Receiver* is as follows:

1. The Sender places a valid data value onto a bus.
2. The Sender then issues a *Request* event.
3. The Receiver accepts the data when it is ready to do so.
4. The Receiver issues an *Acknowledge* event to the Sender.
5. The Sender may then remove the data from the bus and begin the next communication when it is ready to do so.

The data is passed along the bus using a conventional binary encoding, but there are two ways that the Request and Acknowledge events may be signalled:

**Transition signalling**
- AMULET1 uses transition encoding where a change in level (either high to low or low to high) signals an event; this is illustrated in Figure 9.11.

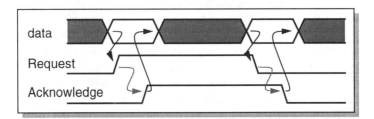

**Figure 9.11**   Transition-signalling communication protocol.

**Level signalling**
- AMULET2 uses level encoding where a rising edge signals an event and a return-to-zero phase must occur before the next event can be signalled; this is illustrated in Figure 9.12 on page 261.

Transition signalling was used on AMULET1 since it is conceptually cleaner; every transition has a role and its timing is therefore determined by the circuit's function. It also uses the minimum number of transitions, and should therefore be power-efficient. However the CMOS circuits used to implement transition control are relatively slow and inefficient, so AMULET2 uses level signalling which employs circuits which are faster and more power-efficient despite using twice the number of

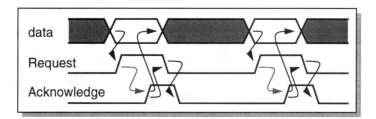

**Figure 9.12**   Level-signalling communication protocol.

transitions, but leave somewhat arbitrary decisions to be taken about the timing of the recovery (return-to-zero) phases in the protocol.

**Self-timed pipelines**

An asynchronous pipelined processing unit can be constructed using self-timing techniques to allow for the processing delay in each stage and one of the above protocols to send the result to the next stage.

When the circuit is correctly designed, variable processing delays and arbitrary external delays can be accommodated; all that matters is the local sequencing of events (though long delays will, of course, lead to low performance).

Unlike a clocked pipeline, where the whole pipeline must always be clocked at a rate determined by the slowest stage under worst-case environmental (voltage and temperature) conditions and assuming worst-case data, an asynchronous pipeline will operate at a variable rate determined by current conditions. It is possible to allow rare worst-case conditions to cause a processing unit to take a little longer. There will be some performance loss when these conditions do arise, but so long as they are rare enough the impact on overall performance will be small.

**Self-timed ARM cores**

Both AMULET processor cores have the same high-level organization as illustrated in Figure 9.13 on page 262. The design is based upon a set of interacting asynchronous pipelines, all operating in their own time at their own speed. These pipelines might appear to introduce unacceptably long latencies into the processor but, unlike a synchronous pipeline, an asynchronous pipeline can have a very low latency.

The operation of the processor begins with the address interface issuing instruction fetch requests to the memory. The address interface has an autonomous address incrementer (the AMULET2 address interface also incorporates a *Jump Trace Buffer* which attempts to predict branches from past behaviour) which enables it to prefetch instructions as far ahead as the capacities of the various pipeline buffers allow.

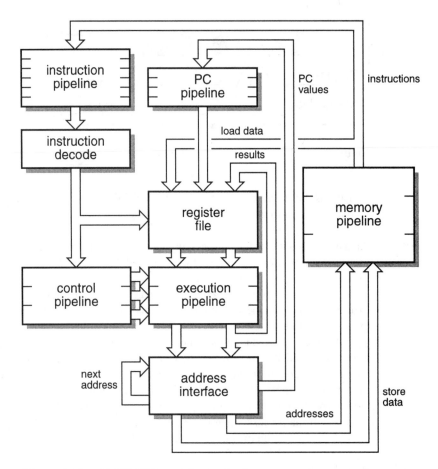

**Figure 9.13**   AMULET internal organization.

**Address
non-
determinism**

Instructions that need to generate a new memory address, such as data transfer instructions and unpredicted branches, calculate the new address in the execution pipeline and then send it to the address interface. Since it arrives with arbitrary timing relative to the internal incrementing loop within the address interface, the point of insertion of the new address into the address stream is non-deterministic, so the processor's depth of prefetch beyond a branch instruction is fundamentally non-deterministic.

**Register coherency**

If the execution pipeline is to work efficiently, the register file must be able to issue the operands for an instruction before the result of the previous instruction has returned. However, in some cases an operand may depend on a preceding result (this is a *read-after-write* hazard), in which case the register file cannot issue the operand until the result has returned unless there is a forwarding mechanism to supply the correct value further down the pipeline.

The register forwarding mechanism used on many RISC processors (including ARM8 and StrongARM) is based upon the characteristics of a synchronous pipeline since it involves comparing the source operand register number in one pipeline stage with the destination register number in another stage. In an asynchronous pipeline the stages are all moving at different times and such a comparison can only be made by introducing explicit synchronization between the stages concerned, thereby losing most of the benefits of asynchronous operation.

**Register locking**

On the AMULET processors register coherency is achieved through a novel form of register locking, based on a register lock FIFO (first-in-first-out queue). The destination register numbers are stored, in decoded form, in a FIFO, until the associated result is returned from the execution or memory pipeline to the register bank.

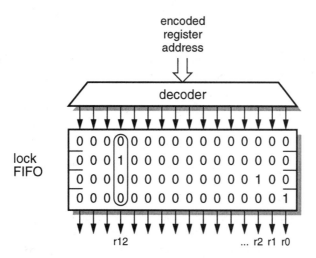

**Figure 9.14**   AMULET register lock FIFO organization.

The organization of the lock FIFO is illustrated in Figure 9.14 on page 263. Each stage of the FIFO holds a '1' in the position corresponding to the destination register. In this figure the FIFO controls 16 registers (in the AMULET chips the FIFO has a column for each physical register, including the ARM banked registers) and is shown in a state where the first result to arrive will be written into r0, the second into r2, the third into r12 and the fourth FIFO stage is empty.

If a subsequent instruction requests r12 as a source operand, an inspection of the FIFO column corresponding to r12 (outlined in the figure) reveals whether or not r12 is valid. A '1' anywhere in the column signifies a pending write to r12, so its current value is obsolete. The read waits until the '1' is cleared, then it can proceed.

The 'inspection' is implemented in hardware by a logical 'OR' function across the column for each register. This may appear hazardous since the data in the FIFO may move down the FIFO while the 'OR' output is being used. However, data moves in an asynchronous FIFO by being duplicated from one stage into the next, only then is it removed from the first stage, so a propagating '1' will appear alternately in one or two positions and it will never disappear completely. The 'OR' output will therefore be stable even though the data is moving.

**AMULET1 register coherency**

AMULET1 depends entirely on the register locking mechanism to maintain register coherency, and as a result the execution pipeline is stalled quite frequently in typical code. (Register dependencies between consecutive instructions are common in typical code since the compiler makes no attempt to avoid them because standard ARM processors are insensitive to such dependencies.)

**AMULET2 register forwarding**

In order to reduce the performance loss due to register dependency stalls, AMULET2 incorporates forwarding mechanisms to handle common cases. As mentioned above, the bypass mechanism used in clocked processor pipelines is inapplicable to asynchronous pipelines, so novel techniques are required. The two techniques used on AMULET2 are:

- A *last result* register. The instruction decoder keeps a record of the destination of the result from the execution pipeline, and if the immediately following instruction uses this register as a source operand the register read phase is bypassed and the value is collected from the last result register.

- A *last loaded data* register. The instruction decoder keeps a record of the destination of the last data item loaded from memory, and whenever this register is used as a source operand the register read phase is bypassed and the value is picked up directly from the last loaded data register. A mechanism similar to the lock FIFO serves as a guard on the register to ensure that the correct value is collected.

Both these mechanisms rely on the required result being available; where there is some uncertainty (for example when the result is produced by an instruction which is conditionally executed) the instruction decoder can fall back on the locking mechanism, exploiting the ability of the asynchronous organization to cope with variable delays in the supply of the operands.

**AMULET2 jump trace buffer**

AMULET1 prefetches instructions sequentially from the current PC value and all deviations from sequential execution must be issued as corrections from the execution pipeline to the address interface. Every time the PC has to be corrected performance is lost and energy is wasted in prefetching instructions that are then discarded.

AMULET2 attempts to reduce this inefficiency by remembering where branches were previously taken and guessing that control will subsequently follow the same path. The organization of the jump trace buffer is shown in Figure 9.15; it is similar to that used on the MU5 mainframe computer developed at the University of Manchester between 1969 and 1974 (which also operated with asynchronous control).

The buffer caches the program counters and targets of recently taken branch instructions, and whenever it spots an instruction fetch from an address that it has stored it modifies the predicted control flow from sequential to the previous branch

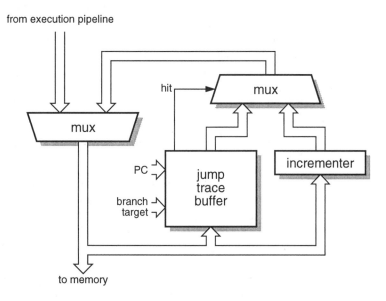

**Figure 9.15**   The AMULET2 jump trace buffer.

**Table 9.4**    AMULET2 branch prediction statistics.

| Prediction algorithm | Correct | Incorrect | Redundant fetches |
|---|---|---|---|
| Sequential | 33% | 67% | 2 per branch (ave.) |
| Trace buffer | 67% | 33% | 1 per branch (ave.) |

target. If this prediction turns out to be correct, exactly the right instruction sequence is fetched from memory; if it turns out to be wrong and the branch should not have been taken, the branch is executed as an 'unbranch' instruction to return to the previous sequential flow.

**Branch statistics**

The effectiveness of the jump trace buffer depends on the statistics of typical branch behaviour. Typical figures are shown in Table 9.4.

In the absence of the jump trace buffer, the default sequential fetch pattern is equivalent to predicting that all branches are not taken. This is correct for one-third of all branches, and incorrect for the remaining two-thirds. A jump trace buffer with around 20 entries reverses these proportions, correctly predicting around two-thirds of all branches and mispredicting or failing to predict around one-third.

Although the depth of prefetching beyond a branch is non-deterministic, a prefetch depth of around three instructions is observed on AMULET1. The fetched instructions are used when the branch is predicted correctly, but are discarded when the branch is mispredicted or not predicted. The jump trace buffer therefore reduces the average number of redundant fetches per branch from two to one. Since branches occur around once every five instructions in typical code, the jump trace buffer may be expected to reduce the instruction fetch bandwidth by around 20% and the total memory bandwidth by 10% to 15%.

Where the system performance is limited by the available memory bandwidth, this saving translates directly into improved performance; in any case it represents a power saving due to the elimination of redundant activity.

**AMULET1 performance**

AMULET1 was developed to demonstrate the feasibility of designing a fully asynchronous implementation of a commercial microprocessor architecture. The prototype chips were functional and ran test programs generated using standard ARM development tools. The test system was an asynchronous version of the ARM PIE (Platform

**Table 9.5**   AMULET1 characteristics.

|                      | AMULET1/ES2      | AMULET1/GPS                  | ARM6            |
|----------------------|------------------|-----------------------------|-----------------|
| **Process**          | 1 μm             | 0.7 μm                      | 1 μm            |
| **Area (mm$^2$)**    | 5.5 x 4.1        | 3.9 x 2.9                   | 4.1 x 2.7       |
| **Transistors**      | 58,374           | 58,374                      | 33,494          |
| **Performance**      | 20.5 kDhrystones | ~40 kDhrystones[a]          | 31 kDhrystones  |
| **Multiplier**       | 5.3 ns/bit       | 3 ns/bit                    | 25 ns/bit       |
| **Conditions**       | 5 V, 20°C        | 5 V, 20°C                   | 5 V, 20 MHz     |
| **Power**            | 152 mW           | N/A[b]                      | 148 mW          |
| **MIPS/W**           | 77               | N/A                         | 120             |

a.  Estimated maximum performance.

b.  The GPS part does not support power measurement.

Independent Evaluation) card which is described in Chapter 13, incorporating a ROM taken from a PIE card.

The performance of the prototypes is summarized in Table 9.5, which shows the characteristics of the devices manufactured on two different process technologies by European Silicon Systems (ES2) and GEC Plessey Semiconductors (GPS). The layout of the 1 μm AMULET1 core is shown in Figure 9.16 on page 268.

The performance figures, based on the Dhrystone benchmark, show a performance which is of the same order as, but certainly no better than, an ARM6 processor built on the same process technology. However, AMULET1 was built primarily to demonstrate the feasibility of self-timed design, which it manifestly does.

**AMULET2**   The characteristics of AMULET2 are discussed further in Section 14.5 on page 382, where its use as a processor core in a prototype embedded system chip (AMULET2e) is described.

At the time of writing AMULET2e is about to be shipped for fabrication, so no AMULET2 silicon has yet been tested. Therefore its performance is less certain than that of AMULET1, but simulations suggest that it should deliver close to 70 kDhrystones under typical conditions, making it faster than any of the ARM cores with simple 3-stage pipelines but slower than the ARM810 (and considerably slower than the StrongARM).

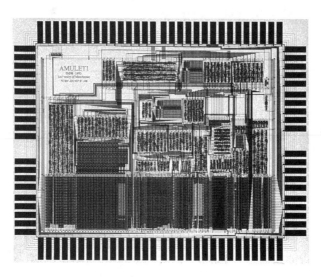

**Figure 9.16**    AMULET1 die plot.

**AMULET
support**

AMULET1 was developed using European Community funding within the Open Microprocessor systems Initiative - Microprocessor Architecture Project (OMI-MAP). AMULET2 was developed within the Open Microprocessor systems Initiative - Deeply Embedded ARM (OMI-DE/ARM) project.

The work also received support in various forms from Advanced RISC Machines Limited, GEC Plessey Semiconductors and VLSI Technology, Inc. Tools from Compass Design Automation were important to the success of both projects, and TimeMill from EPIC Design Technology, Inc. was vital to the accurate modelling of AMULET2.

## 9.5   Examples and exercises

**Example 9.1**   **How should the ARM6 address bus be retimed to interface to static RAM or ROM devices?**

To interface to static memory devices the address pipelining must be removed. This is most simply achieved by connecting *ale* to an inverted *mreq*. In systems where some memory devices benefit from early addresses and some are static, either an external latch should be used to retime the addresses to the static devices or *ale* should be controlled to suit the currently addressed device.

**Exercise 9.1.1**   Consider the design of the control logic required to control *ale* appropriately in a system where some memory devices are static and others require the address as early as possible. Why is this not straightforward?

**Exercise 9.1.2**   Now consider the case where non-sequential cycles take two clock cycles and sequential cycles take one clock cycle. The address timing is critical only in sequential cycles. Design the control logic for *ale*.

**Example 9.2**   **Why does ARM8 require a double-bandwidth memory in order to reduce the average number of clock cycles per instruction (CPI) compared with ARM7?**

Since ARM7 accesses memory on nearly all clock cycles either to fetch an instruction or to transfer data and the number of memory accesses required by a particular code sequence is defined by the instruction set semantics, the only way to reduce the number of clock cycles required for the sequence is to transfer more than one memory word in some clock cycles.

There are several ways to deliver more than one word per cycle. The separate instruction and data caches on StrongARM (described in Section 12.4 on page 329) can each deliver a word per cycle. ARM8 uses a different approach which exploits the sequential nature of many ARM memory accesses. The double-bandwidth memory can deliver two consecutive words in one clock cycle. This is not useful all of the time, since a single word or byte load or store cannot benefit from a 'free' second word. However, instruction fetches are highly sequential and load multiple instructions also use sequential addresses (as do store multiple instructions, though ARM8 does not exploit this), so although the double-bandwidth memory does not double the useful bandwidth, it provides a significant increase.

**Exercise 9.2.1**     Assuming that 75% of all ARM memory accesses are sequential, and taking the dynamic instruction distribution given in Table 1.3 on page 23, compare the maximum possible CPI improvement that can be achieved with separate instruction and data caches with that achievable using double-bandwidth memory.

**Exercise 9.2.2**     How is the above result affected if the double-bandwidth memory is restricted to even word addresses?

**Exercise 9.2.3**     What other factors might limit the effectiveness of the double-bandwidth memory?

# 10 Memory Hierarchy

**Summary of chapter contents**

A modern microprocessor can execute instructions at a very high rate. To exploit this potential performance fully the processor must be connected to a memory system which is both very large and very fast. If the memory is too small, it will not be able to hold enough programs to keep the processor busy. If it is too slow, the memory will not be able to supply instructions as fast as the processor can execute them.

Unfortunately, the larger a memory is the slower it is. It is therefore not possible to design a single memory which is both large enough and fast enough to keep a high-performance processor busy.

It is, however, possible to build a composite memory system which combines a small, fast memory and a large, slow *main* memory to present an external behaviour which, with typical program statistics, appears to behave like a large, fast memory much of the time. The small, fast memory component is the *cache*, which automatically retains copies of instructions and data that the processor is using most frequently. The effectiveness of the cache depends on the *spatial locality* and *temporal locality* properties of the program.

This two-level memory principle can be extended into a memory hierarchy of many levels, and the computer backup (disk) store can be viewed as part of this hierarchy. With suitable *memory management* support, the size of a program is limited not by the computer's main memory but by the size of the hard disk, which may be very much larger than the main memory.

## 10.1   Memory size and speed

A typical computer memory hierarchy comprises several levels, each level having a characteristic size and speed.

- The processor registers can be viewed as the top of the memory hierarchy. A RISC processor will typically have around thirty-two 32-bit registers making a total of 128 bytes, with an access time of a few nanoseconds.

- On-chip cache memory will have a capacity of eight to 32 Kbytes with an access time around ten nanoseconds.

- High-performance desktop systems may have a second-level off-chip cache with a capacity of a few hundred Kbytes and an access time of a few tens of nanoseconds.

- Main memory will be megabytes to tens of megabytes of dynamic RAM with an access time around 100 nanoseconds.

- Backup store, usually on a hard disk, will be hundreds of Mbytes up to a few Gbytes with an access time of a few tens of milliseconds.

Note that the performance difference between the main memory and the backup store is very much greater than the difference between any other adjacent levels, even when there is no secondary cache in the system.

The data which is held in the registers is under the direct control of the compiler or assembler programmer, but the contents of the remaining levels of the hierarchy are usually managed automatically. The caches are effectively invisible to the application program, with blocks or 'pages' of instructions and data migrating up and down the hierarchy under hardware control. Paging between the main memory and the backup store is controlled by the operating system, and remains transparent to the application program. Since the performance difference between the main memory and the backup store is so great, much more sophisticated algorithms are required here to determine when to migrate data between the levels.

An embedded system will not usually have a backing store and will therefore not exploit paging. However, many embedded systems incorporate caches, and ARM CPU chips employ a range of cache organizations. We will therefore look at cache organizational issues in some detail.

**Memory cost**   Fast memory is more expensive per bit than slow memory, so a memory hierarchy also aims to give a performance close to the fastest memory with an average cost per bit approaching that of the slowest memory.

## 10.2 Caches

The first RISC processors were introduced at a time when standard memory parts were faster than their contemporary microprocessors, but this situation did not persist for long. Subsequent advances in semiconductor process technology which have been exploited to make microprocessors faster have been applied differently to improve memory chips. Standard DRAM parts have got a little faster, but mostly they have been developed to have a much higher capacity.

**Processor and memory speeds**

In 1980 a typical DRAM part could hold 4 Kbits of data, with 16 Kbit chips arriving in 1981 and 1982. These parts would cycle at 3 or 4 MHz for random accesses, and at about twice this rate for local accesses (in page mode). Microprocessors at that time could request around two million memory accesses per second.

In 1995 DRAM parts have a capacity of 16 Mbits per chip, with random accesses operating at around 6 MHz. Microprocessors can request a hundred million memory accesses per second. If the processor is so much faster than the memory, it can only deliver its full performance potential with the help of a **cache** memory.

A cache memory is a small, very fast memory that retains copies of recently used memory values. It operates transparently to the programmer, automatically deciding which values to keep and which to overwrite. These days it is usually implemented on the same chip as the processor. Caches work because programs normally display the property of **locality**, which means that at any particular time they tend to execute the same instructions many times (for instance in a loop) on the same areas of data (for instance a stack).

**Unified and Harvard caches**

Caches can be built in many ways. At the highest level a processor can have one of the following two organizations:

- A unified cache.

  This is a single cache for both instructions and data, as illustrated in Figure 10.1 on page 274.

- Separate instruction and data caches.

  This organization is sometimes called a **modified Harvard** architecture as shown in Figure 10.2 on page 275.

Both these organizations have their merits. The unified cache automatically adjusts the proportion of the cache memory used by instructions according to the current program requirements, giving a better performance than a fixed partitioning. On

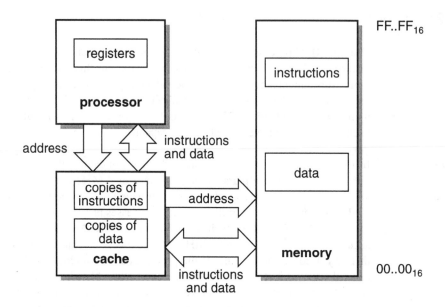

**Figure 10.1**   A unified instruction and data cache.

the other hand the separate caches allow load and store instructions to execute in a single clock cycle.

**Cache performance metrics**
Since the processor can operate at its high clock rate only when the memory items it requires are held in the cache, the overall system performance depends strongly on the proportion of memory accesses which cannot be satisfied by the cache. An access to an item which is in the cache is called a **hit**, and an access to an item which is not in the cache is a **miss**. The proportion of all the memory accesses that are satisfied by the cache is the **hit rate**, usually expressed as a percentage, and the proportion that are not is the **miss rate**.

The miss rate of a well-designed cache should be only a few per cent if a modern processor is to fulfil its potential. The miss rate depends on a number of cache parameters including its size (the number of bytes of memory in the cache) and its organization.

**Cache organization**
Since a cache holds a dynamically varying selection of items from main memory, it must have storage for both the data and the address that the data is stored at in main memory.

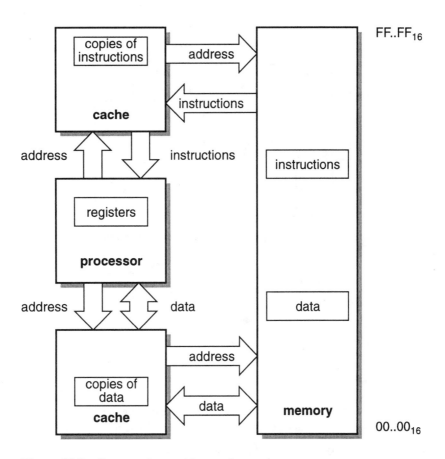

**Figure 10.2**    Separate data and instruction caches.

**The direct-mapped cache**

The simplest organization of these components is the direct-mapped cache which is illustrated in Figure 10.3 on page 276. In the direct-mapped cache a **line** of data is stored along with an address **tag** in a memory which is addressed by some portion of the memory address.

To check whether or not a particular memory item is stored in the cache, the relevant address bits are used to access the cache entry. The top address bits are then compared with the stored tag; if they are equal, the item is in the cache. The lowest address bits can be used to access the desired item within the line.

This, simplest, cache organization has a number of properties that can be contrasted with those of more complex organizations:

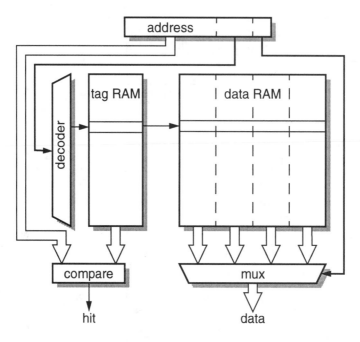

**Figure 10.3**  Direct-mapped cache organization.

- A particular memory item is stored in a unique location in the cache; two items with the same cache address field will contend for use of that location.

- Only those bits of the address which are not used to select within the line or to address the cache RAM need be stored in the tag field.

- The tag and data access can be performed at the same time, giving the fastest cache access time of any organization.

- Since the tag RAM is typically a lot smaller than the data RAM, its access time is shorter, allowing the tag comparison to be completed within the data access time.

A typical direct-mapped cache might store 8 Kbytes of data in 16-byte lines. There would therefore be 512 lines. A 32-bit address would have four bits to address bytes within the line and nine bits to select the line, leaving a 19-bit tag which requires just over one Kbyte of tag store.

When data is loaded into the cache, a **block** of data is fetched from memory. There is little point in having the line size smaller than the block size. If the block size is smaller than the line size, the tag store must be extended to include a valid bit for each block within the line. Choosing the line and block sizes to be equal results in the simplest organization.

**The set-associative cache**

Moving up in complexity, the set-associative cache aims to reduce the problems due to contention by enabling a particular memory item to be stored in more than one cache location. A 2-way set-associative cache is illustrated in Figure 10.4 on page 278. As the figure suggests, this form of cache is effectively two direct-mapped caches operating in parallel. An address presented to the cache may find its data in either half, so each memory address may be stored in either of two places. Each of two items which were in contention for a single location in the direct-mapped cache may now occupy one of these places, allowing the cache to hit on both.

The 8 Kbyte cache with 16 byte lines will have 256 lines in each half of the cache, so four bits of the 32-bit address select a byte from the line and eight bits select one line from each half of the cache. The address tag must therefore be one bit longer, at 20 bits. The access time is only very slightly longer than that of the direct-mapped cache, the increase being due to the need to multiplex the data from the two halves.

When a new data item is to be placed in the cache, a decision must be taken as to which half to place it in. There are several options here, the most common being:

• Random allocation.

The decision is based on a random or pseudo-random value.

• Least recently used (LRU).

The cache keeps a record of which location of a pair was last accessed and allocates the new data to the other one.

• Cyclic.

The cache keeps a record of which location of a pair was last allocated and allocates the new data to the other one.

The set-associative approach extends beyond 2-way up to any degree of associativity, but in practice the benefits of going beyond 4-way associativity are small and do not warrant the extra complexity incurred.

**The fully associative cache**

At the other extreme of associativity, it is possible to design a fully associative cache in VLSI technology. Rather than continuing to divide the direct-mapped cache into ever smaller components, the tag store is designed differently using content addressed memory (**CAM**). A CAM cell is a RAM cell with an inbuilt comparator, so a CAM based tag store can perform a parallel search to locate an address in any location. The organization of a fully associative cache is illustrated in Figure 10.5 on page 279.

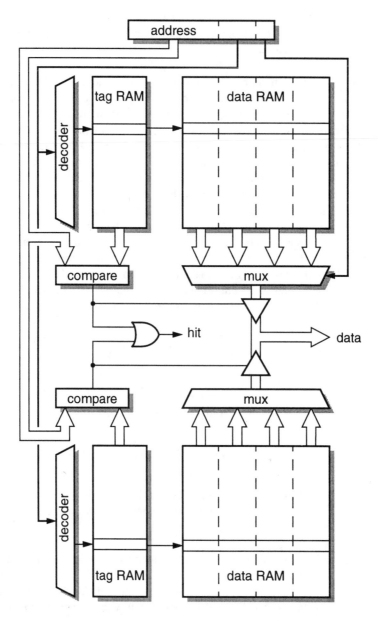

**Figure 10.4**    2-way set-associative cache organization.

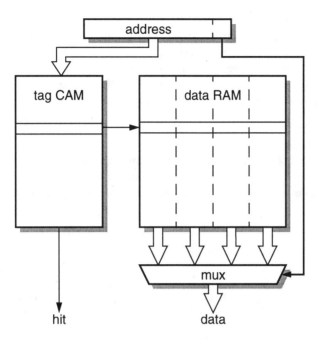

**Figure 10.5**   Fully associative cache organization.

Since there are no address bits implicit in the position of data in the cache, the tag must store all the address bits apart from those used to address bytes within the line.

**Write strategies**

The above schemes operate in an obvious way for read accesses: when presented with a new read address the cache checks to see whether it holds the addressed data; if it does, it supplies the data; if it does not, it fetches a block of data from main memory, stores it in the cache in some suitable location and supplies the requested data to the processor.

There are more choices to make when the processor executes a write cycle. In increasing order of complexity, the commonly used write strategies are:

- **Write-through**.

  All write operations are passed to main memory; if the addressed location is currently held in the cache, the cache is updated to hold the new value. The processor must slow down to main memory speed while the write takes place.

- **Write-through with buffered write**.

  Here all write operations are still passed to main memory and the cache updated as appropriate, but instead of slowing the processor down to main memory speed the write address and data are stored in a **write buffer** which can accept the write information at high speed. The write buffer then transfers the data to main memory, at main memory speed, while the processor continues with its next task.

- **Copy-back**.

  A copy-back cache is not kept coherent with main memory. Write operations update only the cache, so cache lines must remember when they have been modified (usually using a **dirty** bit on each line or block). If a dirty cache line is allocated to new data it must be copied back to memory before the line is re-used.

  The write-through cache is the simplest to implement and has the merit that the memory is kept up to date; the drawback is that the processor must slow to memory speeds on every write transfer. The addition of a write buffer allows the processor to continue until the write traffic exceeds the external write bandwidth. The copy-back cache reduces the external write bandwidth requirement since a location may be written many times before the final value gets written back to memory, but the implementation is considerably more complex and the loss of coherency is hard to manage.

**Cache feature summary**

The various parameters that define the organization of a cache are summarized in Table 10.1. The first of these is the relationship between the cache and the memory management unit (**MMU**) which will be discussed further in the next section; the others have been covered in this section.

**Table 10.1**   Summary of cache organizational options.

| Organizational feature | Options | | |
|---|---|---|---|
| **Cache-MMU relationship** | Physical cache | Virtual cache | |
| **Cache contents** | Unified instruction and data cache | Separate instruction and data caches | |
| **Associativity** | Direct-mapped RAM-RAM | Set-associative RAM-RAM | Fully associative CAM-RAM |
| **Replacement strategy** | Cyclic | Random | LRU |
| **Write strategy** | Write-through | Write-through with write buffer | Copy-back |

## 10.3   Memory management

Modern computer systems typically have many programs active at the same time. A single processor can, of course, only execute instructions from one program at any instant, but by switching rapidly between the active programs they all appear to be executing at once, at least when viewed on a human timescale.

The rapid switching is managed by the operating system, so the application programmer can write his or her program as though it owns the whole machine. The mechanism used to support this illusion is described by the term **memory management unit** (MMU). There are two principal approaches to memory management, called **segmentation** and **paging**.

**Segments**   The simplest form of memory management allows an application to view its memory as a set of segments, where each segment contains a particular sort of information. For instance, a program may have a code segment containing all its instructions, a data segment and a stack segment. Every memory access provides a segment selector and a logical address to the MMU. Each segment has a base address and a limit associated with it. The logical address is an offset from the segment base address, and must be no greater than the limit or an access violation will occur, usually causing an exception. Segments may also have other access controls, for instance the code segment may be read-only and an attempt to write to it will also cause an exception.

The access mechanism for a segmented MMU is illustrated in Figure 10.6 on page 282.

Segmentation allows a program to have its own private view of memory and to coexist transparently with other programs in the same memory space. It runs into difficulty, however, when the coexisting programs vary and the available memory is limited. Since the segments are of variable size, the free memory becomes fragmented over time and a new program may be unable to start, not because there is insufficient free memory, but because the free memory is all in small pieces none of which is big enough to hold a segment of the size required by the new program.

The crisis can be alleviated by the operating system moving segments around in memory to coalesce the free memory into one large piece, but this is inefficient, and most processors now incorporate a memory mapping scheme based on fixed-size chunks of memory called **pages**. Some architectures include segmentation and paging, but many, including the ARM, just support paging without segmentation.

**Paging**   In a paging memory management scheme both the logical and the physical address spaces are divided into fixed size components called pages. A page is usually a few kilobytes in size, but different architectures use different page sizes. The relationship

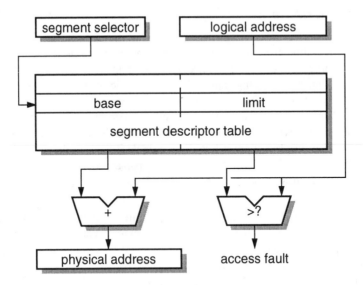

**Figure 10.6**   Segmented memory management scheme.

between the logical and physical pages is stored in **page tables**, which are held in main memory.

A simple sum shows that storing the translation in a single table requires a very large table: if a page is 4 Kbytes, 20 bits of a 32-bit address must be translated, which requires $2^{20}$ x 20 bits of data in the table, or a table of at least 2.5 Mbytes. This is an unreasonable overhead to impose on a small system.

Instead, most paging systems use two or more levels of page table. For example, the top ten bits of the address can be used to identify the appropriate second-level page table in the first-level page table directory, and the second ten bits of the address then identify the page table entry which contains the physical page number. This translation scheme is illustrated in Figure 10.7 on page 283.

Note that with the particular numbers suggested here, if 32 bits are allocated to each directory and page table entry, the directory and each page table happen to occupy exactly 4 Kbytes each, or exactly one memory page. The minimum overhead for a small system is 4 Kbytes for the page directory plus 4 Kbytes for one page table; this is sufficient to manage up to 4 Mbytes of physical memory. A fully populated 32 gigabyte memory would require 4 Mbytes of page tables, but this overhead is probably acceptable with this much memory to work in.

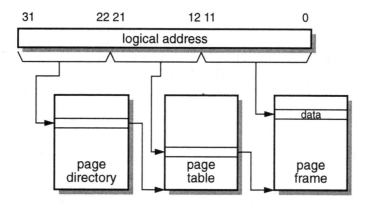

**Figure 10.7**   Paging memory management scheme.

The ARM MMU, described in Section 11.3 on page 294, uses a slightly different allocation of bits from the one described here (and also supports the single-level translation of larger blocks of memory), but the principle is the same.

**Virtual memory**

One possibility with either memory management scheme is to allow a segment or page to be marked as absent and an exception to be generated whenever it is accessed. Then an operating system which has run out of memory to allocate can transparently move a page or a segment out of main memory into backup store, which for this purpose is usually a hard disk, and mark it as absent. The physical memory can then be allocated to a different use. If the program attempts to access an absent page or segment the exception is raised and the operating system can bring the page or segment back into main memory, then allow the program to retry the access.

When implemented with the paged memory management scheme, this process is known as **demand-paged virtual memory**. A program can be written to occupy a virtual memory space that is larger than the available physical memory space in the computer where it is run, since the operating system can wheel bits of program and data in as they are needed. Typical programs work some parts of their code very hard and rarely touch others; leaving the infrequently used routines out on disk will not noticeably affect performance. However, over-exploiting this facility causes the operating system to switch pages in and out of memory at a high rate. This is described as **thrashing**, and *will* adversely affect performance.

**Restartable instructions**

An important requirement in a virtual memory system is that any instruction that can cause a memory access fault must leave the processor in a state that allows the operating system to page-in the requested memory and resume the original program as though the fault had not happened. This is often achieved by making all instructions that access memory **restartable**. The processor must retain enough state to allow the operating system to recover enough of the register values so that, when the page is in main memory, the faulting instruction is retried with identical results to those that would have been obtained had the page been resident at the first attempt.

This requirement is usually the most difficult one to satisfy in the design of a processor whilst retaining high-performance and minimum hardware redundancy.

**Translation look-aside buffers**

The paging scheme described above gives the programmer complete freedom and transparency in the use of memory, but it would seem that this has been achieved at considerable cost in performance since each memory access appears to have incurred an overhead of two additional memory accesses, one to the page directory and one to the page table, before the data itself is accessed.

This overhead is usually avoided by implementing a translation look-aside buffer (**TLB**), which is a cache of recently used page translations. As with instruction and data caches (described in Section 10.2 on page 273), there are organizational options relating to the degree of associativity and the replacement strategy. The line and block sizes usually equate to a single page table entry, and the size of a typical TLB is much smaller than a data cache at around 64 entries. The locality properties of typical programs enable a TLB of this size to achieve a miss rate of a per cent or so. The misses incur the table-walking overhead of two additional memory accesses.

The operation of a TLB is illustrated in Figure 10.8 on page 285.

**Virtual and physical caches**

When a system incorporates both an MMU and a cache, the cache may operate either with virtual (pre-MMU) or physical (post-MMU) addresses.

A virtual cache has the advantage that the cache access may start immediately the processor produces an address, and, indeed, there is no need to activate the MMU if the data is found in the cache. The drawback is that the cache may contain **synonyms**, which are duplicate copies of the same main memory data item in the cache. Synonyms arise because address translation mechanisms generally allow overlapping translations. If the processor modifies the data item through one address route it is not possible for the cache to update the second copy, leading to inconsistency in the cache.

A physical cache avoids the synonym problem since physical memory addresses are associated with unique data items. However the MMU must now be activated on every cache access, and with some MMU and cache organizations the address transla-

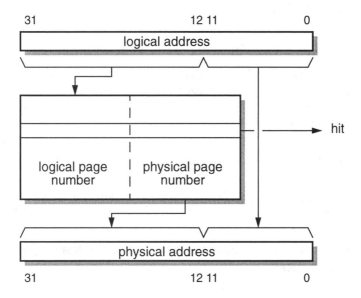

**Figure 10.8** The operation of a translation look-aside buffer.

tion must be completed by the MMU before the cache access can begin, leading to much longer cache latencies.

A physical cache arrangement that neatly avoids the sequential access cost exploits the fact that a paging MMU only affects the high-order address bits, while the cache is accessed by the low-order address bits. Provided these sets do not overlap, the cache and MMU accesses can proceed in parallel. The physical address from the MMU arrives at the right time to be compared with the physical address tags from the cache, hiding the address translation time behind the cache tag access. This optimization is not applicable to fully-associative caches, and only works if the page size used by the MMU is larger than each directly addressed portion of the cache. A 4 Kbyte page, for example, limits a direct-mapped cache to a maximum size of 4 Kbytes, a two-way set-associative cache to a maximum size of 8 Kbytes, and so on.

In practice both virtual and physical caches are in commercial use, the former relying on software conventions to contain the synonym problem and the latter either exploiting the above optimization or accepting the performance cost.

## 10.4   Examples and exercises

**Example 10.1**   **How big can a 4-way physical cache be in a system with 1 Kbyte pages?**

Assume we want to perform the TLB and cache accesses in parallel as described in 'Virtual and physical caches' on page 284.

Each section of the cache can be at most 1 Kbyte, so the maximum total cache size is 4 Kbytes.

**Exercise 10.1.1**   How much memory does the tag store require in this cache if the line size is 16 bytes?

**Exercise 10.1.2**   Estimate the proportions of the areas of the TLB and the data cache tag and data memories in the above example.

**Example 10.2**   **How big would a TLB have to be to contain the translations for all of the physical pages?**

With 4 Kbyte pages, a 1 Mbyte memory contains 256 pages so the TLB needs 256 entries. The TLB need no longer be an automatic cache. Since a TLB miss means that the page is absent from physical memory a disk transfer is required, and the overhead of maintaining the TLB by software is negligible compared with the cost of the disk transfer.

A TLB which covers all physical memory is a form of **inverted page table**, and just such a translation scheme was used on the early ARM memory controller chips used in the Acorn Archimedes machines (see Section 13.3 on page 355). Referring to Figure 10.8 on page 285, the translation hardware can be a CAM; the physical page number store is a simple hard-wired encoder, and the CAM has one entry for each physical page.

The Acorn memory controller chips had CAMs with 128 entries and a page size that varied according to the amount of physical memory in the system. A 1 Mbyte system had 8 Kbyte pages, a 4 Mbyte system had 32 Kbyte pages. To extend beyond 4 Mbytes, the page size stayed at 32 Kbytes and a second memory controller was added. The CAMs were maintained by software, so no complex table-walking hardware was required. The full translation tables were entirely defined by software.

**Exercise 10.2.1**   Estimate the die area of a 128 entry inverted page table compared with a 64 entry TLB, assuming that one bit of CAM requires twice the area of one bit of RAM.

# 11 Architectural Support for Operating Systems

**Summary of chapter contents**

The role of an operating system is to provide an environment where several programs may run concurrently with a minimal risk of unwanted interference between them but with support for safe data sharing. The operating system should also provide a clean interface to the hardware facilities of the machine.

Interference between processes is minimized by memory management and protection schemes which enable each process to access only its own area of memory. The process is given its own view of the system memory, and when a process switch takes place the memory view is dynamically transformed to that of the new process, with all the memory used by the previous process being removed from sight. This requires sophisticated hardware support if it is to operate efficiently.

Data sharing implies a loophole in the protection scheme which must be controlled with great care. Haphazard access to shared structures can lead to the most obscure forms of program misbehaviour, so a disciplined approach must be applied.

Access to hardware facilities often involves a lot of low-level bit manipulation, and rather than require each process to do this independently, the details are usually handled centrally by the operating system. Processes can then access input/output functions at a higher level through system calls.

The ARM architecture incorporates features specifically to support all these aspects of the operating system.

## 11.1  An introduction to operating systems

The role of an operating system is to present a uniform and clean interface between the underlying hardware resources of the machine and the application programs that run on it. The most sophisticated operating systems are those that provide facilities for multiple general-purpose programs run by several different users at the same time.

**Multi-user systems**

It is very inconvenient if a multi-user system requires each program to make allowances for the presence of other programs in the same machine, since the number and type of concurrent programs is unknown and will vary from one run to the next. Therefore a multi-user operating system presents each program with a complete **virtual machine** in which to operate. Each program can be written as though it is the only program running at the time; the only noticeable effect of the presence of other programs is that the program typically takes longer to run.

Although several programs may be present in the machine at one time, the processor has only one set of registers (we are not concerned with multi-processor systems here), so only one program is executing at any particular time. The apparent concurrency is achieved by **time-slicing**, which means that each program takes a turn in the processor. Since the processor operates at very high speeds by human standards, the effect is that over a period of, say, a second each program will have had several goes in the processor so all programs make some progress. The operating system is responsible for **scheduling** (deciding which program runs when), and it may give each program an equal share of the CPU time or it may use **priority** information to favour some programs over others.

A program is switched out of the processor either because the operating system is invoked by a timer interrupt and decides the program has had enough time for now, or because the program has requested a slow peripheral access (such as a disk access) and cannot do any more useful work until it gets a response. Rather than leave the program idling in the processor, the operating system switches it out and schedules another program that can make useful progress.

**Memory management**

In order to create the virtual machine in which a program runs, the operating system must establish an environment where the program has access to its code and data at the memory locations where it expects to find them. Since one program's expectations of the addresses it will use may conflict with another's, the operating system uses memory translation to present the **physical** memory locations where it has loaded the code and data to the program at appropriate **logical** addresses. The program sees the memory through a logical-to-physical address translation mechanism which is managed by the operating system.

**Protection**

Where several users are running programs on the same machine it is highly desirable to ensure that an error in one user's program cannot interfere with the operation of any of the other programs. It is also, unfortunately, necessary to protect against malicious attempts to interfere with other programs.

The memory-mapping hardware which gives each program its own virtual machine can also ensure that a program cannot see any memory belonging to another program, thereby providing a measure of protection. It is not efficient to enforce this too far, however, since sharing areas of memory that contain, for example, libraries of useful functions can save on memory use. A solution here is to make these areas *read-only* or *execute-only* so one program cannot corrupt code that will be used by another.

An obvious route for a malicious user to cause damage to another is to overcome the protection afforded by the memory-management system by assuming operating system status and then changing the translation tables. Most systems address this by providing a privileged system mode which has controlled access and making the translation tables accessible only from this mode.

Designing a computer system to be secure against malicious attacks by clever individuals is a complex issue which requires some architectural support. On the ARM this support is provided by privileged processor modes with controlled access and various forms of memory protection in the memory management units. However few ARMs are used in systems where protection against malicious users is required, so most of the time these facilities are used to catch inadvertent programming errors and thereby help debug the software.

**Resource allocation**

Two programs which are running concurrently may place conflicting demands on system resources. For example, one program may request data from one part of a disk. It will be switched out while the disk drive seeks the data, and the program that gets switched in may immediately request data from a different part of the disk. If the disk drive responds directly to these requests a situation can easily arise where the programs alternately have control and the disk drive oscillates between the two seeks, never having long enough to find either data area, and the system will livelock until the disk drive wears out.

In order to avoid this sort of scenario, all requests for input/output activity are channelled through the operating system. It will accept the request from the first program and then queue up the request from the second program to receive attention once the first has been satisfied.

**Single-user systems**

Where a system serves a single user, still possibly running several programs at the same time, much of the above continues to apply. Although the threat of a malicious user sharing the same machine is removed, it is still very useful for each program to run in its own space so that an error in one program does not cause errors in another. The simplification that arises from removing the concern about the malicious user is that it is no longer necessary to make it impossible for a program to assume system privileges, it should merely be extremely unlikely that this will happen inadvertently.

However, desktop machines that appear to belong to one user are increasingly being connected to computer networks that allow other users to run programs on them remotely. Such machines should clearly be viewed as multi-user and incorporate appropriate levels of protection.

**Embedded systems**

An embedded system is quite different from the single- and multi-user general-purpose system discussed above. It typically runs a fixed set of programs and has no mechanism for introducing new programs. Presumably, then, the problem of the malicious user has been removed.

The operating system continues to play a similar role, giving each active program a clean virtual machine in which to run, providing protection for one program from errors in another and scheduling the use of CPU time.

Many embedded systems operate within real-time constraints which must be allowed to determine scheduling priorities. Cost issues also preclude the use of the operating systems that are popular on general-purpose machines, since these tend to demand large memory resources. This has led to the development of the real-time operating system (**RTOS**) which provides the scheduling and hardware interface facilities required by an embedded system using just a few kilobytes of memory.

Smaller embedded systems may not even be able to bear this cost, or they may have such simple scheduling requirements (for example, one fixed program that runs all the time) that they do not need an 'operating system' at all. Here a simple 'monitor' program suffices, providing a few system functions such as sanitized interfaces to input/output functions. Such systems almost certainly dispense with the memory management hardware and use the processor's logical address to access memory directly. Most of the rest of this chapter is of little relevance to them!

**Chapter structure**

The general principles of memory management were described in the previous chapter. Subsequent sections in this chapter introduce the ARM system control coprocessor and the memory management system it controls. Following this there are sections on the important operating system related issues of synchronization, context switching and the handling of input/output devices, including the use of interrupts.

## 11.2 The ARM system control coprocessor

The ARM system control coprocessor is an on-chip coprocessor, using logical coprocessor number 15, which controls the operation of the on-chip cache or caches, memory management unit, write buffer, prefetch buffer, branch target cache and system configuration signals.

**CP15 instructions**

The control is effected through the reading and writing of the CP15 registers. The registers are all 32 bits long, and access is restricted to MRC and MCR instructions (see Section 5.18 on page 145) which must be executed in supervisor mode. Use of other coprocessor instructions or any attempted access in user mode will cause the undefined instruction trap to be taken. The format of these instructions is shown in Figure 11.1. In most cases the CRm and Cop2 fields are unused and should be zero, though they *are* used in certain operations.

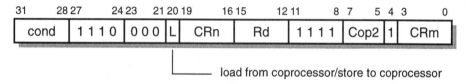

load from coprocessor/store to coprocessor

**Figure 11.1** CP15 register transfer instructions.

**CP15 registers**

CRn is used to specify the register to be read or written. Not all of the 15 logical registers are currently used; those that are not used should not be tampered with! The register structure is illustrated in Table 11.1 on page 292.

In detail, the register functions are as follows:

- **Register 0** (which is read-only) returns identification information.

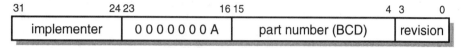

Bits [3:0] contain a revision number, bits [15:4] contain a 3-digit part number in binary-coded decimal, bits [23:16] contain the architecture version ('A' = 0 for version 3, 'A' = 1 for version 4) and bits [31:24] contain the ASCII code of an implementer's trademark (ASCII 'A' = $41_{16}$ indicates ARM Limited, 'D' = $44_{16}$ indicates Digital, and so on).

**Table 11.1**   CP15 register structure.

| Register | Purpose |
|----------|---------|
| 0 | ID Register |
| 1 | Control |
| 2 | Translation Table Base |
| 3 | Domain Access Control |
| 4 | UNUSED |
| 5 | Fault Status |
| 6 | Fault Address |
| 7 | Cache Operations |
| 8 | TLB Operations |
| 9 to 15 | UNUSED |

Some older CPUs do not follow the above register 0 format exactly.

- **Register 1** (which is write-only in architecture version 3 but read-write in version 4) contains several bits of control information which enable system functions and control system parameters.

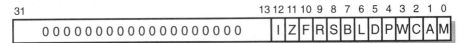

All bits are cleared on reset. If subsequently set, M enables the MMU, A enables address alignment fault checking, C enables the data or unified cache, W enables the write buffer, P switches from 26- to 32-bit exception handling, D switches from 26- to 32-bit address range, L switches to late abort timing, B switches from little- to big-endian byte ordering, S and R modify the MMU system and ROM protection states, F controls the speed of external coprocessor communications, Z enables branch prediction and I enables the instruction cache when this is separate from the data cache.

Note that not all bits are provided in all implementations. Bits [31:13] are unpredictable on read and should be written as zeros.

- **Register 2** (which is write-only in architecture version 3 but read-write in version 4) contains the address of the start of the currently active first-level translation table. This must be aligned on a 16 Kbyte boundary.

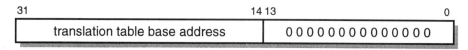

| 31 | 14 13 | 0 |
|---|---|---|
| translation table base address | 0 0 0 0 0 0 0 0 0 0 0 0 0 0 | |

- **Register 3** (which is write-only in architecture version 3 but read-write in version 4) contains 16 2-bit fields, each specifying the access permissions for one of the 16 domains. See 'Domains' on page 294 for further details.

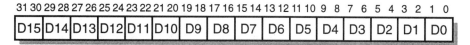

| 31 30 | 29 28 | 27 26 | 25 24 | 23 22 | 21 20 | 19 18 | 17 16 | 15 14 | 13 12 | 11 10 | 9 8 | 7 6 | 5 4 | 3 2 | 1 0 |
|---|---|---|---|---|---|---|---|---|---|---|---|---|---|---|---|
| D15 | D14 | D13 | D12 | D11 | D10 | D9 | D8 | D7 | D6 | D5 | D4 | D3 | D2 | D1 | D0 |

- **Register 5** (which is read-write in architecture version 4, but in version 3 it is read-only and writing to it flushes the whole TLB) indicates the type of fault and the domain of the last data access that aborted.

| 31 | 9 8 7 | 4 3 | 0 |
|---|---|---|---|
| 0 0 0 0 0 0 0 0 0 0 0 0 0 0 0 0 0 0 0 0 0 0 0 | 0 | domain | status |

- **Register 6** (which is read-write in architecture version 4, but in version 3 it is read-only and writing to it flushes a particular TLB entry) contains the address of the last data access that aborted.

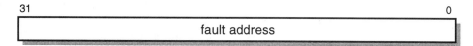

| 31 | 0 |
|---|---|
| fault address | |

- **Register 7** (which is read-write in architecture version 4, but in version 3 it is write-only and simply flushes the cache) is used to perform a number of cache, write buffer, prefetch buffer and branch target cache clean and/or flush operations. The data supplied should be either zero or a relevant virtual address.

  Accesses to register 7 use the Cop2 and CRm fields to specify particular operations; the available functions vary from implementation to implementation.

- **Register 8** (which is read-write in architecture version 4 and unavailable in version 3) is used to perform a number of TLB operations, flushing single entries or the whole TLB and supporting unified or separate instruction and data TLBs.

## 11.3   ARM MMU architecture

An MMU performs two primary functions:

- It translates virtual addresses into physical addresses.
- It controls memory access permissions, aborting illegal accesses.

The ARM MMU uses a 2-level page table with table-walking hardware and a TLB which stores recently used page translations. Where the processor has separate instruction and data caches it is likely also to have separate instruction and data TLBs.

**Memory granularity**

The memory mapping is performed at several different granularities by the same basic mechanism. The units that can be used are:

- **Sections**. These are 1 Mbyte blocks of memory.
- **Large pages**. These are 64 Kbyte blocks of memory, and within a large page access control is applied to individual 16 Kbyte **subpages**.
- **Small pages**. These are 4 Kbyte blocks of memory, and within a small page access control is applied to individual 1 Kbyte subpages.

The normal granularity is the 4 Kbyte small page. Large pages and sections exist to allow the mapping of large data areas with a single TLB entry. Forcing a large data area to be mapped in small pages can, under certain circumstances, cause the TLB to perform inefficiently.

**Domains**

Domains are an unusual feature of the ARM MMU architecture. A domain is a group of sections and/or pages which have particular access permissions. This allows a number of different processes to run with the same translation tables whilst retaining some protection from each other. It gives a much more lightweight process switch mechanism than is possible if each process must have its own translation tables.

The access control is based on two sorts of programs:

- **Clients** are users of domains and must observe the access permissions of the individual sections and pages that make up the domain.
- **Managers** are the controllers of the domain and can bypass the access permissions of individual sections or pages.

At any one time a program may be a client of some domains, a manager of some other domains and have no access at all to the remaining domains. This is controlled by CP15 register 3 which contains two bits for each of the 16 domains describing the

**Table 11.2** Domain access control bits.

| Value | Status | Description |
|-------|--------|-------------|
| 00 | No access | Any access will generate a domain fault |
| 01 | Client | Page and section permission bits are checked |
| 10 | Reserved | Do not use |
| 11 | Manager | Page and section permission bits are not checked |

status of the current program with respect to each domain. The interpretation of the two bits is given in Table 11.2. The relationship of a program to all of the domains can be changed by writing a single new value into CP15 register 3.

**Translation process**

The translation of a new virtual address always begins with a first-level fetch. (We ignore for now the TLB, which is only a cache to accelerate the process described below.) This uses the translation base address held in CP15 register 2. Bits [31:14] of the translation base register are concatenated with bits [31:20] of the virtual address to form a memory address which is used to access the first-level descriptor as shown in Figure 11.2 on page 296.

The first-level descriptor may be either a section descriptor or a pointer to a second-level page table depending on its bottom two bits. '01' indicates a pointer to a second-level page table; '10' indicates a section descriptor. Other values are trapped, and '00' should be used to indicate a descriptor that causes a translation fault ('11' should not be used).

**Section translation**

Where the first-level descriptor indicates that the virtual address translates into a section, the domain ('Domain' in the section descriptor) is checked and, if the current process is a client of the domain, the access permissions ('AP' in the section descriptor) are also checked. If the access is permissible, the memory address is formed by concatenating bits [31:20] of the section descriptor with bits [19:0] of the virtual address. This address is used to access the data in memory. The full section translation sequence is shown in Figure 11.3 on page 297.

The operation of the access permission bits (AP) is described in 'Access permissions' on page 297, and the operation of the bufferable (B) and cacheable (C) bits is described in 'Cache and write buffer control' on page 300.

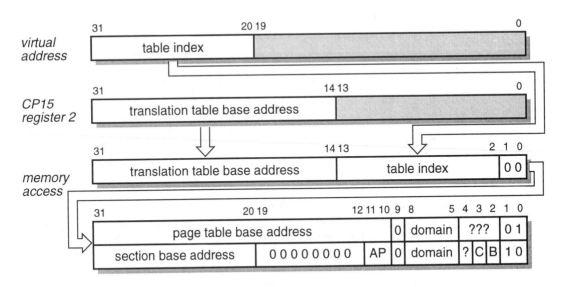

**Figure 11.2** First-level translation fetch.

**Page translation**

Where the first-level descriptor indicates that the virtual address translates into a page, a further access is required to a second-level page table. The address of the second-level page descriptor is formed by concatenating bits [31:10] of the first-level descriptor to bits [19:12] of the virtual address.

The second-level page descriptor may be a large (64 Kbyte) page descriptor or a small (4 Kbyte) page descriptor, depending on its bottom two bits. '01' indicates a large page; '10' indicates a small page. Other values are trapped, and '00' should be used to generate a translation fault ('11' should not be used).

The page base address is held in bits [31:12] of the page descriptor; a large page descriptor will have bits [15:12] equal to zero. Bits [11:4] contain two access permission bits ('AP0-3') for each of the four subpages, where a subpage is a quarter of the size of the page. Bits [3:2] contain the 'bufferable' and 'cacheable' bits. (Bits marked '?' have implementation specific uses.)

The overall translation sequence for a small page is shown in Figure 11.4 on page 298. The translation sequence for a large page is similar except bits [15:12] of the virtual address are used both in the page table index and in the page offset. Each page table entry for a large page must therefore be copied 16 times in the page table for every value of these bits in the page table index.

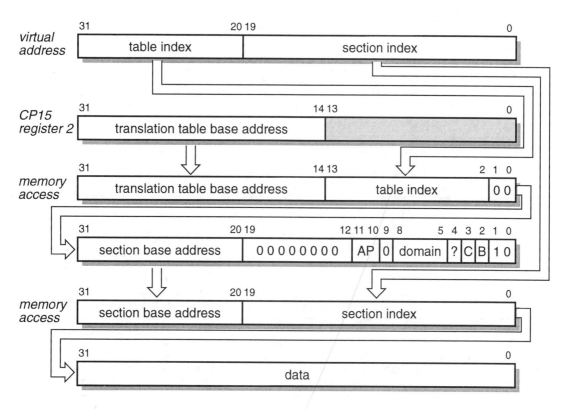

**Figure 11.3** Section translation sequence.

**Access permissions**

The AP bits for each section or subpage are used together with the domain information in the first-level descriptor, the domain control information in CP15 register 3, the S and R control bits in CP15 register 1 and the user/supervisor state of the processor to determine whether a read or write access to the addressed location is permissible. The permission checking operation proceeds as follows:

1. If alignment checking is enabled (bit 1 of CP15 register 1 is set) check the address alignment and fault if misaligned (that is, if a word is not aligned on a 4-byte boundary or a half-word is not aligned on a 2-byte boundary).

2. Identify the domain of the addressed location from bits [8:5] of the first-level descriptor. (Fetching the first-level descriptor will fault if the descriptor is invalid.)

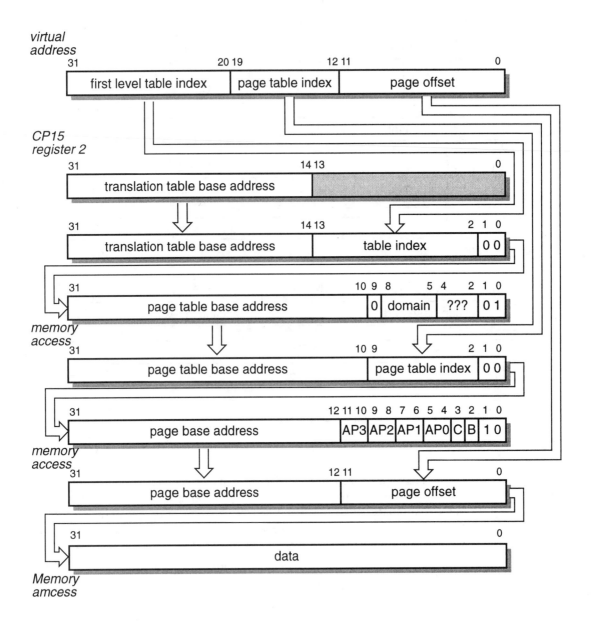

**Figure 11.4**  Small page translation sequence.

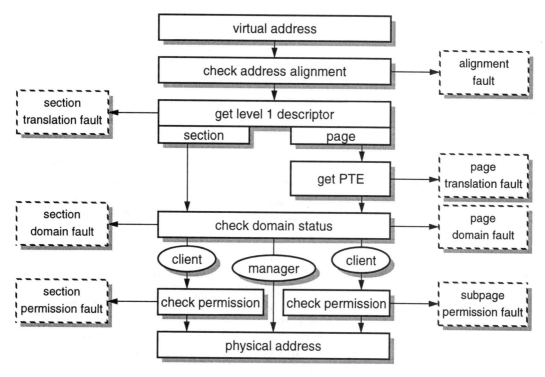

**Figure 11.5** Access permission checking scheme.

3. Check in CP15 register 3, the domain access control register, whether the current process is a client or manager of this domain; if neither, fault here.

4. If a manager of this domain, proceed ignoring access permissions. If a client, check the access permissions against Table 11.3 on page 300 using the S and R bits from CP15 register 1. Fault if access is not permitted, otherwise continue to access data.

The permission checking scheme is illustrated in Figure 11.5 which shows the various faults that can be generated in the course of an address translation. The MMU may generate alignment, translation, domain and permission faults. In addition, the external memory system may fault on cache line fetches, uncached or unbuffered accesses (aborts on buffered writes are not supported) and translation table accesses. These faults are all called *aborts* and are handled by the processor as prefetch or data abort exceptions, depending on whether the access was for an instruction or for data.

**Table 11.3**  Access permissions.

| AP | S | R | Supervisor | User |
|----|---|---|------------|------|
| 00 | 0 | 0 | No access | No access |
| 00 | 1 | 0 | Read only | No access |
| 00 | 0 | 1 | Read only | Read only |
| 00 | 1 | 1 | Do not use | |
| 01 | - | - | Read/write | No access |
| 10 | - | - | Read/write | Read only |
| 11 | - | - | Read/write | Read/write |

A fault on a data access causes the fault status register (CP15 register 5) and the fault address register (CP15 register 6) to be updated to provide information on the cause and location of the fault. A fault on an instruction access only causes an exception if and when the instruction is executed (it may not be executed since it may be fetched just after a taken branch), and it does not update the fault status and address registers. The fault address may be deduced from the return address in the link register.

**Cache and write buffer control**

The C and B bits in the section and second-level page descriptors control whether the data in the section or page may be copied into a cache and/or written back to memory through a write buffer.

Where the cache uses a write-through scheme, C controls whether or not the data is cacheable and B controls whether or not writes may be buffered. Where the cache uses a copy-back scheme the 'cached, unbuffered' combination may alternatively be used to specify a 'write-through, buffered' behaviour. (This cache terminology is described in 'Write strategies' on page 279.)

**External faults**

Note that the processor cannot recover from external faults signalled on buffered writes, because by the time the fault is signalled the processor may have executed several instructions and is therefore unable to recover its state to retry the faulting store instruction. Where recovery is required (for example, to allow the processor to retry a store instruction following a bus fault) unbuffered writes must be used.

In typical ARM applications there are no potentially recoverable sources of external faults, so this is not an issue.

# 11.4 Synchronization

A standard problem in a system which runs multiple processes that share data structures is to control accesses to the shared data to ensure correct behaviour.

For example, consider a system where a set of sensor values is sampled and stored in memory by one process and used at arbitrary times by another. If it is important that the second process always sees a single snapshot of the values, care must be taken to ensure that the first process does not get swapped out and the second swapped in when the values are only partially updated. The mechanisms used to achieve this are called **process synchronization**. What is required is *mutually exclusive* access to the data structure.

**Mutual exclusion**

A process which is about to perform an operation on a shared data structure, where the operation requires that no other process is accessing the structure, must wait until no other process *is* accessing the data and then set some sort of lock to prevent another process from accessing it until it has finished the operation.

One way to achieve mutual exclusion is to use a particular memory location to control access to a data structure. For example, the location could contain a Boolean value indicating whether or not the data structure is currently in use. A process which wishes to use the data structure must wait until it is free, then mark it as busy while it uses the data, then mark it as free again when it has finished using it. The problem is that an interrupt can arise between the structure becoming free and it being marked as busy. The interrupt causes a process switch, the new process sees the structure is free, marks it as busy, changes it a bit and then another interrupt returns control to the first process which is in a state where it believes, now incorrectly, that the structure is free.

A standard solution to this problem is to disable interrupts while the Boolean is tested and set. This works, but on a processor with a protected supervisor mode (such as the ARM) user-level code cannot disable interrupts, so a system call is required, which takes several clock cycles to complete and return control to the user process.

**SWAP**

A more efficient solution is to use an **atomic** (that is, uninterruptable) 'test and set' instruction. The ARM 'SWAP' instruction (see Section 5.12 on page 137) is just such an instruction which is included in the instruction set for exactly this purpose. A register is set to the 'busy' value, then this register is swapped with the memory location containing the Boolean. If the loaded value is 'free' the process can continue; if it is 'busy' the process must wait, often by **spinning** (repeating the test until it gets the 'free' result) on the lock.

Note that this is the *only* reason for including SWAP in the ARM instruction set. It does not contribute to the processor's performance and its dynamic frequency of use is negligible. It is there just to provide this functionality.

## 11.5   Context switching

A process runs in a **context**, which is all the system state that must be established for the process to run correctly. This state includes:

- The values of all of the processor's registers, including the program counter, stack pointer, and so on.
- The values in the floating-point registers, if the process uses them.
- The translation tables in memory (but not the contents of the TLB since it is just a cache of the values in memory and will automatically reload active values as they are used).
- Data values used by the process in memory (but not the values in the cache since they will automatically be reloaded when required).

When a process switch takes place, the context of the old process must be saved and that of the new process restored (if it is resuming rather than starting for the first time).

**When to switch**

Context switching may occur as a result of an external interrupt, for example:

- A timer interrupt causes the operating system to make a new process active according to a time-slicing algorithm.
- A high-priority process which is waiting for a particular event is reactivated in response to that event.

Alternatively, a process may run out of useful work and call the operating system to be made dormant until an external event occurs.

In all cases, the operating system is given or takes control and is responsible for saving the old and restoring the new context. In an ARM-based system, this will normally take place while the processor is in supervisor mode.

**Register state**

If all context switches take place in response to IRQs or internal faults or supervisor calls, and the supervisor code does not re-enable interrupts, the process register state may be restricted to the user-mode registers. If context switches may take place in response to FIQs or supervisor code does re-enable interrupts, it may be necessary to save and restore some of the privileged mode registers as well.

The 'architectural support' for register saving and restoring offered on the ARM recognizes the difficulty of saving and restoring user registers from a privileged mode and provides special instructions to assist in this task. These instructions are the special forms of the load and store multiple instructions (see Section 5.11 on page 135) which allow code running in a non-user mode to save and restore the user registers from an area of memory addressed by a non-user mode register.

Without these instructions, an operating system would have to switch into user mode to save or restore the banked user registers and then get back through the protection barrier into supervisor mode. Though possible, this solution is inefficient.

## Floating-point state

The floating-point registers, whether held in a hardware coprocessor or maintained in memory by a software emulator, represent part of the state of any process that uses them. Rather than add to the context switching overhead by saving and restoring them on every process swap, the operating system simply disables user-level use of the floating-point system when a process that uses floating-point is swapped out. If the new process attempts to use the floating-point system, the first use will trap. At that point the operating system will save the old process state and restore the new, then it will re-enable the floating-point system and the new process can use it freely.

Thus the floating-point context switch overhead is incurred only when strictly necessary.

## Translation state

Where the old and new processes have independent translation tables a *heavy-weight* process switch is required. The complete translation table structure can be switched simply by changing the base address of the first-level page table in CP15 register 2, but since this will invalidate existing TLB and (virtually addressed) cache entries, these must be flushed. The TLB and an instruction or write-through data cache can be flushed simply by marking all entries as invalid, which on an ARM processor chip requires a single CP15 instruction for each TLB or cache, but a copy-back cache must be purged of all dirty lines which may take many instructions.

(Note that a physically addressed cache avoids this problem, but to date all ARM CPUs have used virtually addressed caches.)

Where the old and new processes share the same translation tables a *light-weight* process switch is required. The 'domain' mechanism in the ARM MMU architecture allows the protection state of 16 different subsets of the virtual address space to be reconfigured with a single update of CP15 register 3.

In order to ensure that the cache does not represent a leak in the protection system, a cache access must be accompanied by a permission check. This could be achieved by storing the domain and access permission information along with the data in each cache line, but current ARM processors check permissions using information in the MMU concurrently with the cache access.

## 11.6    Input/Output

The input/output (I/O) functions are implemented in an ARM system using a combination of memory-mapped addressable peripheral registers and the interrupt inputs. Some ARM systems may also include direct memory access (**DMA**) hardware.

**Memory-mapped peripherals**

A peripheral device, such as a serial line controller, contains a number of registers. In a memory-mapped system, each of these registers appears like a memory location at a particular address. (An alternative system organization might have I/O functions in a separate address space from memory devices.) A serial line controller may have a set of registers as follows:

- A transmit data register (write only); data written to this location gets sent down the serial line.

- A receive data register (read only); data arriving along the serial line is presented here.

- A control register (read/write); this register sets the data rate and manages the RTS (request to send) and similar signals.

- An interrupt enable register (read/write); this register controls which hardware events will generate an interrupt.

- A status register (read only); this register indicates whether read data is available, whether the write buffer is full, and so on.

To receive data, the software must set up the device appropriately, usually to generate an interrupt when data is available or an error condition is detected. The interrupt routine must then copy the data into a buffer and check for error conditions.

**Memory-mapped issues**

Note that a memory-mapped peripheral register behaves differently from memory. Two consecutive reads to the read data register will probably deliver different results even though no write to that location has taken place. Whereas reads to true memory are **idempotent** (the read can be repeated many times, with identical results) a read to a peripheral may clear the current value and the next value may be different. Such locations are termed **read-sensitive**.

Programs must be written very carefully where read-sensitive locations are involved, and, in particular, such locations must *not* be copied into a cache memory.

In many ARM systems I/O locations are made inaccessible to user code, so the only way the devices can be accessed is through supervisor calls (SWIs) or through C library functions written to use those calls.

**Direct Memory Access**

Where I/O functions have a high data bandwidth, a considerable share of the processor's performance may be consumed handling interrupts from the I/O system. Many systems employ DMA hardware to handle the lowest level I/O data transfers without processor assistance. Typically, the DMA hardware will handle the transfer of blocks of data from the peripheral into a buffer area in memory, interrupting the processor only if an error occurs or when the buffer becomes full. Thus the processor sees an interrupt once per buffer rather than once per byte.

Note, however, that the DMA data traffic will occupy some of the memory bus bandwidth, so the processor performance will still be reduced by the I/O activity (though far less than it would be if it were handling the data traffic on interrupts).

**Fast Interrupt Request**

The ARM fast interrupt (FIQ) architecture includes more banked registers than the other exception modes (see Figure 2.1 on page 41) in order to minimize the register save and restore overhead associated with handling one of these interrupts. The number of registers was chosen to be the number required to implement a software emulation of a DMA channel.

If an ARM system with no DMA support has one source of I/O data traffic that has a significantly higher bandwidth requirement than the others, it is worth considering allocating the FIQ interrupt to this source and using IRQ to support all the other sources. It is far less effective to use FIQ for several different data sources at the same time, though switching it on a coarse granularity between sources may be appropriate.

**Interrupt latency**

An important parameter of a processor is its **interrupt latency**. This is a measure of how long it takes to respond to an interrupt in the worst case. For the ARM6 the worst case FIQ latency is determined by the following components:

1. The time for the request signal to pass through the FIQ synchronizing latches; this is three clock cycles (worst case).

2. The time for the longest instruction (which is a load multiple of 16 registers) to complete; this is 20 clock cycles.

3. The time for the data abort entry sequence; this is three clock cycles. (Remember that data abort has a higher priority than FIQ but does not mask FIQs out; see 'Exception priorities' on page 116.)

4. The time for the FIQ entry sequence; this is two clock cycles.

The total worst-case latency is therefore 28 clock cycles. After this time the ARM6 is executing the instruction at 0x1C, the FIQ entry point. These cycles may be sequential or non-sequential, and memory accesses may be further delayed if they address slow memory devices. The best-case latency is four clock cycles.

The IRQ latency calculation is similar but must include an arbitrary delay for the longest FIQ routine to complete (since FIQ is higher priority than IRQ).

**Cache - I/O interactions**

The usual assumption is that a cache makes a processor go faster. Normally this is true, if the performance is averaged over a reasonable period. But in many cases interrupts are used where worst-case real-time response is critical; in these cases a cache can make the performance significantly worse. An MMU can make things worse still!

Here is the worst-case interrupt latency sum for the ARM710 which we will meet in the next chapter. The latency is the sum of:

1.  The time for the request signal to pass through the FIQ synchronizing latches; this is three clock cycles (worst case) as before.

2.  The time for the longest instruction (which is a load multiple of 16 registers) to complete; this is 20 clock cycles as before, but...

    ...this could cause the write buffer to flush, which can take up to 12 cycles, then incur three MMU TLB misses, adding 18 clock cycles, and six cache misses, adding a further 24 cycles. The original 20 cycles overlap the line fetches, but the total cost for this stage can still reach 66 cycles.

3.  The time for data abort entry sequence; this is three clock cycles as before, but...

    ...the fetches from the vector space could add an MMU miss and a cache miss, increasing the cost to 12 cycles.

4.  The time for the FIQ entry sequence; this is two clock cycles as before, but...

    ...it could incur another cache miss, costing six cycles.

The total is now 87 clock cycles, many of which are non-sequential memory accesses. So note that automatic mechanisms which support a memory hierarchy to speed up general-purpose programs *on average* often have the opposite effect on *worst-case* calculations for critical code segments.

**Reducing latency**

How can the latency be reduced when real-time constraints simply must be met?

*   A fixed area of fast on-chip RAM (for example, containing the vector space at the bottom of memory) will speed up exception entry.

*   Sections of the TLB and cache can be **locked down** to ensure that critical code segments never incur the miss penalty.

Note that even in general-purpose systems where the cache and MMU are generally beneficial there are often critical real-time constraints, for example for servicing disk data traffic or for managing the local area network. This is especially true in low-cost systems with little DMA hardware support.

**Other cache issues**

There are other things to watch out for when a cache is present, for example:

- Caching assumes that an address will return the same data value each time it is read until a new value is written. I/O devices do not behave like this; each time you read them they give the next piece of data.

- A cache fetches a block (which is typically around four words) of data at a time from sequential addresses. I/O devices often have different register functions at consecutive addresses; reading them all can give unpredictable results.

Therefore the I/O area of memory is normally marked as uncacheable, and accesses bypass the cache. In general caches interact badly with any *read-sensitive* devices. Display frame buffers also need careful consideration and are often made uncacheable.

**Operating system issues**

Normally, all the low-level detail of the I/O device registers and the handling of interrupts is the responsibility of the operating system. A typical process will send data to the serial port by loading the next byte into r0 and then making the appropriate supervisor call; the operating system will call a subroutine called a **device driver** to check for the transmit buffer being empty, that the line is active, that no transmission errors occur, and so on. There may even be a call which allows the process to pass a pointer to the operating system which will then output a complete buffer of values.

Since it takes some time to send a buffer full of data down a serial line, the operating system may return control to the process until the transmit buffer has space for more data. An interrupt from the serial line hardware device returns control to the operating system, which refills the transmit buffer before returning control to the interrupted process. Further interrupts result in further transfers until the whole buffer has been sent.

It may be the case that the process which requested the serial line activity runs out of useful work, or an interrupt from a timer or another source causes a different process to become active. The operating system must be careful, when modifying the translation tables, to ensure that it does not make the data buffer inaccessible to itself. It must also treat any requests from the second process to output data down the serial line with caution; they must not interfere with the ongoing transfer from the first process. **Resource allocation** is used to ensure that there are no conflicts in the use of shared resources.

A process may request an output function and then go inactive until the output has completed, or it may go inactive until a particular input arrives. It can lodge a request with the operating system to be reactivated when the input/output *event* occurs.

## 11.7   Example and exercises

**Example 11.1   Why, on the ARM, can user-level code not disable interrupts?**

To allow a user to disable interrupts would make building a protected operating system impossible. The following code illustrates how a malicious user could destroy all the currently active programs:

```
        MSR     CPSR_f, #&c0        ; disable IRQ and FIQ
HERE    B       HERE                ; loop forever
```

Once interrupts are disabled there is no way for the operating system to regain control, so the program will loop forever. The only way out is a hard reset, which will destroy all currently active programs.

If the user cannot disable interrupts the operating system can establish a regular periodic interrupt from a timer, so the infinite loop will be interrupted and the operating system can schedule other programs. This program will either time-out, if the operating system has an upper limit on the amount of CPU time it is allowed to consume, or it will continue to loop whenever it gets switched in, running up a large bill on a system with accounting.

**Exercise 11.1.1**   What minimum level of protection must be applied to the bottom of memory (where the exceptions vectors are located) in a secure operating system?

**Exercise 11.1.2**   If the ARM had no SWAP instruction, devise a hardware peripheral that could be used to support synchronization. (Hint: standard memory will not work; the location must be read-sensitive.)

# *12* ARM Processor Chips

---

**Summary of chapter contents**

Although ARM processor cores are often used as macrocells in application specific complex system-level chips, there are also a number of standard product CPU chips where the processor macrocell shares the silicon area with cache and memory management functions.

These CPU chips are targeted at higher performance applications such as the Acorn Risc PC platforms, Online Media's set-top box products and the Apple Newton MessagePad.

A high-end embedded application may use one of these integrated processor chips if it requires the maximum possible performance or needs sophisticated memory management support. Also, if an application will not be produced in sufficient volume to warrant the development of a specific system-level chip then a stand-alone ARM CPU may be the logical choice. However, a high-volume medium performance embedded application is likely to be more cost-effective if it employs a custom chip incorporating an ARM processor macrocell.

The ARM CPUs described here include the ARM600, the ARM610 (developed for the first Apple Newton product), the ARM700 and ARM710, the ARM810 (which is based on the ARM8 processor core) and the very high performance StrongARM. These CPUs encompass a range of pipeline and cache organizations and form a useful illustration of the issues which arise when designing high-performance processors for low-power applications.

---

## 12.1   The ARM600 and ARM610

The ARM600 is a general-purpose 32-bit microprocessor based on an ARM6 processor core. It incorporates a 4 Kbyte 64-way associative mixed instruction and data cache, a memory management unit, a write buffer and support for on- and off-chip coprocessors. It also incorporates JTAG test circuitry (this was described in detail in Section 8.2 on page 221).

The organization of the chip is illustrated in Figure 12.1. Internal address and data buses connect the processor core to the cache, and most instruction and data references are satisfied by the cache. A read which misses the cache goes off chip to external memory and a 16-byte block of data is loaded into the cache using fast memory modes where available. The cache uses a write-through strategy, so all writes go to external memory, but the write buffer allows the processor to proceed without waiting

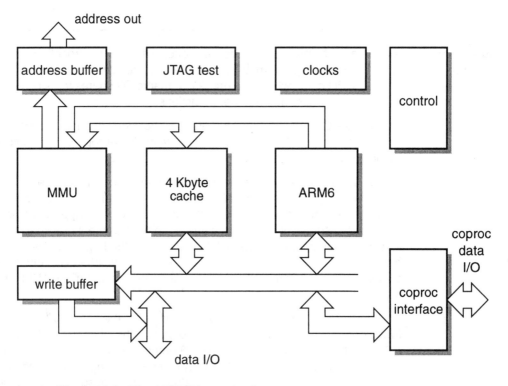

**Figure 12.1**   The ARM600 organization.

for the memory in most cases. The on-chip cache and MMU are controlled by system coprocessor 15 as described in Section 11.2 on page 291, and the coprocessor interface supports the connection of further, off-chip coprocessors.

**The ARM600 cache**

The choice of organization for a cache requires the consideration of several factors as discussed in Section 10.2 on page 273, including the size of the cache, the degree of associativity, the line and block sizes, the replacement algorithm, and the write strategy (here write-through was chosen for simplicity). Detailed architectural simulations are required to analyse the effects of these choices on the performance of the cache.

The ARM600 inherited its cache organization from the ARM3, the first ARM chip to incorporate an on-chip cache, where detailed studies were carried out into the effects of these parameters on performance and bus use. These studies used specially-designed hardware to capture address traces whilst running several benchmark programs on an ARM2; software was then used to analyse these traces to model the behaviour of the various organizations. (Today special hardware is generally unnecessary since desktop machines have sufficient performance to simulate large enough programs without hardware support.)

The study started by setting an upper bound on the performance benefit that could be expected from a cache. A 'perfect' cache, which always contains the requested data, was modelled to set this bound. Any real cache is bound to miss some of the time, so it cannot perform any better than one which always hits.

Three forms of perfect cache were modelled using realistic assumptions about the cache and external memory speeds (which were 20 MHz and 8 MHz respectively): caches which hold either just instructions, mixed instructions and data, or just data. The results are shown in Table 12.1, normalized to the performance of a system with no cache. They show that instructions are the most important values to hold in the cache, but including data values as well can give a further 25% performance increase.

**Table 12.1**   'Perfect' cache performance.

| Cache form | Performance |
|---|---|
| No cache | 1 |
| Instruction-only cache | 1.95 |
| Instruction and data cache | 2.5 |
| Data-only cache | 1.13 |

Although a decision was taken early on that the cache write strategy would be write-through (principally on the grounds of simplicity), it is still possible for the cache to detect a write miss and load a line of data from the write address. This 'allocate on write miss' strategy was investigated briefly, but proved to offer a negligible benefit in exchange for a significant increase in complexity, so it was rapidly abandoned. The problem was reduced to finding the best organization, consistent with chip area and power constraints, for a unified instruction and data cache with allocation on a read miss.

Various different cache organizations and sizes were investigated, with the results show in Figure 12.2. The simplest cache organization is the direct-mapped cache, but even with a size of 16 Kbytes, the cache is significantly worse than the 'perfect' case. The next step up in complexity is the dual set associative cache; now the performance of the 16 Kbyte cache is within a per cent or so of the perfect cache. But at the time of the design of the ARM600 (1990) a 16 Kbyte cache required a large chip area, and the 4 Kbyte cache does not perform so well. (The results depend strongly on the program used to generate the address traces used, but these are typical.)

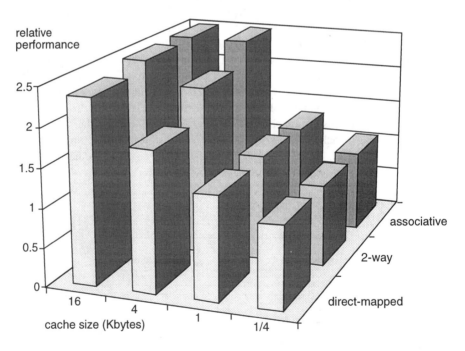

**Figure 12.2**   Unified cache performance as a function of size and organization.

Going to the other extreme, a fully associative cache performs significantly better at the smaller size, delivering the 'perfect' performance on the benchmark program used for the tests. Here the replacement algorithm is random; LRU (least recently used) gives very similar results.

The cache model was then modified to use a quad-word line which is necessary to reduce the area cost of the tag store. This change had minimal effect on the performance.

The fully associative cache requires a large CAM (Content Addressable Memory) tag store which is likely to consume significant power, even with a quad-word line. The power can be reduced a lot by segmenting the CAM into smaller components, but this reduces the associativity. An analysis of the sensitivity of the system performance on the degree of associativity, using a 4 Kbyte cache, is shown in Figure 12.3. This shows the performance of the system for all associativities from fully (256-way) associative down to direct-mapped (1-way). Although the biggest performance increase is in going from direct-mapped to dual-set associative, there are noticeable improvements all the way up to 64-way associativity.

It would therefore appear that a 64-way associative CAM-RAM cache provides the same performance as the fully associative cache whilst allowing the 256 CAM

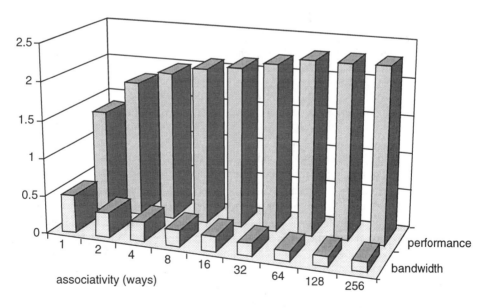

**Figure 12.3**   The effect of associativity on performance and bandwidth requirement.

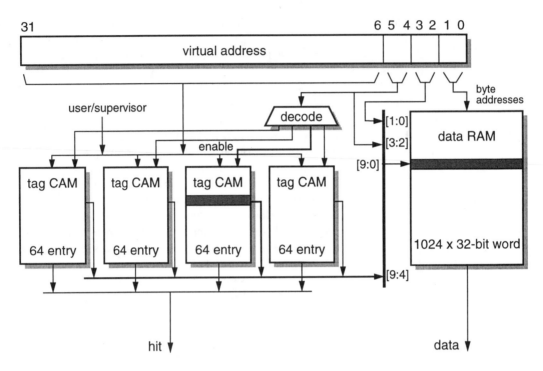

**Figure 12.4**  ARM600 cache organization.

entries to be split into four sections to save power. The external memory bandwidth requirement of each level of associativity is also shown in Figure 12.3 (relative to an uncached processor), and note how the highest performance corresponds to the lowest external bandwidth requirement. Since each external access costs a lot of energy compared with internal activity, the cache is simultaneously increasing performance and reducing system power requirements.

The organization of the cache is therefore that shown in Figure 12.4. The bottom two bits of the virtual address select a byte within a 32-bit word, the next two bits select a word within a cache line and the next two bits select one of the four 64-entry CAM tag stores. The rest of the virtual address is presented to the selected tag store (the other tag stores are disabled to save power) to check whether the data is in the cache, and the result is either a miss, or a hit together with the address of the data in the cache data RAM.

**Cache control FSM**

The ARM600 operates with two clocks. The **fast** clock defines the processor cycle time when it is operating from the cache or writing to the write buffer; the **memory** clock defines the speed when the processor is accessing external memory. The clock supplied to the core switches dynamically between these two clock sources, which may be asynchronous with respect to each other. There is no requirement for the memory clock to be a simple subdivision of the fast clock, though if it is the processor can be configured to avoid the synchronization overhead.

Normally the processor runs from the cache using the fast clock. When a cache miss occurs (or a reference is made to uncacheable memory), the processor synchronizes to the memory clock and either performs a single external access or a cache line-fill. Because switching between the clocks incurs an overhead for the synchronization (to reduce the risk of metastability to an acceptable level), the processor checks the next address before deciding whether or not to switch back to the fast clock.

The finite state machine that controls this activity is shown in Figure 12.5 on page 316. Following initialization, the processor enters the *Check tag* state running from the fast clock. Depending on whether or not the addressed data is found in the cache, the processor can proceed in one of the following ways:

- So long as the address is non-sequential, does not fault in the MMU and is either a read found in the cache or a buffered write, the state machine remains in the *Check tag* state and a data value is returned or written every clock cycle.

- When the next address is a sequential read in the same cache line or a sequential buffered write, the state machine moves to the *Sequential fast* state where the data may be accessed without checking the tag and without activating the MMU. This saves power, and exploits the *seq* signal from the processor core (see 'Memory interface' on page 246). Again a data value is read or written every clock cycle.

- If the address is not in the cache or is an unbuffered write an external access is required. This begins in the *Start external* state. Reads from uncacheable memory and unbuffered writes are completed as single memory transactions in the *External* state. Cacheable reads perform a quad-word line fetch, after fetching the necessary translation information if this was not already in the MMU.

- Cycles where the processor does not use memory are executed in the *Idle* state.

At several points in the translation process it may become clear that the access cannot be completed and the *Abort* state is entered. Uncacheable reads and unbuffered writes may also be aborted by external hardware.

**The ARM600 MMU**

The ARM600 memory management unit implements the ARM memory management architecture described in Section 11.3 on page 294 using the system control coprocessor described in Section 11.2 on page 291.

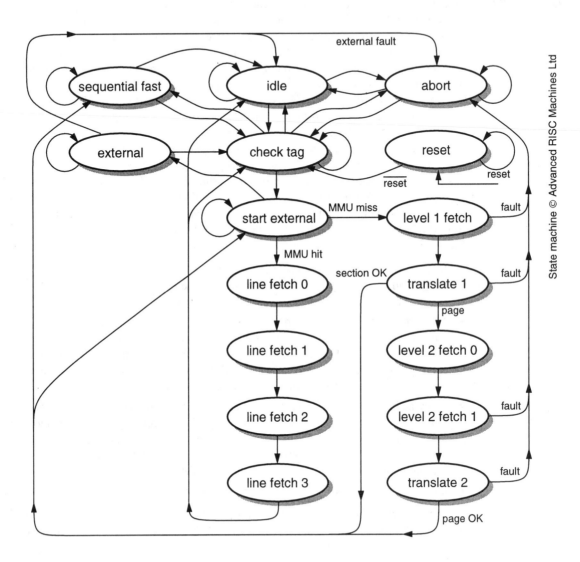

**Figure 12.5**   ARM600 cache control state machine.

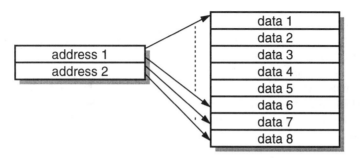

**Figure 12.6**   Write buffer mapping example.

The translation look-aside buffer (TLB) is a 32-entry associative cache of recently used translations which accelerates the translation process by removing the need for the 2-stage table look-up in a high proportion of accesses.

**The ARM600 write buffer**

The write buffer holds two addresses and eight data words. Each address may be associated with any number of the data words, so the write buffer may hold one word (or byte) of data to write to one address and seven words to write to another address, or two blocks of four words to write to different addresses, and so on. The data words associated with a particular address are written to sequential memory locations starting at that address. (Clearly multiple data words associated with one address are generated principally by store multiple register instructions, the only other potential source being a data transfer from an external coprocessor.)

The mapping is illustrated in Figure 12.6, which shows the first address holding six data words and the second two. The write buffer becomes full either when both addresses are used or when all eight data words are full.

The processor can write into the buffer at the fast (cache) clock speed and continue executing instructions from the cache while the write buffer stores the data to memory at the memory clock rate. The processor is therefore fully decoupled from the memory speed so long as the instructions and data it needs are in the cache and the write buffer is not full when it comes to perform a write operation. The write buffer gives a performance benefit of around 15% for a modest hardware cost.

The principle drawback of the write buffer is that it is not possible to recover from external memory faults caused by buffered writes since the processor state is not recoverable. The processor can still support virtual memory since translation faults are detected in the on-chip MMU, so the exception is raised before the data gets to the write buffer. But, for example, a memory error correction scheme based on software error recovery cannot be supported if buffered writes are enabled.

**Coprocessor interface**

The interface for the on-chip system coprocessor is relatively simple. Only single-word coprocessor register transfers (data movements between ARM registers and CP15 registers) are supported, and the standard ARM coprocessor hand-shake described in Section 4.4 on page 101 suffices.

The support provided by the ARM600 for off-chip coprocessors is rather more complex. Since the ARM coprocessor model is based upon the coprocessor seeing the ARM instruction stream, which in the main comes from the cache, this requires all the traffic from the cache to the ARM core to be exported off chip to the coprocessor. There are two problems in this:

- Sending high-bandwidth traffic off chip dissipates a lot of power due to the high off-chip track capacitances. Since coprocessor instructions make up a small proportion of this traffic, most of this power is wasted.

- Getting the data to the coprocessor in a single clock cycle time, most of which is taken up with the cache access time, is not possible without compromising the fast clock rate (which would affect the performance of all instructions, not just those for execution by the coprocessor).

The solution to these problems adopted in the ARM600 is to introduce a 1-clock pipeline delay between the on-chip cache data bus and the external coprocessor bus. This gives the chip a whole clock cycle to get coprocessor instructions through the pins and to the coprocessor. Furthermore, it gives the ARM600 time to identify the real coprocessor instructions and to substitute the same null instruction for all the others, thereby reducing the number of transitions on the external bus (to zero in the absence of any coprocessor instructions) and saving the wasted power.

Running the external coprocessors one clock cycle behind the ARM introduces a 1-cycle stall whenever a coprocessor instruction is encountered so that the handshake can be completed, and although data transfers *to* the coprocessor can run down the same pipeline, transfers *from* the coprocessor require the coprocessor to run *ahead* of the ARM. This reduces the performance of code which uses the coprocessors, but more importantly it means that supporting external coprocessors has no impact on code which makes no use of them.

**The ARM610**

The ARM610 is a variant of the ARM600 produced, initially, for use in the Apple Newton MessagePad. The difference between the ARM600 and the ARM610 is that the latter omits the support for external coprocessors which is included on the former (though it retains the on-chip system control coprocessor, CP15). Although the external coprocessor support logic does not occupy a particularly significant area on the ARM600, its omission allows a physical reorganization of the on-chip function blocks that results in a more compact silicon layout.

A more impressive difference is in the packaging of the chip. The ARM610 is packaged in a 144-pin 'thin quad flat pack'. This package is 2 centimetres square and only 1.6 millimetres thick (so thin, in fact, that the silicon wafer has to be ground down in thickness in order that the chip will fit in the package). Such a small package cannot be expected to dissipate much heat, but the ARM610 running with a 25 MHz fast clock dissipates at most 500 mW and typically much less, which is comfortably within the capabilities of the package. It has several other features that suit it to low-power applications such as portable battery-powered equipment:

- Its operation is fully static, so it can operate with a clock of any frequency from 0 Hz up to the specified maximum frequency, which provides the sort of flexibility required by the designer low-power system.

- Its small size and low power dissipation make it easy to design into physically small products with minimal cooling requirements.

- The on-chip cache reduces external instruction and data traffic, saving power. (Remember that off-chip traffic uses far more power than on-chip traffic because off-chip capacitances are higher.)

- The segmented CAM structure reduces the on-chip power consumption.

Although the design was originally driven by the requirements of the Apple Newton, the ARM610 remains a general-purpose low-power low-cost processor which has a wide range of potential applications, and in addition to its role in the Newton it has been used in the Acorn Risc PC desktop system and in a number of other products.

**ARM610 silicon**

The ARM610 was originally designed on a 1 μm CMOS process but it has subsequently been shrunk onto a 0.6 μm process. Figure 12.7 on page 320 shows a photograph of an ARM610 die, with an overlay indicating the major functional areas.

The largest share of the core area is taken by the cache which comprises a 4 Kbyte RAM block and the CAM address tag store. Both of these blocks employ memory structures which are very regular, so a high transistor density is achieved.

The ARM6 processor core is physically the same as that used in the ARM60 chip (see Figure 9.3 on page 248) reflected about a horizontal axis.

The MMU includes the TLB which is another dense memory structure, and less dense control logic which performs the table walking to reload the TLB on a translation miss.

The smaller areas identified in Figure 12.7 are the JTAG test access port (TAP) controller, the write buffer and the cache control logic.

The remaining die area is taken up by the pad ring which here, as on the ARM60, occupies a considerable proportion of the total silicon area.

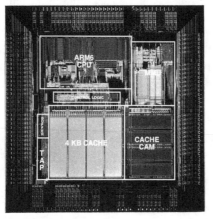

© VLSI Technology, Inc.

**Figure 12.7**   ARM610 die photograph.

The principal characteristics of the chip are summarized in Table 12.2. The figures presented are for the 0.6 μm part as this has largely displaced the older 1 μm part. Of particular note is the very small total die size which is approximately half the area of the first ARM processor chips fabricated in 3 μm CMOS in 1985 which had no cache, MMU or JTAG test circuitry.

The ARM6 core accounts for approximately 33,000 of the total transistor count.

The MIPS rating is based upon the Dhrystone 2.1 benchmark and is the number of Dhrystones the processor can deliver at the maximum clock frequency divided by 1,757. (Therefore an ARM610 can deliver 52,700 Dhrystones per second at 33 MHz.)

**Table 12.2**   ARM610 characteristics.

| | | | | | |
|---|---|---|---|---|---|
| **Process** | 0.6 μm | **Transistors** | 358,931 | **MIPS** | 30 |
| **Metal layers** | 2 | **Die area** | 26 mm$^2$ | **Power** | 500 mW |
| **Vdd** | 5 V | **Clock** | 0 to 33 MHz | **MIPS/W** | 60 |

## 12.2   The ARM700 and ARM710

The ARM700 is very similar to the ARM600 and the ARM710 to the ARM610. The ARM700 and 710 use the ARM7 core, which is an ARM6 core re-engineered to incorporate circuit design changes to enable it to operate reliably from a 3.3 volt power supply (ARM6 requires a 5 volt supply). The principal organizational and physical differences are as follows:

- The translation look-aside buffer (TLB) has 64 entries instead of the 32 on the ARM 600.

- The write buffer holds four addresses and eight data items instead of two addresses and eight data items. Its data capacity is therefore the same, but it can hold the output from more single word or byte write instructions.

- The ARM700 cache is larger and differently organized, holding 8 Kbytes of instructions and data in a 4-way set-associative 8-word line structure instead of 4 Kbytes in a 64-way associative 4-word line structure. (ARM710 variants have reverted to a 4-word line, however.)

- The ARM700 and 710 have been designed for 3 volt operation, giving 192 MIPS/watt against 60 MIPS/watt for the ARM610. (The power-efficiency depends on $Vdd^2$, so reducing the supply from 5 volts to 3.3 volts gives almost a factor three improvement in power-efficiency; see Section 1.7 on page 30.)

- Circuit-level improvements support a clock rate increased from 33 MHz (for the 0.6 μm ARM610) to 40 MHz (for the 0.6 μm ARM710).

**The ARM700 cache**

The organization of the ARM700 cache is illustrated in Figure 12.8 on page 322. Bits [10:5] of the virtual address are used to index into each of the four tag stores. The tags contain bits [31:11] of the virtual addresses of the corresponding data, so these tags are compared with bits [31:11] of the current virtual address. If one of the tags matches, the cache has hit and the corresponding line can be accessed from the data RAM using the same index (bits [10:5] of the virtual address) together with two bits which encode the number of the tag store which produced the matching tag. Virtual address bits [4:2] select the word from the line and, if a byte access is requested, bits [1:0] select the byte from the word.

It is interesting to compare the ARM600 and 700 cache organizations, since they illustrate the sorts of issues that arise in designing a cache for both good performance and low power operation. Although there is, as yet, no final word on the correct way to design a cache for this sort of application, the designer can be guided by the following observations on the examples presented in these ARM chips.

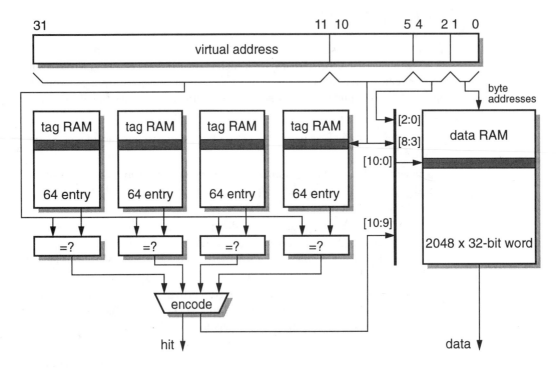

**Figure 12.8**   The ARM700 cache organization.

**Cache speed**   High associativity caches give the best hit rate, but require sequential CAM then RAM accesses which limits how fast the cycle time can become. Caches with a lower associativity can perform parallel tag and data accesses to give faster cycle times, and although a direct mapped cache has a significantly lower hit rate than a fully associative one, most of the associativity benefits accrue going from direct-mapped to 2- or 4-way associative; beyond 4-way the benefits of increased associativity are small. However a fully associative CAM-RAM cache is much simpler than a 4-way associative RAM-RAM cache.

**Cache power**   CAM is somewhat power-hungry, requiring a parallel comparison with every entry on each cycle. Segmenting the cache by reducing the associativity a little and activating only a subsection of the CAM reduces the power cost significantly for a small increase in complexity.

In a static RAM the main users of power are the analogue sense-amplifiers. A 4-way cache must activate four times as many sense-amplifiers in the tag store as a direct-mapped cache; if it exploits the speed advantage offered by parallel tag and data accesses, it will also uses four times as many sense-amplifiers in the data store. (RAM-RAM caches can, alternatively, perform serial tag and data accesses to save power, only activating a particular data RAM when a hit is detected in the corresponding tag store.) Waste power can be minimized by using self-timed power-down circuits to turn off the sense-amplifiers as soon as the data is valid, but the power used in the sense-amplifiers is still significant.

**Sequential accesses**

Where the processor is accessing memory locations which fall within the same cache line it should be possible to bypass the tag look-up for all but the first access. The ARM generates a signal which indicates when the next memory access will be sequential to the current one, and this can be used, with the current address, to deduce that the access will fall in the same line. (This does not catch every access within the same line, but it catches nearly all of them and is very simple to implement.)

Where an access will be in the same line, bypassing the tag look-up increases the access speed and saves power. Potentially, sequential accesses could use slower sense-amplifiers (possibly using standard logic rather than analogue circuits) and save considerable power.

**Power optimization**

The cache designer must remember that the goal is to minimize the overall system power, not just the cache power. Off-chip accesses cost a lot more energy than on-chip accesses, so the first priority must be to find a cache organization which gives a good hit rate. Deciding between a highly associative CAM-RAM organization or a set-associative RAM-RAM organization requires a detailed investigation of all of the design issues, and may be strongly influenced by low-level circuit issues such as novel ways to build power-efficient sense-amplifiers or CAM hit detectors.

Exploiting sequential accesses to save power and to increase performance is always a good idea. Typical dynamic execution statistics from the ARM show that 75% of all accesses are sequential, and since sequential accesses are fundamentally easier to deal with, this seems to be a statistic that should not be overlooked. Where power-efficiency is paramount, it may be worth sacrificing performance by making non-sequential accesses take two clock cycles; this will only reduce performance by about 25% and may reduce the cache power requirements by a factor of two or three.

An interesting question for research into low power is to ask whether the best cache organization for power-efficiency is necessarily the same as the best organization for high performance.

© GEC Plessey Semiconductors

**Figure 12.9**   ARM700 die photograph.

**ARM700 silicon**   A photograph of the ARM700 die is shown in Figure 12.9 and the principal character-istics of the ARM700 chip are summarized in Table 12.3. The part is delivered in a 160-pin plastic quad flat pack.

**Table 12.3**   ARM700 characteristics.

| | | | | | |
|---|---|---|---|---|---|
| **Process** | 0.8 μm | **Transistors** | 578,977 | **MIPS** | 18/30 |
| **Metal layers** | 2 | **Die area** | 68 mm$^2$ | **Power** | 118/611 mW |
| **Vdd** | 3.3/5 V | **Clock** | 0 to 20/33 MHz | **MIPS/W** | 152/49 |

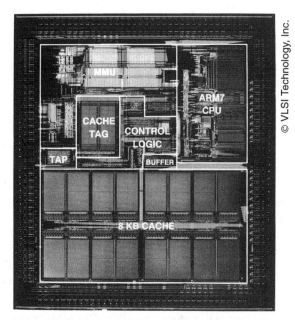

© VLSI Technology, Inc.

**Figure 12.10**　ARM710 die photograph.

**ARM710
silicon**

A photograph of the ARM710 die is shown in Figure 12.10 and the principal characteristics of the chip are summarized in Table 12.4. The die area is half that of the ARM700, mainly due to the smaller process technology (0.6 μm against 0.8 μm). The removal of the coprocessor interface logic makes a small contribution, as does the reduction in pin count from 160 to 144.

The MIPS rating used here, and elsewhere in this book, is based upon the performance of the chip running the Dhrystone 2.1 benchmark.

**Table 12.4**　ARM710 characteristics.

| Process | 0.6 μm | Transistors | 570,295 | MIPS | 23/36 |
|---|---|---|---|---|---|
| Metal layers | 2 | Die area | 34 mm$^2$ | Power | 120/500 mW |
| Vdd | 3.3/5 V | Clock | 0 to 25/40 MHz | MIPS/W | 192/72 |

## 12.3 The ARM810

The ARM810 is a high-performance ARM CPU chip with an on-chip cache and memory management unit. It is the first implementation of the ARM instruction set developed by ARM Limited to use a fundamentally different pipeline structure from that used on the original ARM chip designed at Acorn Computers and carried through to ARM6 and ARM7.

The ARM8 core is the integer processing unit used in the ARM810. It was described in Section 9.3 on page 254. The ARM810 adds the following on-chip support to the basic CPU:

- An 8 Kbyte virtually-addressed unified instruction and data cache using a copy-back (or write-through, controlled by the page table entry) write strategy and offering a double-bandwidth capability as required by the ARM8 core. The cache is 64-way associative, and constructed from 1 Kbyte components to simplify the future development of a smaller cache for an embedded system chip or a larger cache on a more advanced process technology. It is designed so that areas of the cache can be 'locked down' to ensure that speed-critical sections of code, which arise in many embedded applications, do not get flushed.

- A memory management unit conforming to the ARM MMU architecture described in Section 11.3 on page 294 using the system control coprocessor described in Section 11.2 on page 291.

- A write buffer to allow the processor to continue while the write to external memory completes.

The organization of the ARM810 is illustrated in Figure 12.11 on page 327.

**Double-bandwidth cache**

The core's double-bandwidth requirement is satisfied by the cache; external memory accesses use conventional line refill and individual data transfer protocols. Double-bandwidth is available from the cache only for sequential memory accesses, so it is exploited by the prefetch unit for instruction fetches and by the core for load multiple register instructions.

Since the pipeline organization used on ARM6 uses the memory interface almost every cycle, some way must be found to increase the available memory bandwidth if the CPI (the number of clocks per instruction) of the processor is to be improved. The StrongARM (described in the next section) achieves an increased bandwidth by incorporating separate instruction and data caches, thereby making double the bandwidth potentially available (though not all of this bandwidth can be used since the ARM generates instruction traffic with around twice the bandwidth of the data traffic, so the effective increase in bandwidth is approximately 50%). The ARM810 delivers an

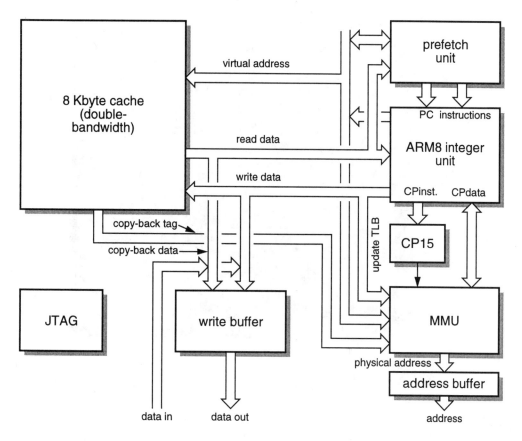

**Figure 12.11** ARM810 organization.

increased bandwidth by returning two sequential words per clock cycle which, since typically around 75% of an ARM's memory accesses are sequential, increases the use-able bandwidth by about 60%. Although the ARM810 approach gives more band-width, it also creates more opportunity for conflict between instruction and data accesses; evaluating the relative merits of the two approaches is not straightforward.

As the cache uses a copy-back write strategy and is virtually addressed, evicting a dirty line requires an address translation. The mechanism used on the ARM810 is to send the virtual tag to the MMU for translation.

© VLSI Technology, Inc.

**Figure 12.12**    ARM810 die photograph.

**ARM810 silicon**

A photograph of an ARM810 die is shown in Figure 12.12. The ARM8 core datapath is visible at the top of the photograph with its control logic immediately below. The MMU TLB is in the top right hand corner and the eight 1 Kbyte cache blocks occupy the bottom area of the chip.

The characteristics of the ARM810 are summarized in Table 12.5.

**Table 12.5**    ARM810 characteristics.

| | | | | | |
|---|---|---|---|---|---|
| **Process** | 0.5 μm | **Transistors** | 836,022 | **MIPS** | 86 |
| **Metal layers** | 3 | **Die area** | 76 mm$^2$ | **Power** | 500 mW |
| **Vdd** | 3.3 V | **Clock** | 0 to 72 MHz | **MIPS/W** | 172 |

## 12.4　The StrongARM

The StrongARM CPU was developed by Digital Equipment Corporation in collaboration with ARM Limited. It is the first ARM processor to use a *modified-Harvard* (separate instruction and data cache) architecture, and is the highest performance ARM available at the time of writing.

**Digital
Alpha
background**

Digital are, perhaps, best known in the microprocessor business for their range of 'Alpha' microprocessors which are 64-bit RISC processors that operate at very high clock rates. The ability to sustain these clock frequencies is a result of advanced CMOS process technology, carefully balanced pipeline design, a very thoroughly engineered clocking scheme and in-house design tools that give unusually good control of all these factors.

The same approach has been applied to the design of StrongARM, with the added objective of achieving exceptional power-efficiency.

**StrongARM
organization**

The organization of StrongARM is shown in Figure 12.13 on page 330. Its main features are:

- A 5-stage pipeline with register forwarding.
- Single-cycle execution of all common instructions except 64-bit multiplies, multiple register transfers and the swap memory and register instruction.
- A 16 Kbyte 32-way associative instruction cache with 32-byte line.
- A 16 Kbyte 32-way associative copy-back data cache with 32-byte line.
- Separate 32-entry instruction and data translation look-aside buffers.
- An 8-entry write buffer with up to 16 bytes per entry.
- Pseudo-static operation with low power consumption.

The processor uses system control coprocessor 15 to manage the on-chip MMU and cache resources, and incorporates JTAG boundary scan test circuitry for testing printed circuit board connectivity (the JTAG 'in-test', for in-circuit testing of the device itself, is not supported).

The first StrongARM chips are implemented on Digital's 0.35 μm CMOS process, using three layers of metal. They use around 2.5 million transistors on a 50 mm$^2$ die (which is very small for a processor of this performance) and deliver 200 to 250 Dhrystone MIPS with a 160 to 200 MHz clock, dissipating half to just under one watt using a 1.65 V to 2 V supply.

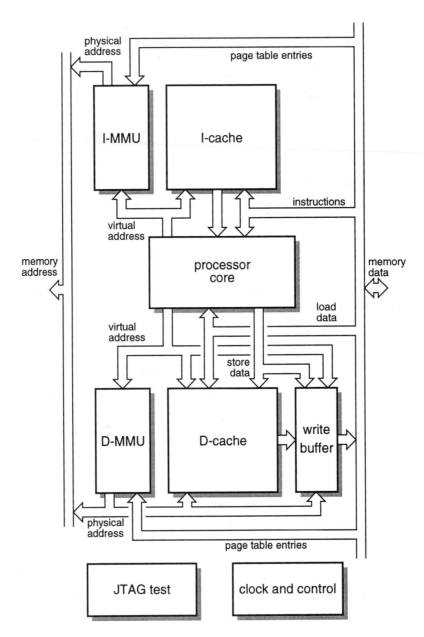

**Figure 12.13**    StrongARM organization.

**The StrongARM processor core**

The processor core employs a 'classic' 5-stage pipeline with full bypassing (register forwarding) and hardware interlocks. The ARM instruction set requires some instruction decoding to take place before the register bank read accesses can begin, and it also requires a shift operation in series with the ALU, but both of these additional logic functions are fitted within their respective pipeline stages and do not add to the pipeline depth. The pipeline stages are:

1. Instruction fetch (from the instruction cache).
2. Instruction decode and register read; branch target calculation and execution.
3. Shift and ALU operation, including data transfer memory address calculation.
4. Data cache access.
5. Result write-back to register file.

The organization of the major pipeline components is illustrated in Figure 12.14 on page 332. The shaded bars delimit the pipeline stages and data which passes across these bars will be latched at the crossing point. Data which feeds around the end of a bar is being passed back or forward across pipeline stages, for example:

- The register forwarding paths which pass intermediate results on to following instructions to avoid a register interlock stall caused by a read-after-write hazard.
- The PC path which forwards pc + 4 from the fetch stage of the *next* instruction, giving pc + 8 for the current instruction, to be used as r15 and in the branch target calculation.

**Pipeline features**

Of particular note in this pipeline structure are:

- The need for three register read ports to enable register-controlled shifts and store with base plus index addressing to issue in one cycle.
- The need for two register write ports to allow load with auto-index to issue in one cycle.
- The address incrementer in the execute stage to support load and store multiple instructions.
- The large number of sources for the next PC value.

This last point reflects the many ways the ARM architecture allows the PC to be modified as a result of its visibility as r15 in the register bank.

**PC modification**

The most common source of the next PC is the PC incrementer in the fetch stage; this value is available at the start of the next cycle, allowing one instruction to be fetched each cycle.

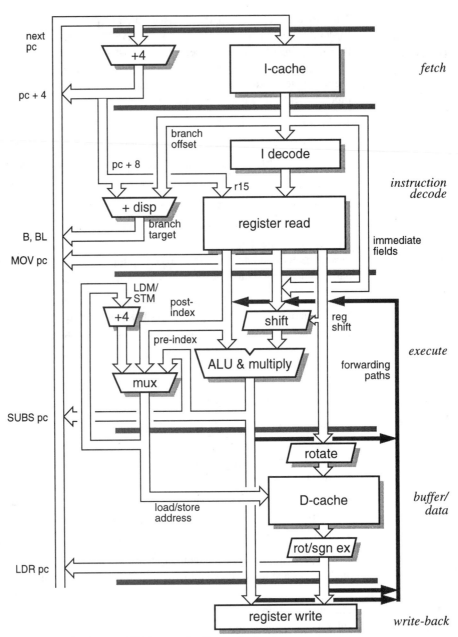

**Figure 12.14**    StrongARM core pipeline organization.

The next most common source of the PC is the result of a branch instruction. The dedicated branch displacement adder computes the target address during the instruction decode stage, causing a taken branch to incur a one cycle penalty in addition to the cycle taken to execute the branch itself. Note that the displacement addition can take place in parallel with the instruction decode since the offset is a fixed field within the instruction; if the instruction turns out not to be a branch the computed target is simply discarded.

A common code sequence, for instance to control the exit from a loop, is:

```
CMP     r0, #0
BNE     label
..
```

The operation of the pipeline during this sequence is shown in Figure 12.15. Note how the condition codes become valid just in time to avoid increasing the branch penalty; the instruction immediately following the branch is fetched and discarded, but then the processor begins fetching from the branch target. The target address is generated concurrently with the condition codes that determine whether or not it should be used.

The same one cycle penalty applies to branch and link instructions which take the branch in the same way but use the execute and write stages to compute pc + 4 and write it to r14, the link register. It also applies to the normal subroutine return instruction, MOV pc, lr, where the target address comes from the register file rather than from the branch displacement adder, but it is still available at the end of the decode stage.

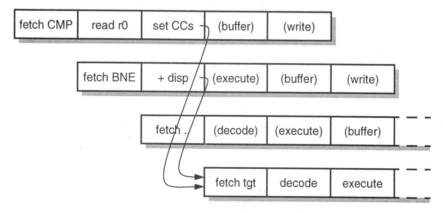

**Figure 12.15** StrongARM loop test pipeline behaviour.

If the return address must be computed, for example when returning from an exception, there is a two cycle penalty since the ALU result is only available at the end of the execute stage, and where the PC is loaded from memory (from a jump table, or subroutine return from stack) there is a three cycle penalty.

**Forwarding paths**

The execution pipeline includes three forwarding paths to each register operand to avoid stalls when read-after-write hazards occur. Values are forwarded from:

1. The ALU result.
2. Data loaded from the data cache.
3. The buffered ALU result.

These paths remove all data-dependency stalls except when a loaded data value is used by the following instruction, in which case a single cycle stall is required.

**Abort recovery**

It might seem that one of these paths could be avoided if the ALU result were written into the register file in the following stage rather than buffering it and delaying the write to the last stage. The merit of the delayed scheme is that data aborts can occur during the data cache access, perhaps requiring remedial action to recover the base register value (for instance when the base register is overwritten in a load multiple sequence before the fault is generated). This scheme not only allows recovery but supports the cleanest recovery mechanism, leaving the base register value as it was at the start of the instruction and removing the need for the exception handler to undo any auto-indexing.

**Multiplier**

A feature of particular note is the StrongARM's multiplication unit which, despite the processor's high clock rate, computes at the rate of 12 bits per cycle giving the product of two 32-bit operands in one to three clock cycles. The high-speed multiplier gives StrongARM considerable potential in applications which require significant digital signal processing performance.

**Instruction cache**

The I-cache holds 16 Kbytes of instructions in 512 lines of eight instructions (32 bytes). The cache is 32-way associative (using a CAM-RAM organization) with a cyclic replacement algorithm and uses the processor's virtual address. The block size is the same as the line size, so whole lines are loaded from memory at a time. Individual areas of memory may be marked as cacheable or uncacheable using the memory management tables, and the cache may be disabled and flushed (in its entirety) under software control.

**Data cache**
The data cache uses a similar organization to the instruction cache but with added functions to cope with data stores (instructions are read-only). It has a capacity of 16 Kbytes with 512 32-byte lines arranged as a 32-way virtually-addressed associative cache with cyclic replacement. The block size is also 32 bytes. The cache may be disabled by software and individual regions of memory may be made uncacheable. (Making I/O regions uncacheable is usually a good idea.)

The data cache uses a copy-back write strategy, and has two dirty bits per line so that when a line is evicted from the cache all, half or none of it is written to memory. The use of two dirty bits rather than one reduces memory traffic since the 'half dirty' case is quite common. The cache stores a copy of the physical address with each line for use when the line is written back to memory, and evicted lines are placed into the write buffer.

Since the cache uses a copy-back write strategy, it is sometimes necessary to cause all dirty lines to be written back to memory. On StrongARM this is achieved using software to load new data into every line, causing dirty lines to be evicted.

**Synonyms**
As with any virtually-addressed cache, care must be taken to ensure that all cacheable physical memory locations have unique virtual addresses that map to them. When two different virtual addresses map to the same physical location the virtual addresses are **synonyms**; where synonyms exist, neither virtual address should be cacheable.

**Cache consistency**
The separate instruction and data caches create the potential for the two caches to have inconsistent copies of the same physical memory location. Whenever a region of memory is treated as (writeable) data at one time and as executable instructions at another, great care must be taken to avoid inconsistencies.

A common example of this situation is when a program is loaded (or copied from one memory location to another) and then executed. During the load phase the program is treated as data and passes through the data cache. When it is executed it is loaded into the instruction cache (which may have copies of previous instructions from the same addresses). To ensure correct operation:

1.  The load phase should be completed.
2.  The entire data cache should be 'cleaned' (by loading new data into every line as described above) or, where the addresses of the affected cache lines are known, these lines may be explicitly cleaned and flushed.
3.  The instruction cache should be flushed (to remove obsolete instructions).

Alternative solutions might involve making certain regions of memory uncacheable during the load phase.

Note that this is not a problem for literals (data items included in the instruction stream) which are quite common in ARM code. Although a block of memory may be loaded into both caches since it contains a mixture of instructions and literals, so long as individual words (or bytes) are treated consistently as *either* instructions *or* data, there will be no problem. It is even acceptable for the program to change the value of a literal (though this is rarely used and is probably bad practice) so long as it does not affect the values of instructions which may be in the instruction cache. It is better practice, however, to avoid literals altogether and to keep data in data areas that are separate from code areas which contain instructions.

**Compiler issues**

The separation of the instruction and data caches should be observed by the compiler, which should pool constants across compiler units rather than placing them at the end of each routine. This minimizes the pollution of the data cache with instructions and of the instruction cache with data.

**The write buffer**

The write buffer smooths out small peaks in the write data bandwidth, decoupling the processor from stalls caused by the memory bus saturating. A large peak that causes the buffer to fill will stall the processor. Independent writes to the same 16-byte area are merged within the write buffer, though only to the last address written into the buffer. The buffer stores up to eight addresses (each address aligned to a 16-byte boundary), copying the virtual address for use when merging writes and the physical address to address the external memory, and up to 16 bytes of data for each address (so each address can handle a dirty half-line or up to four registers from a single store multiple).

The write buffer may be disabled by software, and individual memory regions may be marked as bufferable or unbufferable using the MMU page tables. All cacheable regions are bufferable (evicted cache lines are written through the write buffer) but uncacheable regions may be bufferable or unbufferable. Normally the I/O region is unbufferable. An unbuffered write will wait for the write buffer to empty before it is written to memory.

Data reads that miss the data cache will be checked against entries in the write buffer to ensure consistency, but instruction reads are not checked against the write buffer. Again, great care is needed whenever memory locations which have been used as data are to be used as instructions.

**MMU organization**

StrongARM incorporates the standard ARM memory management architecture, using separate translation look-aside buffers (TLBs) for instructions and data. Each TLB has 32 translation entries arranged as a fully associative cache with cyclic replacement. A TLB miss invokes table-walking hardware to fetch the translation and access permission information from main memory.

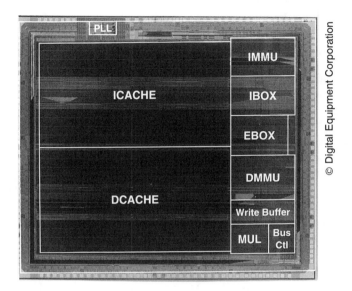

© Digital Equipment Corporation

**Figure 12.16**    StrongARM die photograph.

**StrongARM silicon**

A photograph of a StrongARM die is shown in Figure 12.16 with an overlay indicating the major functional areas. The die area is, not surprisingly, dominated by the instruction cache (ICACHE) and the data cache (DCACHE). Each cache has its own MMU (IMMU and DMMU). The processor core has the instruction issue unit (IBOX) and the execution unit (EBOX) with high-speed multiplication hardware (MUL). The write buffer and external bus controller complete the processor logic.

The high-frequency on-chip clock is generated by a phase-locked loop (PLL) from an external 3.68 MHz clock input.

The characteristics of the StrongARM are summarized in Table 12.6.

**Table 12.6**    StrongARM characteristics.

| Process | 0.35 μm | Transistors | 2,500,000 | MIPS | 201/251 |
|---------|---------|-------------|-----------|------|---------|
| Metal layers | 3 | Die area | 50 mm$^2$ | Power | 450/900 mW |
| Vdd | 1.65/2 V | Clock | 160/200 MHz | MIPS/W | 448/279 |

## 12.5   Example and exercises

**Example 12.1**   **Why was a 64-way associative cache used on the ARM600?**

The ARM600 was designed in 1990, at which time the maximum size of cache that would fit on a reasonably low cost CPU was around 4 Kbytes. At around this size, the organization of the cache has a significant influence on the hit rate and hence the processor's performance. In simulations a fully associative 4 Kbyte cache gave 65% better performance than a direct-mapped cache of the same size and 15% better performance than a 4-way set-associative 4 Kbyte cache.

However, a fully associative 4 Kbyte cache with a 4-word line size requires a 256-entry content addressable memory (CAM) tag store, and the 256-entry CAM consumes considerable power performing 256 tag look-ups in parallel. Reducing the associativity to 64 ways has minimal impact on the performance while reducing the CAM power by a factor of four.

Hence the choice of a 64-way associative cache was driven by the objective of maximizing performance, tempered by the need to control the power dissipation.

**Exercise 12.1.1**   Discuss the impact of the following cache features on performance and power dissipation:

1. Increasing associativity by splitting the tag and data RAMs into multiple blocks which perform parallel look-ups.
2. Serializing the tag and data RAM accesses.
3. Exploiting sequential access patterns to bypass the tag look-up and to optimize the data RAM access mechanism.
4. Including separate data and instruction caches (as on StrongARM).
5. Providing two sequential words per clock cycle (as on ARM810).

**Exercise 12.1.2**   Explain why an on-chip write buffer cannot be used with an off-chip memory management unit.

**Exercise 12.1.3**   Why, as processor speeds rise relative to memory speeds, does it become increasingly important to use a copy-back rather than a write-through cache write strategy?

# 13 ARM Systems

**Summary of chapter contents**

This chapter introduces the principles of building ARM processor chips into systems and contains a number of examples of systems built around ARM processor chips. The final chapter describes the use of ARM processor cores within embedded system chips.

The simplest example of an ARM system is the Platform Independent Evaluation (PIE) card developed by ARM Limited to allow users to run programs on ARM hardware as cheaply and easily as possible. The card incorporates a small amount of memory and a serial interface to a host machine which will normally be running the cross-development toolkit. There are no other custom devices on the card, only a few readily available programmable logic devices, so it is a basic introduction to getting an ARM processor running using only standard parts.

Although the PIE card design embodies considerable experience of working with the ARM, it represents a level of design that should be (and has been) achievable in a good student project over a few months.

The other examples described here are considerably more complex products, incorporating large custom integrated circuits to improve the system performance and/or reduce the build cost. They represent a major investment of design effort on the part of the companies that developed these products, and such development is clearly not to be undertaken lightly!

## 13.1 The ARM memory interface

In this section we look at the general principles involved in connecting an ARM processor to a memory system built from standard memory parts. The efficiency of the memory interface is an important determinant of the system performance, so these principles must be well understood by the designer who wishes to develop a high-performance system.

**ARM bus signals**

ARM processor chips vary in the details of their bus interfaces, but they are generally similar in nature. The memory bus interface signals include the following:

- A 32-bit address bus, $A[31:0]$, which gives the byte address of the data to be accessed.

- A 32-bit bidirectional data bus, $D[31:0]$, along which the data is transferred.

- Signals which specify whether the memory is needed ($\overline{mreq}$) and whether the address is sequential ($seq$); these are issued in the previous cycle (see Figure 9.2 on page 247) so that the memory control logic can prepare appropriately.

- Signals which specify the direction ($\overline{r/w}$) and size ($\overline{b/w}$ on earlier processors; $mas[1:0]$ on later processors) of the transfer.

- Bus timing and control signals ($abe$, $ale$, $ape$, $dbe$, $lock$, $bl[3:0]$).

**Simple memory interface**

The simplest form of memory interface is suitable for operation with ROM and static RAM (**SRAM**). These devices require the address to be stable until the end of the cycle, which may be achieved by disabling the address pipeline (tying $ape$ low) on later processors or retiming the address bus (connecting $ale$ to $\overline{mclk}$) on earlier processors. The address and data buses may then be connected directly to the memory parts as shown in Figure 13.1 on page 341 which also shows the output enable signals ($\overline{RAMoe}$ and $\overline{ROMoe}$) and the write enables ($\overline{RAMwe}$).

This figure illustrates the connection of 8-bit memory parts, which are a standard configuration for SRAMs and ROMs. Four parts of each type are required to form a 32-bit memory and an individual device is connected to a single byte section of the bus. The notation on the figure shows the device's bus numbering inside the device and the bus wires to which it is connected outside the device, so, for example, the SRAM shown nearest the ARM has its pins $D[7:0]$ connected to bus pins $D[31:24]$ which are connected to the ARM's pins $D[31:24]$.

Since the bottom two address lines, $A[1:0]$, are used for byte selection, they are used by the control logic and not connected to the memory. Therefore the address lines on the memory devices are connected to $A[2]$ and upwards, the precise number used

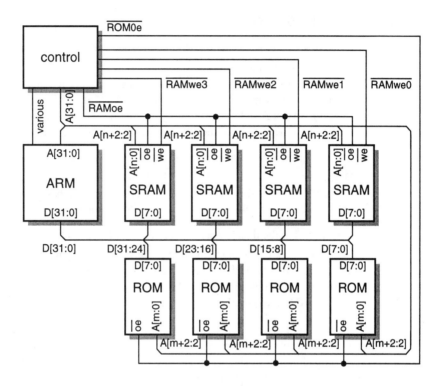

**Figure 13.1**   A basic ARM memory system.

depending on the size of the memory part (for example, a 128 Kbyte ROM part will use *A[18:2]*).

Although the ARM performs reads of both bytes and words, the memory system can ignore the difference (at the cost of some power wastage) and always simply supply a word quantity. The ARM will extract the addressed byte and ignore the remainder of the word. Therefore the ROMs do not need individual enables and using 16-bit devices causes no problems. Byte *writes*, however, do require individual byte enables, so the control logic must generate four byte write enable controls. This makes the use of wider RAMs difficult (and inefficient) unless they incorporate separate byte enables, since writing an individual byte would require a read-modify-write memory operation. Since many processors require support for writing bytes, it is likely that if RAMs do become available with a data width greater than a byte, they will incorporate individual byte enables.

**Control logic**     The control logic performs the following functions:

- It decides when to activate the RAM and when to activate the ROM.

  This logic determines the system memory map. The processor starts from location zero after a reset, so it must find ROM there since the RAM is uninitialized. The simplest memory map therefore enables the ROM if *A[31]* is low and the RAM if it is high. (Most ARM systems change the memory map shortly after start-up to put the RAM at the bottom of memory so that the exception vectors can be modified.)

- It controls the byte write enables during a write operation.

  During a word write all the byte enables should be active, during a byte write only the addressed byte should be activated, and where the ARM supports half-words a half-word write should activate two of the four enables.

- It ensures that the data is ready before the processor continues.

  The simplest solution is to run *mclk* slowly enough to ensure that all the memory devices can be accessed within a single clock cycle. More sophisticated systems may have the clock set to suit RAM accesses and use wait states for (typically slower) ROM and peripheral accesses.

  The logic required for the above functions is quite straightforward and is illustrated in Figure 13.2 on page 343. (All this logic can be implemented using a single programmable logic device.) Perhaps the trickiest aspect of the design relates to the bidirectional data bus. Here it is very important to ensure that only one device drives the bus at any time, so care is needed when turning the bus around for a write cycle, or when switching between reading from the ROM and reading from the RAM. The solution illustrated in the figure activates the appropriate data source when *mclk* is high and turns all sources off when *mclk* is low, so *dbe*, the processor's data bus enable, should also be connected to *mclk*. This is a very conservative solution which will often compromise the performance of the system by limiting the maximum clock frequency that can be used.

  Note that this design assumes that the ARM outputs are stable to the end of the clock cycle, which will be the case on newer processors with the address pipeline enable (*ape*) control input tied low. Older processors should use *ale* = $\overline{mclk}$ to retime the address outputs, but will need an external transparent latch which is open when *mclk* is low to retime $\overline{r/w}$ and $\overline{b/w}$ (which replaces *mas[1]*, and *mas[0]* is tied low).

  This simple memory system makes no use of $\overline{mreq}$ (or *seq*); it simply activates the memory on every cycle. This is safe since the ARM will only request a write cycle on a genuine memory access. The $\overline{r/w}$ control remains low during all internal and coprocessor register transfer cycles.

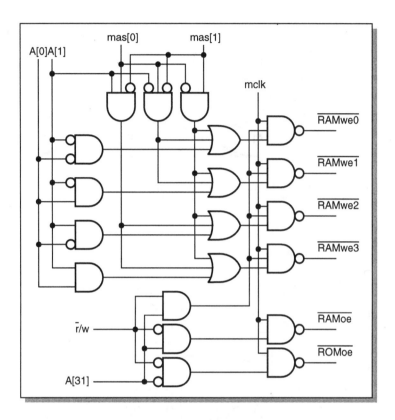

**Figure 13.2** Simple ARM memory system control logic.

**Wait states**
If we try to speed up the clock in this system it will stop working when the slowest path fails. This will normally be the ROM access. We can get a lot more performance from the system if the clock is tuned to the RAM access time and wait states are introduced to allow the ROM more access time. Usually the ROM will be allowed a fixed number of clock cycles per access, the exact number being determined by the clock rate and the ROM data sheet. We will assume an access time of four clock cycles.

The memory control logic must now incorporate a simple finite state machine to control the ROM access. A suitable state transition diagram is shown in Figure 13.3 on page 344. The three ROM states are used to stretch the ROM access time to four cycles by asserting the ARM's $\overline{wait}$ input. A design problem here is that since the addresses have been retimed to become valid early in the current cycle and $\overline{wait}$ must

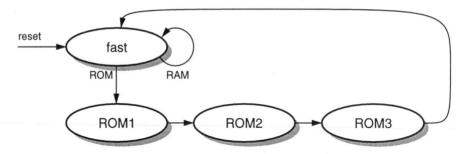

**Figure 13.3**    ROM wait control state transition diagram.

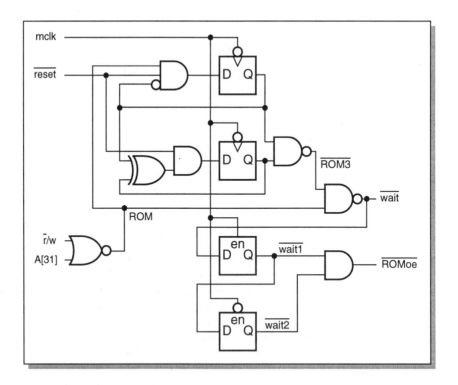

**Figure 13.4**    ROM wait state generator circuit.

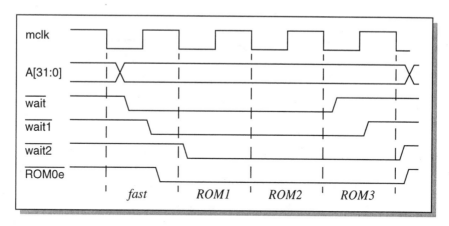

**Figure 13.5** The timing diagram for the ROM wait state logic.

be asserted before *mclk* rises, $\overline{wait}$ cannot be generated as a simple state machine output since there is no clock edge that can be used to generate it. Another problem is to generate a stretched $\overline{ROMoe}$ signal that is glitch-free.

A possible circuit is shown in Figure 13.4 on page 344. The state machine is a synchronous counter which uses the two edge-triggered flip-flops. Only the state ROM3 is of significance, since it de-activates $\overline{wait}$ which is otherwise active whenever a ROM access is detected. The two level-sensitive latches are used to generate a clean, stretched $\overline{ROMoe}$ using $\overline{wait}$ as the starting point. A timing diagram for this circuit is shown in Figure 13.5, which should clarify the operation of the logic.

**Sequential accesses**

If the system is to operate even faster it may not be possible to decode a new address and perform a RAM access in a single clock cycle. Here an extra cycle can be inserted whenever an unknown address is issued to allow time for address decoding. The only addresses that are not unknown are sequential ones, but these represent around 75% of all addresses in a typical program.

We should also now begin to recognize cycles that do not use the memory, since there is no reason why they should not operate at the full clock rate. A suitable state transition diagram is shown in Figure 13.6 on page 346.

**DRAM**

The cheapest memory technology (in terms of price per bit) is dynamic random access memory (**DRAM**). 'Dynamic' memory stores information as electrical charge on a capacitor where it gradually leaks away (over a millisecond or so). The memory data must be read and rewritten ('refreshed') before it leaks away. The responsibility for

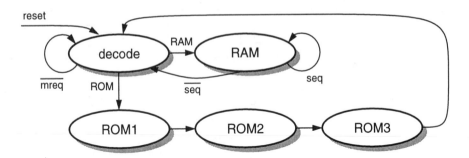

**Figure 13.6**  State transition diagram with a wait state for address decoding.

refreshing the memory usually lies with the memory control logic, not the processor, so it is not of immediate concern to us here. What is of concern is the internal organization of the memory which is shown in Figure 13.7 on page 347.

Like most memory devices, the storage cells in a DRAM are arranged in a matrix which is approximately square. Unlike most other memory devices, this organization is exposed to the user. The matrix is addressed by *row* and by *column*, and a DRAM accepts the row and column addresses separately down the same **multiplexed address bus**. First the row address is presented and latched using the active-low **row address strobe** signal ($\overline{ras}$), then the column address is presented and latched using the active-low **column address strobe** ($\overline{cas}$). If the next access is within the same row, a new column address may be presented without first supplying a new row address. Since a $\overline{cas}$-only access does not activate the cell matrix it can deliver its data two to three times faster than a full $\overline{ras}$-$\overline{cas}$ access and consumes considerably less power. It is therefore very advantageous to use $\overline{cas}$-only accesses whenever possible.

The difficulty is in detecting early enough in the memory access that the new address is in the same row as the previous address. Performing a comparison of the relevant bits of the new address with the corresponding bits of the previous address is almost always too slow.

**ARM address incrementer**

The solution adopted on the ARM exploits the fact that most addresses (typically 75%) are generated in the address incrementer. The ARM address selection logic (shown in Figure 13.8 on page 348) picks the address for the next cycle from one of four sources. One of these sources is the incrementer. The ARM indicates to the outside world whenever the next address is coming from the incrementer by asserting the

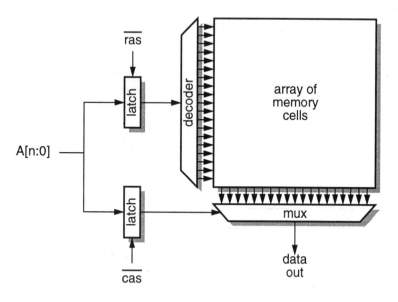

**Figure 13.7** DRAM memory organization.

*seq* output. External logic can then look at the previous address to check for row boundaries; if the previous address is *not* at the end of a row and the *seq* signal is asserted then a $\overline{cas}$-only memory access can be performed.

Although this mechanism will not capture all accesses which fall within the same DRAM row, it does find most of them and is very simple to implement and exploit. The *seq* signal and the previous address are all available over half a clock cycle before the cycle in question, giving the memory control logic plenty of time.

A typical DRAM timing diagram is shown in Figure 13.9 on page 348. The first, non-sequential access takes two clock cycles as the row address is strobed in, but subsequent sequential addresses use a $\overline{cas}$-only access and operate in a single clock cycle. (Note that early address timing is now used, with *ape* or *ale* high.)

The other use of the *seq* signal, to indicate a cycle which will use the same address as the preceding internal or coprocessor register transfer cycle, can also be exploited to improve DRAM access times. The DRAM access is started in the preceding cycle, which is only possible because *seq* is available so early. Typical timing is illustrated in Figure 13.10 on page 349. ($\overline{wait}$ is inactive during this sequence.)

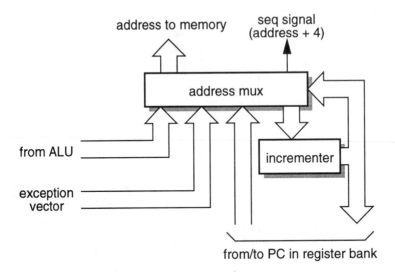

**Figure 13.8**   ARM address register structure.

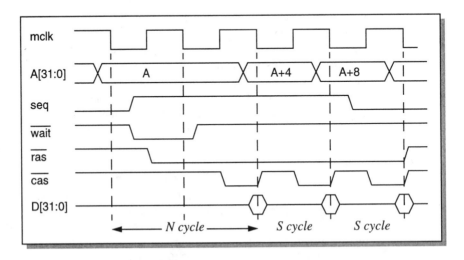

**Figure 13.9**   DRAM timing illustration.

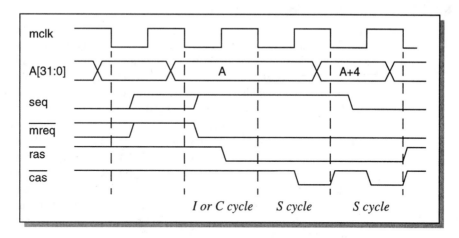

**Figure 13.10**   DRAM timing after an internal cycle.

**Peripheral access**

Most systems incorporate peripheral devices in addition to the memory components described so far. These often have slow access speeds, but can be interfaced using techniques similar to those described above for ROM access.

Further examples will arise as we consider real system examples, particularly in the next section where we consider the design of the ARM Platform Independent Evaluation (PIE) card.

## 13.2   The Platform Independent Evaluation card

The ARM Limited Platform Independent Evaluation (PIE) card is a minimal ARM system which can be connected to a host computer via a standard serial interface. If the host system is running the ARM software development tools, ARM programs can be compiled or assembled and downloaded into the PIE card where they can be executed on the ARM processor and debugged.

The software development tools work with the software on the PIE card to make running code on the card appear very similar to running it on the ARMulator on the host, making the transition from emulation to hardware as transparent as possible.

Physically, the PIE card is a short 8-bit PC expansion card which may be plugged into a PC expansion slot. If it is plugged into a PC it will take power from the PC through the plug-in connector. If it is not plugged into a PC it can be powered from a bench supply through power connectors on the card. A photograph of the card is shown in Figure 13.11 on page 351.

**Components**     The card incorporates the following components:

- An ARM60 processor (which is an ARM6 integer core with a JTAG test interface).
- Four 8-bit SRAMs (Static RAMs).
- An 8-bit EPROM (Electrically-Programmable ROM) containing 'Demon' (the debug monitor software which communicates with the host) and three 8-bit latches which are used to build 32-bit instructions from multiple EPROM accesses.
- A serial interface controller and a serial line driver chip.
- Two GAL (Generic Array Logic) devices to decode the address map and control the memory access times.
- A clock oscillator.
- Three standard inverter and logic ICs for clock buffering and so on.

**Interfaces**     The interfaces provided on the card are:

- The 8-bit PC expansion connector, used here only for power.
- The 9-pin D-type serial line connector.
- Connections for a logic analyser to all the system buses and control information.
- Power connectors for a bench supply.

The card also has a reset button, a light emitting diode (LED) and various configuration links.

**Figure 13.11**    The ARM PIE card.

## The ROM pipeline

The PIE card uses a single 8-bit EPROM together with three 8-bit latches which are used to form EPROM words. This saves space on the circuit board compared with using four EPROM chips, and eases the development of replacement EPROM code. The cost is a large increase in the EPROM access time, since it must be accessed four times for each word of data. The standard PIE configuration operates with a 20 MHz clock, and at this rate each EPROM byte access takes three clock cycles, so a full 32-bit access takes 12 clock cycles.

The hardware configuration of the EPROM is shown in Figure 13.12 on page 352. The processor word address ($A[16:2]$) is extended by adding a byte count ($B[1:0]$) generated by the control logic to access one byte within the word. When this byte is available it is latched into the first register on the rising edge of the byte clock ($Bck$), then the byte address is decremented to access the next byte. The register chips include an output enable control which is turned on whenever the EPROM is active (that is, when $\overline{rom}$ is low).

Throughout this process the processor is halted, until three bytes have been clocked into the latches and the fourth is available directly on the EPROM outputs, whereupon the ARM is released and it accepts the full word of data.

PIE card © Advanced RISC Machines Limited

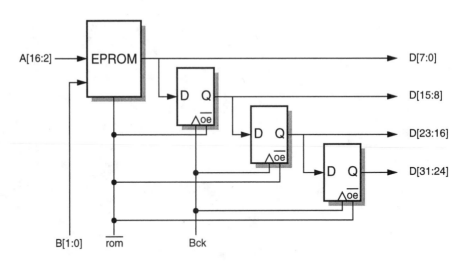

**Figure 13.12**   The PIE card EPROM pipeline.

**Initialization**

In normal operation the PIE memory map has SRAM at the bottom of the address space. This gives the maximum flexibility for modifying the exception handlers and good speed on exception entry. However it is not satisfactory immediately after power on, since the first thing the processor does is a reset entry which takes it into uninitialized RAM locations. Therefore a hardware reset forces a different memory map with the EPROM appearing at the bottom of the address space. This map persists until there is a write access to the bottom quarter of the address space, whereupon memory map switches to the standard form. The two memory maps are illustrated in Figure 13.13 on page 353.

The software entered at reset should branch up to the normal EPROM location before attempting any writes to RAM, then it can begin to initialize the RAM.

**Memory timing**

The memory timing state machine follows the principles outlined earlier in this chapter. All non-sequential accesses have a decode cycle followed by a number of access cycles, the number being determined by the access time of the addressed device:

- SRAM accesses take two cycles since the SRAM has an access time of 85 ns.
- EPROM accesses take 12 cycles, three for each of four byte accesses.
- Accesses to the serial controller also take 12 cycles.
- Accesses to external peripherals (on piggy-back cards connected through the logic analyser connectors) indicate completion on a dedicated signal.

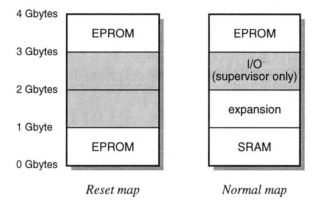

**Figure 13.13** PIE card memory maps.

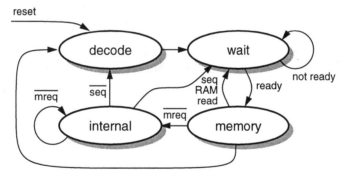

**Figure 13.14** PIE card memory access state transition diagram.

Internal cycles proceed at the full clock rate, and the only optimized timings are those for sequential RAM reads which follow internal or RAM read cycles; these bypass the decode cycle.

The state transition diagram is shown in Figure 13.14. A separate counter controls the exit from the Wait state when an EPROM or I/O access takes place, but a RAM access exits immediately. The $\overline{wait}$ input to the ARM processor is active in the Decode and Wait states and inactive in the other two states.

**Demon**        The ARM debug monitor 'Demon' provides a low-level programming and debugging environment on the PIE card. It supports the ARM Remote Debug Protocol, allowing a user to set and clear breakpoints (in RAM), read and modify the ARM's registers, read and modify the contents of RAM and load and run programs. These operations are controlled from a remote host running the ARM software development tools and connected to the PIE card via a serial communications channel.

Demon also provides support for programs running on the PIE card by establishing a number of operating system facilities which those programs can use. These facilities are available as supervisor calls (accessed using the SWI instruction) and support character input (from the host keyboard) and output (to the host display), file transfer (using the host's file system) and other functions.

**PIE card
extensions**    The PIE card is often used as the starting-point for developing a hardware emulator of a complex system chip based on an ARM processor core. A 'piggy-back' board can be connected through the logic analyser ports and peripheral macrocells can be mounted on this second card. Where peripheral macrocells are not available 'off the shelf', they can be emulated using electrically-programmable logic devices (**EPLDs**) or field-programmable gate arrays (**FPGAs**).

A flexible development environment can be based on a PIE card and a second card with several programmable devices such as Xilinx EPLDs. The peripheral macrocells are designed in VHDL (a standard hardware description language) and the Xilinx configuration file is generated automatically from the VHDL using synthesis techniques. When the designs have been debugged, the same VHDL source can be used to synthesize semi-custom implementations of the peripheral cells using gate array or standard cell technology and then merged with an ARM core and memory components for fabrication.

An emulator built this way may not have the full performance of the final chip, but it should easily come within a factor of ten of this performance, which is many orders of magnitude closer than a software simulation will come.

## 13.3  The Acorn Archimedes

The first complete system to incorporate an ARM processor was the Acorn Archimedes desktop computer, which was introduced in 1987.

The Archimedes employs four custom chips, the ARM being one of these. The other three are:

- MEMC, the memory and DRAM controller.

  The Archimedes memory management architecture is simpler than the ARM MMU architecture. MEMC contains an 'inverted' page table, where a 64-entry CAM holds the virtual address corresponding to each physical page (and the physical page size varies with the size of the physical memory). Therefore a virtual address can either hit in the CAM and be translated immediately, or it misses and a page fault is generated. The intermediate case, where a TLB misses and page table walking hardware is invoked does not arise since the CAM is effectively a TLB which covers all the physical memory.

  MEMC also incorporates the DRAM address multiplexers and $\overline{ras}$ and $\overline{cas}$ timing generators, so DRAM chips can be connected with no further interface components.

- VIDC, the video and sound controller.

  The video frame buffer is in the main DRAM memory, giving the ARM high bandwidth access for animation. VIDC has an 8-word FIFO buffer for the video data stream. When the buffers is half empty, it requests more data from MEMC which supplies a quad-word burst in response (using DRAM page mode). VIDC supports a number of different video timing, resolution and bits per pixel options, and includes the data serializer, a 16-entry colour map and digital to analogue converters.

  The sound system operates similarly, though at much lower bandwidths, to give eight sound channels with independent stereo positioning using 8-bit logarithmic data samples. The exponential analogue to digital converter is again on the chip.

- IOC, the I/O subsystem controller.

  The main high-speed processor to memory data bus is ill-suited to the direct connection of slow peripheral devices, so these are connected to a slower I/O bus which is controlled by IOC. The chip incorporates a number of simple I/O functions, such as a serial interface to a keyboard and some counter/timers, and also has a hand-shake interface to MEMC to define the access timing for particular peripheral devices.

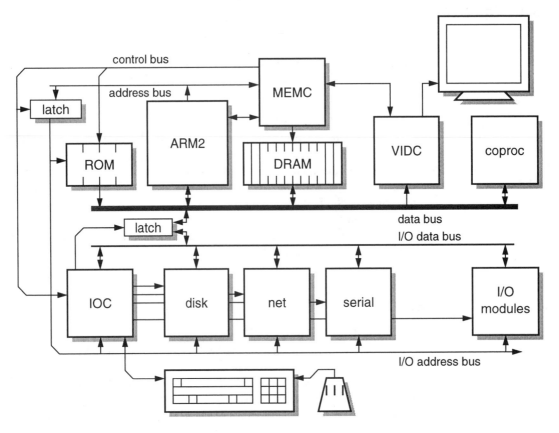

**Figure 13.15**    Archimedes system organization.

The overall system block diagram is illustrated in Figure 13.15.

The ARM2 is configured to produce early addresses for MEMC to optimize DRAM timing, and an external address latch buffers and retimes the address bus for the ROMs and I/O devices.

The main data bus operates at 4 MHz for non-sequential cycles and 8 MHz for sequential cycles, with sequential runs restricted to quad-word blocks. The memory bandwidth is therefore 25.6 Mbytes per second, shared between the processor and the video system. In 1987 this gave a remarkable processor and graphics performance by the standards of the day for a sub-$1,500 system.

## 13.4   The Acorn Risc PC

As semiconductor process technology develops, the functionality that can be incorporated in a single chip increases. This causes the partitioning of functions between the major chips in a system to change. The most noticeable change in the organization of the ARM-based products from Acorn is the migration of the memory management function from a separate chip in the Archimedes onto the processor chip in the Risc PC. The memory control functions (DRAM timing, and so on) which previously shared the space on the memory controller chip with the memory management functions now share space with the I/O functions, so the four system chips of the Archimedes are reduced to three on the Risc PC, while the functionality in each area is greatly enhanced. A photograph of the Risc PC is shown in Figure 13.16, and the system organization is illustrated in Figure 13.17 on page 359.

Risc PC © Acorn Computers Limited

**Figure 13.16**   The Acorn Risc PC.

**Risc PC CPU**       The system is built around the ARM710 CPU (though earlier Risc PCs used the
                      ARM610) which is on a plug-in card, and there are two CPU card slots in current
                      Risc PCs. The second CPU slot may be occupied by another ARM, a digital signal
                      processing chip or some other special-purpose processor (such as an MPEG decoder
                      for compressed digital video), or a different general-purpose processor such as an
                      Intel486 to support standard PC application software.

                      The second CPU shares all the memory and I/O components with the first, so the
                      added cost of supporting PC software is the 486 chip, a bus interface chip and the cir-
                      cuit card itself.

                      The ARM710 incorporates an 8 Kbyte mixed instruction and data cache, a mem-
                      ory management unit and a write buffer (see Section 12.2 on page 321). The cache
                      decouples the processor from the bus, a result of which is that the ARM710 does not
                      use all the available bus bandwidth, so connecting a second CPU which also has a
                      cache (such as the 486) will not prevent either CPU from delivering near maximum
                      performance much of the time, though there will be occasions when both are attempt-
                      ing to access memory when one must be impeded by the other.

                      The plug-in CPU card makes upgrading the processor straightforward, for exam-
                      ple enabling an easy upgrade route to StrongARM when these chips become available.

**The video**        The other source of demand for system bandwidth is the video subsystem. The video
**subsystem**        output is generated by a VIDC20 (Video Controller version 2) chip which was also
                      designed by ARM Limited. A fully configured Risc PC uses VRAM to support the
                      video data stream. VRAM (Video RAM) is a special form of DRAM with an on-chip
                      shift register which latches a row of data (see 'DRAM' on page 345 and Figure 13.7
                      on page 347 for an explanation and illustration of a 'row') and then shifts it out
                      through dedicated pins, leaving the normal data port available for processor accesses.
                      VIDC20 accepts 64-bit wide data from the VRAM shift registers at 21.33 MHz, giv-
                      ing a video data bandwidth of just over 170 Mbytes per second.

                      Lower-cost Risc PC systems can work without VRAM, in which case the video
                      data is accessed from the DRAM using the main data bus and then passed to VIDC20
                      through the buffer drawn next to the VRAM in Figure 13.17. This route is also used in
                      all Risc PCs for the lower bandwidth data streams used by VIDC20 to generate the
                      hardware cursor and the audio outputs. The VRAM module is then offered as a simple
                      upgrade to the basic machine.

                      VIDC20 incorporates a 256-entry colour look-up table to generate 8-bit levels
                      for each of the red, green and blue on-chip video drivers, plus some logical control bits
                      which may be used to mix external video sources. Alternatively, the video data stream
                      may drive the video outputs directly to give the full $2^{24}$ colours on the same screen. All
                      the video timing is fully programmable, and displays from television quality up to
                      1,600 by 1,024 pixels may be generated using pixel depths of 1, 2, 4, 8, 16 or 32 bits

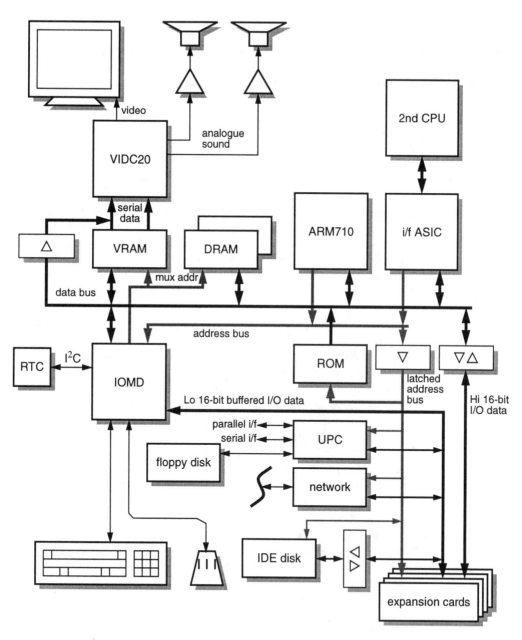

**Figure 13.17** Risc PC system organization.

per pixel (subject to bandwidth limitations at the highest resolutions). The wide range of possible pixel clock rates (from 8 MHz to 135 MHz) is accommodated by using a frequency synthesizer based on a simple off-chip voltage controlled oscillator and on-chip frequency dividers and a phase comparator.

The sound output is either based on 8-bit logarithmic samples played through an 8-bit exponential digital to analogue converter (DAC) on VIDC20, with switching control which allows eight time-multiplexed channels to have independent stereo positions, or a stream of 16-bit samples can be sent to an off-chip CD quality stereo DAC.

## The I/O and memory subsystem

The I/O and memory subsystem is controlled by IOMD (the I/O Memory Device). This chip takes the physical address bus from the processor(s) and generates the multi-plexed address for the DRAM and VRAM, along with the memory control signals ($\overline{ras}$, $\overline{cas}$, and so on). It includes direct memory access (DMA) hardware to generate the addresses for the video, cursor and sound channels, so when the data buffers in VIDC20 have sufficient space for another data burst, VIDC20 sends a request to IOMD which controls the DRAM or VRAM accordingly. DMA channels are also available to support I/O data transfers.

The physical address bus is latched externally to retime it suitably for the system ROM and I/O devices. IOMD interfaces the bottom 16 bits of the I/O data bus to the main data bus, and external latches can be used to extend the I/O data bus to 32 bits if required. (IOMD handles 32-bit accesses to 16-bit peripherals directly.)

The basic system peripherals are controlled by a standard 'Universal Peripheral Controller' (UPC) of the sort widely used by PC manufacturers, which incorporates floppy disk, serial line and parallel printer port interfaces.

The hard disk uses an 'IDE' (Integrated Drive Electronics) interface where all the peripheral intelligence is in the controller in the disk drive itself, so only a 16-bit data bus buffer and a few address lines are required to complete the interface. The net-work interface, which may be for a standard Ethernet, Acorn's proprietary Econet, or some other network, uses standard peripheral devices.

Further expansion is available through plug-in cards, for example to give an interface for a CD-ROM drive.

IOMD handles a number of peripheral functions directly, incorporating a clocked serial interface for an IBM PS/2 compatible keyboard, quadrature mouse tracking hardware and an I$^2$C serial interface for a real-time clock (RTC), battery-backed memory, and so on. (The I$^2$C bus is also available to the expansion cards through the normal connector.)

**Software**
The Risc PC runs Acorn's proprietary RISC OS operating system which supports cooperative multitasking within a desktop environment based on a window user-interface and a mouse pointing device. There is a wide range of software available to run under RISC OS including personal productivity tools such as spreadsheets and wordprocessors, multimedia support including software-based real-time video decompression, and a vast range of educational curriculum software resulting from Acorn's dominant position in the UK educational computing market since its inception with the introduction of the BBC microcomputer in 1982.

RISC OS operates from ROM in the Risc PC. This is unusual – most operating systems of this sophistication operate from RAM and must be reloaded from the hard disk every time the machine is switched on. The advantages of a ROM-based operating system include cost (ROM has a lower price per bit than RAM) and a faster start-up. If the system has no hard disk, the advantages become much greater.

With a 486 processor in the second CPU slot, the Risc PC will also run industry-standard business software packages.

**ARM7500**
The three major components of the Risc PC (the ARM710, VIDC20 and IOMD) have been merged with relatively minor changes into a single chip, the ARM7500, which is described in Section 14.4 on page 378. The ARM7500 has been used as the basis of low-cost versions of the Risc PC and of other products which exploit Risc PC technology in different market areas.

**Online Media**
An off-shoot of Acorn, Online Media was established to develop products for the video-on-demand market. Their set-top boxes enable consumers to watch films and television programmes when they wish, not when the schedules dictate. The technology used combines the Risc PC system architecture with an ATM (Asynchronous Transfer Mode) network and video decompression hardware to deliver programme material (and computer programs) from a remote video filestore to the consumer's television.

As the set-top box does not require a hard disk drive, the ability of RISC OS to operate from ROM plays a significant role in keeping costs down.

**Network Computer**
Another related product is the Network Computer, developed by Acorn as the reference design to a specification defined by Oracle. This product offers very low-cost access to the Internet using a standard television as the display device.

## 13.5   The Apple Newton

The Apple Newton MessagePad is an early member of a new class of product described by Apple as a 'Personal Digital Assistant'. Products in this class are expected to be significantly smaller and lighter than a typical portable computer, offering the user access to electronic information such as personal diary data, address and phone number lists, notes taken at meetings, and given a suitable radio data link or telephone connection, access to electronic mail and other centrally provided services.

A major objective with the Newton was to open up a market outside established computer users by providing a user-interface that is very simple to use. The small size objective precludes the use of a conventional keyboard in any case. The Newton designers therefore adopted a pen and paper metaphor; the user operates a stylus with the characteristics of a pen on a screen which responds like a sheet of paper. To accept input in this form, and particularly to recognize handwritten input in the form of cursive script, requires considerable computing power.

A photograph of an Apple Newton is shown in Figure 13.18 on page 363.

**Choice of
ARM CPU**

The low weight objective precludes the use of large batteries, so the computing power must be available at low power consumption and it must be managed with considerable care. Apple chose the ARM processor as offering the best balance of characteristics for this role. They were instrumental in establishing ARM Limited as a separate company in 1990 in order to create the resource needed to advance the ARM design from the ARM3 to the ARM610, adding the full 32-bit addressing and memory management functions they required for the Newton.

The ARM MMU architecture, while fairly conventional overall, incorporates a number of features which were driven by the Newton requirements (though they are probably equally suited to other tight, low-power applications). The assignment of permissions at the granularity of 1 Kbyte subpages improves the performance of small memory systems, and the domain-based memory management avoids frequent TLB and cache flushes, thereby saving power and increasing performance.

The ARM610 cache was exactly that used on the ARM3. The small size kept the chip small and therefore low-cost, with the 64-way associativity and the relatively dense ARM code compensating for the small size to keep the hit-rate high.

**Hardware
organization**

The hardware organization of the Newton MessagePad is illustrated in Figure 13.19 on page 364. The ARM610 CPU is supported by an application specific integrated circuit (ASIC) which includes a DMA controller, timers, and clock control and interrupt control circuits. The other principal components are the system ROM and RAM, a serial interface which supports a range of protocols including Apple's LocalTalk local

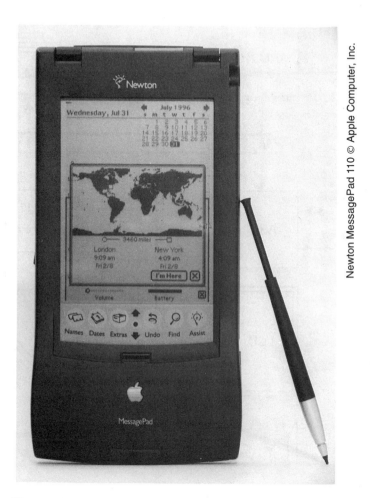

Newton MessagePad 110 © Apple Computer, Inc.

**Figure 13.18**   The Apple Newton MessagePad 110.

area network, an analogue to digital converter (ADC) used to measure the position of the stylus on the digitizing tablet, and a loudspeaker driven from an 8-bit digital sound stream.

The system ASIC includes interfaces for an infrared link and a PCMCIA card (a standard plug-in card format) slot and is responsible for maintaining a real-time clock and for supplying the operating clocks to the ARM610.

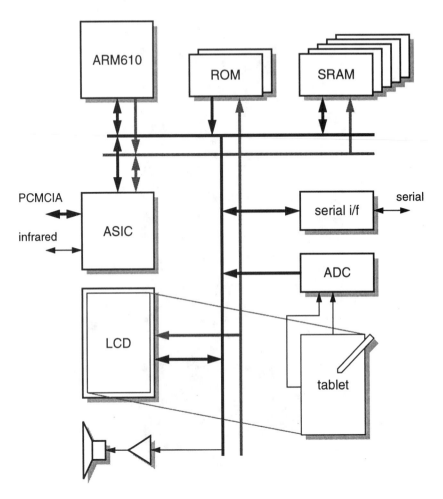

**Figure 13.19**   The Newton MessagePad hardware organization.

**Saving
power**

Of course, the processor is not the only component that uses significant battery power. On the Newton the liquid crystal display (LCD) and the digitizing tablet (an overlay on the LCD that detects when and where the stylus is touching the screen) are potential power drains. A typical LCD system has a controller which scans a frame buffer and sends a high bit-rate data stream to the LCD row and column drivers all the time that the display is active, consuming over 100 mW of power just to display a static image. In the Newton MessagePad, the frame buffers are integrated into the LCD row and column drivers, reducing the power for a static image to below 5 mW.

The digitizing tablet samples the stylus position up to 80 times a second, which consumes 17 mA and uses 10% of the ARM CPU processing power. Whenever the operating system knows that the stylus is in an area of the display that requires lower sensitivity (as defined by the current application), the sample rate is reduced to save power.

The system is entirely event driven. Whenever the processor runs out of useful work to do, its clocks are stopped. An interrupt restarts them instantaneously. The system ASIC uses ripple counters for event timers, as they use less power than synchronous counters. Every ASIC function uses a gated clock at the lowest frequency required for its function, and all ASIC clocks drop to 1.5 MHz while the system is idle awaiting an event. In addition, the sound amplifier is turned off whenever it is not needed.

## System issues

As the user can remove the batteries at any time, a very robust data storage scheme is required to ensure that a consistent state is maintained. Hence the system has a complete transaction-based object-oriented database built in.

To keep options open for the future, the software is written in the 'NewtonScript' interpreted byte code. This makes porting the applications to a platform which uses a different instruction set straightforward. NewtonScript is a dynamic, object-oriented language. The byte code is very dense, minimizing the system memory requirements.

Newton applications run in a single 32-bit address space and work with data held in a persistent object store. Data is stored in a compressed form and dynamically decompressed and cached upon demand. Again, data compression reduces the system memory requirements.

The micro-kernel controls tasks using a pre-emptive scheduler that switches tasks about 50 times a second. The single address space allows task switching without flushing the virtual cache or the TLB, while the domain system maintains protection and the ARM MMU subpages give fine-grained memory access control.

## Low-power design

The Newton illustrates the many facets of low-power product design. The choice of the ARM as the processor was only one of many design decisions which had to be carefully thought through. Every aspect of the system was considered from first principles to identify opportunities to save power. The Newton incorporates innovations at many levels, including the display technology, the control of the digitizing tablet, the memory-management organization and both the system and the application software.

System design is always challenging. Low-power system design introduces an additional parameter which must be traded-off against the usual factors of performance, weight, size, design cost, production cost and time to market.

## 13.6  Examples and exercises

**Example 13.1**    **Design the state transition graph which interfaces an ARM processor to dynamic RAM to generate the cycles shown in Figures 13.9 and 13.10 on pages 348 and 349.**

In each *mclk* cycle the dynamic memory is either doing nothing (a processor internal or coprocessor transfer cycle), performing a sequential access (a processor S-cycle) or performing the first or second half of a non-sequential access (a processor N-cycle).

The memory controller state machine will change state on the falling edge of *mclk*, so an N-cycle requires two states. However the second half of an N-cycle looks exactly like an S-cycle, so these two states can be merged.

The state transition diagram below shows how the system could be designed. An N-cycle starts in 'wait' where the processor's $\overline{wait}$ input is activated, then finishes in 'CAS' where the DRAM column address strobe ($\overline{cas}$) is active. An S-cycle remains in 'CAS'. Note the transition from 'internal' to 'CAS' on *mreq.seq* which corresponds to the optimization illustrated in Figure 13.10 on page 349.

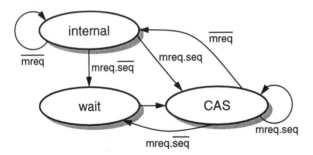

Note that this state diagram does not allow for the fact that DRAM rows have limited size, so $\overline{cas}$-only accesses must not go beyond the end of a row. This is easily incorporated by combining each *seq* test with a suitable check on the old address (but watch the address timing!).

**Exercise 13.1.1**    Design the state machine logic and show how $\overline{wait}$, $\overline{ras}$, $\overline{cas}$ and the DRAM row/column address multiplexer control are produced.

Hints:

- the state machine can generate $\overline{wait}$ and the DRAM row/column address multiplexer control directly.

- $\overline{cas}$ is enabled in the 'CAS' state, but requires a timing input to generate the correct pulse shape (for example, $\overline{cas} = \overline{casenable.mclk}$ where $casenable$ is active in the 'CAS' state).
- $\overline{ras}$ is a little trickier since it must be activated during 'Wait' and possibly 'Internal' and held on through the 'CAS' states; it must also remain firmly low throughout its active period with no glitches. The technique used to hold $\overline{ROMoe}$ stable in Figure 13.4 on page 344 may be modified to achieve this.

**Exercise 13.1.2**  Extend the state transition diagram shown above to control a system which contains both DRAM and 4-cycle access ROM.
Hints:

- the address is valid and may be decoded in the 'Wait' state, though it must also be checked before making the optimized transition from 'Internal' to 'CAS'.
- $\overline{ras}$ should only be activated in 'Wait' or 'Internal' if DRAM is addressed.

**Exercise 13.1.3**  Design the logic for the state machine described in the previous exercise and its control outputs.

## Example 13.2  Extend the state transition diagram shown above to allow a second bus master (such as a video controller) to gain control of the memory.

The video controller will issue a request for the bus which must be recognized, causing the ARM to relinquish control of the bus at a safe point, whereupon the request may be granted.

It is not usually necessary (nor desirable) to grant the request immediately. If the ARM is running S-cycles it is more efficient to wait until the end of the sequential burst before considering the request (it may be desirable to limit sequential activity to less than a full DRAM row to reduce the latency here). It is *not* adequate to arbitrate the bus only during internal cycles as the ARM can go for a long time without executing an internal cycle. However the ARM can be allowed to continue executing internal cycles while the video controller accesses memory.

In the state transition diagram below, the video controller request (vrq) is granted in 'grantI' and 'grantW', and the processor continues to execute internal cycles in 'grantI' but waits in 'grantW'. Whilst it is waiting the internal clock is disabled by $\overline{wait}$, so $\overline{mreq}$ and $seq$ cannot change and it is not necessary to make subsequent state transitions depend on them.

This diagram can be simplified at a small loss of efficiency by removing 'grantI' and always stopping the ARM when the video controller is using the bus, and can be

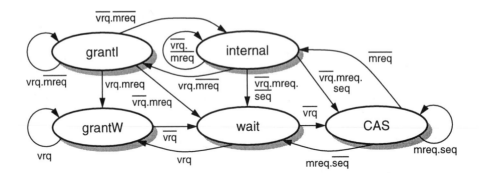

enhanced with a small increase in complexity by allowing transitions out of 'CAS' directly to 'grantI' and 'grantW' when *vrq* is active. (Note, though, that the looping transition back into 'CAS' should not normally depend on *vrq*.)

**Exercise 13.2.1**   Design the logic for this state machine and its control outputs.

**Exercise 13.2.2**   So far, the state machine grants the bus to the video controller but does not help it access the DRAM. Modify the state diagram so that each video request causes four DRAM accesses (using page mode) before control is returned to the ARM.

**Exercise 13.2.3**   Design the logic which controls the DRAM for both video and ARM accesses.

# 14 Embedded ARM Processor Cores

**Summary of chapter contents**

Increasingly the trend in embedded system design is to integrate all the major system functions apart from some memory components into a single chip. The benefits in terms of component costs, reliability and power-efficiency are considerable. The development that makes this possible is the advance in semiconductor process technology which now allows chips incorporating millions of transistors to be built cheaply, and within a few years will allow tens of millions of transistors on a chip.

So, the era of complex systems on a single chip is upon us. The ARM has played a leading role in the opening of this era since its very small core size leaves more silicon resource available for the rest of the system functions. In this chapter we look at several examples of ARM-based 'systems on chips', but we are, in fact, only scratching the surface of this domain. The next few years will see a flood of embedded applications based around ARM processor cores.

Designing a 32-bit computer system is a complex undertaking. Designing one on a single chip where it must be 'right first time' is still very challenging. There is no formula for success, but there are many very powerful design tools available to assist the designer. As in most engineering endeavours, one can only get so far by studying the problem and the experiences of others. Understanding an existing design is far easier than creating a new one. Developing a new system on a chip is one of today's greatest challenges in digital electronics.

## 14.1 GEC Plessey Semiconductors Butterfly microcontroller

GEC Plessey Semiconductors (GPS) was an early ARM semiconductor partner and has manufactured a number of ARM standard products such as the ARM610 used in the Apple Newton MessagePad. In 1995 they announced a range of ARM-based microcontrollers aimed at the communications market for use in products such as digital telephones, set-top boxes and entertainment systems.

A standard microcontroller product called Butterfly has been produced, from which application-specific variants can be designed to meet customer requirements. The microcontroller is based on the GPS BμILD (Bus for μcontroller Integration in Low-power Designs) modular bus architecture, which is similar to, but not the same as, the ARM Limited Advanced Microcontroller Bus Architecture (AMBA) which was described in Section 8.5 on page 234. (GPS and ARM Limited are now moving BμILD and AMBA towards a common open standard.)

The rapid development of application-specific microcontrollers is based on the re-use of macrocells which are designed in VHDL, then synthesized and automatically laid out on a structured array which includes a 'hard' ARM7 core macrocell. (The ARM7 core is 'hard' because its physical layout is fixed.) The BμILD bus supports modular test and characterization, and also provides a modular application-level debugging methodology.

**Bus masters**    The organization of the Butterfly chip is shown in Figure 14.1 on page 371. There is an ARM7 core and two additional BμILD bus masters on the chip:

- The 4-channel **DMA controller** relieves the ARM7 of the duty of transferring blocks of data between memory and peripherals. Each channel can handle one stream of data between a block of memory and a peripheral, or a pair of channels can be used for memory to memory or peripheral to peripheral transfers. The memory address can be anywhere in the 32-bit space and blocks of data up to 65 Kbytes can be handled by a single transfer in units of bytes, half-words or words and bursts can deliver transfer rates up to 100 MBytes per second.

- The **BμILD broadcast module** provides a dedicated 4-bit diagnostic port in order to facilitate real-time debugging of application code. This port can be used to identify the current BμILD bus master and the type of bus cycle that is taking place during each clock cycle.

**System management modules**    In addition to these bus master modules, Butterfly has a number of modules which primarily perform on-chip system management functions:

- The **phase-locked loop** (PLL) balances the mark-space ratio of the memory clock and reduces skew between clock and I/O signals, improving set-up and hold

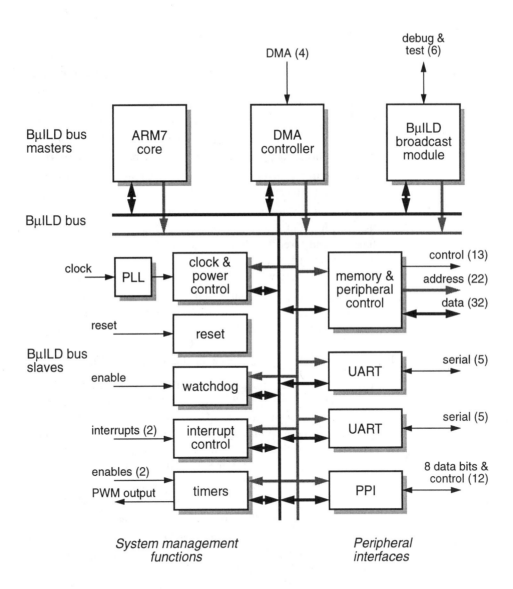

**Figure 14.1**   Butterfly microcontroller organization.

margins. In times-four mode the PLL and on-chip oscillator circuitry jointly produce a very stable system clock from a low-cost external crystal.

- The **clock control module** contains registers which determine independently for each module on the chip whether or not it is clocked in each of the 'run' and 'stand-by' (power-down) modes. When 'stand-by' mode is requested, the BµILD broadcast module is asked to close down bus activity in an orderly way and then to wait in a minimum power configuration until an interrupt causes it to reactivate.

- The chip includes a power-on **reset module** to initialize system components and to bring the BµILD bus up in a orderly way. There is also an external reset pin.

- The **interrupt controller** manages 15 different interrupt sources which may be configured for polarity and edge or level sensitivity where appropriate.

- The **watchdog timer** is present to detect hardware and software failures that cause the system to fail. It is a counter which, if not regularly cleared by software, will time-out and reset the chip. Occasional failures due, for example, to externally generated electrical noise will therefore not cause the system to crash permanently since the watchdog will cause recovery within a defined time.

- There are four independent 32-bit **timers** with an 8-bit prescaler. They can be configured for periodic or single-shot output. Two may be combined to generate a pulse-width modulated (PWM) output for audio signal generation.

**Peripheral modules**

Finally, the chip also incorporates a number of peripheral modules:

- The **memory and peripheral controller** interfaces to off-chip memory and peripherals which may be 8, 16 or 32 bits wide. The controller supports four off-chip memory segments of 4 Mbytes each, with programmable wait state generation. The map may be changed after reset to allow the boot ROM (which must initially reside at the bottom of memory space to provide the ARM reset vector) to be replaced by faster RAM (to speed up the interrupt response time).

- Each of the two **UART** modules supports a full duplex asynchronous serial channel with programmable baud rate, support for XON/XOFF protocol and double-buffering on both transmit and receive channels.

- The **programmable peripheral interface** (PPI) supports eight general-purpose I/O pins which may be individually addressed or grouped into a byte with buffer full and empty flags. Any input transition can cause an interrupt, so the interface can support a further eight external interrupt sources.

**Package**

Butterfly is packaged in a 28 mm square 144-pin plastic quad flat pack. It operates at 25 MHz at 5 volts or 15 MHz at 3.3 volts.

## 14.2   The VLSI Ruby II Advanced Communication Processor

VLSI Technology, Inc., were the first ARM semiconductor partner and were instrumental, along with Acorn Computers Limited and Apple Computer, Inc., in setting up ARM Limited as a separate company. Their relationship with the ARM predates the existence of ARM Limited, since they fabricated the very first ARM processors in 1985 and licensed the technology from Acorn Computers in 1987.

VLSI have manufactured many standard ARM-based chips for Acorn Computers and produced ARM610 chips for Apple Newtons. They have also produced several ARM-based designs for customer specific products and a number which they have made available as standard parts. The Ruby II chip is one such standard part which is intended for use in portable communications devices.

**Ruby II organization**

The organization of Ruby II is illustrated in Figure 14.2 on page 374. The chip is based around an ARM core and includes 2 Kbytes of fast (zero wait state) on-chip SRAM. Critical routines can be loaded into the RAM under application control to get the best performance and minimum power consumption. There is a set of peripheral modules which share a number of pins, including a PCMCIA interface, four byte-wide parallel interfaces and two UARTs. A mode select block controls which combination of these interfaces is available at any time, and byte-wide FIFO buffers decouple the processor from having to respond to every byte which is transferred.

A synchronous communications controller module supports a range of standard serial communication protocols, and a serial controller module provides a software controlled data port which can be used to implement various serial control protocols such as the $I^2C$ bus defined by Philips which enables a range of serial devices such as battery-backed RAM, real-time clock, $E^2PROM$ and audio codecs to be connected.

The external bus interface supports devices with 8-, 16- and 32-bit data buses and has flexible wait state generation. The counter-timer block has three 8-bit counters connected to a 24-bit prescaler, and an interrupt controller gives programmable control of all on- and off-chip interrupt sources. The chip has four power-management modes:

1. On-line – all circuits are clocked at full speed.
2. Command – the ARM core runs with 1 to 64 wait states but all other circuitry runs at full speed. An interrupt switches the system into on-line mode immediately.
3. Sleep – All circuitry is stopped apart from the timers and oscillators. Particular interrupts return the system to on-line mode.
4. Stopped – all circuits (including the oscillators) are stopped. Particular interrupts return the system to on-line mode.

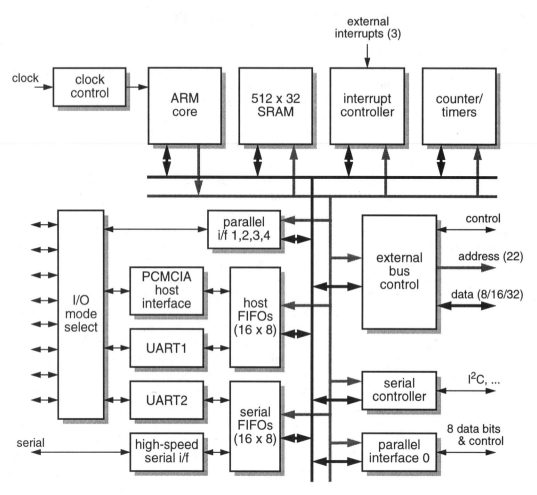

**Figure 14.2** Ruby II advanced communication controller organization.

**Packaging** The Ruby II is available in 144- and 176-pin thin quad flat packs and can operate at up to 32 MHz at 5 volts. At 20 MHz using 32-bit 1 wait state memory the chip consumes 30 mA in on-line mode, 7.9 mA in command mode, 1.5 mA in sleep mode and 150 μA in stop mode.

## 14.3   The VLSI ISDN Subscriber Processor

The VLSI ISDN Subscriber Processor (VIP) is a programmable engine for **ISDN** (Integrated Services Digital Network; a digital telephony standard) subscriber communications. The design was developed by Hagenuk Gmbh for use in their ISDN product range and subsequently licensed back to VLSI Technology for sale as an **ASSP** (Application Specific Standard Part). It incorporates most of the circuitry required to implement a full-feature ISDN terminal, supporting voice, data and video services down the same digital line. The sort of applications it is targeted at include:

- ISDN terminal equipment, such as domestic and digital PABX telephones, H.320 videophones and integrated PC communications.

- ISDN to **DECT** (Digital European Cordless Telephone) controllers, allowing a number of cordless telephones to link to each other and to an ISDN line for domestic and business use.

- ISDN to PCMCIA communication cards.

The VIP chip incorporates the specialized interfaces required to connect to the ISDN S0-interface, support for telephony interfaces such as a numeric keypad, a number display, a microphone and an earphone, digital links for external signal processors or codecs, and power management features such as a programmable clock and an analogue to digital converter to monitor the battery state.

The ARM6 core performs general control and ISDN protocol functions. A 3 Kbyte on-chip RAM operates without wait states at the full processor clock rate of 36.864 MHz. Critical code routines can be loaded into this RAM as required, for example, the signal processing routines required to support hands-free operation.

**VIP organization**

The organization of the VIP chip is illustrated in Figure 14.3 on page 376 and a typical system configuration is shown in Figure 14.4 on page 377.

**Memory interface**

The external memory interface supports 8-, 16- and 32-bit off-chip static RAMs and ROMs and 16- and 32-bit dynamic RAMs. The addressable memory is divided into four ranges, each of which operates with a programmable number of wait states (where the minimum is one wait state giving a 54 ns access time).

**S0-interface**

The on-chip ISDN S0-interface allows connection to an S0-interface bus via isolating transformers and surge protection. The on-chip functions include a phase-locked loop for data and clock recovery, framing, and low-level protocols. The 192 Kbit/s raw data rate includes two 64 Kbit/s B channels and one 16 Kbit/s D channel. In telephony

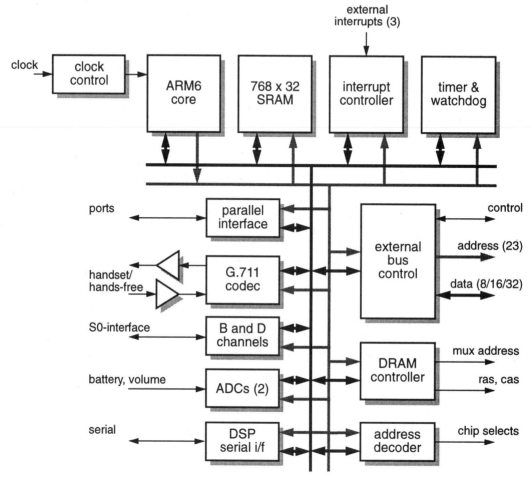

**Figure 14.3**   VIP organization.

applications the B channels carry 8-bit speech samples at an 8 KHz sample rate and the D channel is used for control purposes.

**Codec**         The G.711 codec includes an on-chip analogue front end that allows direct connection to both a telephone handset and a hands-free microphone and speaker. The input and output channels have independently programmable gains. The amplification stages have power-down modes to save power when they are inactive.

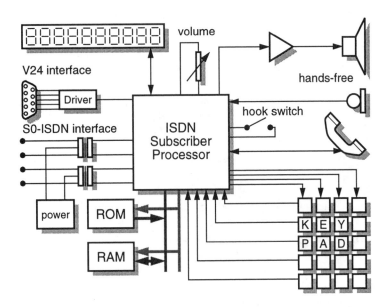

**Figure 14.4**  Typical VIP system configuration.

**ADCs**

The on-chip analogue to digital converters are based upon timing how long it takes to discharge a capacitor to the input voltage level. This is a very simple way to measure slowly varying voltages, requiring little more than an on-chip comparator, an output to charge the capacitor at the start of the conversion and a means of measuring the time from the start of the conversion to the point where the comparator switches. Typical uses would be to measure the voltage from a volume control potentiometer or to check the battery voltage in a portable application.

**Keypad interface**

The keyboard interface uses parallel output ports to strobe the columns of the keypad and parallel input ports with internal pull-down resistors to sense the rows. An OR gate on the inputs can generate an interrupt. If all the column outputs are active, any key press will generate an interrupt whereupon the ARM can activate individual columns and sense individual rows to determine the particular key pressed.

**Clocks and timers**

The chip has two clock sources. Normal operation is at 38.864 MHz, with 460.8 KHz used during power-down. A watchdog timer resets the CPU if there is no activity for 1.28 seconds, and a 2.5 ms timer interrupts the processor from sleep mode for DRAM refresh and multitasking purposes.

## 14.4   The ARM7500

The ARM7500 is a highly integrated single-chip computer which combines the major components of the Acorn Risc PC (apart from the memory) onto a single chip. It is the first such system chip to employ as its processor macrocell a full ARM CPU, including cache and memory management, rather than just the basic integer processor core.

The principal macrocells on the chip are:

- The ARM CPU core.
- The video and sound macrocell.
- The memory and I/O controller.

Each of these macrocells embodies considerable system functionality.

**The ARM CPU core**

The ARM CPU core contains most of the functionality of the ARM710 CPU (see Section 12.2 on page 321), the only compromise to allow room for the other macrocells being a reduction in the size of the cache from 8 Kbytes to 4 Kbytes.

The CPU is based around the ARM7 integer core, with a 4 Kbyte 4-way set-associative mixed instruction and data cache, a memory management unit based on a 2-level page table with a 64-entry translation look-aside buffer and a write buffer.

**The video and sound macrocell**

The video controller can generate displays using a pixel clock of up to 120 MHz (which is generated by a simple off-chip voltage controlled oscillator using an on-chip phase comparator). It includes a 256-entry colour palette with on-chip 8-bit digital-to-analogue converters for each of the red, green and blue outputs and additional control bits for external mixing and fading. A separate hardware cursor is supported, and the output can drive a high-resolution colour monitor or a single- or double-panel grey-scale or colour liquid crystal display. The display timing is fully programmable.

The sound system can generate eight independent channels of 8-bit (logarithmic) analogue stereo sound, played through an on-chip exponential digital-to-analogue converter. Alternatively, 16-bit sound samples can be generated through a serial digital channel and an external CD-quality digital-to-analogue converter.

The data channels for the video, cursor and sound streams are generated using the DMA controllers in the memory and I/O controller.

**The memory and I/O controller**

The memory controller supports the direct connection of up to four banks of DRAM and two banks of ROM. Each bank can be programmed to be 16 or 32 bits wide and the memory controller will make double accesses for 32-bit quantities in 16-bit banks.

The DRAM controller uses page mode accesses for sequential cycles in bursts of up to 256 transfers and supports a range of DRAM refresh modes, and the ROM controller also supports burst-mode where suitable devices are used. Three DMA controllers handle data streams for the video, cursor and sound channels.

The I/O controller manages a 16-bit off-chip I/O bus (which is expandable to 32 bits using external buffers) and a number of on-chip interfaces. The off-chip bus supports simple peripheral devices, intelligent peripheral modules, PC-style peripherals and an interface for PCMCIA cards.

The on-chip interfaces include four analogue comparators which can be used to support four analogue input channels, two serial ports intended for keyboards and/or mice, counter-timers, eight general-purpose open-drain I/O lines and a programmable interrupt controller. Power management facilities are also available.

**System diagram**

There are many variations on how this chip could be used, but a typical system organization is illustrated in Figure 14.5 on page 380.

**Applications**

The ARM7500 has many potential applications in multimedia and portable computing systems. It has already been used in low-cost versions of the Acorn Risc PC and in the Online Media interactive video set-top box. Its principal limitation compared with the normal Risc PC chip set is restricting the video data stream to normal DRAM, whereas high-resolution displays on the standard Risc PC use VRAM. This precludes the use of large numbers of colours on displays with high resolutions, but with liquid crystal displays or monitors of television, VGA or super-VGA resolution the restriction is not apparent. It is really only at resolutions of 1,280 by 1,024 and above that the number of colours becomes severely restricted because of the bandwidth limitations of standard DRAM.

Since interactive video and games machines use TV quality displays, and portable computers use liquid crystal displays at VGA (640 by 480 pixel) resolution, the ARM7500 is ideally suited to these applications. Its high integration and power-saving features make it suitable for hand-held test equipment, and its high quality sound and graphics are good characteristics for multimedia applications.

**Network Computer**

Perhaps the highest profile application of the ARM7500 at the time of writing is the Network Computer. Acorn has developed a system design, based on the ARM7500, for a sub-$500 box to give consumer access to the Internet using a standard television as the display. The system requirements were defined by Oracle and the Acorn reference design was the first to meet the functionality and cost targets.

The design has been licensed to several manufacturers world-wide, and the ARM7500 seems poised to make a significant contribution to the broadening of Internet access into the consumer marketplace.

A version of the ARM7500 with built-in floating-point hardware, the ARM7500FE, is being developed for future Network Computer products.

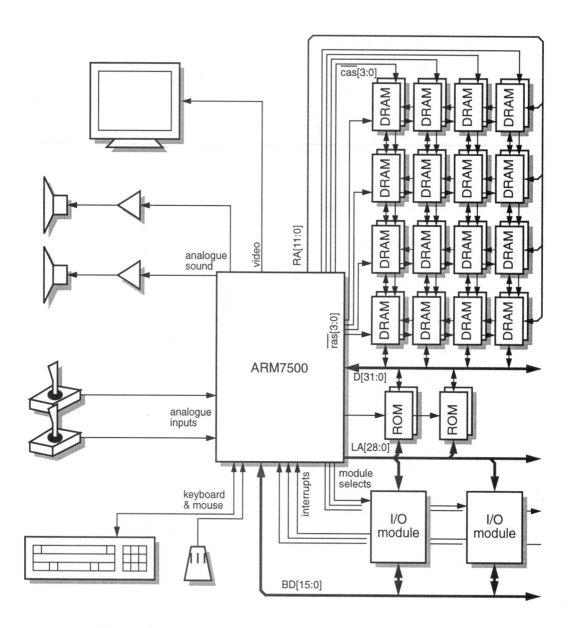

**Figure 14.5** Typical ARM7500 system organization.

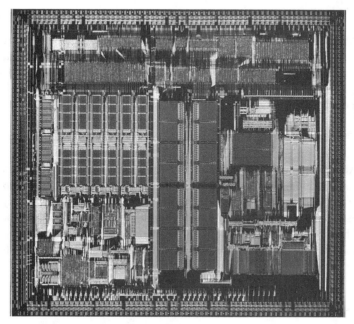

© VLSI Technology, Inc.

**Figure 14.6**   ARM7500 die photograph.

**ARM7500
silicon**

A photograph of an ARM7500 die is shown in Figure 14.6 and the characteristics of
the device are summarized in Table 14.1. Note the ARM7 core in the lower right-hand
corner of the die occupying only five per cent of the die area.

   This high functionality requires a large number of pins to connect to external
devices. The ARM7500 is packaged in a 240-pin plastic quad flat pack which is
32 millimetres square.

**Table 14.1**   ARM7500 characteristics.

| Process | 0.6 μm | Transistors | 550,000 | MIPS | 30 |
|---|---|---|---|---|---|
| Metal layers | 2 | Die area | 70 mm$^2$ | Power | 690 mW |
| Vdd | 5 V | Clock | 0 to 33 MHz | MIPS/W | 43 |

## 14.5   AMULET2e

AMULET2e is an AMULET2 processor core (see Section 9.4 on page 259) combined with 4 Kbytes of memory, which can be configured either as a cache or a fixed RAM area, and a flexible memory interface (the *funnel*) which allows 8-, 16- or 32-bit external devices to be connected directly, including memories built from DRAM. The internal organization of AMULET2e is illustrated in Figure 14.7.

**Timing reference**

The absence of a reference clock in an asynchronous system makes timing memory accesses an issue that requires careful consideration. The solution incorporated into AMULET2e uses a single external reference delay connected directly to the chip and configuration registers, loaded at start-up, which specify the organization and timing properties of each memory region. The reference delay will normally reflect the external SRAM access time, so the RAM will be configured to take one reference delay. The ROM, which is typically much slower, may be configured to take several reference delays. (Note that the reference delay is only used for off-chip timing; all on-chip delays are self-timed.)

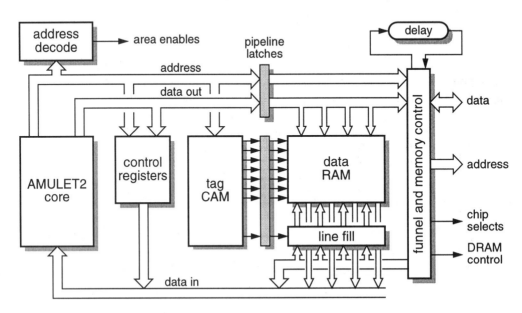

**Figure 14.7**   AMULET2e internal organization.

**AMULET2e cache**

The cache comprises four 1 Kbyte blocks, each of which is a fully associative random replacement store with a quad-word line and block size. A pipeline register between the CAM and the RAM sections allows a following access to begin its CAM look-up while the previous access completes within the RAM; this exploits the ability of the AMULET2 core to issue multiple memory requests before the data is returned from the first. Sequential accesses are detected and bypass the CAM look-up, thereby saving power and improving performance.

Cache line fetches are non-blocking, accessing the addressed item first and then allowing the processor to continue while the rest of the line is fetched. The line fetch automaton continues loading the line fetch buffer while the processor accesses the cache. There is an additional CAM entry that identifies references to the data which is stored in the line fetch buffer. Indeed, this data remains in the line fetch buffer where it can be accessed on equal terms to data in the cache until the next cache miss, whereupon the whole buffer is copied into the cache while the new data is loaded from external memory into the line fetch buffer.

**AMULET2e clock**

Although the processor operates without a clock there are times when an accurate time reference is required, for example to ensure that DRAMs are refreshed often enough. AMULET2e incorporates a clock oscillator and counter/timer for this purpose, but this will typically run at 32 KHz and use negligible power and therefore not negate the potential power savings from asynchronous operation.

**AMULET2e systems**

AMULET2e has been configured to make building small systems as straightforward as possible. As an example, Figure 14.8 on page 384 shows a PIE card incorporating AMULET2e. The only components, apart from AMULET2e itself, are four SRAM chips (though the system could equally well have been designed to operate with just one, at lower performance), one ROM chip, a UART and an RS232 line interface. The UART uses a crystal oscillator to control its bits rate and to provide a real-time clock, but all the system timing functions are controlled by AMULET2e using the single reference delay.

The ROM contains the standard PIE Demon debug monitor code and the host computer, at the other end of the RS232 serial line, runs the standard ARM development tools. This system demonstrates that using an asynchronous processor need be no more difficult than using a conventional clocked processor provided that the memory interface has been carefully thought out.

**A self-timed future?**

The AMULET chips are presently research prototypes and are not about to replace synchronous ARM cores in commercial production. However, there is a resurgence of world-wide interest in the potential of asynchronous design styles to save power and to offer a more modular approach to the design of computing hardware.

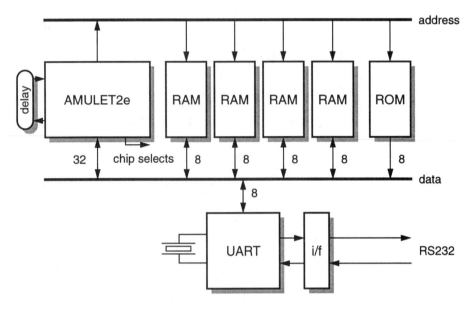

**Figure 14.8**   AMULET2e PIE card organization.

The power savings which result from removing the global clock, leaving each subsystem to perform its own timing functions whenever it has useful work to perform, are clear in theory but there are few demonstrations that the benefits can be realized in practice with circuits of sufficient complexity to be commercially interesting. The AMULET research is aimed directly at adding to the body of convincing demonstrations of the merits of asynchronous technology.

It is also clear that, should asynchronous technology gain acceptance as a low-power design style, the AMULET work places the ARM architecture in the vanguard of the asynchronous assault on the stronghold of the global clock.

An obstacle to the widespread adoption of self-timed design styles is the knowledge-base of the existing design community. Most IC designers have been trained to have a strong aversion to asynchronous circuits because of the difficulties that were experienced by the designers of some early asynchronous computers. These difficulties resulted from an undisciplined approach to self-timed design, and modern developments offer asynchronous design frameworks which overcome most of the problems inherent in what is, admittedly, a more anarchic approach to logic design than that offered within the clocked framework.

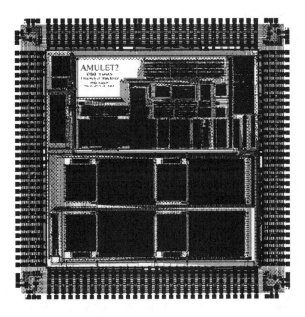

**Figure 14.9**    AMULET2e die plot.

The next few years will tell whether or not AMULET and similar developments around the world can demonstrate the sort of advantages that will cause designers to throw away most of their past education and learn a new way to perform their duties.

**AMULET2e silicon**

A plot of the AMULET2e die is shown in Figure 14.9 and the characteristics of the device are summarized in Table 14.2. The AMULET2 core uses 93,000 transistors, the cache 328,000 and the remainder are in the control logic and pads.

**Table 14.2**    AMULET2e characteristics.

| **Process** | 0.5 µm | **Transistors** | 454,000 | **MIPS** | 40 |
|---|---|---|---|---|---|
| **Metal layers** | 3 | **Die area** | 41 mm$^2$ | **Power** | 140 mW |
| **Vdd** | 3.3 V | **Clock** | none | **MIPS/W** | 285 |

## 14.6  Examples and exercises

**Example 14.1**  **Estimate the performance improvement which results from running a critical DSP routine in zero wait state on-chip RAM instead of two wait state off-chip RAM.**

Typical DSP routines are dominated by multiply-accumulate computations. A code sequence might be:

```
          ..                              ; initialize
LOOP     LDR     r0, [r3], #4            ; get next data value
         LDR     r1, [r4], #4            ; and next coefficient
         MLA     r5, r0, r1, r5         ; accumulate next term
         SUB     r2, r2, #1             ; decrement loop counter
         BNE     LOOP                   ; loop if not finished
```

This loop requires seven instruction fetches (including two in the branch shadow) and two data fetches. On a standard ARM core the multiply takes a data dependent number of computation cycles, evaluating two bits per cycle. If we assume 16-bit coefficients and order the multiplication so that the coefficient determines the number of cycles, the multiply will require eight internal cycles. Each load also requires an internal cycle.

If the data and coefficients are always in on-chip memory, the loop takes 19 clock cycles if executed from on-chip RAM, with 14 additional wait state cycles if executed from two wait state off-chip RAM.

The use of on-chip RAM therefore speeds the loop up by around 75%.

Note that this speed-up is a lot less than the factor three that might be expected from simply comparing memory access speeds.

**Exercise 14.1.1**  Estimate the power saving that results from using the on-chip RAM. (Assume that on-chip accesses cost 2 nJ and off-chip accesses 10 nJ.)

**Exercise 14.1.2**  Repeat the estimates assuming the external memory is restricted to 16 bits wide.

**Exercise 14.1.3**  Repeat the estimates for both 32- and 16-bit external memory assuming that the processor supports Thumb mode (and the program is rewritten to use Thumb instructions) and high-speed multiplication.

**Example 14.2** **Survey the designs presented in this chapter and summarize the power-saving techniques employed on the system chips described here.**

Firstly, all the system chips display a high level of integration which saves power whenever two modules on the same chip exchange data.

All the chips are based around an ARM core which is, itself, very power-efficient.

Though none of the chips has enough on-chip memory to remove the need for off-chip memory completely, several have a few kilobytes of on-chip RAM which can be loaded with critical routines to save power (and improve performance).

Several of the chips incorporate clock control circuitry which reduces the clock frequency (or stops the clock altogether) when the chip is not fully loaded, and switches the clock to individual modules off when they are inactive.

AMULET2e operates fully asynchronously, avoiding the need for a free-running clock altogether. The self-timed circuits only use power when doing useful work.

All the chips are based upon static or pseudo-static CMOS technology where, with a little care, digital circuits only consume power when they switch. Some of the chips also incorporate analogue functions which require continuous bias currents, so these circuits can usually be powered down when they are inactive.

**Exercise 14.2.1** In embedded systems there is usually no 'reset' button to restart a system that has crashed. What techniques are used to recover from software crashes?

**Exercise 14.2.2** Several of the chips described in this chapter incorporate counter/timer modules. What are these used for?

**Exercise 14.2.3** The ARM7500 has an on-chip cache, AMULET2e has on-chip memory which can be configured either as a cache or as directly addressed memory, and Ruby II and VIP simply have directly addressed on-chip memory. Explain the difference between on-chip RAM and an on-chip cache and explain why the designers of these chips made the choices that they did.

# Appendix: Computer Logic

**Computer logic**

Computer design is based upon Boolean logic where a signal on a wire has one of two values: **true** or **false**. Typically a voltage near ground represents 'false' and one near the supply voltage represents 'true', however any representation that can reliably reflect two different states can be used. 'True' is sometimes called logic '1' and 'false' logic '0'.

**Logic gates**

A logic gate produces a function of one or more logic inputs. A 2-input 'AND' gate, for example, produces a 'true' output if the first input is 'true' AND the second input is 'true'. Since each input is either 'true' or 'false', there are only four possible input combinations, and the complete functionality of the gate can be expressed in a **truth table** as shown in Figure A.4 on page 390, which also shows the logic symbol for an AND gate.

An AND gate can be extended to more than two inputs (though current CMOS technology limits the practical **fan-in** to four inputs, reducing to three inputs on some sub-micron process technologies). The output is a '1' when all the inputs are '1', and the output is '0' when at least one input is '0'.

An OR gate is defined similarly, giving a '0' when all the inputs are '0' and a '1' when at least one input is a '1'. The logic symbol and truth table for a 2-input OR gate are shown in Figure A.5 on page 390.

A vital logic component is the inverter. This has one input and produces the opposite output. Its logic function is NOT. The output is false ('0') if the input is true ('1') and *vice versa*. An AND gate with an inverter on the output is a NAND (NOT AND) gate, and an OR gate with an inverter on the output is a NOR (NOT OR) gate.

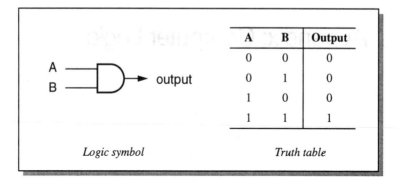

**Figure A.4**    The logic symbol and truth table for an AND gate.

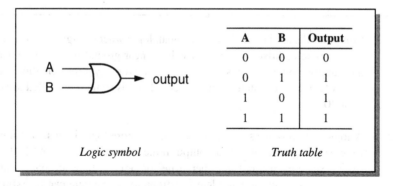

**Figure A.5**    The logic symbol and truth table for an OR gate.

In fact conventional simple CMOS gates are inherently inverting, so NAND is simpler than AND, the latter being formed by adding an inverter to the former, and similarly OR gates are formed from NOR gates by adding inverters.

**Boolean algebra**

All logic circuits can be constructed using only 2-input NAND gates. This stems from the rules of Boolean algebra. First, observe that if both inputs of a NAND gate are connected to the same signal, the output is the inverse of the input, so we have an inverter. Next, connect an inverter to each input of a NAND gate. A brief examination of the truth table reveals that the resulting circuit performs the OR function.

Often logic equations are written using the notation of conventional arithmetic, using '·' for AND and '+' for OR. Thus 'A AND (B OR C)' is written 'A·(B + C)'. Logical inversion is denoted by an overbar: 'A NAND B' is written '$\overline{A \cdot B}$'. This notation is very convenient provided that the context makes it clear that an equation is a Boolean logic equation where 1 + 1 = 1.

**Binary numbers**

Numbers are usually represented in computers in binary notation (there is a more complete discussion of data types and number representation in Section 6.2 on page 161). Here, instead of using the familiar base 10 number notation where each digit is in the range 0 to 9 and positions have values which scale by factors of 10 (units, tens, hundreds,...), binary numbers have digits which are either 0 or 1 and positions have values that scale by factors of 2 (units, twos, fours, eights, sixteens,...). Since each binary digit (**bit**) is restricted to one of two values it can be represented by a Boolean value, and the complete binary number is represented by a set of Boolean values.

**Binary addition**

The sum of two single-bit binary numbers can be formed using the logic gates we have met already. If both bits are zero the sum is zero; the sum of a one and a zero is one, but the sum of two ones is two, which is represented in binary notation by the two bits '10'. An adder for two single-bit inputs must therefore have two output bits: a **sum** bit with the same weight as the input bits and a **carry** bit which has twice that weight.

If the inputs are A and B, the sum and carry are formed as follows:

$$sum \quad = A \cdot \overline{B} + \overline{A} \cdot B \qquad \qquad \text{Equation 16}$$

$$carry \ = A \cdot B \qquad \qquad \text{Equation 17}$$

The sum function arises frequently in digital logic and is called the **exclusive OR** or XOR function. It is 'exclusive' because it is true if A is true, or B is true, but not if they are both true. It has its own logic symbol which is shown in Figure A.6 on page 392 along with a (non-obvious) implementation which uses four NAND gates.

An adder for N-bit binary numbers can be constructed from single-bit adders, but all bits except the first may have to accept a carry input from the next lower stage. Each bit of the adder produces a sum and a carry-out from the inputs and the carry-in:

$$sum_i \quad = A_i \cdot \overline{B_i} \cdot \overline{C_{i-1}} + \overline{A_i} \cdot B_i \cdot \overline{C_{i-1}} + \overline{A_i} \cdot \overline{B_i} \cdot C_{i-1} + A_i \cdot B_i \cdot C_{i-1} \qquad \text{Equation 18}$$

$$C_i \quad = A_i \cdot B_i + A_i \cdot C_{i-1} + B_i \cdot C_{i-1} \qquad \qquad \text{Equation 19}$$

Here the equations apply for $i = 1$ to $N$ and $C_0$ is zero.

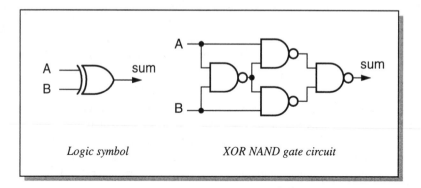

*Logic symbol*                    *XOR NAND gate circuit*

**Figure A.6**   The logic symbol and NAND circuit for an XOR gate.

**Multiplexers**   A common requirement in a processor implementation is to select the source of an operand from a number of alternative inputs on a cycle-by-cycle basis. The logic component that performs this function is a **multiplexer** (or simply a 'mux'). A 2-input multiplexer has a Boolean *select* input ($S$) and two binary input values $A_i$ and $B_i$, where $1 \leq i \leq N$ and $N$ is the number of bits in each binary value. When $S$ is zero, the output $Z_i$ should equal $A_i$ and when $S$ is one $Z_i$ should equal $B_i$. This is a straight-forward logic function:

$$Z_i \quad = \overline{S} \cdot A_i + S \cdot B_i \qquad\qquad\qquad\qquad \text{Equation 20}$$

**Clocks**   Almost all processors are controlled by a free-running timing reference signal called a **clock** (but not quite all; see Section 9.4 on page 259 for details of the AMULET processor cores that operate without any external timing reference signal). The clock controls the state changes within the processor.

Generally, all the state is held within **registers**. During the clock cycle **combinatorial** logic (logic whose outputs depend only on the current input values) works out the next state values using Boolean logic gates as described above. At the end of the clock cycle the active clock edge causes all the registers to switch simultaneously to the next state. For maximum performance the clock frequency is set at the highest rate at which all the combinatorial logic can be guaranteed to complete, under worst-case conditions, in time for the next active clock edge.

**Sequential circuits**   A register stores the state between active clock edges and changes its contents on the active edge. It is a **sequential** logic circuit; its outputs depend not only on the current input values, but also on how they have changed in the past.

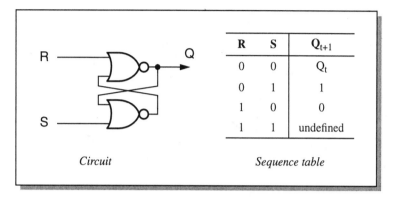

| R | S | $Q_{t+1}$ |
|---|---|-----------|
| 0 | 0 | $Q_t$ |
| 0 | 1 | 1 |
| 1 | 0 | 0 |
| 1 | 1 | undefined |

*Circuit*　　　　　　*Sequence table*

**Figure A.7**　An R-S flip-flop circuit and sequence table.

The simplest sequential circuit is the R-S (**Reset-Set**) flip-flop. This is a circuit whose output is set high whenever the *Set* input is active and is reset low whenever the *Reset* input is active. If both inputs are active at the same time the flip-flop behaviour depends on the implementation; if both are inactive the flip-flop *remembers* the last state it was put into. An implementation of an R-S flip-flop using two NOR gates is shown in Figure A.7 with its sequence table; this is no longer a simple truth table since the output is not a combinatorial function of the current input values.

**Transparent latches**

A transparent (or **D-type**) latch has a data input (*D*) and an enable signal (*En*); the output follows the *D* input whenever *En* is high, but remains constant at whatever value applied just before *En* went low while *En* stays low. This can be constructed from an R-S flip-flop by generating *R* and *S* from *D* and *En* as shown in Figure A.8 on page 394.

In principle it should be possible to build any sequential circuit using a D-type latch provided the combinatorial logic between stages is slow enough. Applying a very short positive pulse to *En* will let the next state data through the latch and then hold it before the combinatorial logic has time to respond to the new values. However, in practice this turns out to be a very hard way to build a reliable circuit.

**Edge-triggered latches**

There are various ways to build more reliable latching circuits, most of which require each signal to pass through two transparent latches per clock cycle. In the simplest of these, the second latch is placed in series with the first and operates with the inverse enable function. At all times, one latch or the other is holding and the other is transparent. On one clock edge, where the first latch goes opaque and the second goes

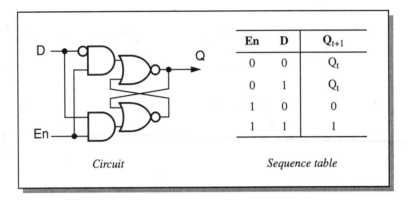

| En | D | $Q_{t+1}$ |
|----|---|-----------|
| 0  | 0 | $Q_t$     |
| 0  | 1 | $Q_t$     |
| 1  | 0 | 0         |
| 1  | 1 | 1         |

*Circuit*                                      *Sequence table*

**Figure A.8**    A D-type transparent latch circuit and sequence table.

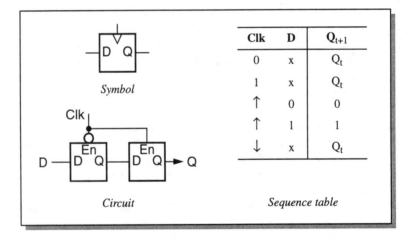

| Clk | D | $Q_{t+1}$ |
|-----|---|-----------|
| 0   | x | $Q_t$     |
| 1   | x | $Q_t$     |
| ↑   | 0 | 0         |
| ↑   | 1 | 1         |
| ↓   | x | $Q_t$     |

*Circuit*                                      *Sequence table*

**Figure A.9**    A D-type edge-triggered latch symbol, circuit and sequence table.

transparent, the input data value propagates through to the output. It is then held through the full cycle until the same edge in the following cycle. This is therefore an **edge-triggered latch**; its logic symbol, circuit and sequence table are shown in Figure A.9. (In the table an 'x' in an input column indicates that the input has no effect on the output.)

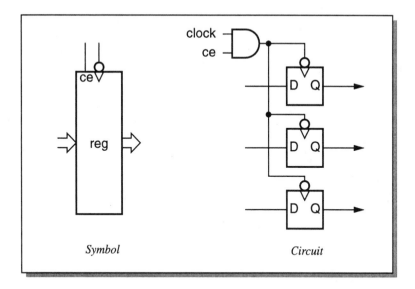

**Figure A.10** A register with a clock enable control signal.

Edge-triggered latches require very careful design, since they are not simply combinatorial logic circuits and their function depends critically on the dynamic properties of the circuit elements. If constructed, as suggested above, from two transparent latches in series, there are various *race conditions* which must be avoided. But, with good tools, reliable latches can be designed, and once a reliable latch is available, sequential circuits of arbitrary complexity can be constructed.

**Registers**  A set of edge-triggered (or equivalent) latches which jointly store the state of a binary value through a clock cycle is termed a **register**. A flexible form of register is connected to a free-running clock and has a 'clock enable' control input so that control logic can decide on a cycle-by-cycle basis whether or not to update the register's contents. A simple way to build such a register is to add a gate on the common clock line to the edge-triggered latches. If we use negative-edge triggered latches, an AND gate will remove the entire high-going clock pulse provided the enable input is low before the clock goes high and stays low until the clock has gone low again. (These are the **set-up** and **hold** conditions for the enable input.) If the enable is, itself, produced from a similar register running off the same clock, it will meet these constraints. The register circuit is shown in Figure A.10.

# Glossary

**ACM**
*Association for Computing Machinery*; the American association for computing professionals.

**Acorn Computers Limited**
The UK company where the ARM processor was developed between 1983 and 1985. Acorn also developed the BBC microcomputer, which established the wide-spread educational use of computers in the UK, and the Archimedes range of ARM-based computers which followed the BBC micro into the schools market.

**ADC**
*Analogue to Digital Converter*; an electronic circuit which takes an input which may vary continuously within a specified range and converts it into an $n$-bit binary number which approximates the input to one of $2^n$ discrete values within that range.

**ALU**
*Arithmetic-Logic Unit*; the component in a processor that performs the arithmetic (addition, subtraction, and sometimes including multiplication and division) and logic (shift, bit-wise AND, and so on) operations.

**AMBA**
*Advanced Microcontroller Bus Architecture*; an open standard for an on-chip bus which connects the various modules used to build a complex embedded system chip.

**AMULET**
*Asynchronous Microprocessor Using Low-Energy Technology*; this term is used to describe the prototype asynchronous implementations of the ARM architecture developed at the University of Manchester.

**ANSI**          *American National Standards Institute*; the American standards body which has defined many useful conventions which are widely used in computing, for example *ASCII* and ANSI standard C.

**APCS**          *ARM Procedure Call Standard*; a calling convention defined by ARM Limited to allow procedures generated by different compilers (or written in assembly language) to call each other.

**ARM**           *Advanced RISC Machine* (formerly *Acorn RISC Machine*); a 32-bit microprocessor based on RISC design principles (see *RISC*).

**ARM Limited**   *Advanced RISC Machines Limited*; the company spun out from Acorn in 1990 to develop the ARM technology. Based in Cambridge, England.

**ASCII**         *American Standard for Computer Information Interchange*; a standard way to represent printable and print control characters in 7-bit binary numbers (often extended to 8-bit fields in today's computers).

**ASIC**          *Application-Specific Integrated Circuit*; a *VLSI* device designed for a particular application, usually for a particular customer.

**ASSP**          *Application-Specific Standard Part*; a *VLSI* device designed for a particular application which is sold as a standard component by the semiconductor manufacturer. Often the chip will have been developed as an *ASIC*, but then in response to market demand the manufacturer will have come to an agreement with the original customer to make the chip available to other customers.

**BBC**           The *British Broadcasting Corporation*; the UK public service radio and television broadcasting company. The BBC is funded mainly through licence fees which are a compulsory feature of television ownership in the UK. Their charter includes a duty to educate the public, and in 1982 they produced a popular series called 'The Computer Programme' based around the BBC micro which was commissioned for the series.

**BCD**           *Binary Coded Decimal*; a way to represent a number by encoding each decimal digit as its binary equivalent.

**BCS**           The *British Computer Society*; the UK association for computing professionals.

**C**             The *C* programming language, widely used for general-purpose and embedded system development.

**CAM**    *Content Addressable Memory*; this is memory which contains a number of different data items and is accessed by presenting a data value which is compared with all the stored items to see if there is a match. If there is a match, the address of the matched location is output; otherwise the CAM signals a 'miss'. It is also described as *associative memory*, and is an important component of an associative cache or *TLB*.

**CISC**    *Complex Instruction Set Computer*; a term created at the same time as *RISC* to describe earlier architectures which do not have the characteristics of RISCs. Typically a CISC has a variable instruction length mini-computer style instruction set with many addressing modes, memory-to-memory operations and support for many data types.

**CMOS**    *Complementary Metal Oxide Semiconductor*; the predominant technology used for modern integrated circuits, CMOS combines *NMOS* and *PMOS* field-effect transistors on the same chip. This gives the technology active signal drive in both directions, hence fast switching, and near zero power dissipation when it is not switching.

**CPI**    *Cycles Per Instruction*; a measure of processor efficiency based on the number of clock cycles divided by the number of instructions in a typical code sequence.

**CPSR**    *Current Program Status Register*; an *ARM* register which contains the condition code bits, interrupt disable flags and processor operating mode bits.

**CPU**    The *Central Processing Unit*; a term used somewhat imprecisely to refer to the processor in a computer. It might be just the processor core, or it might include the on-chip MMU and cache, and possibly the main memory as well.

**DAC**    *Digital to Analogue Converter*; an electronic circuit which converts a digital signal, usually presented in binary form on $n$ wires, into an analogue signal presented as one of $2^n$ values on a single wire.

**DECT**    *Digital European Cordless Telephone*; a European standard for cordless telephones where speech is transferred in digital form between the handset and a local base-station through a radio link.

**DRAM**    *Dynamic Random Access Memory*; the lowest price per bit form of *RAM*, used as the main memory in most computer systems. The data is stored as charge on a capacitor and leaks away in a few milliseconds (hence *dynamic*); to store for longer periods the DRAM must be *refreshed* periodically, which means it must be read while it is still valid and then rewritten to restore the full charge.

**EPLD**            *Electrically-Programmable Logic Device*; a general-purpose logic chip which has a large number of gates whose connectivity is defined by the state of on-chip memory cells. These cells may be reprogrammed to change the logic function of the device. (See also *FPGA*, which is a one-time configurable device.)

**EPROM**           *Electrically-Programmable Read Only Memory*; a *ROM* which can be programmed by applying suitable electrical signals. Usually it can be erased and reprogrammed many times.

**FPA**             *Floating-Point Accelerator*; additional hardware to speed up floating-point operations, for example, the ARM FPA10.

**FPASC**           *Floating-Point Accelerator Support Code*; the software which is run in an ARM system which includes an FPA10 floating-point accelerator. The FPA10 implements a subset of the ARM floating-point instruction set in hardware, and requires the FPASC to handle the remaining instructions.

**FPE**             *Floating-Point Emulator*; the software which is run in an ARM system which does not include an FPA10 floating-point accelerator to support the ARM floating-point instruction set.

**FPGA**            *Field-Programmable Gate Array*; a general-purpose logic chip which has a large number of gates whose connectivity is defined by the state of one-time programmable on-chip components such as anti-fuses. (See also *EPLD*, which is a reprogrammable device.)

**FPSR**            *Floating-Point Status Register*; a user-visible register in the ARM floating-point architecture which controls various options and indicates error conditions.

**FPU**             *Floating-Point Unit*; the component in a processor that carries out the floating-point operations.

**GPS**             *GEC Plessey Semiconductors*; an ARM semiconductor partner who manufacture a range of ARM CPUs and system chips. (In other contexts GPS may stand for *Global Positioning by Satellite*, a location system based on triangulating on low-orbit satellites.)

**IC**              *Integrated Circuit*; a semiconductor device where several (up to several million) transistors have been printed during the same manufacturing process. An IC is sometimes referred to as a 'chip'.

**IDE**
*Integrated Drive Electronics*; an interface for a hard disk drive where all the intelligence is in the drive electronics and the host computer interface comprises a data bus and a few address lines.

**IEE**
The *Institution of Electrical Engineers*; the UK professional association for electronics (and electrical) engineers. The IEE sponsors colloquia and publishes journals in the computing area.

**IEEE**
The *Institute of Electrical and Electronics Engineers, Inc.*; the American professional association for electronics and electrical engineers. Membership is not restricted to US nationals, and the IEEE is very active in sponsoring international conferences and publishing journals in the computing area, often in collaboration with the ACM.

**I/O**
*Input/Output*; the activity of transferring data between the computer and its environment through a peripheral device.

**IOC**
*I/O Controller*; the chip designed by Acorn Computers to handle the I/O functions in the Archimedes products.

**IOMD**
*I/O Memory Device*; the chip designed by ARM Limited to handle memory and peripheral accesses, used in the Acorn Risc PC.

**ISDN**
*Integrated Services Digital Network*; an international standard for digital telephony where speech is sent as a 64 Kbit/s data stream. The standard also defines control protocols.

**JTAG**
*Joint Test Action Group*; the committee which defined the test standard based on a serial interface which is used on many ARM chips.

**LRU**
*Least-Recently Used*; this term describes an algorithm for choosing which value in an associative cache or *TLB* to evict in order to make room for a new value.

**MEMC**
*Memory Controller*; the memory management and *DRAM* controller designed by Acorn Computers for the Archimedes products.

**MFLOPS**
*Millions of Floating-Point Operations Per Second*; a measure of the performance of a computer when executing floating-point operations.

**MIPS**
*Millions of Instructions Per Second*; a measure of the rate at which a processor can execute its own instructions. Since different instruction sets have different semantic

content per instruction, comparing two processors on the basis of their native MIPS rating is meaningless. Benchmark programs attempt to provide a basis for valid comparison, and 'Dhrystone MIPS' is a normalized rating that is (arguably) more valid.

**MMU**     *Memory Management Unit*; the part of the processor that translates the virtual address into the physical address, using page tables in memory. It includes the table-walking hardware and the *TLB*.

**NMOS**    *N-type Metal Oxide Semiconductor*; a semiconductor technology that pre-dates *CMOS* that was used to build some 8- and 16-bit microprocessors. It supports a logic family with active pull-down and passive pull-up outputs, and gates with a low output draw current even when not switching. NMOS transistors are used, with *PMOS* transistors, to form CMOS. NMOS transistors are more effective than PMOS transistors, which is why NMOS superseded PMOS as the technology of choice for microprocessors, but the combination of the two in CMOS, though more complex to manufacture, is greatly superior to either in both speed and power-efficiency.

**PC**      *Program Counter*; the register in a processor that holds the address of the next instruction to be fetched. Usually the context should differentiate this use from the next.

**PC**      *Personal Computer*; although apparently generic, this term is now used to refer to desktop computers which are compatible with the IBM PC, which means, *inter alia*, that they use a processor with the Intel x86 instruction set architecture.

**PCMCIA**  *Personal Computer Memory Card International Association*; the organization responsible for a physical form and interface standard for cards which plug into PCs (and other portable equipment, such as the Apple Newton). Despite the name, the standard is not limited to memory cards; various peripheral interface cards are also conformant. PCMCIA cards are often referred to simply as 'PC-cards'.

**PIE card** *Platform Independent Evaluation* card; a simple ARM system with RAM, ROM and a serial interface to connect to a host machine which is running the ARM software development tools.

**PMOS**    *P-type Metal Oxide Semiconductor*; a semiconductor technology that pre-dates *CMOS* and *NMOS* that was used to build early 4-bit microprocessors. It supports a logic family with active pull-up and passive pull-down outputs, and gates with a high output draw current even when not switching. PMOS transistors are used, with NMOS transistors, to form CMOS.

**PSR**        *Program Status Register*; the register in a processor that holds various bits of information such as the condition codes, the interrupt disable bits and the operating mode bits. The ARM has a *CPSR* (Current Program Status Register), and an *SPSR* (Saved Program Status Register) for each non-user mode.

**RAM**        *Random Access Memory*; a misnomer, since *ROM* is also random access, RAM is used to refer to the read-write memory used to store programs and data in a computer; the term is also used to describe the semiconductor components used to build this memory and also used in structures such as caches and *TLBs*.

**RISC**       *Reduced Instruction Set Computer*; a processor with an architecture with certain characteristics based on ideas expounded around 1980 by Patterson (U.C. Berkeley), Ditzel (Bell Laboratories) and Hennessy (Stanford University).

**ROM**        *Read Only Memory*; the fixed program store in a computer, also used to describe the semiconductor devices which may be used in this role. Contrast with *RAM*.

**RS232**      A particular standard for asynchronous serial communications, enabling the connection of modems, printers, and communication with other machines.

**RTC**        *Real-Time Clock*; a clock source which allows a computer to work out the time of day, date, and so on. Normally this is a small battery-backed system with a low frequency crystal oscillator which runs all the time, even when the computer itself is turned off.

**RTL**        *Register Transfer Level*; an abstract view of a hardware system such as a processor where multi-bit values are viewed as flowing between registers along buses.

**RTOS**       *Real-Time Operating System*; an operating system that supports programs that must satisfy external timing constraints. These are often small (a few kilobytes) and well-suited to use in embedded systems.

**SPSR**       *Saved Program Status Register*; an *ARM* register used to save the values of the *CPSR* when an exception occurs.

**SRAM**       *Static Random Access Memory*; more expensive than *DRAM*, this form of *RAM* holds its data in flip-flops which do not require refreshing. SRAM has a lower access time than DRAM and can retain its contents indefinitely with almost no power dissipation. It is used for most RAM functions on processor chips, such as cache and *TLB* memory, and may be used for the main memory in some smaller embedded systems.

**TLB**
*Translation Look-aside Buffer*; a cache of recently used page table entries which avoids the overhead of page table-walking on every memory access.

**UART**
*Universal Asynchronous Receiver/Transmitter*; a peripheral device that interfaces a serial line (typically with an RS232 signalling protocol) to a processor bus.

**UPC**
*Universal Peripheral Controller*; a chip used by many *PC* manufacturers which integrates floppy disk, serial line and parallel printer interface functions. It is also used in the Acorn Risc PC.

**VHDL**
*VHSIC Hardware Description Language* (where VHSIC expands to *Very High-Speed Integrated Circuit*); a standard language for describing hardware at a behavioural or structural level which is supported by most semiconductor design tool companies.

**VIDC**
*Video Controller*; a chip designed at Acorn Computers for the Archimedes computer. VIDC handles video and sound output.

**VIDC20**
*Video Controller version 2.0*; the video and sound chip used on the Acorn Risc PC, and capable of generating high-quality video output in a number of applications.

**VLSI**
*Very Large Scale Integration*; the process of putting a lot of transistors onto a single chip. There was an attempt to categorize chip transistor counts as SSI, MSI, LSI (Small, Medium and Large Scale Integration), VLSI, and so on, on the basis of orders of magnitude, but process technology advanced faster than new terms could be coined. The next term, ULSI (Ultra Large Scale Integration) never gained widespread use, and would probably now be obsolete anyway.

**VLSI Technology Inc.**
VLSI Technology Inc., sometimes abbreviated to just *VLSI*, manufactured the first ARM chips designed at Acorn Computers and, with Acorn and Apple, established ARM Limited as a separate company in 1990. VLSI was the first ARM semiconductor partner and manufactures a range of ARM-based CPUs and system chips.

**VM**
*Virtual Memory*; the address space that the program runs in which is mapped to physical memory by the *MMU*. The virtual space may be larger than the physical space, and parts of the virtual space may be paged out onto a hard disk or may not exist anywhere.

**VRAM**
*Video Random Access Memory*; a form of *DRAM* with on-chip shift registers to give high-bandwidth access to sequential data for generating video displays.

# Bibliography

**ARM texts**
- ARM Limited, *ARM datasheets*.

  Datasheets are available on all the ARM processors, some from ARM's semiconductor partners and some over the Internet from ARM's World Wide Web site at http://www.arm.com/.

- ARM Limited, *ARM Software Development Toolkit: Reference Manual*, *Programming Techniques* and *Windows Toolkit Guide*.

  These manuals accompany Toolkit version 2.0 and offer substantial assistance to the ARM programmer. *Programming Techniques* documents obvious and non-obvious ways to get the best from the ARM chip, whether programming in C or assembler.

- Furber, *VLSI RISC Architecture and Organization*, Marcel Dekker, New York, USA, 1989. ISBN 0-8247-8151-1.

  This book describes a range of RISC architectures including extended details of the ARM2.

- van Someren and Atack, *The ARM RISC Chip - A Programmer's Guide*, Addison-Wesley, Wokingham, England, 1993. ISBN 0-201-62410-9.

  This is an introduction to the ARM6 instruction set with a useful reference section.

**Thumb**
- Segars, Clarke and Goudge, 'Embedded Control Problems, Thumb, and the ARM7TDMI', *IEEE Micro*, **15** (5), October 1995, pages 22–30.

  A paper describing the philosophy and performance of the Thumb instruction set.

**RISC architecture**

- Patterson and Ditzel, 'The Case for the Reduced Instruction Set Computer', ACM SIGARCH *Computer Architecture News*, **8** (6), October 1980, pages 25–33.

  The seminal paper that questioned the trend towards ever-increasing complexity in processor design.

- Katevenis, *Reduced Instruction Set Computer Architectures for VLSI*, MIT Press, Cambridge, MA, USA, 1985. ISBN 0-262-11103-9.

  A detailed account of the Berkeley RISC designs and an ACM Doctoral Dissertation Award winner.

- Hennessy and Patterson, *Computer Architecture - A Quantitative Approach*, 2nd edition, Morgan Kaufmann, San Francisco, CA, USA, 1990. ISBN 1-55860-329-8.

  This is the authoritative text on mainstream RISC design, written by the two people with primary responsibility for making RISC happen.

- Patterson and Hennessy, *Computer Organization and Design - The Hardware/ Software Interface*, Morgan Kaufmann, San Francisco, CA, USA, 1994. ISBN 1-55860-281-X.

  Following the considerable success of *Computer Architecture - A Quantitative Approach* by the same authors (but in a different order!), this book goes into the basics in rather more detail.

**CMOS design**

- Weste and Eshraighan, *Principles of CMOS VLSI Design, A Systems Perspective*, 2nd edition, Addison-Wesley, Reading, MA, USA, 1993. ISBN 0-201-53376-6.

  This is an authoritative text on transistor-level CMOS design, covering physical layout, circuits and systems issues. Most professional CMOS designers keep a copy to hand at all times.

**Self-timed logic**

- Birtwistle and Davis (editors), *Asynchronous Circuit Design*, Proceedings of the 1993 VIIth Banff High Order Workshop, Springer, 1995. ISBN 3-540-19901-2, 0-387-19901-2.

  Chapter 5, *Computing without Clocks: Micropipelining the ARM Processor*, pages 211-262, by S. B. Furber, describes the AMULET1 organization in some detail. Other chapters in the book give background on asynchronous logic design and describe alternative approaches to the 'micropipelines' used in the AMULET designs.

**Endianness**
- Cohen, 'On Holy Wars and a Plea for Peace', *Computer*, **14** (10), October 1981, IEEE Computer Society Press, pages 48–54.

  The article which raised the issue of big- and little-endian byte ordering and established the endian terminology by analogy with *Gulliver's Travels*.

**C language**
- Kernighan and Ritchie, *The C Programming Language*, 2nd edition, Prentice Hall, Englewood Cliffs, NJ, USA, 1988. ISBN 0-13-110362-8.

  This is a standard reference book for C; note that the second edition covers ANSI standard C which the first edition did not.

- Harbison and Steele, *A C Reference Manual*, 2nd edition, Prentice Hall, Englewood Cliffs, NJ, USA, 1987. ISBN 0-13-109802-0.

  This C text is more extensive than Kernighan and Ritchie, and therefore less succinct. Again, it is the second edition that covers ANSI standard C.

- Koenig, *C Traps and Pitfalls*, Addison-Wesley, Reading, MA, USA, 1989. ISBN 0-201-17928-8.

  A text describing how to avoid the standard pitfalls in C programming; useful for C programmers at all levels of experience.

- ANSI, *American National Standard for Information System Programming Language C*, X3J11/90-013, Feb. 14, 1990.

  Available from your national standards body, this is the definitive reference on ANSI standard C. However the texts mentioned above are adequate for most purposes.

# Index